**THE
SEARCH
FOR**

empowerment

THE SEARCH FOR

empowerment

Social Capital as Idea and Practice at the World Bank

Edited by

Anthony Bebbington
Michael Woolcock
Scott E. Guggenheim and
Elizabeth A. Olson

Kumarian
Press, Inc.

The Search for Empowerment: Social Capital as Idea and Practice at the World Bank

Published in 2006 in the United States of America by Kumarian Press, Inc., 1294 Blue Hills Avenue, Bloomfield, CT 06002 USA

The text of this book is set in Palatino and Palatino Light

Design, production, and editorial services were provided by Publication Services, Inc., Champaign, Illinois.

Printed in the United States of America by McNaughton & Gunn, Inc. Text printed with vegetable oil-based ink.

∞ The paper used in this publication meets the minimum requirements of the American National Standard for Information Sciences—Permanence of Paper for printed Library Materials, ANSI Z39.48-1984

Library of Congress Cataloging-in-Publication Data

The search for empowerment : social capital as idea and practice at the World Bank / Anthony Bebbington ... [et al.] ; edited by Michael Woolcock, Scott E. Guggenheim, and Elizabeth A. Olson.
    p. cm.
 Includes bibliographical references and index.
 ISBN-13: 978-1-56549-215-8 (alk. paper)
 1. World Bank. 2. Social capital (Sociology) 3. Economic development projects. 4. Economic development--Social aspects. I. Bebbington, Anthony, 1962- II. Woolcock, Michael J. V., 1964- III. Guggenheim, Scott E. (Scott Evan), 1955- IV. Olson, Elizabeth A., PhD.
HG3881.5.W57S36 2006
302--dc22
                    2006004695

CONTENTS

LIST OF ABBREVIATIONS AND ACRONYMS

Abbreviation	Full Title	Chapter(s)
AFR	Africa	1
AMUCSS	Asociacion Mexicana de Uniones de Credito del Sector Social	8
ARC	Agrarian Reform Community	8
ARCDP	Agrarian Reform Communities Development Project	8
BA	Beneficiary Assessment	7
BRAC	Bangladesh Rural Advancement Committee	8
BSB	Bangladesh Sericulture Board	8
BSF	Bangladesh Silk Foundation	8
BSRTI	Bangladesh Sericulture Research and Training Institute	8
CARE	Cooperative for American Relief Everywhere	6
CDD	Community-Driven Development	7
CDF	Comprehensive Development Framework	4
CODENPE	Consejo de Desarrollo de las Nacionalidades y Pueblos del Ecuador	6
CONAIE	Confederación Nacional Indígena de Ecuador	6
CONFENIAE	Confederación de las Nacionalidades Indígenas de la Amazonia Ecuatoriana	6
CONPLADEIN	Consejo Nacional de Planificación de Desarrollo de los Pueblos Indígenas y Negros	6
DAR	Department of Agrarian Reform	8

Abbreviation	Full Title	Chapter(s)
DEC	Development Economics	1
DENR	Department of Environment and Natural Resources	8
DfID	Department for International Development	1
DRG	Development Research Group	1
EAP	East Asia and the Pacific	1
ECA	Europe and Central Asia	1
ELF	Ethnolinguistic Fractionalization	2
ESSD	Environmentally and Socially Sustainable Development	1
FOPAR	Fondo Participativo de Inversión Social	7
FOSIS	Fondo de Solidaridad e Inversión Social	7
GoE	Government of Ecuador	6
HD	Human Development	1
IAF	Inter-American Foundation	6
IBRD	International Bank for Reconstruction and Development	1
ICSID	International Center for Settlement of Investment Disputes	1
IDA	International Development Association	1
IDB	Inter-American Development Bank	6
IDT	Inpres Desa Tertinggal	5
IFAD	International Fund for Agricultural Development	6
IFC	International Finance Corporation	1
ILO	International Labor Organization	6
INDA	Instituto Nacional de Desarrollo Agrario	6
INEFAN	Instituto Ecuatoriano Forestal y de Areas Naturales	6
JSIF	Jamaica Social Investment Fund	7
KDP	Kecamatan Development Project	1, 5

Abbreviation	Full Title	Chapter(s)
LCR	Latin America and the Caribbean	1
LKMD	Lembaga Ketahan Masyarakat Desa	5
LLI	Local Level Institutions	2, 5
LMD	Lembaga Musyawarah Desa	5
MIGA	Multilateral Investment Guarantee Association	1
MNA	Middle East and North Africa	1
MOT	Ministry of Textiles	8
NGO	Nongovernmental Organization	1
NICE	National Index of Civic Engagement	2
NTT	Nusa Tenggara Timur	5
NUSAF	Northern Uganda Social Action Fund	7
OECD	Organisation for Economic Cooperation and Development	3
OED	Operations Evaluation Department	1, 8
OSG	Organización de Segundo Grado	6
PA	Protected Area	8
PAHO	Pan American Health Organizations	6
PAMB	Protected Area Management Board	8
PID	Public Information Document	8
PO	Private Organization	8
PREM	Poverty Reduction and Economic Management	1
PRODEPINE	Proyecto de Desarrollo de los Pueblos Indígenas y Afroecuatorianos	6
PRSP	Poverty Reduction Strategy Paper	4
PSD	Private Sector Development and Infrastructure	1
ROSCA	Rotating Savings and Credit Association	3
RSDF	Romanian Social Development Fund	7
SAR	South Asia	1
SDV	Social Development	1
SENAIME	Secretaría Nacional de Asuntos Indígenas y Minorías Étnicas	6

Abbreviation	Full Title	Chapter(s)
SF	Social Fund	7
SRP	Social Recovery Project	7
UNDP	United Nations Development Programme	5
UNESCO	United Nations Educational, Scientific, and Cultural Organization	6
UNIDO	United Nations Industrial Development Organization	3
WDR	World Development Report	10
WVS	World Values Survey	2

PREFACE AND ACKNOWLEDGMENTS

During the final weeks when we were putting this manuscript to bed, two things happened. Tragically, Gloria Davis, who had nurtured so much of the social development agenda at the World Bank, passed away far too young. Shortly thereafter, the debate on who would be the president of the World Bank from mid-2005 onward gained pace and intensity, as the United States made its formal nomination. Institutions are far more than individuals; that's the basis for the very concept of institution. But institutions are built, steered, and governed by people. To use a well-worn phrase, "people matter"—in determining not just the effects of development projects, but also the effects of development institutions. Gloria mattered a great deal to the themes discussed in this book, and the three of us who knew her well each owe her great debts that we cannot now repay. This book—dedicated to her and two other colleagues—represents a small recognition of those debts.

There are two other individuals we wish to acknowledge, who have been important players in the arguments, debates, and struggles we have tried to cover in this book. Michael Cernea, the first sociologist in the World Bank, initiated many of these arguments and through intellectual flair, bureaucratic cunning, and sheer stubbornness extended the border of the thinkable and doable within the Bank more than any other social scientist. We also owe debts to Michael, and we know that the work we have done in the Bank would not have been possible but for his prior work there.

Next there is Ashraf Ghani, once principal anthropologist in the Bank, later Minister of Finance of Afghanistan, and now chancellor of Kabul University. Ashraf has been a close friend, colleague, and inspiration to all of us. He insisted on academic rigor in his work in the institution, and was an intimidating sparring partner for any who crossed his path and dared to suggest that social structures were anything but central to the development process.

This book is dedicated to these three heroes of ours—all former academics turned Bank social scientists and intellectual activists. They are individuals who have made a difference, whose arguments have mattered, and whose conceptual choices and insistencies have helped nudge the institution in more human directions. However, as this week's other discussion surrounding an individual at the Bank—the new president—makes palpably clear, some individuals have far more power than others and reflect particular power positions in global society. This tension—between arguments over concepts and the struggles of committed individuals on the one hand, and the much more deeply embedded power and political economic relationships within the institution on the other—frames this book. It is left for the reader to decide whether the arguments over one concept—social capital—have been significant in the face of these broader relationships of which the Bank is a part. It is also up to the reader to decide whether the efforts of social scientists within the institution have been well invested.

Individuals have also mattered greatly in bringing this book to fruition over the several years it has taken us to complete it. We are grateful to the following people, in no particular order, for the different ways in which they helped and supported this project: Gloria Davis, Ashraf Ghani, Gary Gaile, Rachel Silvey, Marcia Signer, Susan Johnson, Karen Hunt, Joyce Chinsen, Mike Edwards, Jim Lance, Nana Chandrakirana, Denise Humphreys Bebbington, Connie Woolcock, Brian King, and Michael Watts. The project was generously supported by a grant from the Ford Foundation, and has been supported institutionally by the University of Manchester, the University of Colorado at Boulder, and the World Bank. We are grateful to Oxford University Press for allowing us to use a revised version of a previously published paper. Finally, we also dedicate this book to our families, with our love: to Denise, Anna and Carmen, Connie, Jenna and Nathan, Ed and Callan, and Nana.

Anthony Bebbington, Manchester, UK
Scott Guggenheim, Jakarta, Indonesia
Elizabeth Olson, Lancaster, UK
Michael Woolcock, Washington, DC, USA

April 2005

CONTRIBUTORS

ANTHONY BEBBINGTON is Professor in the Institute for Development Policy and Management in the School for Environment and Development at the University of Manchester, UK.

JULIE VAN DOMELEN was, until mid-2005, Lead Social Protection Specialist in the Africa Region and in the Human Development Network, World Bank.

MICHAEL EDWARDS is Director of the Governance and Civil Society Program, Ford Foundation, USA.

JONATHAN FOX is Professor of Latin American and Latino Studies at the University of California, Santa Cruz.

JOHN GERSHMAN is Senior Analyst at the Interhemispheric Resource Center and Adjunct Professor at New York University's Robert F. Wagner School for Public Service.

SCOTT GUGGENHEIM is Lead Social Development Specialist in the East Asia and Pacific Region, and in the Environmentally and Socially Sustainable Development Network, World Bank.

JEFFREY HAMMER is Lead Economist in the World Bank's South Asia Environment and Social Unit, based in New Delhi, and has previously worked in the Bank's Research Department.

DAVID LEWIS is Reader in Social Policy at the London School of Economics and Political Science, UK.

DEEPA NARAYAN is Senior Advisor in the Poverty Reduction and Economic Management Network, World Bank, currently based in India.

MARTIEN VAN NIEUWKOOP is Lead Operations Officer in the Africa Region and in the Environmentally and Socially Sustainable Development Network, World Bank.

ELIZABETH OLSON is Lecturer in the Department of Geography, Lancaster University, UK.

LANT PRITCHETT is Lead Economist in the World Bank's South Asia Environment and Social Unit, based in New Delhi, and has previously worked in the Bank's Research Department.

M. SHAMEEN SIDDIQI is Rights and Social Justice Coordinator with CARE-Bangladesh.

JORGE UQUILLAS is Senior Sociologist, Latin America Region, and in the Environmentally and Socially Sustainable Development Network, World Bank.

MICHAEL WOOLCOCK is Senior Social Scientist in the Development Research Group of the World Bank.

CHAPTER ONE

THE IDEAS-PRACTICE NEXUS IN INTERNATIONAL DEVELOPMENT ORGANIZATIONS
Social Capital at the World Bank

Anthony Bebbington
Scott Guggenheim
Michael Woolcock

How and why do conceptual and linguistic shifts occur in international development bureaucracies? How do those shifts relate to changes in what those organizations actually *do*? What are the relationships between what we might call discursive shifts—changes in constellations of ideas, practices, and techniques—and development outcomes? Such questions are of critical importance. Critiques of development have suggested that discourse plays a significant role in structuring development practice (Ferguson 1990; Escobar 1995; Bebbington 2000; Mitchell 2002).[1] If this is so, then the ways in which discourses are fashioned, debated, and argued over, as well as the ways in which discursive practices intersect with material practices inside development institutions, become important objects of analysis. They are also important for questions of strategy, for if discourse is indeed so significant, then understanding the conditions under which it might change in particular ways and help give rise to new types of institutional action becomes a critical point of entry for actors aiming to challenge and ultimately refashion dominant ideas in development bureaucracies.

One of the reform battles that has been waged since the mid-1980s in many multilateral and bilateral development agencies has been to incorporate ideas of social development into understandings of development that have otherwise been influenced by ideas from neoclassical economics, engineering, agricultural science, and other, more technical fields. In these struggles, advocates of social development have attempted to

1

introduce concerns such as participation, gender equity, rights, and empowerment into conventional discourses that have tended to distrust such "touchy-feely," "woolly," and qualitative issues.

In certain bureaucracies considerable progress has been made, as Gardner and Lewis (2000) suggest for the case of the British government's Department for International Development (DfID). Even the discourses of certain multilateral bureaucracies have been changed—witness the ongoing elaboration of and experimentation with the United Nations Development Program's Human Development Index. In this multilateral domain, however, such changes have been fewer and more limited, and certain institutions have moved especially slowly—perhaps, above all, the multilateral development banks and international financial institutions, including the International Monetary Fund, the World Bank, the InterAmerican Development Bank, the Asian Development Bank, and the African Development Bank.

This is the point of departure for this book. In writing it, our research questions have been fourfold.

1. Is it possible to improve the purchase of a set of social development ideas within a large development bureaucracy, and if so, how can this be done? More specifically, can theoretical and analytical concepts give greater specificity to, and enhance the leverage of, longer-standing substantive concerns for fostering participation, empowerment, social inclusion, and the role of local associations in the development process?

2. Through what processes can such pro–social development change occur within large development bureaucracies? Indeed, is it at all possible for such change to occur in any real (rather than cosmetic) sense? A significant body of thought suggests that change is unlikely, if not impossible, in such organizations.[2] Such thought is not merely inspired by pessimism and a deeply felt dislike of such institutions; it also has a solid empirical base.

3. In such efforts to usher in change, how are pro–social development coalitions created and sustained, and what factors determine their efficacy? Likewise, how do the agendas—normative, strategic, and tactical—of such coalitions change in the process of pursuing their goals? And if, in the final instance, their initiatives have effects that are not those initially intended, how and why does this mismatch between intent and effect occur?

4. What are the structural, contextual, and institutionally specific conditions under which arguments over the means, ends, and very meaning of "development" emerge within such institutions? How do such arguments change the ways in which problems are framed,

ultimately leading to changes in institutional discourses and practices? In which parts of development bureaucracies do these arguments have such effects, and in which do they not?

Our specific approach to addressing these questions is to look at the following set of interrelated phenomena: the ways in which the concept of
social capital (see Box 1.1) and its role in development have been debated
at the World Bank; the ways in which these debates have shaped, and
been shaped by, project practice (or what are referred to within the Bank
as "operations"); and the ways (however uneven, partial, and incomplete)
in which the concept has made (or might make) a significant difference in
the quality and poverty impact of development programs promoted by the
Bank.

In this sense, the book attempts to ground the general questions just
outlined by addressing the efficacy of a particular concept within a specific
organizational context. In that the book focuses on the internal dynamics
of the Bank, it serves as something of a complement to Jonathan Fox and
David Brown's (1998) edited collection *The Struggle for Accountability*,
which also focused on the World Bank but was particularly interested in
the ways in which grassroots movements and nongovernmental organizations (NGOs) have been able to demand more accountability from the
Bank on social and environmental issues (see also Clark et al. 2003). *The
Struggle for Accountability*—particularly its concluding chapter—discussed
the important role of insider reformists in any such process of institutional
change (and as allies of external pressure groups), but its empirical material focused mainly on articulations between the Bank and other actors.
Our study takes the opposite (but complementary) tack and focuses on
such reformists.[3] And just as Fox and Brown's collection raised issues that
are relevant to issues of policy and institutional change that extend
beyond the confines of the Bank, our intent is that this collection, though
based on the Bank, also have resonance for broader theoretical and strategic discussions.

Although this is a case study approach, it is, of course, not any old case
study. The fact that the collection deals with a debate within the World Bank
raises the intellectual and policy stakes considerably. On the one hand, it is
possible that the adoption of a certain set of ideas by the Bank can create a sort of umbrella that can help other actors (such as those within
developing-country public bureaucracies) pursue concerns that might
otherwise have been difficult to pursue within their own governments.
On the other hand, the fact that it is the Bank—and not another, less
polemical and publicly visible organizations—that is adopting the concept
of social capital raises legitimate questions about the motivations and reasons behind such adoption and about the likelihood that the term will be
co-opted by stronger forces within the institution. This attracts the critical
scrutiny of external observers, thus threatening to debunk the concept so

---

Box 1.1   Defining "Social Capital"

As the subtitle of this book implies, we are primarily interested here in understanding the ways in which the *idea* of "social capital" has been appropriated as part of a strategy for advancing, justifying, and defending social themes and project *practices* within the World Bank. We are less concerned with endorsing (or rejecting) one particular or narrow definition among the many offered. Chapter 2, by Woolcock and Narayan, explores the broader constellation of conceptual frameworks that have emerged connecting social capital to economic development and the policy options to which they give rise. The reader is referred to this chapter for a more detailed discussion of these particular points.[1]

Nevertheless, given that social capital is the central object of our attention and has been both praised and damned for its capacity to embrace a broad range of issues, it is appropriate to allocate some space at the outset to clarifying what we mean by this term. The literature itself offers two quite distinct views (Woolcock 2003). For most academic sociologists, social capital refers to the resources—information, tips, reputations, credit—that flow through a network; it is, if you will, the "electricity." For writers such as Pierre Bourdieu, social capital is a resource ("capital") just like other, more familiar resources (land, money, education)—that is, it can be used to enhance one's wealth and status, to marginalize others, or both. For political scientists such as Robert Putnam, on the other hand, the primary focus is on the nature and extent of the network structure itself; from this perspective, social capital refers to the "wires." Their concern is more with understanding how and why particular networks are structured, the consequences for those who are and those who are not members of these networks, and what can be done (via policy and other instruments) to shape social networks so that they are conducive to building more democratic, supportive, and inclusive communities.

These views are not inherently incompatible, and it is the task of a more general theory of social capital to show how these elements and others that form the corpus of the conceptual debates surrounding this term can (if possible) be reconciled. For present purposes, we are content to draw on both themes to argue that social capital refers to the assets of groups that reside within their relationships. These assets, of course, cannot be understood apart from the broader political and cultural context in which they reside. Nonetheless, they constitute a key component of people's identities and the strategies they deploy for survival and mobility, and as such, these assets powerfully shape these people's interests and aspirations.

1. See also Farr (2004) for a comprehensive intellectual history of "social capital."

that it loses legitimacy and efficacy. Taking a position between these two views, we suggest that the social capital discussion can and sometimes has served as something of a Trojan horse for other changes (though it is important not to claim too much in this regard; see also Mosse 2004). We also suggest that there have indeed been many motivations behind the adoption of the social capital rhetoric within the Bank and that not all of these motivations favor the advancement of a social development agenda. The book, then, inquires into the implications of complicated institutional politics.

Ideas, Institutions, and Contingencies: Room for Maneuvering in Development

In its most general sense, this book is intended to speak to the growing body of work in development studies that—from a variety of disciplinary, methodological, and political perspectives—addresses the workings of large-scale institutions. More specifically, it speaks to that work that aims to "get inside" development organizations in order to analyze the ways in which discourse and organizational practices are developed. Yet more specifically—though of major importance, we feel—it is part of a literature that seeks to understand the capacity that networks of people working within such organizations have for fostering innovation and change in policy and practice (Hirschmann 1963). This is a body of work that—while fully recognizing the weight of political economy and other sources of path-dependent constraints on development possibilities—holds that there are contingencies in the process of development and that some of these contingencies are the effects of people's deliberate efforts to create space for change and then use it. At their best, these are not approaches based on voluntaristic, overly optimistic views of human agency. They do, however, emphasize the reflexive, tactical, and strategic dimensions of human agency (as well as the routine ones), and they explore how the exercise of such agency, and the negotiations that go on at the interfaces among a range of actors, are central to both the reproduction and change of institutions.[4]

As noted earlier, one critical body of work here focuses on discourses of development, a literature that has been effective in pointing to the ways in which understandings of development, once framed and codified, exercise great influence over what is and is not done in the name of development (Ferguson 1990; Escobar 1995; Mitchell 2002). More specifically, these approaches emphasize that the discursive positions of dominant institutions consistently exclude reflections on political economy and politics and thus lead to technical interventions that, even if well intentioned, can never succeed in addressing the problems they set out to tackle, because they are unable to act upon the "real" source of those problems.

John Harriss (2002) has suggested that something very similar is afoot in the rise of the social capital discourse within the World Bank—that it is one more attempt at "depoliticizing development." These critiques have resonated very widely, yet they leave hanging the questions of how such discourses emerge in a given institutional context and of how, in actuality, discursive practices intersect with material practices of intervention—indeed, how change of any kind is brought about within large organizations. If these interpretations are right in suggesting that such institutions will always generate discourses that divert attention from politics, then it becomes interesting to look at what happens when groups within an institution attempt to draw attention to certain dimensions of the political process surrounding development.

James Scott's (1998) important study of the ways in which states "see" delivers a somewhat similar interpretation. He draws attention to the ways in which states need to make landscapes, populations, and other domains of intervention and control "legible" in order to be able to act upon them. This process of making abstract entities and processes legible involves considerable simplification, be it in how forest ecologies are re-created, land tenure systems legislated, or development plans conceptualized. Scott insists that these simplifications consistently prevent the state from recognizing the practical, iterative, local knowledge (what he refers to as *mêtis*) that allows people to make systems work. As a consequence, attempts by the state and other large, powerful bureaucracies to develop and implement simplified blueprints for "schemes to improve the human condition" consistently fail because they do not allow the space that people need to adapt, modify, and make functional such blueprints. While in Ferguson's analysis the discourses of centralizing institutions exclude politics, in Scott's they exclude practical knowledge. Either way, interventions derived from those readings of the world lead to effects that are not consonant with their stated (development) objectives and thus, in Scott's language, "fail."

Of course, there is no shortage of examples of development debacles in schemes emanating from large bureaucracies, and this helps substantiate such arguments, not least because in most cases an important source of failure is said to lie in the tendency of such institutions to produce inflexible blueprints for development. As both Scott and Ferguson remind us, though, more important than talking about failure is to inquire into why such things happen the way they do. That said, it is also important to inquire into why schemes emanating from such bureaucracies sometimes *do* seem to work, and sometimes very well, in the sense that they meet development goals that their authors, and a broader community, consider desirable. Inquiries into such cases suggest the need to elaborate more fully the internal workings of such bureaucracies and how, within their realms, ideas translate into actions.

In this respect, the longer-standing body of work on policy implementation (e.g., Grindle 1986, 1997; Grindle and Thomas 1991) and Judith Tendler's (1997) influential work on good government in Brazil open up lines of inquiry. This research has shown how ideas are translated, often in unexpected ways, in the process of implementation and that bureaucrats and field staff are active agents in that process of translation (see also Long and Long 1992). In land reform and rural development programs, for instance, this translation has often frustrated program implementation and turned such programs into things they were not intended to be (Grindle 1986). In some cases, however, the political commitments of certain staff have led to far more intensive implementations of land reform (and thus more radical interpretations of what land reform was meant to be) than were anticipated by the policy ideas underlying it (Cleaves and Scurrah 1980).

Of course, in such cases bureaucrats may continue to implement policies with a model in mind that misinterprets, or at least excludes recognition of, certain elements of the social reality in which they are intervening. Indeed, this argument has been made precisely to explain the ways in which land reforms have often generated resistance within the very populations they were intended to assist. Nonetheless, the implication is that it is not quite good enough to associate a discourse with a centralized bureaucracy and expect the ways in which it is implemented to cohere with that centralized vision. Indeed, it is not only citizens and workers who have *mêtis*, the practical knowledge necessary to make things really work; bureaucrats and government technicians have their own particular forms of *mêtis* (and, likewise, the practical knowledge to change how things work to make them more in line with their own view of the world).

Tendler's (1997) work illustrates this point very nicely, emphasizing the ways in which both the ideologues and foot soldiers of public programs operate and think about their work. She also demonstrates the ways in which bureaucrats and project staff can, under certain conditions, become sufficiently embedded in the societies in which they are intervening that their understandings move ever closer to those of the people with whom they are working. She also shows, quite explicitly, that this can translate into highly positive human development outcomes. Her analysis suggests—in a way similar to some of Grindle's work—that, in order to understand how bureaucracies frame and implement development interventions, it is critical to understand the internal sociology of those bureaucracies. Only then is it possible to explain the emergence of certain ideas, the particular ways in which they are linked to interventions, and the conditions under which space for innovative action is struggled over, opened up, sustained, and also closed.

As these chapters suggest, it is important to trace the life of ideas within bureaucracies and the ways in which actors mobilize and act on ideas in attempts to influence the policymaking process (Campbell 2002).

Although some such work has been done, Campbell suggests that the causal processes involved remain underspecified—just as, indeed, the causal links between social capital and good government are underspecified in Putnam's (1993) study of democracy in Italy, which effectively launched the idea of "social capital" onto an international stage. Indeed, on the basis of this observation, Campbell identifies the need for research that focuses on "identifying the actors who seek to influence policy making with their ideas, ascertaining the institutional conditions under which these actors have more or less influence, and understanding how political discourse affects the degree to which policy ideas are communicated and translated into practice" (2002: 21).

These various insights into the internal dynamics of development bureaucracies—and Campbell's (2002) call to understand in much more detail the causal processes through which discursive and material practices are linked—resonate with the increasing number of calls for ethnographies of development organizations. In their masterful synthesis of the relationships between the social sciences and international development, Cooper and Packard (1997) noted that one of the largest gaps in academic knowledge of development relates to the inner workings of development agencies—of all types (see also Watts 2001; Markowitz 2001). Only with such knowledge, they implied, would it be possible to understand the processes through which ideas affect practices and organized discourses on development. In an offshoot project, Peters (2001) took that call to heart and, collecting people who had worked within development projects, pursued the ways in which development practices were engineered in particular institutional settings (though ones that were primarily nongovernmental). More recently, Lewis et al. (2003) brought together writings in anthropology and organizational theory to suggest the importance of ethnographic study of organizational culture in development interventions. They suggest that organizational culture is constantly being produced, sometimes tending toward integration, often toward fragmentation. This fragmentation, indicative of a range of cultures within development organizations, is an important reason that projects fail and ideas stated in project documents often are not realized, especially ideas that are novel and institutionally contentious.

These calls for ethnographies that would trace the causal processes through which texts are produced and particular ideas and practices become prominent within development organizations are closely related to the well-established tradition of actor-oriented approaches to development, which owe much to Norman Long (Long 1992; Long and Long 1992; Arce and Long 2000). This work has, like Tendler's, thrown considerable light on how national and local development bureaucracies function and how this functioning leads almost inevitably to significant slippages between the development goals laid down in policy and project documents, the goals pursued in operational practice, and the personal goals pursued by "clients" and local bureaucrats in the course of implementing (or "performing") projects (Long 1992: 34). Indeed, the emphasis of this work on slippage between development text and effect is a salutary warning to those tactical reformists (such as social scientists in the Bank; see Mosse 2004) who commit themselves to influencing the texts of an institution as a means of changing it. Given the myriad other external and internal forces affecting what is actually done through an institution such as the Bank (e.g., Alkire 2004), such an emphasis on ideas in the abstract may simply not be enough. Thus, in the actor-oriented approach, analysis of practice must accompany analysis of text if one is to understand fully how development organizations produce ideas, how slippage occurs in their translation into practice, and the material effects.

In their different ways these distinct (but linked) approaches to analyzing the institutions of development inform both the argument and the approach of this book. They have led us to include chapters addressing general struggles and negotiations over ideas within the World Bank as well as chapters exploring the relationships between ideas and actions within particular project contexts. They have led to what we intend to convey as a quite guarded, but still real, optimism about the scope for change and the room for maneuvering within a large development organization such as the Bank. Finally, they have led to an approach that combines the insights of insiders—with their own *mêtis*, as well as their own biases—and those of outsiders, with different sorts of bias and possibly more room for maneuvering (but less scope for immediate impact) in the ways in which they can frame problems (Mosse 2004). Before we proceed to those chapters, however, it is important to say something about both the history and the organizational structure of the Bank, for each of these topics is not only complex but also partly determinant of the forms that debates over social development and social capital have taken in the institution.

Mapping the World Bank: History, Structure, Organization, Actors

The structure of the World Bank is daunting enough for its employees, let alone outsiders, but a rendering of the mechanisms by which ideas do or do not engage with institutional practice, and the extent to which relations between actors within and outside are central to those mechanisms, requires us to provide at least a basic mapping of that structure and a sense of its historical evolution. Given the size and organizational complexity of the Bank, a simple insider/outsider distinction is inadequate for understanding how ideas enter the institution and are disseminated (or not) within it. Before this mapping is explored in further detail, however, it is worthwhile to review, albeit schematically, how the Bank's current institutional structure and mandate came to be.[5]

The World Bank, since its founding at the end of World War II, has been a member organization of the United Nations, along with the International Monetary Fund. In general terms, the original division of labor between the Bank and the Fund was such that the Bank would assume responsibility for more "micro" projects designed to foster long-term development, while the Fund would address more short-term "macro" economic issues (such as runaway inflation or currency crises) and fiscal stabilization. The name World Bank is actually an overarching label for five constituent organizations, namely the International Bank for Reconstruction and Development (IBRD, the largest and best-known part, which offers loans and technical advice to low-income countries), the International Finance Corporation (IFC, which assists with commercial business development), the Multilateral Investment Guarantee Association (MIGA, which acts as a global insurance agency for national governments), the International Development Association (IDA, which provides grants and "soft loans" to the world's poorest countries), and the International Center for Settlement of Investment Disputes (ICSID). The IBRD and IDA constitute the World Bank proper, while the ICSID, IFC, and MIGA are "affiliates" that "are closely associated with the World Bank" to form the World Bank Group (World Bank Group 2005).

As implied by the IBRD title, the primary mission of the World Bank in the early decades of its existence was "reconstruction" of physical infrastructure, in the first instance in war-torn Europe and Japan. Indeed, the Bank's first loan was actually made to France. Once that task was accomplished, however, and its successes duly celebrated, attention quickly turned to undertaking similar ventures, using similar approaches, in the poorer nations (see Box 1.2). In light of the relatively quick revival of the Japanese economy, and even the rapid gains obtained via state-led industrialization in the Soviet bloc countries, the core problem of underdevelopment in Asia, Africa, and Latin America was largely defined as an "objects gap" (Romer 1993) with respect to investment and infrastructure—a gap that a large international agency, with its growing cadre of construction and finance "experts," seemed well equipped to fill.

Under the leadership of Robert McNamara in the late 1960s through the 1970s, the core mission of the Bank was re-articulated as one of poverty reduction, with agricultural extension specialists joining engineers and macroeconomists on the Bank's staff. During this period the instrument of choice continued to be large projects designed and implemented by external technocrats—in particular, large-scale integrated rural development projects.

In the 1980s, however, technological changes and geopolitical forces led to a shift in how "the problem" of underdevelopment was conceived. It was now an "ideas gap" characterized by "bad policies," "weak capacity," and "low human development," for which "the solution" was some combination of structural adjustment loans and standardized programs to expand health care and education. Structural adjustment loans typically disbursed large amounts of money, but their funds were conditional on domestic policy reforms—in particular, reforms related to the liberalization of trade, reductions in the size of the public sector, privatizations of state-owned assets, the introduction of cost recovery mechanisms in service delivery, and so forth. The design, sequencing, and timing of these reforms and programs remained largely determined by outside "experts."

The end of the Cold War ushered in a new, if somewhat delayed and ultimately contested, period for reframing the problem of and the solution(s) to development. In the early 1990s many claimed that history had delivered an unequivocal verdict in favor of "the market," and for a while, low-income and transition countries alike were besieged with all manner of advice on how to build "market-friendly" economies. Faced with a choice between making incremental or rapid reform, the most influential

---

**Box 1.2   Phases in Dominant Conceptions of
Development at the World Bank**

Very broadly, dominant lines of development thought in the World Bank have gone through eras characterized by their formative ideas (Kapur et al. 1997; Mallaby 2004):

- *Development is about engineering and physical infrastructure.* This idea prevailed in the era of large investments in dams, roads, electricity, ports, and the like.
- *Development is about poverty (version 1).* The Bank in the era of Robert McNamara's presidency (following his tenure as U.S. Secretary of Defense) saw a direct link between poverty, rural unrest, and communism and responded by investing massively in rural development.
- *Development is about policy reform.* This was the theme during the period of structural adjustment, an era that looked at the McNamara years, saw little impact on poverty reduction or economic growth, and concluded that the best way to address poverty was to foster growth.
- *Development is about poverty (version 2).* The Wolfensohn years have been characterized by a multidimensional understanding of both the causes and consequences of poverty, an understanding that exists in uneasy interaction with a continued commitment to policy reform, economic growth, and adjustment lending. This is also the period in which debates on social capital became significant within the institution.

voices stressed the virtues of "shock therapy," invoking aphorisms such as "you can only jump a canyon in a single bound" to make their case.[6]

By the mid-1990s, however, the more painful lesson was that "institutions"—in all their various guises—were crucial for making economies, societies, and polities work. The development challenge was now framed as one of building, reforming, and sustaining institutions. The growing voice of erstwhile marginalized groups (on the demand side, one might say), coupled with influential scholarly work (on the supply side) on the power of information asymmetries and the importance of context-specific knowledge, combined to establish a new conceptual and political space for debating the means, ends, and definitions of development. In an important development, a new president—James Wolfensohn—arrived at the helm of the World Bank in this period, a president less deferential to economic orthodoxy than his predecessors (despite his impeccable Wall Street credentials), willing to embrace a more holistic view of the development challenge, and, crucially, committed to giving social development perspectives a formal voice within the Bank in those deliberations and corresponding lending activities.[7] An upshot was the creation in 1996 of the Social Development Department,[8] whose challenges and opportunities to establish legitimacy within the organization are ongoing, but whose struggles required a language that—at least in its earliest stages—cast a good share of its lot with the idea of social capital. This is one of the contexts within which the politics and practice of the idea of social capital at the World Bank—the basis of this book—has played itself out.

Another is the internal organizational structure of the Bank itself, a basic familiarity with which is crucial to understanding whether and how ideas gain (or lose) traction. Today the World Bank has approximately ten thousand employees, three-quarters of whom are based in Washington, the others working out of Resident Missions in the Bank's member countries. The head of a Resident Mission is called a Country Director, and he or she is responsible for managing the various Bank-funded development projects in that country. Country programs are themselves located in one of six regions, organized institutionally as Vice Presidencies within the Bank: sub-Saharan Africa (AFR), Middle East and North Africa (MNA), Europe and Central Asia (ECA), South Asia (SAR), East Asia and the Pacific (EAP), and Latin America and the Caribbean (LCR) (World Bank Group 2005). Some staff have regionwide, or at least multicountry, responsibilities, whereas others work only with one country. The latter type of person is increasingly, though not always, located within the country rather than in Washington, whereas regional staff are more likely to be based in Washington. The administrative, analytical, and operational work of the Bank is managed by several different networks, the most important for our purposes being Human Development (HD), Environmentally and Socially Sustainable Development (ESSD), Poverty Reduction and Economic Management (PREM), and Private Sector Development and Infrastructure (PSD). Most professional staff in the Bank are mapped both to a region and to a sectoral network, though some are mapped only to a sectoral network and operate in units with responsibilities that cut across regions. These networks serve as wider professional communities (linking people with particular professional specialties) and also constitute an important part of career structures in the institution—although staff can and do move across networks, very many progress (or not) within their particular network.

Some research in the Bank is conducted within these networks on themes related to the substantive core of the network. However, the bulk (in budget, staff, and output terms) of the research and data management activities of the Bank is coordinated by the Development Economics (DEC) Vice Presidency, its two most visible departments being the Development Research Group and the Data Management Group. More evaluation-oriented studies are conducted from the Bank's Operations Evaluation Department (OED). OED reports directly to the Executive Directors, serving as a sort of internal auditor. Historically, the possibility of deploying the idea of social capital to understand development theory and practice better, and thereby increase the intellectual leverage of "social" concepts more generally, was conceived in the Social Development Department (or SDV, part of the ESSD network[9]), but the idea came to prominence across the Bank more generally under the leadership of Deepa Narayan (a former member of SDV) when she moved to the Poverty Group in PREM (a network, importantly, dominated by economists).

Overlaid on this organizational matrix are various "Communities of Practice," or groups that come together around a particular issue of interest at the intersection of research, policy, and lending that does not otherwise fit neatly into a single unit or department. These groups are known as Thematic Groups in Bank terminology,[10] and their core principle is to provide resources and spaces for individuals who want to explore particular issues in greater depth, engaging both their internal colleagues from across a range of sectors and regions, and (importantly) their counterparts outside the Bank. Of these, the Social Capital Thematic Group was, in the late 1990s and early 2000s, especially prominent. Its activities have included hosting online discussions, managing a website (complete with a bibliography and survey tools), a visiting-scholar series, in-country workshops, and an international conference. Its work fed directly into the Bank's Voices of the Poor series and its Empowerment Agenda (empowerment being the third, and most controversial, pillar of the 2000 World Development Report on poverty).

Most external actors who engage with the Bank do so through one of the networks, an individual Task Manager, or a Thematic Group. They have an impact at the time on one subsection of a larger, complex whole, much of which is difficult to identify from the outside (and even from the inside). Thus, any claim (or implication) that a given body of work by one or a group of employees represents "World Bank policy" is not accurate; even the high-profile World Development Reports are, formally, staff documents, not statements of official organization policy. For Bank employees, "having an impact" entails not just mobilizing one's peers and immediate colleagues but seeking to forge coalitions and networks that span the analytical, policy, and (crucially) operational worlds of the institution. As the chapters in this volume attempt to show, the rise and spread of the influence of the idea of social capital and practices linked to it entailed alliance building both among individuals in key positions across different realms within the Bank's organizational matrix *and* with influential external scholars and practitioners.

Plotting Social Development at the World Bank[11]

"Social development" has been the umbrella term at the Bank for the promotion of participation, civil society, empowerment, and social transformation. Since 1996 the Bank has had both a Social Development Department and a Social Development professional family. This embodiment of the concept in a set of institutional arrangements is, however, relatively recent, and for a long period the pursuit of social development concerns was undertaken from different corners of the institution.

The first sociologist hired to the Bank, Michael Cernea, was recruited by the Rural Development Department in 1974[12] to enhance the effectiveness of rural development projects (this being the period under McNamara, when the Bank prioritized rural development as an instrument of poverty reduction). Cernea was recruited in particular for his expertise in rural institutions and peasant societies, and he soon became a voice lobbying for recruitment of additional social scientists. This was a slow process, and by the late 1980s there were still only a dozen or so social scientists scattered widely across the Bank. They were linked informally through the Sociology Group, headed by Cernea, which met periodically and typically drew between twenty and fifty people to brown-bag lunches and other presentations.

Much of the work of this group focused at a project level, and—reflecting the then portfolio of Bank-funded programs—was largely rural in emphasis. Thematically, many people in this group were concerned with the roles of people and local associations in development, especially in natural resource management. The edited collection *Putting People First: Sociological Variables in Rural Development* (Cernea 1985) is a good reflection of these concerns, with chapters focusing on irrigation associations, social forestry, and farmers' groups. One of the main operational concerns at the time was to find ways of increasing people's participation in projects, but the group also had a substantive, theoretical objective. This objective was to make explicit the interactions among sociological and other variables in the development process and to change the way the institution understood development. In Cernea's words, the larger task was to challenge the "economic reductionism" in the institution's theory of development.

Putting People First is also illustrative in another sense, in that its chapters were written by both Bank staff and non-Bank researchers working closely with the nascent social team at the Bank. This strategy of building insider-outsider alliances has characterized the history of the social development community at the Bank. Indeed, as Fox and Brown (1998) argue, such cross-boundary relationships have played an important role in opening up spaces in the institution that, in turn, have given more room to those within the Bank who have been committed to social development. Two initiatives that emerged in the late 1980s and early 1990s are illustrative and important in this regard.

The first was an initiative that sought to promote and ultimately institutionalize concerns for participation in the Bank. Non-Bank actors—in particular NGOs—had been increasingly vocal in calling on the institution to open up its project cycle and other activities to the participation of poor people and, more generally, of developing-country citizens and civil-society actors. One response to this was the establishment of a Bank-wide Learning Group on Participatory Development in 1990, led by the NGO Unit, to accelerate understanding of participatory processes within the institution and to explore ways of increasing participation in Bank programs. This group combined both "social" staff and others with shared commitments and met informally around periodic meetings, breakfasts, visiting speakers, and the like. The initiative produced syntheses of experiments with participation in Bank projects (Bhatnagar and Williams 1992). The next steps were to commission papers on participation from people both within and outside the Bank and to convene, in 1994, a very visible conference on participation that brought together Bank staff and externals and led to a working paper series on participation and later a *Participation Sourcebook* (World Bank 1996).

The second process, unfolding during the same period and involving many of the same people, grew out of the growing international criticism of the social and environmental impacts of large-scale Bank-funded infrastructure projects. One of the most controversial projects involved a series of proposed dams on the Narmada River in western India, though there were other large "disaster" projects that also attracted much criticism (such as the Polonoreste project in Brazil and transmigration in Indonesia). In response to growing concerns about the environmental and social impacts of these projects, environment divisions were formed in each of the four regions as part of a major Bank reorganization in 1987. These divisions eventually came to include social as well as environmental expertise, and their work revolved around mitigating the negative effects of projects on people. A second, slightly later response came when the

Bank management (nudged along in some measure by Cernea) requested that he lead a review of experiences with resettlement across the institution. This so-called Resettlement Review (published in 1993) was very critical of the Bank's operation in this sphere and highlighted the many ways in which resettlement had created poverty and in which the Bank had not followed its own internal guidelines.

These two initiatives were important in several respects beyond their particular subject matter. First, they brought a number of people into the institution, several of whom would in later years see the social capital discussion as a means of deepening these concerns for participation, consultation, and the analysis of social relationships prior to project design. Second, they created momentum for institutional change. In particular, in 1993 the Bank created a Division for Social Policy and Resettlement within the Environment Department whose mandate was to monitor resettlement, to ensure the enforcement of Bank policies that sought to reduce the harm that development interventions might otherwise effect, and to broaden the place of social analysis and policy in the Bank.[13]

The year 1993 saw, then, the release of the Resettlement Review, the creation of the Division for Social Policy and Resettlement, and the publication of Robert Putnam's *Making Democracy Work* (1993), the book that would propel the concept of social capital to both the academic and public limelight. Putnam argued that the main factor explaining the quality of regional government performance and responsiveness in Italy was the density and quality of civic associations. These associations, he argued, both bred a capacity to engage politically and nurtured networks of trust, linking people within civil society and people working in government (see Chapter 2 for more detail). These networks of trust and cooperation he referred to as *social capital*.

The book quickly gained traction in the Bank, both in DEC and in the Vice Presidency for Environmentally Sustainable Development, within which most social development staff then sat.[14] Indeed, by 1994 Bank publications were referring to the importance of social capital as an asset for development (Serageldin and Steer 1994). In these early days, some social development staff viewed social capital as a concept to help frame their belief in participation and local organization, whereas some economists began to see it as potentially useful in taking them beyond the limitations of game theory in explaining patterns of cooperation and "success" in Bank projects (see Chapter 3). Institutionally, the concept became yet more visible when, in 1996, Cernea persuaded the still-new president of the World Bank (Wolfensohn) to commission a Social Development Task Force to explore the importance of social development for the Bank and the potential for increasing its significance within the institution. As an input into its thinking, the Task Force organized a dozen working groups to look at certain key topics; one of these looked at social capital (World Bank 1996, 1997). One of the ultimate effects of the Task Force was the creation in 1997 of a Social Development Department.

By the time of the creation of the Social Development Department, then, the concept of social capital was being discussed quite widely. It was certainly not the only discussion within the social development family, or even the one on which most people could find agreement. It did, however, occupy a central conceptual position in the family's efforts to talk about its understanding of development. At a more personal level, it also occupied a pivotal place in the ways in which key players in social development at the Bank were talking about development at the time, particularly Gloria Davis (the Director of Social Development) and Deepa Narayan (see Chapter 2). Some of the most visible work of the new Social Development Department and family thus hinged around social capital, with two large research initiatives: one on local-level institutions and development (Grootaert 1999), and another on social capital (the so-called Social Capital Initiative; Grootaert and van Bastelaer 2002).

In many respects this fascination with local associations simply continued themes that Cernea had addressed when he first joined the Bank: the emphasis on institutions and social relations and the challenge to the economism of Bank theory. The language, however, was not the same. It thus becomes critical to ask whether this shift in language has made any difference. Had it helped carry forward any further the concerns of Cernea, those of the Participation Learning Group, and those of the Resettlement Review? In the ongoing battle to embed social development in the institution, has the concept opened up new fronts (as advocates hoped), or has it in fact ceded space (as critics suggest is more likely)? These are the themes addressed by the chapters of this book.

Mapping the Chapters

We noted earlier that this text might be thought of as a complement to Fox and Brown's (1998) study of the articulations between the World Bank, NGOs, and grassroots movements. In that collection, the editors combined essays from practitioners (in that case, civil society activists) and academic researchers. This collection has followed a similar strategy and brings together contributions from researchers and people who have been (to varying degrees) insiders in the institution. Indeed, the "map" of the Bank introduced in the preceding section—a mapping both of the formal institutional structure of the Bank and of the social and professional positions that define actors' degree of identification with, and location within or outside, the institution—is helpful for introducing the book's chapters. It serves to locate them and explain what they do and do not say, what they are and are not able to say, and how directly they influence what the Bank actually does.[15]

Following this introduction, the book is divided into three broad sections, with conclusions in Section IV. The first section, which includes three chapters, does two main things. It discusses the conditions under and ways in which the social capital debate has been framed within the World Bank, as well as reflecting ways in which the ferment has been viewed by different sorts of Bank insider. Importantly, the chapters do not discuss the framing of the debate in the broader academy. Though the two framings are obviously related—not least because some of the key actors have been involved in each context—they are not the same. The focus here is on the framings that have occurred within the Bank and, indeed, within particular parts of the institution.

Chapter 2 discusses ways in which social capital has been conceptualized and suggests specific ways in which it might be most productively framed within a development organization such as the Bank. Written by two of the main propagators of the social capital discussion in the institution, it provides a summary of how the concept has been understood by the social development family at the Bank. Although, as of this writing, Deepa Narayan works in the Poverty Reduction and Economic Management network, she has long maintained close links with the Social Development Department and has worked there in the past, in particular on issues of participation and, later, when beginning her own work on social capital.[16] She has also pushed the empowerment agenda at the institution, and the chapter traces ways in which the social capital debates fed into and helped structure elements of the empowerment discussion.

The third chapter is written by two Bank economists (Jeffrey Hammer and Lant Pritchett), who have spent much of their careers in the Bank as research economists. Their chapter complements Chapter 2 in that it discusses ways in which Bank economists have approached social capital, and both the theoretical and the institutional reasons they have found it to be of any interest. The conclusion of the chapter is more guarded, suggesting that the term *social capital* may be of limited use in the future. However, Hammer and Pritchett suggest that the term has helped to introduce a concern for a "social something" in the work of many Bank economists that did not exist in the past, and that concern is likely to endure, as shown, for example, in the stress on "relationships of accountability" in high-profile documents such as the 2004 World Development Report on service delivery (World Bank 2003).

Chapter 4, by Michael Edwards, takes a more interpretive tack. If the prior two chapters discuss some of the conceptual reasons the concept gained traction in the Bank, Edwards is more interested in exploring some of the strategic reasons. The analysis is based on his own year or so working within the Civil Society Unit of the World Bank (he works now with the Ford Foundation) and watching the social capital debate unfold around him. It is a "street corner society" (Whyte 1943) sort of ethnographic take on these processes, coupled with a critique of how far the debate can, and cannot, go in terms of bringing issues of social power to the Bank's agenda.

Whereas the first section of the book is dominated by people who have spent long periods working at "the center" of the Bank, largely on issues of research and policy, the second section, "Operationalizing Social Capital Ideas," is dominated by people with much closer links to projects. This section is concerned with the ways in which some of the conceptual arguments over social capital have traveled to—or been drawn in by—operational staff. Sometimes these staff have found the ideas helpful for framing project interventions, at other times for communicating project ideas within the Bank, and at still other times for evaluating and interpreting the effects that projects have had, thus contributing to discussions about how future projects ought to (or might) be conceptualized. These chapters discuss some of the different links between a concept and its practice, though at the same time they suggest ways in which material practices (of and within operations) affect discursive practices—both those of Task Managers and those enacted at the center of the Bank.

Chapter 5 discusses the largest—in both geographical and financial terms—Bank-funded project to have been influenced by the social capital discussion: the Kecamatan (sub-district) Development Project (KDP) in Indonesia. This project (now in its third phase and eighth year) was made possible in a very real sense by prior research on village-level social capital in Indonesia. This study—which understood social capital both as the "horizontal" capacity to act collectively within a village and as the "vertical" linkages between village groups and external actors (such as other villages, NGOs, and the government)—provided empirical material with which to argue that it was worth investing in these different forms of "social capital" as part of a poverty reduction strategy (Chandrakirana 1998; Grootaert 1999). In the chapter, Scott Guggenheim discusses the ways in which this research about social capital interacted with certain political economic conjunctures in both Indonesia and the Bank to create the space that made KDP possible.

The next chapter in this section deals with an indigenous development project in Ecuador, an operation that was the Bank's first effort to support the strengthening of indigenous people's organizations and to work much more directly with such organizations. The authors, sociologist Jorge Uquillas and economist Martien Van Nieuwkoop, discuss how the project staff—while initially understanding their function in terms of indigenous people's policy within the Bank—began to frame their objectives and impacts in terms of social capital formation. They did so in order to communicate the project more broadly within the Bank and also to try to overcome the otherwise implicit sense that the indigenous people's agenda (and people who worked on it) were exceptionalist and thus marginal within the institution. Social capital provided a language for generalizing the significance of the program beyond the small group of Bank staff concerned with indigenous people's issues. Both authors, in this case, are very much on the inside of the Bank; at the time of writing, each was based in the Latin American Department and was involved in the conceptualization, management, and monitoring of the project. Yet it is also significant that Uquillas is Ecuadorian and has, in previous positions, worked directly with indigenous organizations in Ecuador. In a significant sense, his experience beyond the Bank helped make this project possible, for, based on this experience, Uquillas was committed, within the institution, to making a project of this nature possible.

The seventh chapter addresses the case of social funds in the World Bank. Social funds are aimed at distributing resources quickly to local initiatives intended to reduce poverty in the context of ongoing structural adjustments. They have been designed to disburse resources quickly and (in general) directly to local organizations (nongovernmental and governmental). They have been hotly contested,[17] some arguing that, rather than being poverty reduction instruments, they have been complicit in adjustment programs, serving to dissipate protest while at the same time continuing to weaken traditional line agencies by bypassing them. Supporters, however, suggest that they have been vehicles for strengthening local organizational capacity and also for poverty reduction. In this chapter Julie Van Domelen, who has been involved with social funds since the first Bank-sponsored fund in Bolivia in 1986, discusses the general experience with social funds, explores the extent to which they have built local organizational capacity, and reflects on how far the social capital debate in the Bank has helped inform the work of social funds. Having been involved in a range of social fund operations, she was for a long time based in the Social Protection Unit of the Human Development Network, where she played a more advisory and analytical role. She is now Lead Social Protection Specialist in the Bank's Africa Region.

The third section of the book, "Evaluating Operations Through a Social Capital Lens," includes chapters that have been written from outside the World Bank, primarily by academic researchers who have used themes raised by the social capital debate in their efforts to assess World Bank operations. Not surprisingly, these external views are somewhat more skeptical and critical. They suggest the many obstacles to Bank projects delivering on a social development agenda, in particular as it applies to questions of participation and empowerment. There are many factors behind this, among them incentives and practices within the Bank, government agencies, and even NGOs, as well as the rough-and-tumble of national politics and related politics of gender, ethnicity, and class. Interestingly, however, in some ways these studies turn the social capital lens back on the Bank. Though not in each case using that terminology, they do suggest that if this concept really is a means to help people within the Bank think more carefully about power, social relationships, and the complexities of organizations, then in many Bank operations it is not having this effect.

The first chapter in this section is by Jonathan Fox and John Gershman. Although writing from an academic position, Fox has a long history of doing research on the World Bank (Fox 1997; Fox and Brown 1998; Clark et al. 2003) and also performing research funded by the Bank (e.g., Fox and Aranda 1996). During 1996 he also participated (as did Bebbington) in discussions within the World Bank regarding the ways in which the concept of social capital might contribute to a social development agenda (World Bank 1996). He is thus an outsider with something of an "in" and a more nuanced knowledge of the institution than most other Bank watchers. In their chapter, Fox and Gershman inquire into the institutional conditions that make it possible for World Bank projects to contribute to social capital, in the form of both "horizontal social capital on the ground" and "intersectoral social capital that bridges social and institutional divides" (Fox and Gershman, this volume).[18] In particular, they are interested in how flows of money related to Bank-funded operations affect relationships of power. They base their argument on an analysis of projects in the Philippines and Mexico, with a special focus on how Bank projects affect the relationships between government agencies and autonomous social organizations.

The next chapter shares this interest in the ways in which Bank-funded interventions affect both the capacities and power of autonomous social organizations and also the relationships between these organizations, government, and other types of organizations (such as NGOs). David Lewis and M. Shameen Siddiqi consider the ways in which a relatively small Bank-supported project concerned with promoting commercial silk production affected relationships between the local Bank office, government agencies, private foundations, several NGOs, and village-based women's groups involved in silk production. The authors write from positions completely external to the Bank, having had no prior contact. This outsider location did not necessarily translate into especially critical conclusions, though the study suggests ways in which the organizational culture of the World Bank jeopardizes any possibility that the Bank might deliver on the sorts of empowerment agendas that have grown out of work on social capital (Chapter 2). They also ask whether a social capital lens—at least in the form in which it is often used—is sufficient for unveiling the types of power and dependency relations that structure transactions in rural Bangladesh. They suggest that, to the extent that such relations are not addressed head on, projects are highly unlikely to deliver on an empowerment agenda. Indeed, they see few empowerment effects of the project they discuss.

Following these empirical chapters—written from different positions vis-à-vis the World Bank—Chapter 10 in Section IV, written by ourselves, reads across the contributions to this collection. It reflects on the different ways in which the concept of social capital appears to have been used in the Bank, the extent to which the concept has influenced broader debates and practices in the institution, and the extent to which this might have made a material difference in the lives of people in areas affected by Bank programs. It also moves the discussion back to a more general level by reflecting on the implications of these cases and experiences for thinking about the roles of ideas and reformists in fostering change in large-scale development institutions.

The studies suggest very strongly that, even if the debate on social capital has opened up some space for change, and has in some cases led to important changes in projects and their effects, there are many obstacles to carrying social development concerns through to practice in World Bank–funded (and likely other) operations. Many of these structural constraints relate to factors that some have hoped the social capital debate (within the Bank at least) would make more explicit: questions of power, real politics, institutional incentives, and so forth. The sense is that even if the concept of social capital *could* illuminate some of these issues (though not all contributors agree on this), it will take more than a discursive shift within the Bank for the institution to engage more fully with these issues (cf. Alkire 2004). It will also require pressure from outside. Indeed, just as Fox and Brown, whose primary concern was the effect of external pressure on Bank behavior, conclude that "insider-outsider reform coalitions" (1998: 534) are of acute importance in eliciting any shift in Bank practice, our focus on internal sources of change brings us necessarily to the same conclusion. Working from within the Bank to change discourse, and hence practice, is important, but it is not and never will be enough if the goal is (as indeed it must be) to elicit more than partial, patchy, and incomplete changes in how the Bank sees the world, how it acts upon it, and how it transforms it.

Notes

1. We discuss this literature later in this chapter; see also Bebbington et al. (2004).
2. See, for example, Fine (2001) and Harriss (2002).
3. In a recent paper, Fox (2004: 1) continues to sustain this argument: "[P]ro-poor reform initiatives are likely to have broader and deeper institutional impacts if they are accompanied by processes of strategic interaction between policy makers and civil society counterparts."
4. See, among others, Giddens (1984), Long and Long (1992), Arce and Long (2000), and Bebbington (2000).
5. For a more detailed treatment of the Bank's institutional history, see Pincus and Winters (2002) and Kapur et al. (1997).

6. See Adams and Brick (1993) for a satirical dialogue on the nature and content of such encounters.
7. See Mallaby (2004) for a history of the Wolfensohn years at the World Bank.
8. For further details on this aspect and the ways in which the social development agenda "co-evolved" with these broader shifts in Bank policy and practice, see the following chapters of this book and the paper by Gloria Davis (2004), the founding director of the Social Development Department.
9. See Davis (2004) on the evolution of various social ideas and strategies in SDV.
10. This is a central element of the Bank's efforts to reposition itself not merely as a financial lending institution but as a Knowledge Bank, able to disseminate data, ideas, and "good practice" around the globe quickly and cheaply. The Bank has been highly praised for this work (see, for example, Wenger and Snyder 2000).
11. This section draws heavily on Davis (2004), which provides both an institutional and a personal history of social development, and Bebbington et al. (2004).
12. Thanks to Michael Cernea for interviews regarding this period.
13. For the Bank's most recent work on this issue, see the *Involuntary Resettlement Sourcebook* (World Bank 2004), a compendium of lessons learned from a range of resettlement initiatives.
14. It is important to note that, at the time, Putnam was a close advisor to both Ismail Serageldin (head of the Environment Department) and Michael Bruno (the Bank's Chief Economist). The details of these connections are outlined in Bebbington et al. (2004).
15. Among the authors, Anthony Bebbington is the most "outside" of the Bank, working from an academic position. He has, however, spent two periods (a total of 19 months) working as a social scientist in the Social Development Department (1999–2000) and its precursor, the Social Policy and Resettlement Division (1995–1996). On both occasions his mandate was to work within the social capital debate, conducting and managing research and participating in working groups and other fora. Michael Woolcock is based in the Development Research Group (DRG) and is one of the two non-economists in what is otherwise viewed as the largest economics faculty in the world. The DRG plays a critical role in the management and analysis of development data and thus, concomitantly, the adjudication of new ideas; some argue that it is the epicenter of the Bank's efforts to uphold what Wade (1996) has called "paradigm maintenance." In many cases, however, its staff move in and out of academic positions, or (as in the case of Woolcock) hold adjunct academic positions at the same time they work for the World Bank. The adjudication function of the DRG is thus always potentially unstable, especially when people leave and begin to publish in ways that contest elements of Bank orthodoxy (as in the case of William Easterly). Scott Guggenheim, an anthropologist, currently works within the social development family, based in the East Asia Region and specifically in Jakarta. Having worked in the "center" in the past, his current position places him squarely in operations, sometimes as Task Manager and other times as senior advisor.

16. Since writing this piece, Narayan has moved and is now based in the World Bank's office in New Delhi.
17. See, for instance, recent policy fora in the *Journal of International Development* (2002: vol 14, no. 5) and the *World Bank Economic Review* (2002: vol. 16, no. 2). See also Tendler (2000a, 2000b) and Rawlings et al. (2003).
18. The notion of *intersectoral social capital* is very similar to the concept of *linking social capital*, discussed in Chapter 3.

References

Adams, Walter, and James W. Brick. 1993. *Adam Smith goes to Moscow: A dialogue on radical reform.* Princeton, NJ: Princeton University Press.

Alkire, Sabina. 2004. Culture, poverty and external intervention. In *Culture and public action: A cross-disciplinary perspective on development policy,* edited by Vijayendra Rao and Michael Walton. Stanford, CA: Stanford University Press, pp. 185–209.

Arce, Alberto, and Norman Long, eds. 2000. *Anthropology, development and modernities.* London: Routledge.

Bebbington, Anthony. 2000. Re-encountering development: Livelihood transitions and place transformations in the Andes. *Annals of the Association of American Geographers* 90(3):495–520.

Bebbington, Anthony, Scott Guggenheim, Elizabeth Olson, and Michael Woolcock. 2004. Exploring social capital debates at the World Bank. *Journal of Development Studies* 40(5):33–64.

Bhatnagar, Bhuvan, and Aubrey Williams, eds. 1992. *Participatory development and the World Bank: Potential directions for change.* World Bank Discussion Paper 183. Washington, DC: World Bank.

Campbell, John. 2002. Ideas, politics and public policy. *Annual Review of Sociology* 28:21–38.

Cernea, Michael, ed. 1985 (rev. 1991)*Putting people first: Sociological variables in rural development.* Oxford: Oxford University Press.

Chandrakirana, Kamala. 1998. Local capacity and its implications for development: The case of Indonesia. Mimeo. Jakarta: World Bank.

Clark, Dana, Jonathan Fox, and Kay Treakle, eds. 2003. *Demanding accountability: Civil-society claims and the World Bank Inspection Panel.* Lanham, MD: Rowman and Littlefield.

Cleaves, Peter, and Martin Scurrah. 1980. *Agriculture, bureaucracy and the military.* Ithaca, NY: Cornell University Press.

Cooper, Frederick, and Randall Packard, eds. 1997. *International development and the social sciences: Essays on the history and politics of knowledge.* Berkeley: University of California Press.

Davis, Gloria. 2004. *A history of the Social Development Network in the World Bank, 1973–2002.* Social Development Paper No. 56. Washington, DC: World Bank, Social Development Department.

Escobar, Arturo. 1995. *Encountering development:The making and unmaking of the Third World.* Princeton, NJ: Princeton University Press.

Farr, James. 2004. Social capital: A conceptual history. *Political Theory* 32(1):6–33.

Ferguson, James. 1990. *The anti-politics machine: Development, depoliticization and bureaucratic power in Lesotho*. New York: Cambridge University Press.

Fine, Ben. 2001. *Social capital versus social theory: Political economy and social science at the turn of the millennium*. London: Routledge.

Fox, Jonathan. 1997. The World Bank and social capital: Contesting the concept in practice. *Journal of International Development* 9(7):963–971.

Fox, Jonathan. 2004. Empowerment and institutional change: Mapping "virtuous circles" of state-society interaction. In *Power, rights, and poverty: Concepts and connections*, edited by Ruth Alsop. Washington, DC: World Bank; London: UK Department for International Development.

Fox, Jonathan, and Josefina Aranda. 1996. *Decentralization and rural development in Mexico: Community participation in Oaxaca's Municipal Funds Program*. La Jolla: University of California, San Diego, Center for US-Mexican Studies Contemporary Monograph Series.

Fox, Jonathan, and L. David Brown. 1998. *The struggle for accountability: The World Bank*. Cambridge, MA: MIT Press.

Gardner, Katy, and David Lewis. 2000. Dominant paradigms overturned or "business as usual"? Development discourse and the White Paper on international development. *Critique of Anthropology* 20(1):15–29.

Giddens, Anthony. 1984. *The constitution of society: Outline of the theory of structuration*. Cambridge, UK: Polity Press.

Grindle, Merilee. 1986. *State and countryside*. Baltimore: Johns Hopkins University Press.

Grindle, Merilee. 1997. Divergent cultures? When public organizations perform well in developing countries. *World Development* 25(4):481–495.

Grindle, Merilee, and John Thomas. 1991. *Public choices and policy change: The political economy of reform in developing countries*. Baltimore: Johns Hopkins University Press.

Grootaert, Christiaan. 1999. *Social capital, household welfare and poverty in Indonesia*. Local Level Institutions Working Paper No. 6. Washington DC: World Bank, Social Development Department.

Grootaert, Christiaan, and Thierry van Bastelaer, eds. 2002. *The role of social capital in development: An empirical assessment*. Cambridge, UK: Cambridge University Press.

Harriss, John. 2002. *De-politicizing development: The World Bank and social capital*. London: Anthem Press.

Hirschman, Albert. 1963. *Journeys toward progress: Studies of economic policymaking in Latin America*. New York: Twentieth Century Fund.

Kapur, Devesh, John P. Lewis, and Richard Webb, eds. 1997. *The World Bank: Its first half century*. Washington, DC: Brookings Institution.

Lewis, David, Anthony Bebbington, Simon Batterbury, Alpa Shah, Elizabeth Olson, Shameen Siddiqi, and Sandra Duvall. 2003. Practice, power and meaning: Frameworks for studying organisational culture in multi-agency rural development projects. *Journal of International Development* 15:541–557.

Long, Norman. 1992. From paradigm lost to paradigm regained? The case for an actor-oriented sociology of development. In *Battlefields of knowledge: The inter-*

locking of theory and practice in social research and development, edited by Norman Long and Ann Long, London, Routledge, pp. 16–43.

Long, Norman, and Ann Long, eds. 1992. *Battlefields of knowledge: The interlocking of theory and practice in social research and development*. London: Routledge.

Mallaby, Sebastian. 2004. *The world's banker: A story of failed states, financial crises, and the wealth and poverty of nations*. New York: Penguin Books.

Markowitz, Lisa. 2001. Finding the field: Notes on the ethnography of NGOs. *Human Organization* 60(1):40–46.

Mitchell, Timothy. 2002. *Rule of experts: Egypt, techno-politics, modernity*. Berkeley: University of California Press.

Mosse, David. 2004. Social analysis as product development: Anthropologists at work in the World Bank. In *The development of religion/the religion of development*, edited by A. Kumar Giri, O. Salemink, and A. van Harskamp. Delft: Eburon Academic Publishers.

Peters, Pauline. 2001. *Development encounters: Sites of participation and knowledge*. Cambridge, MA: Harvard University Press.

Pincus, Jonathan, and Jeffrey Winters, eds. 2002. *Reinventing the World Bank*. Ithaca, NY: Cornell University Press.

Putnam, Robert. 1993. *Making democracy work: Civic traditions in modern Italy*. Princeton, NJ: Princeton University Press.

Rawlings, Laura, Lynne Sherburne-Benz, and Julie Van Domelen. 2003. *Evaluating social funds: A cross-country analysis of community interventions*. Washington, DC: World Bank.

Romer, David. 1993. Objects gaps and ideas gaps in development economics. *Journal of Monetary Economics* 32(3):543–573.

Scott, James. 1998. *Seeing like a state: How certain schemes to improve the human condition have failed*. New Haven, CT: Yale University Press.

Serageldin, Ismail, and Andrew Steer, eds. 1994. *Making development sustainable: From concepts to action*. Environmentally Sustainable Development Occasional Paper No.2. Washington, DC: World Bank.

Tendler, Judith. 1997. *Good governance in the tropics*. Baltimore: Johns Hopkins University Press.

Tendler, Judith. 2000a. Why are social funds so popular? In *Local dynamics in an era of globalization*, edited by Shahid Yusuf, Simon Evenett, and Weiping Wu. New York: Oxford University Press, pp. 114–129.

Tendler, Judith. 2000b. Safety nets and service delivery: What are social funds really telling us? In *Social development in Latin America: The politics of reform*, edited by Joseph Tulchin and Allison Garland. Boulder, CO: Lynne Rienner, pp. 87–118.

Wade, Robert. 1996. Japan, the World Bank, and the art of paradigm maintenance: *The East Asian Miracle* in political perspective. *New Left Review* 217:3–36.

Watts, Michael. 2001. Development ethnographies. *Ethnography* 2(2):283–300.

Wenger, Etienne, and William Snyder. 2000. Communities of practice: The organizational frontier. *Harvard Business Review* 78(1):139–145.

Whyte, William Foote. 1943. *Street corner society: The social structure of an Italian slum*. Chicago: University of Chicago Press.

Woolcock, Michael. 2003. Social capital. In *Encyclopedia of community: From the village to the virtual world,* edited by Karen Christensen and David Levinson. Thousand Oaks, CA: Sage, pp. 1258–1262.

World Bank. 1996. Social Capital. Report of the Satellite Group on Social Capital. Mimeo. Washington, DC: World Bank, Environment Department.

World Bank. 1997. *Social development and results on the ground.* Task Group Report. Washington, DC: World Bank.

World Bank. 2003. *World development report 2004: Making services work for poor people.* New York: Oxford University Press.

World Bank. 2004. *Involuntary resettlement sourcebook: Planning and implementation in development projects.* Washington, DC: World Bank.

World Bank Group. 2005. About us. Available online at http://web.worldbank.org/ WBSITE/EXTERNAL/EXTABOUTUS/0,,pagePK:50004410~piPK :36602~theSitePK:29708,00.html. Accessed October 28, 2005.

SECTION ONE

FRAMING SOCIAL CAPITAL

SOCIAL CAPITAL: IMPLICATIONS FOR DEVELOPMENT THEORY, RESEARCH, AND POLICY REVISITED[1]

Michael Woolcock
Deepa Narayan

What is social capital? How does it affect economic development? How do we know? What are the implications for theory, research, and policy? These questions lie at the heart of recent attempts to make sense of the burgeoning social capital literature, and to ascertain its usefulness as a basis for incorporating "the social dimension" more directly into academic and policy discussions of economic development. In this chapter we endeavor to answer each of these questions. In so doing, we aim to provide both an overview of the scholarship on social capital for those unfamiliar with the term, and to bring a sense of coherence and direction for those embarking on new empirical research and policy analysis.[2]

The paper proceeds as follows. We begin by exploring the basic intuition behind the idea of social capital and its manifestations in everyday life. We then present a definition of social capital, introduce its significance for understanding development outcomes, and place the central claims of social capital scholars in the context of earlier theoretical approaches. In the second section we review the empirical evidence in support of four perspectives on the relationship between social capital and economic development. The third section explores findings from recent survey instruments specifically designed to measure social capital, and spells out the policy implications consistent with them. The final section renews a call for multidisciplinary approaches to development theory, research, and policies that facilitate the attainment of more equitable, accountable, and inclusive outcomes.

What Is Social Capital?

"It's not what you know, it's *who* you know." This common aphorism sums up much of the conventional wisdom regarding social capital. It is wisdom born of our experience that gaining membership to exclusive clubs requires inside contacts, that close competitions for jobs and contracts are usually won by those with "friends in high places." When we fall on hard times, we know it is our friends and family who constitute the final "safety net." Conscientious parents devote hours of time to the school board and to helping their kids with homework, only too aware that a child's intelligence and motivation alone are not enough to ensure a bright future. Less instrumentally, some of our happiest and most rewarding hours are spent talking with neighbors, sharing meals with friends, participating in religious gatherings, and volunteering on community projects.

Intuitively, then, the basic idea of "social capital" is that one's family, friends, and associates constitute an important asset, one that can be called upon in a crisis, enjoyed for its own sake, and (when necessary) leveraged for material gain. What is true for individuals, moreover, also holds for groups. Those communities endowed with a diverse stock of social networks and civic associations will be in a stronger position to confront poverty and vulnerability (Moser 1996; Krishna 2002), resolve disputes (Schafft and Brown 2000; Varshney 2002), or take advantage of new opportunities (Narayan and Pritchett 1999; Isham 2002).[3] Conversely, the *absence* of social ties can have an equally important impact. Office workers, for example, fear being left "out of the loop" on important decisions; ambitious professionals recognize that getting ahead in a new venture typically requires an active commitment to "networking" (Burt 2005). A defining feature of being poor, moreover, is that one is not a member of— or is even actively excluded from—certain social networks and institutions, ones that could be used to secure good jobs and decent housing (Wilson 1987, 1996).

Our intuition and everyday language recognize an additional feature of social capital, however. Social capital has costs as well as benefits; social ties can be a liability as well as an asset. Most parents, for example, worry that their teenage children will "fall in with the wrong crowd," that peer pressure and a strong desire for acceptance can induce them to take up harmful habits. Even close family members can "overstay their welcome." At the institutional level, many countries and organizations (including the World Bank) have laws discouraging nepotism, in explicit recognition that personal connections can be used to unfairly discriminate, distort, and corrupt. In our everyday language and life experience, in short, we find that the social ties we have can be both a blessing and a blight, while those we do *not* have can deny us access to key resources. These features of social capital, we will show, are well documented by the empirical evidence, and have important implications for economic development and poverty reduction.

These examples allow us to pose a more formal definition of social capital. For us, social capital refers to the norms and networks that enable people to act collectively. This simple definition serves a number of purposes. First, it allows us to focus on the sources, as opposed to the consequences, of social capital (Portes 1998) while recognizing that important features of social capital, such as trust and reciprocity, are developed in an iterative process. Second, this definition allows us to incorporate different dimensions of social capital and to recognize that communities can have access to more or less of them. The poor, for example, may have a close-knit and intensive stock of "bonding" social capital that they leverage to "get by" (Briggs 1998; Holzmann and Jorgensen 1999) but be lacking in the more diffuse and extensive "bridging" social capital deployed by the non-poor to "get ahead" (Kozel and Parker 1998; Barr 2002; Narayan 2002). Moreover, as we shall see, such an approach allows us to argue that it is different *combinations* of these dimensions that are responsible for the range of outcomes we cited above, and to incorporate a dynamic component in which optimal combinations change over time. Third, while this definition presents the community (as opposed to individuals, households, or the state) as the primary unit of analysis, it allows for the fact that social capital nonetheless can be appropriated by individuals and households (as members of a given community), and that how communities themselves are structured turns in large part on their relationship with the state. Weak, hostile, or indifferent governments have a profoundly different effect on community life and development projects, for example, than governments that respect civil liberties, uphold the rule of law, honor contracts, and resist corruption (Isham and Kaufmann 1999).

This conceptualization of the role of social relationships in development represents an important departure from earlier theoretical approaches, and therefore has important implications for contemporary development research and policy. Until the 1990s, the major theories of development held rather narrow, even contradictory, views of the role of social relationships in economic development, and offered little by way of constructive policy recommendations. In the 1950s and 1960s, for example, modernization theory regarded traditional social relationships and ways of life as an impediment to development. When modernization theorists explained "the absence or failure of capitalism," Moore (1997: 289) correctly notes, "the focus [was] on social relations as obstacles." As an influential United Nations (1951) document of the time put it, for development to proceed,

> ancient philosophies have to be scrapped; old social institutions have to disintegrate; bonds of caste, creed and race have to burst; and large numbers of persons who cannot keep up with progress have to have their expectations of a comfortable life frustrated. (cited in Escobar 1995: 3)

This view gave way in the 1970s to the arguments of dependency and world systems theorists, who held social relations among corporate and political elites to be a primary mechanism of capitalist exploitation. The social characteristics of poor countries and communities were defined almost exclusively in terms of their relations to the means of production, and the inherent antipathy between the interests of capital and labor. Little mention was made of the possibility (or desirability) of mutually beneficial relationships between workers and owners, of the tremendous variation in success enjoyed by developing countries, or of political strategies other than "revolution" by which the poor could improve their lot. Communitarian perspectives,[4] on the other hand, with their emphasis on the inherent beneficence and self-sufficiency of local communities, underestimated the negative aspects of communal obligations, overestimated the virtues of isolationism and self-sufficiency, and neglected the importance of social relations in constructing effective and accountable formal institutions. For their part, neoclassical and public choice theories—which were the most influential in the 1980s and early 1990s—assigned no distinctive properties to social relations per se. These perspectives focused on the strategic choices of rational individuals interacting under various time, budgetary, and legal constraints, holding that groups (including firms) existed primarily to lower the transactions costs of exchange; given undistorted market signals, the optimal size and combination of groups would duly emerge.

For the major development theories, then, social relations have been construed as singularly burdensome, exploitative, liberating, or irrelevant. Reality, unfortunately, does not conform so neatly to these descriptions and their corresponding policy prescriptions. Events in the post–Cold War era—from ethnic violence and civil war to financial crises and the acknowledgment of widespread corruption—have demanded a more sophisticated appraisal of the virtues, vices, and vicissitudes of "the social dimension" as it pertains to the wealth and poverty of nations. The social capital literature, in its broadest sense, represents a first approximation to the answer to this challenge. It is a literature to which all the social science disciplines have contributed, and it is beginning to generate a remarkable consensus regarding the role and importance of institutions and communities in development. Indeed, we shall argue that one of the primary benefits of the idea of social capital is that it is allowing scholars, policymakers, and practitioners from different disciplines to enjoy an unprecedented level of cooperation and dialogue (Brown and Ashman 1996; Brown 1998).

Four Perspectives on Social Capital
and Economic Development

The letter and spirit of social capital has a long intellectual history in the social sciences (see Platteau 1994; Woolcock 1998; Farr 2004), but the sense in which it is used today dates back ninety years to the writings of Lyda J. Hanifan, then the superintendent of schools in West Virginia. Writing on the importance of community participation to enhancing school performance, Hanifan (1916: 130) explained this positive relationship by invoking the concept of social capital, describing it as

> those tangible substances [that] count for most in the daily lives of people: namely good will, fellowship, sympathy, and social intercourse among the individuals and families who make up a social unit. . . . If [an individual comes] into contact with his neighbor, and they with other neighbors, there will be an accumulation of social capital, which may immediately satisfy his social needs and which may bear a social potentiality sufficient to the substantial improvement of living conditions in the whole community.

After Hanifan, the idea of social capital disappeared for several decades but was "re-invented" in the 1950s by a team of urban sociologists (see Sealy et al. 1956), in the 1960s by an exchange theorist (Homans 1961) and an urban scholar (Jacobs 1961), and in the 1970s by an economist (Loury 1977).[5] None of these writers, interestingly, cited earlier work on the subject, but all apparently felt the need to use the same umbrella term to encapsulate the vitality and significance of community ties. The seminal research of James Coleman (1987, 1988, 1990) on education and especially Robert Putnam (1993a, 1995) on civic participation and institutional performance, however, has provided the inspiration for most of the current work, which has since coalesced around studies in nine primary fields: (1) families and youth behavior problems; (2) schooling and education; (3) community life ("virtual" and civic); (4) work and organizations; (5) democracy and governance; (6) general cases of collective action problems; (7) public health and environment issues; (8) crime and violence; and (9) economic development.[6] It is to the findings and lessons from this final category, and related work in political economy and new institutional economics, that we now turn in more detail.[7]

The literature on social capital and economic development is expanding rapidly,[8] and it is helpful to trace out the evolution of that literature and to identify the various perspectives that are emerging. We argue that there are essentially four such perspectives. While each is making an important contribution, we find that one in particular enjoys the strongest empirical support, is in the best position to articulate a coherent multidisciplinary research agenda, and is able to propose a realistic set of policy recommendations pertaining to poverty reduction. Our analysis updates and extends the perspectives outlined by the World Bank's interdisciplinary Social Capital Group, first convened in January 1996, which highlighted three general perspectives on social capital (see Grootaert 1997; Serageldin and Grootaert 2000).[9]

The Communitiarian View

The first perspective, which we will call the *communitarian* view, equates social capital with local-level organizations, namely associations, clubs, and civic groups. This view, measured most simply by the number and density of these groups in a given community, implies that social capital is essentially "good," that "more is better," and that its presence always has a positive effect on a community's welfare. This perspective has made important contributions to analyses of poverty by stressing the centrality of social ties in helping the poor manage risk and vulnerability. As Dordick (1997) notes, the poor have "something left to lose," namely each other.

In their celebration of community and civil society, however, many enthusiasts of this view of social capital have ignored its important "downside" (Portes and Landolt 1996). For example, where communities or networks are isolated, parochial, or working at cross-purposes to society's collective interests (e.g., ghettos, gangs, drug cartels), "productive" social capital is replaced by what Rubio (1997)—discussing the case of Colombia—calls "perverse" social capital, which greatly hinders development. There are certainly many benefits associated with being a member of a highly integrated community, but there are also significant costs, and for some—for example, bright girls taken out of village schools in India because of community expectations—the costs of their "connections" may greatly outweigh the benefits. In the case of organized crime syndicates in Latin America and Russia, such groups may generate large negative externalities for the rest of society in the form of lost lives, wasted resources, and pervasive uncertainty. The communitarian perspective also implicitly assumes that "communities" are homogeneous entities that automatically include and benefit all members. The extensive literature on caste inequality, ethnic exclusion, and gender discrimination (e.g., Narayan and Shah 2000)—phenomena often produced and maintained by community pressures—suggests otherwise.

Evidence from the developing world demonstrates why merely having high levels of social solidarity or informal groups does not necessarily lead to economic prosperity. In Kenya a participatory poverty assessment found over 200,000 community groups in rural areas, but most were unconnected to outside resources and were unable to lift the poor out of poverty (Narayan and Nyamwaya 1996). A World Bank report on Rwanda (World Bank 1989) cited the existence of more than

3,000 registered cooperatives and farmers groups, and an estimated 30,000 informal groups, yet these groups were unable to prevent one of history's most gruesome civil wars. Similarly, in many Latin American countries indigenous groups are often characterized by high levels of social solidarity, but nonetheless experience high levels of poverty because they lack the resources and access to power that is necessary to shift the rules of the game in their favor (Narayan 2002). This is also the case in Haiti, where social capital, "rich at the local level," is employed by peasant groups to "meet labor requirements, gain access to land, protect clientship in the marketplace, promote mutual aid, assure protection from state authorities, and generally manage risk." Even so, these groups cannot overcome the crippling effects of colonialism, corruption, "geographical isolation, political exclusion, and social polarization" (all quotes from White and Smucker 1998: 1–3).

The Networks View

In the light of these concerns, a second perspective on social capital can be identified that attempts to account for both its "upside" and "downside." This view stresses the importance of vertical as well as horizontal associations between people, and relations within and among other organizational entities such as community groups and firms. Building on the seminal work of Granovetter (1973), it recognizes that intra-community (or "strong") ties are needed to give families and communities a sense of identity and common purpose (Astone et al. 1999). This view also stresses, however, that without inter-community (or "weak") ties that cross various social divides—for example, those based on religion, class, ethnicity, gender, and socioeconomic status—strong horizontal ties can become a basis for the pursuit of narrow sectarian interests.[10] In the recent popular literature, these two forms of social capital have come to be called "bonding" and "bridging" social capital (Gittell and Vidal, 1998). Different combinations of these dimensions, it is argued, are responsible for the range of outcomes that can be attributed to social capital. This more nuanced perspective, which we call the *networks* view, regards the tension between social capital's virtues and vices as a defining property, one that explains in part why scholars and policymakers have been so persistently ambivalent about its potential as a theoretical construct and policy instrument.

The networks view of social capital, most closely associated with the work of sociologists Pierre Bourdieu (1986), Ronald Burt (1992, 1997, 1998), Alejandro Portes (Portes and Sensenbrenner 1993; Portes 1995, 1997, 1998), and Douglas Massey (Massey and Espinosa 1997; Massey 1998), is characterized by two key propositions. First, social capital is a double-edged sword. On the one hand, it can provide a range of valuable services for community members, ranging from babysitting and house minding to job referrals and emergency cash. But there are also costs, in that those same ties can place considerable noneconomic claims on members' sense of obligation and commitment that have negative economic consequences. Group loyalties may be so strong that they isolate members from information about employment opportunities, foster a climate of ridicule toward efforts to study and work hard, or siphon off hard-won assets (for example, to support recent co-ethnic immigrants). Portes and Sensenbrenner (1993) cite the case of prosperous Asian immigrants who had Anglicized their names in order to divest themselves of communal obligations to supporting subsequent cohorts.[11] Second, the sources of social capital need to be distinguished from the consequences derived from them. Imputing only desirable outcomes to social capital, or equating them with it, ignores the possibility that these outcomes may be being attained at another group's expense, that given outcomes may be suboptimal, or that desirable outcomes attained today may come at the price of significant costs tomorrow.

These results have given rise to the logical conclusion that there must be two basic dimensions of social capital at the community level, namely "strong" intra-community ties ("bonds") and "weak" extra-community networks ("bridges"); both are needed to avoid tautological claims regarding the efficacy of social capital.[12] (Without this distinction, for example, an argument could be put forward that successful groups were distinguished by their dense community ties, neglecting the possibility that the same ties could be *preventing* success in another, otherwise similar group.) Accordingly, the networks view argues that communities can be characterized by their endowments of these two dimensions of social capital, and that different combinations of these dimensions account for the range of outcomes associated with social capital (see Figure 2.1).

Figure 2.1   Dimensions of Social Capital at the Community Level

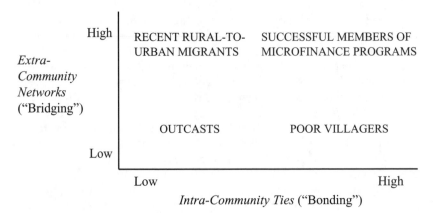

Furthermore, as community members' welfare changes over time, so does the optimal "calculus" of costs and benefits associated with particular combinations of bonds and bridges. Poor entrepreneurs, for example, once heavily dependent on their immediate neighbors and friends (for example, their "bonding" social capital) for credit, insurance, and support, require access to more extensive product and factor markets as their businesses expand (cf. Fafchamps and Minten 2002). Economic development, from this perspective, takes place when an ongoing "coupling and decoupling" social mechanism is in place (Granovetter 1995). This mechanism allows individuals initially to draw on the benefits of close community membership, but in doing so also ensures that they acquire the skills and resources to participate in more extensive networks that transcend their community, thereby progressively incorporating them into mainstream economic life.

These insights can be demonstrated graphically and applied to poverty reduction more generally. Figure 2.2 shows that as the diversity of the social networks of the poor expands, so too does their welfare. The social capital residing in a given network can be leveraged or utilized more efficiently, which is essentially the principle behind group-based credit programs such as the well-known Grameen Bank in Bangladesh (cf. Van Bastelaer 1999). Poor village women lacking material collateral are given loans on the basis of their membership in a small peer group, which helps them start or expand a small business and thereby improve their families' welfare (*A* in Figure 2.2). But the economic returns to any given network soon reach a limit (*B*), especially when the network is characterized by high endowments of "bonding" social capital. If the network continues to expand—for example, through the arrival into urban slums of subsequent cohorts from the village—its resources may become overwhelmed, reducing well-being for long-established members (*C*). Similarly, long-term members of group-based credit programs may find that obligations and commitments to their colleagues become an obstacle to further advancement, especially for the more ambitious (Woolcock 1999a). In these circumstances, a solution for many poor people is partially to divest themselves of their immediate community ties (*D*) and to move where networks are potentially more diverse (for example, where "bridging" social capital is more abundant) and hence economic opportunities are more promising (*E*). Migration from villages to cities is the most dramatic example, but Portes and Sensenbrenner's (1993) name-changing Asian immigrants are doing essentially the same thing.

The networks view has been employed with great effect in recent development research. Kozel and Parker's (1998) analysis of poor communities in rural north India, for example, reports that social groups among poor villagers serve vital protection, risk management, and solidarity functions. It is the more extensive and leveraged networks of the nonpoor, by contrast, that are used for strategic advantage and the advancement of

Figure 2.2 Social Capital and Poverty Transitions

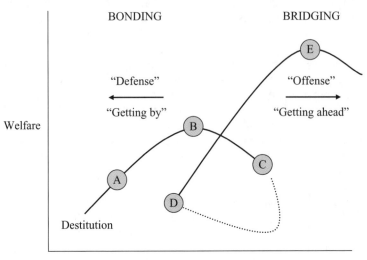

Source: Woolcock (1999b).

material interests. Crudely put, the networks of the poor play "defense" while those of the nonpoor play "offense" (cf. Briggs 1998). Barr (2002) reports strikingly similar results from her work on the relationship between the structure of business networks and enterprise performance in Africa. Poor entrepreneurs, operating small local firms in traditional industries, form what she calls "solidarity networks," sharing personal information about members' conduct and intentions, the primary function of which is to reduce risk and uncertainty. Larger regional firms, on the other hand, coalesce into "innovation networks," sharing knowledge about technology and global markets with the explicit goal of enhancing enterprise productivity, profit, and market share (see also Van Dijk and Rabellotti 1997; Fafchamps and Minten 2002). Far from dismissing the vitality of traditional village groups in poor communities (the modernization view) or romanticizing it (the communitarian view), the networks view in effect recognizes that these groups can both help and hinder economic advancement.

From the networks perspective, the clear challenge to social capital theory, research, and policy is thus to identify the conditions under which the many positive aspects of "bonding" social capital in poor communities can be harnessed and its integrity retained (and, if necessary, its negative aspects dissipated) while simultaneously helping the poor gain access to formal institutions and a more diverse stock of "bridging" social capital. It

is a process fraught with multiple dilemmas, however, especially for external NGOs, extension services, and development agencies, since it may
entail altering social systems that are the product of long-standing cultural traditions or powerful vested interests (cf. Klitgaard 1990: 12).

The particular strength of the networks view is its conduciveness to
detailed policy discussions, on the basis of compelling empirical evidence
and detailed assessments of the veracity of competing explanations. This
view, however, minimizes the "public good" nature of social groups,
regarding any benefits of group activity as primarily the property of the
particular individuals involved. As such it is highly resistant to arguments
that social capital can (or should) be measured across larger social aggregates, such as societies or nations (Portes 1998). Neither does it explicitly
incorporate macro-level institutions, such as the state, and their capacity
to both shape and be shaped by local communities. To be sure, the networks perspective recognizes that weak laws and overt discrimination can
undermine efforts by poor minorities to act in their collective interest, but
the role communities play in shaping institutional performance generally,
and the enormous potential of positive state-society relations in particular, is largely ignored.

The Institutional View

A third perspective on social capital, which we call the *institutional* view,
argues that the vitality of community networks and civil society is largely
the product of the political, legal, and institutional environment. Whereas
the communitarian and networks perspectives largely treat social capital
as an independent variable giving rise to various "goods" and "bads," the
institutional view puts the emphasis on social capital as a dependent variable. This view argues that the very capacity of social groups to act in their
collective interest depends crucially on the quality of the formal institutions under which they reside (North 1990), and that emergent qualities
such as high levels of "generalized trust" (as measured, for example, by
the World Values Survey), in turn, correspond to superior rates of economic growth. It also stresses that the performance of states and firms
themselves depends on their own internal coherence, credibility, and
competence, and their external accountability to civil society.

Research from the institutional view has two variants that have
yielded remarkably similar results. The first approach encompasses com-
parative-historical case studies and is exemplified in the work of Theda
Skocpol (1995, 1996). It argues that if the state is demonstrably ill suited to
assuming full responsibility for all aspects of modern economic life, then it
is erroneous to pit states and societies against one another in a zero- or
negative-sum game—for example, to argue that firms and communities
thrive to the extent that governments retreat. On the contrary, Skocpol
shows, civil society thrives to the extent that the state actively encourages

it. Judith Tendler's (1997) work on the political economy of decentralization in Brazil similarly stresses the importance of "good government" for making local programs work.

The second and increasingly influential approach uses quantitative cross-national studies of the effects of government performance and social divisions on economic performance. Within the social capital field, Knack and Keefer (1995, 1997) pioneered the way by creating indices from a range of measures of institutional quality compiled by various investment agencies and human rights groups. They showed that items such as "generalized trust," "rule of law," "civil liberties," and "bureaucratic quality" were positively associated with economic growth. In a recent survey and extension of this literature, Knack (2002: 70–71) concludes that social capital—defined in this institutional way—"not only improves economic performance, it is progressive, in the sense that it helps the poorer classes more than it helps the richer classes."

Collier and Gunning (1999) employ a variation of this view in their analyses of the causes of slow growth in Africa (see also Collier 1999, 2002; Temple 1998). Distinguishing between "civic" and "government" social capital, they show that slow growth occurs in societies with both high levels of ethnic fragmentation and weak political rights.[13] Although he does not employ the terminology of social capital, Rodrik's (1999a, 1999b) important work makes a similar argument, demonstrating that economies with divided societies and weak institutions of conflict management respond sluggishly to shocks. Easterly (2001) also reports that societies able to generate and sustain a "middle class consensus" are those most likely to produce stable and positive rates of growth. The related literature on "social capabilities" and development (for example, Temple and Johnson 1998; Hall and Jones 1999) tells a similar story.

A number of empirical and methodological questions can be raised about these studies, but in the aggregate their message is becoming clearer and louder. Rampant corruption, frustrating bureaucratic delays, suppressed civil liberties, vast inequality, divisive ethnic tensions, and failure to safeguard property rights (to the extent they exist at all) are increasingly recognized as major impediments to generating greater prosperity. In countries where these conditions prevail, there is little to show for well-intentioned efforts to build schools, hospitals, roads, and communications infrastructure, and to encourage foreign investment (World Bank, 1998, 2003). Investments in "civic" and "government" social capital are thus highly complementary to investments in more orthodox forms of capital accumulation.

The very strength of the institutional view in addressing macro policy concerns, however, is also a weakness in that it lacks a micro component. Freedoms, rights, and liberties, for example, are entities necessarily granted by governments; coherent and competent bureaucracies are several steps removed from the lives of the poor in urban slums or isolated rural villages, and may take decades to be constructed. In providing broad statistical evidence for the importance of social capital, the subtlety, richness, and enormous variation gleaned from case studies of individual countries and community contexts is lost, as are the voices of those most directly affected by weak public institutions, namely the poor.

The Synergy View

In recognition of this disconnect, a number of scholars have recently proposed what might be called the *synergy* view, which attempts to integrate the compelling work emerging from the networks and institutional camps. While the synergy view traces its intellectual antecedents to earlier work in comparative political economy and anthropology, its most influential body of research was published in a special issue of *World Development* (1996). The contributors to this volume examined cases from India, Mexico, Russia, South Korea, and Brazil in search of the conditions fostering developmental "synergies"—for example, dynamic professional alliances and relationships—between and within state bureaucracies and various civil society actors.

Three broad conclusions emerged from these studies:

- Contra some public choice and communitarian theorists, neither the state nor societies are inherently good or bad; governments, corporations, and civic groups are "variables" in terms of the impact they can have on the attainment of collective goals.
- States, firms, and communities alone do not possess the resources needed to promote broad-based, sustainable development; complementarities and partnerships forged both within and across these different sectors are required. Identifying the conditions under which these synergies emerge (or fail to emerge) is thus a central task of development theory and practice.
- Of these different sectors, the state's role in facilitating positive developmental outcomes is the most problematic and important. This is so because the state is not only the ultimate provider of public goods (stable currencies, public health, universal education) and the final arbiter and enforcer of the rule of law (property rights, due process, freedom of speech and association); it is also the actor best situated to facilitate enduring alliances across the boundaries of class, ethnicity, race, gender, politics, and religion. Communities and firms also have an important role to play in their own right, in creating the conditions that produce, recognize, and reward good governance. In otherwise difficult institutional environments, community leaders able to identify and engage "pockets of efficiency" within the state become agents of more general reform (Fox 1992).

Evans (1992, 1995, 1996), one of the primary contributors to this view, concludes that synergy between government and citizen action is based on *complementarity* and *embeddedness.* Complementarity refers to mutually supportive relations between public and private actors, and is exemplified in frameworks of rules and laws that protect rights to associate, or more humble measures such as the provision of transport by the state to facilitate exchanges among community associations. Embededdness refers to the nature and extent of the ties connecting citizens and public officials. The classic examples are from irrigation, in which the lowest-level officials are from the community being served; they are enmeshed in local social relations and hence are under pressure by the community to perform and be responsive to them. Importantly, this enmeshment works only where the actions of public officials are simultaneously bound by performance-oriented organizational environments characterized by competence, coherence, and credibility.[14] As the case of Russia amply demonstrates, weak public institutions and deep cleavages between the powerful and ordinary citizens can lead to political instability, rampant corruption, high inflation, rising inequality, and capital flight (Rose 1998).

Developing these ideas further, Woolcock (1998) and Narayan (1999) integrate the core ideas of bridging social capital and state functioning, arguing that different combinations result in different outcomes, whether at the community, district, regional, or national level (see Figure 2.3). The framework is particularly helpful in capturing some of the dynamic aspects of state-society relations and suggests that different interventions are needed for different combinations of governance and bridging social capital in a group, community, or society. In societies (or communities) with good governance and high levels of bridging social capital, there is complementarity between state and society; economic prosperity and social order are likely. But when a society's social capital inheres mainly in primary social groups disconnected from one another, the more powerful groups dominate the state, to the exclusion of other groups. Such societies are characterized by latent conflict and include countries in Latin America with large excluded indigenous populations. In these circumstances, a key task for subordinate groups and activists is to forge broad, coherent coalitions (Keck and Sikkink 1998), and nurture relations with allies in positions of power (Fox and Brown 1998); should they be successful, rights and resources previously denied them may begin to accrue. Similarly, if the state opens up to excluded groups and explicitly build bridges between them, there may be movement toward quadrant 1 in Figure 2.3.

Alternatively, state-society relations may degenerate into conflict, violence, war or anarchy, with a gradual breakdown of the state and "warlords," local mafia, and guerilla movements allowed to become substitutes for the power and authority of the state. Rebuilding Rwanda, for example, will involve building bridges and forging a measure of reconciliation

Figure 2.3   Relationship Between Bridging Social Capital and Governance

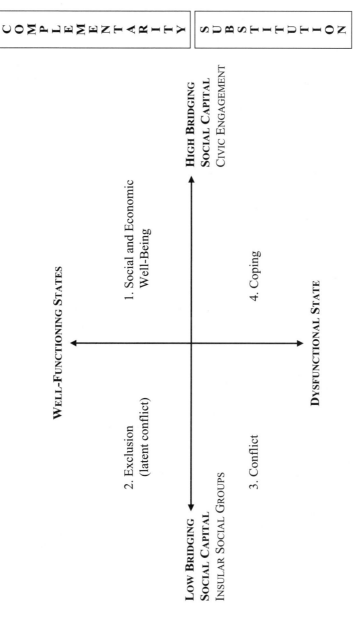

Source: Narayan (2002).

45

between two ethnic groups before economic prosperity and peace can be sustained. When societies or communities are characterized by poor governance and abundant bridging social capital, the informal networks become substitutes for the failed state and form the basis of coping strategies. This is the case in both Togo and Benin, where women, denied access to formal credit, have begun investing in informal revolving credit societies; in Tanzania, in the absence of police, some villages have started their own nightly security guard systems (Narayan et al. 2000).

The synergy view stresses that inclusive development takes place when representatives of the state, the corporate sector, and civil society establish common fora through which they can identify and pursue common goals. Social capital is thus treated as a mediating variable; it is shaped by public and private institutions, and yet has important impacts of development outcomes. This makes "investing" in social capital an inherently contentious and contested—that is to say, political—process, one in which the role of the state is crucial, not marginal. Moreover, the fundamental social transformation of economic development—from traditional kinship-based community life to societies organized by formal institutions and arm's-length exchange—itself alters the calculus of costs and benefits associated with the particular dimensions of social capital, and thus the desirable combinations of these dimensions at any given moment (cf. Berry 1993). But development struggles are not always won by the most powerful, nor must a challenge to authority always entail violent conflict. Similarly, patient efforts by intermediaries to establish partnerships between associations of the poor and outsiders can reap significant dividends (Isham et al. 1995). As Uphoff (1992: 273) astutely recognizes,

> paradoxical though it may seem, "top-down" efforts are usually needed to introduce, sustain, and institutionalize "bottom-up" development. We are commonly constrained to think in "either-or" terms—the more of one the less of the other—when both are needed in a positive-sum way to achieve our purposes.

The synergy view suggests three central tasks for theorists, researchers, and policy makers. The first is to identify the nature and extent of the social relationships characterizing a particular community, its formal institutions, and the interaction between them. The second is to develop institutional strategies based on an understanding of these social relations, particularly the extent of bonding and bridging social capital in a society or community. The third task is to identify ways and means by which positive manifestations of social capital—widespread cooperation, trust, institutional efficiency—can offset, and/or be created from, its negative manifestations—sectarianism, isolationism, nepotism. Put another way, the challenge is to transform situations where a community's social capital "substitutes" for weak, hostile, or indifferent formal institutions into ones in which the two realms "complement" one another.

Table 2.1 summarizes the key elements of the four perspectives on social capital and development, along with their corresponding policy prescriptions. The differences between them consist primarily of the unit of analysis on which they focus; their treatment of social capital as an independent, dependent, or mediating variable; and the extent to which they incorporate a theory of the state. The largest and most influential bodies of work have emerged from the networks and institutional perspectives, with the most recent approaches seeking a synthesis in the form of the synergy view. In the next section, we examine various practical attempts at the World Bank and elsewhere to build instruments to measure social capital and demonstrate its significance for development projects and policy.

How Does Social Capital Affect Economic Development?

Several recent innovative studies have attempted to quantify social capital and its contribution to economic development. As indicated previously, social capital scholarship is very rich in part because it draws on a variety of methodological approaches that have important roles in interpreting, challenging, and refining each other's findings (cf. Tarrow 1995). Arriving

Table 2.1   Four Views of Social Capital: Key Actors and Policy Prescriptions

Perspective	Key Actors	Policy Prescriptions
Communitarian view Local associations	Community groups Voluntary sector	"Small is beautiful" Recognize social assets of the poor
Networks view Intra- ("bonding") and inter- ("bridging") community ties	Entrepreneurs Business groups "Information brokers"	Decentralization Creation of enterprise zones "Bridging" social divides
Institutional view Political and legal institutions	Private and public sector	Grant civil and political liberties Transparency, accountability
Synergy View Community networks *and* state-society relations	Community groups, civil society, firms, and states	Co-production, complementarity Participation, linkages "Scaling up" local organizations

at more concrete policy recommendations, however, requires more comparative research using precise measures of social capital to examine within-country and across-country variations in poverty reduction, government performance, ethnic conflict, and economic growth. In this section, we examine some of the measures that have been employed to date, evaluating their usefulness and their limitations for development theory and policy.

It should be stressed from the outset that there are a number of reasons why obtaining a single "true" measure of social capital is probably not possible. First, as we have seen, the most comprehensive definitions of social capital are multidimensional, incorporating different levels and units of analysis. Second, the nature and forms of social capital change over time, as the balance shifts between informal organizations and formal institutions. And third, no long-standing cross-country surveys were initially designed to measure "social capital," leaving contemporary researchers to compile indices from a range of approximate items (measures of trust, confidence in government, voting trends, social mobility, modern outlook, hours spent volunteering, etc.). New surveys currently being tested may produce more direct and accurate indicators across and within countries.[15]

Measuring social capital may be difficult, but several excellent studies—using different types and combinations of qualitative and quantitative research methodologies—have nonetheless identified useful measures of and proxies for social capital. We review briefly some of the studies that have attempted to quantify social capital for the purpose of deriving measures that can be aggregated beyond the community level.

One clear and commonly used measure of social capital is membership in informal and formal associations and networks. In developing countries generally, and rural areas in particular, measures to capture the informal give-and-take through community-wide festivals, sports events, and other traditional methods of fostering connectedness are very important. The national participatory poverty assessment in Tanzania included a household poverty and social capital survey based on 1,400 households in eighty-seven villages across Tanzania (Narayan, 1997). Based on data from this survey, Narayan and Pritchett (1999) developed an index of social capital at the household and community level that included both density and characteristics of informal and formal groups and networks to which people belonged. The dimensions of this index included group functioning, contributions to groups, participation in decision making, and heterogeneity of membership. A series of measures was also constructed on interpersonal trust and changes over time. These measures demonstrated that for Tanzanian villagers, social capital was indeed both "social" and "capital," generating returns that exceeded those to human capital.

In tandem with the Tanzania study, the Social Development Department of the World Bank launched the Local Level Institutions study in three countries: Indonesia, Bolivia, and Burkina Faso. In addition to the measures used in the Tanzania study, the LLI study included more detailed qualitative information on service delivery issues, with subsequent quantification of these variables. Results from these studies demonstrate that the questionnaire items do in fact capture different dimensions of social capital at the household and community level, that certain dimensions of social capital contribute significantly to household welfare, and that social capital is the capital of the poor. The most important variables in these studies are density of associations, heterogeneity of membership in associations, and active participation in them (see Grootaert 1999; Grootaert and Narayan 1999).

Another manifestation of social capital includes norms and values that facilitate exchanges, lower transaction costs, reduce the cost of information, permit trade in the absence of contracts, and encourage responsible citizenship and the collective management of resources (Fukuyama 1995). Ronald Inglehart's (1997) work on the World Values Survey (WVS) is the most comprehensive in this area. With economists being drawn into the social capital issue, the most used questions from the World Values Survey have become the questions on generalized trust (for example, "Generally speaking, would you say that most people can be trusted or that you can't be too careful in dealing with people?"). Knack and Keefer (1997), for example, use WVS trust data from twenty-nine countries to show the positive relationship between trust and levels of investment in a country.

While there has been a recent proliferation of research attempting to identify the nature of the relationships between social variables and development, everyone recognizes that the quality of the data is less than ideal. With mounting pressure to provide simple measures of inherently complex and interdependent relationships, there is a very real danger that expectations will exceed capacity, and that hastily assembled, poorly conceived measures will jeopardize the agenda they purport to serve. We recognize these dangers, even as we maintain that the goal of having valid and reliable cross-national measures of social capital is a desirable one. We feel that the best way to strike the balance between quality and quantity measures is to begin by unbundling social capital into its dimensions, and to generate new data sets on social capital that are comparable across many countries.

Four recent studies attempt to develop indices of social capital at the national or subnational level. In the United States, spurred by Robert Putnam's "bowling alone" thesis (Putnam 1995, 2000), several new surveys of civic engagement have been conducted, in addition to the data already collected in surveys by the private sector to measure consumer preferences and changes in lifestyles. The National Commission on Philanthropy and

Civic Renewal (1998), in collaboration with researchers from the University of Connecticut, has developed a National Index of Civic Engagement (NICE) based on a national sample of 1,000 people. This index includes five dimensions: the giving climate, community engagement, charitable involvement, the spirit of voluntarism, and active citizenship. Related work has been done by the National Commission on Civic Renewal (1998), housed at the University of Maryland, which has developed an Index of National Civic Health. This index measures and combines trends over the past quarter century in political participation, political and social trust, associational membership, family integrity, and stability and crime.[16]

In exploring the roots and determinants of Hindu and Muslim riots in India, Varshney (2002) focuses on the role of intercommunal networks. In cities where Hindus and Muslims have little interaction, Varshney shows that latent communal conflict has few channels for peaceful resolution and periodically descends into violence; in cities where there are overlapping associational memberships and frequent everyday interaction, on the other hand, conflict is anticipated and dissipated. This research was based on six Indian cities carefully arranged in three matched pairs that were similar in terms of Hindu-Muslim demographic composition and dissimilar in that one city experienced recurrent riots while the other city remained calm. Varshney's work shows that diversity can be a source of strength where there are social ties transcending different community boundaries.

To assess social capital at the community level, Onyx and Bullen (2000) developed a questionnaire for the state of New South Wales (Australia) from which they isolated eight underlying factors as constituting social capital. The eight factors (identified through factor analysis) were participation in local community, proactivity in social context, feelings of trust and safety, neighborhood connections, family and friend connections, tolerance of diversity, value of life, and work connections. Based on an individual's social capital score, the authors could predict the community to which the person belonged, thus raising the prospects for the use of this instrument planning and monitoring community development activities.

Building on this work, attempts are now under way at the World Bank to develop social capital instruments that can be used as diagnostic tools at the community level and across countries.[17] Because the forms of social capital are society specific and change over time, such instruments must focus on a range of dimensions of social capital, assuming that different forms and combinations of dimensions of social capital will be important in different societies. Such instruments have recently been piloted in Ghana and Uganda (Narayan 1998), and by the World Bank's Social Capital Initiative[18] in Panama and India (Krishna and Shrader 1999). Both instruments include a variety of questionnaires and open-ended methods to collect data at the household and community level.

Analyses of the Uganda and Ghana data reveal that the dimensions underlying social capital are strikingly similar even when the context is quite different. The Ghana study draws on a sample of 1,471 rural and urban households while the Uganda study focuses on 950 poor households in slum communities in the city of Kampala in Uganda. Factor analyses reveals a similar underlying structure and clustering of variables (see Figure 2.4).

Figure 2.4   Measuring Social Capital in Communities

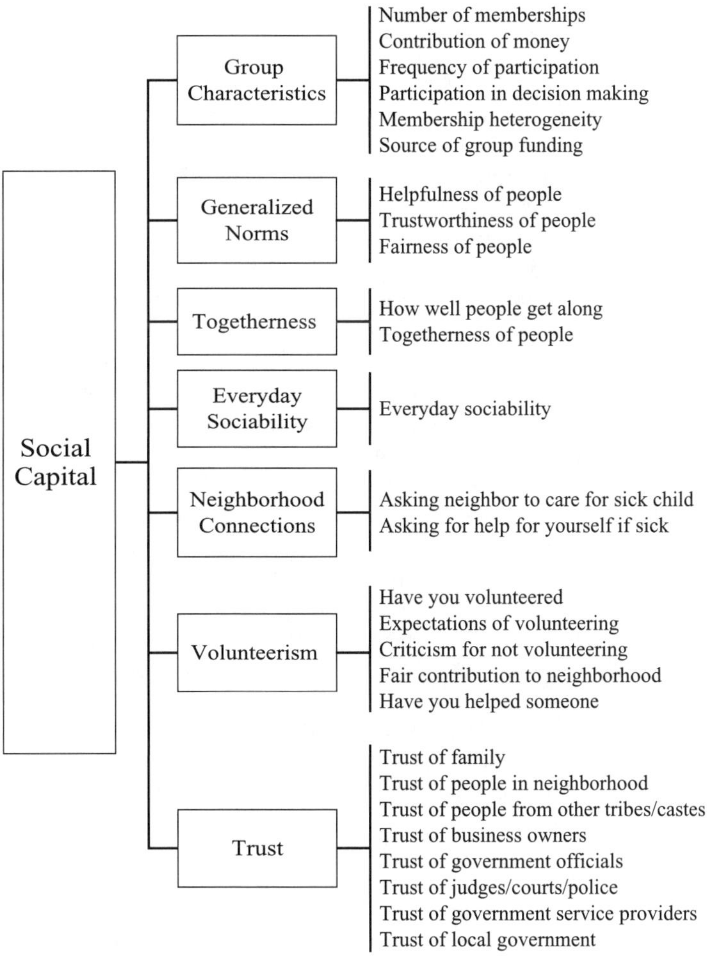

Social Capital	Group Characteristics	Number of memberships Contribution of money Frequency of participation Participation in decision making Membership heterogeneity Source of group funding
	Generalized Norms	Helpfulness of people Trustworthiness of people Fairness of people
	Togetherness	How well people get along Togetherness of people
	Everyday Sociability	Everyday sociability
	Neighborhood Connections	Asking neighbor to care for sick child Asking for help for yourself if sick
	Volunteerism	Have you volunteered Expectations of volunteering Criticism for not volunteering Fair contribution to neighborhood Have you helped someone
	Trust	Trust of family Trust of people in neighborhood Trust of people from other tribes/castes Trust of business owners Trust of government officials Trust of judges/courts/police Trust of government service providers Trust of local government

Source: Narayan and Cassidy (1999).

What Are the Implications for Development Theory and Policy?

In this section, we consider some of the implications of social capital research for development theory and policy. We stress that these implications are necessarily preliminary, and invite others to refine, correct, or expand upon them.

The first implication for development theory is that the concept of social capital offers a way to bridge sociological and economic perspectives, thereby providing potentially richer and better explanations of economic development. In a world beset with ethnic conflict, political tensions, and financial crisis, no single discipline can hope to provide (if ever it could) either a full accounting of these problems or realistic prescriptions for change. Dialogue across disciplinary, sectoral, and professional lines alike is crucial for both conceptual and operational advancement. A second implication is that economic growth is shaped by the nature and extent of social interactions between communities and institutions. This has important implications for development policy, in which attention to the embeddedness of economic life in the social and political environment has until recently been largely absent. Similarly, our review affirms that understanding how "outside" agencies can facilitate sustainable poverty alleviation in diverse (and often poorly understood) communities remains one of the great challenges of development. Having a project that is technically and financially sound is a necessary but insufficient condition for its acceptance by poor communities.

Recent work by the World Bank and the development community at large on social development, participation, institutions, and governance has laid the building blocks to help us move forward.[19] Six broad recommendations can be offered. First, for development interventions in all sectors and at all levels (especially the country level), social institutional analysis should be used to correctly identify the range of stakeholders and their interrelations. Understanding how their power and political interests will be affected by proposed policy interventions is a vital consideration, since all policy interventions occur in a social context characterized by a delicate mix of informal organizations, networks, and institutions. Special attention is necessary in the design of interventions to the potential for dominant groups to mobilize in ways that undermine the public good.

Second, it is critical to invest in the organizational capacity of the poor and to support the building of "bridges" across communities and social groups. The latter is particularly important, since many decisions affecting the poor are not made at the local level. To this end, the use of participatory processes can facilitate consensus building and social interaction among stakeholders with diverse interests and resources. Finding ways and means by which to transcend social divides so as to build social cohesion and trust is crucial for economic development. One of the great virtues of the idea and discourse of social capital is that it provides a common language for these different stakeholders, enabling them to communicate more openly with one another.

Third, a social capital perspective adds its voice to those calling for information disclosure policies at all levels to encourage informed citizenship and accountability of both private and public actors who purport to serve the public good. Fourth, emphasis should be placed on improving physical access and modern technology to foster communication and information exchange across social groups to complement social interaction based on face-to-face interchange. Fifth, development interventions should be viewed through a social capital lens, and assessments of their impact should include the potential effects of the intervention on the social capital of poor communities. As we have seen, the social networks of the poor are one of the primary resources they have for managing risk and vulnerability, and outside agents therefore need to find ways to complement these resources, rather than substitute for them.

Finally, social capital should be seen as a component of orthodox development projects, from dams and irrigation systems to local schools and health clinics. Where poor communities have direct input into the design, implementation, management, and evaluation of projects, returns on investments and the sustainability of the project are enhanced (Esman and Uphoff 1984). In this sense, "the social dimensions" of development are at the core of everything the Bank—and every other development agency—does.

Conclusion

While it is too soon to announce the arrival of a new development "paradigm," it is not unreasonable to claim that there is a remarkable, if often unacknowledged, consensus emerging about the importance of social relations in development. In unpacking the literature on social capital and development, we have sought to convey a recurring message that social relations are key in mobilizing other growth-enhancing resources. We have stressed that social capital does not exist in a political vacuum, that the nature and extent of the interactions between communities and institutions hold the key to understanding the prospects for development in a given society. We have argued that social capital can be used to support or undermine the public good. We have stated that perhaps the most important example of social capital at work, in the absence of formal insurance mechanisms and financial instruments, is the use of social connections by the poor as the primary means of protection against risk and vulnerability.

In many respects we are still in the early stages of research on social capital and development, but we cannot wait until we know all there is to know about social capital before acting. Rather, to foster further knowledge and understanding of social capital, we should adopt a learning-by-doing stance. For the World Bank and the development community at large, this implies more rigorous evaluations of project and policy impact on social capital, additional efforts to unbundle the mechanisms through which social capital works, and increased understanding of the determinants of social capital itself.

It would be the ultimate irony if those people most interested in researching and generating social capital did not themselves foster trust, openness, and a willingness to share information, ideas, and opportunities in this field. It is in this spirit that we invite readers to access, use, and contribute to the World Bank's extensive knowledge base of ongoing research around the world in the social capital domain. It is only through collaborative efforts—with all that this entails regarding struggle, perseverance, negotiation, and mutual willingness to learn—that genuine progress will be made.

Notes

1. The views expressed in this paper are those of the authors alone, and should not be attributed to the World Bank, its Executive Directors, or the countries they represent. This chapter is a revised and updated version of a paper originally published in the *World Bank Research Observer* in September 2000. Copyright permission to reproduce those passages that remain unchanged has been secured from Oxford University Press. For helpful comments on the original draft of this paper, we thank John Blaxall, Jonathan Fox, Christiaan Grootaert, Bill Mulford, Vijayendra Rao, Anders Rudkvist, and four anonymous reviewers. Please direct all correspondence to Michael Woolcock, mwoolcock@worldbank.org, and Deepa Narayan, dnarayan@worldbank.org, at the World Bank, 1818 H St. NW, Washington, DC.

2. Earlier reviews of social capital as it pertains to economic development issues can be found in Platteau (1994), Hyden (1997), Grootaert (1997), and Woolcock (1998). For dissenting views, see Harriss and De Renzio (1997), Fox (1997), Durlauf (1999), and Fine (1999, 2001). Durlauf and Fafchamps (2004) present the most comprehensive review of the social capital literature from a strictly economic perspective. Comprehensive general introductions to social capital theory and research can be found in Halpern (2004) and Burt (2005).

3. A more detailed discussion of the role of social capital in shaping responses to poverty (and risk management strategies) is provided in World Bank (2000).

4. This perspective encapsulates the views of the South Commission and Amatai Etzioni, among others. On the doctrine of self-reliance, a key theme of communitarians, see Rist (1997: Chapter 8).

5. A complementary approach was also being developed by the French sociologist Pierre Bourdieu in the 1970s, though Anglo-American scholars did not become fully aware of this until the late 1980s.

6. For citations on the first eight fields, see Woolcock (1998) and Foley and Edwards (1999).

7. Putnam (1993b) and Coleman (1994) were also among the first to outline the challenge to development scholars posed by social capital theory.

8. Isham et al. (2002) present a graphic documenting the exponential rise in social capital publications during the late 1990s.

9. A major product of this group is the collection of papers in Dasgupta and Serageldin (2000).

10. This was also the essence of Banfield's (1958) notion of "amoral familism" and Hirschman's (1958) concerns about "group-focused" development.

11. A happier example of assimilation, in which community ties remain more or less intact, is that of American Jews; on this, see Gold (1995). See also, among others, Zhou and Bankston (1994) and Sanders and Nee (1996).

12. This idea has its origins in Georg Simmel, who wrote extensively on the social boundaries separating "insiders" and "outsiders." Simmel (1971 [1908]: 253, 255) also recognized that development and an expanding division of labor produced

   > a need and an inclination to reach out beyond the original spatial, economic, and mental boundaries of the group and, in connection with the increase in individualization and concomitant mutual repulsion of group elements, to supplement the original centripetal forces of the lone group with a centrifugal tendency that forms bridges with other groups.

13. Most of the work investigating the effects of ethnic heterogeneity on growth uses the so-called ethnolinguistic fractionalization (ELF) index, a product of Soviet social science in the 1960s. For an attempt to improve this measure by incorporating the political significance of particular ethnic groups, see Posner (2004). For further work on the importance of bureaucratic structures to economic performance, see Unger (1998) and Evans and Rauch (1999).

14. For related work in this vein, see Fox (1996), Heller (1996), and Ostrom (1996).

15. Grootaert et al. (2004) present a comprehensive household survey tool that draws on and integrates the lessons of previous efforts (inside and outside the World Bank) to measure social capital quantitatively.

16. The governments of Australia, Canada, and the United Kingdom have been especially active in seeking to construct national measures of social capital (see, for example, Government of Canada 2005).

17. The quantitative assessment tool is outlined in Grootaert et al. (2004); a complementary qualitative instrument is provided in Dudwick et al. (2006).

18. The World Bank's Social Capital Initiative was a $1.2 million project sponsored by the government of Denmark. Several monographs produced for the initiative have been cited in this paper; these and several others can be found in Grootaert and Van Bastelaer (2002a, 2002b).

19. Within the World Bank, the largest operational manifestation of social capital has been in the portfolio of loans collectively referred to as "community driven development" (CDD) projects. See www.worldbank.org/cdd.

References

Astone, Nan Marie, Constance Nathanson, Robert Schoen, and Young Kim. 1999. Family demography, social theory, and investment in social capital. *Population and Development Review* 25(1):1–31.

Banfield, Edward O. 1958. *The moral basis of a backward society.* New York: Free Press.

Barr, Abigail. 2002. The functional diversity and spillover effects of social capital. *Journal of African Economies* 11(1):90–113.

Berry, Sara. 1993. *No condition is permanent: The social dynamics of agrarian change in sub-Saharan Africa.* Madison: University of Wisconsin Press.

Bourdieu, Pierre. 1986 [1983]. The forms of capital. In *Handbook of theory and research for the sociology of education,* edited by John Richardson. Westport, CT: Greenwood Press.

Briggs, Xavier de Souza. 1998. Brown kids in white suburbs: Housing mobility and the multiple faces of social capital. *Housing Policy Debate* 9(1):177–221.

Brown, L. David. 1998. Creating social capital: Nongovernmental development organizations and intersectoral problem solving. In *Private action and the public good,* edited by Walter W. Powell and Elisabeth Clemens. New Haven, CT: Yale University Press.

Brown, L. David, and Darcy Ashman. 1996. Participation, social capital, and intersectoral problem solving: African and Asian cases. *World Development* 24(6):1477–1495.

Burt, Ronald. 1992. *Structural holes: The social structure of competition.* Cambridge, MA: Harvard University Press.

———. 1997. The contingent value of social capital. *Administrative Science Quarterly* 42:339–365.

———. 1998. The gender of social capital. *Rationality and Society* 10(1):5–46.

———. 2005. *Brokerage and closure: An introduction to social capital.* New York: Oxford University Press.

Coleman, James. 1987. Norms as social capital. In *Economic imperialism: The economic method applied outside the field of economics,* edited by Gerard Radnitzky and Peter Bernholz. New York: Paragon House.

———. 1988. Social capital in the creation of human capital. *American Journal of Sociology* 94:S95–S120.

———. 1990. *Foundations of social theory.* Cambridge, MA: Harvard University Press.

———. 1994. A rational choice perspective on economic sociology. In *The handbook of economic sociology,* edited by Neil Smelser and Richard Swedberg. Princeton, NJ: Princeton University Press.

Collier, Paul. 1999. The political economy of ethnicity. In *Annual Bank Conference on Development Economics 1998.* Washington, DC: World Bank.

———. 2002. Social capital and poverty: A microeconomic perspective. In *The role of social capital in development: An empirical assessment,* edited by Christiaan Grootaert and Thierry Van Bastalaer. New York: Cambridge University Press.

Collier, Paul, and Jan Willem Gunning. 1999. Explaining African economic performance. *Journal of Economic Literature* 37(March):4–111.

Dasgupta, Partha, and Ismail Serageldin. 2000. *Social capital: A multifaceted perspective.* Washington, DC: World Bank.

Dordick, Gwendolyn. 1997. *Something left to lose: Personal relations and survival among New York's homeless.* Philadelphia: Temple University Press.

Dudwick, Nora, Kathleen Kuehnast, Veronica Nyhan Jones, and Michael Woolcock. 2006. *Analyzing social capital in context: A guide to using qualitative methods and data.* Washington, DC: World Bank. (Processed.)

Durlauf, Steven. 1999. The case "against" social capital. *Focus* 20(3):1–5.

Durlauf, Steven, and Marcel Fafchamps. 2004. *Social capital.* NBER Working Paper No. 10485. Cambridge, MA: National Bureau for Economic Research.

Easterly, William. 2001. The middle class consensus and economic development. *Journal of Economic Growth* 6(4):317–335.

Escobar, Arturo. 1995. *Encountering development: The making and unmaking of the Third World.* Princeton, NJ: Princeton University Press.

Esman, Milton, and Norman Uphoff. 1984. *Local organizations: Intermediaries in rural development.* Ithaca, NY: Cornell University Press.

Evans, Peter. 1992. The state as problem and solution: Predation, embedded autonomy, and structural change. In *The politics of economic adjustment,* edited by Stephan Haggard and Robert Kaufman. Princeton, NJ: Princeton University Press.

———. 1995. *Embedded autonomy: States and industrial transformation.* Princeton, NJ: Princeton University Press.

———. 1996. Government action, social capital and development: Reviewing the evidence on synergy. *World Development* 24(6):1119–1132.

Evans, Peter, and James Rauch. 1999. Bureaucracy and growth: A cross-national analysis of the effects of "Weberian" state structures on economic growth. *American Sociological Review* 64(5):748–765.

Fafchamps, Marcel, and Bart Minten. 2002. Returns to social network capital among traders. *Oxford Economic Papers* 54(2):173–206.

Farr, James. 2004. Social capital: A conceptual history. *Political Theory* 32(1):6–33.

Fine, Ben. 1999. The developmental state is dead—Long live social capital? *Development and Change* 30:1–19.

———. 2001. *Social capital versus social theory: Political economy and social science at the turn of the millennium.* London and New York: Routledge.

Foley, Michael, and Bob Edwards. 1999. Is it time to disinvest in social capital? *Journal of Public Policy* 19(2):141–173.

Fox, Jonathan. 1992. Democratic rural development: Leadership accountability in regional peasant organizations. *Development and Change* 23(2):1–36.

———. 1996. How does civil society thicken? The political construction of social capital in rural Mexico. *World Development* 24(6):1089–1103.

———. 1997. The World Bank and social capital: Contesting the concept in practice. *Journal of International Studies* 9(7):963–971.

Fox, Jonathan, and L. David Brown, eds. 1998. *The struggle for accountability: The World Bank, NGOs, and grassroots movements.* Cambridge, MA: MIT Press.

Fukuyama, Francis. 1995. *Trust: The social virtues and the creation of prosperity.* New York: Free Press.

Gittell, Ross, and Avis Vidal. 1998. *Community organizing: Building social capital as a development strategy*. Newbury Park, CA: Sage.

Gold, Steven. 1995. Gender and social capital and Israeli immigrants in Los Angeles. *Diaspora* 4(3):267–301.

Government of Canada. 2005. *Social capital as a public policy tool: Project report*. Ottawa: Government of Canada, Policy Research Initiative.

Granovetter, Mark. 1973. The strength of weak ties. *American Journal of Sociology* 78:1360–1380.

Granovetter, Mark. 1995. The economic sociology of firms and entrepreneurs. In *The economic sociology of immigration: Essays on networks, ethnicity and entrepreneurship*, edited by Alejandro Portes. New York: Russell Sage Foundation.

Grootaert, Christiaan. 1997. Social capital: The missing link? In *Expanding the measure of wealth*. ESD Monograph Series No. 20. Washington, DC: World Bank. (Reissued in 1998 as Working Paper No. 3 of the World Bank's Social Capital Initiative.)

Grootaert, Christiaan. 1999. *Social capital, household welfare, and poverty in Indonesia*. Local Level Institutions, Working Paper No. 6. Washington, DC: World Bank.

Grootaert, Christiaan, and Deepa Narayan. 1999. *Social capital in Burkina Faso*. Local Level Institutions Study. Washington, DC: World Bank

Grootaert, Christiaan, Deepa Narayan, Veronica Nyhan Jones, and Michael Woolcock. 2004. *Measuring social capital: An integrated questionnaire*. Working Paper No. 18. Washington, DC: World Bank.

Grootaert, Christiaan, and Thierry Van Bastelaer, eds. 2002a. *The role of social capital in development: An empirical assessment*. New York: Cambridge University Press.

Grootaert, Christiaan, and Thierry Van Bastelaer, eds. 2002b. *Understanding and measuring social capital: A multidisciplinary tool for practitioners*. Washington, DC: World Bank.

Hall, Robert, and Charles Jones. 1999. Why do some countries produce so much more output per worker than others? *Quarterly Journal of Economics* 114(1):83–116.

Halpern, David. 2004. *Social capital*. Cambridge: Polity Press

Hanifan, Lyda J. 1916. The rural school community center. *Annals of the American Academy of Political and Social Science* 67:130–138.

Harriss, John, and Paolo De Renzio. 1997. "Missing Link" or analytically missing? The concept of social capital. *Journal of International Development* 9(7):919–937.

Heller, Patrick. 1996. Social capital as a product of class mobilization and state intervention: Industrial workers in Kerala, India. *World Development* 24(6):1055–1071.

Hirschman, Albert. 1958. *The strategy of economic development* New Haven, CT: Yale University Press.

Holzmann, Robert, and Steen Jorgensen. 1999. *Social protection as social risk management*. Social Protection Discussion Paper No. 9901. Washington, DC: World Bank.

Homans, George. 1961. *Social behavior: Its elementary forms*. New York: Harcourt, Brace and World.

Hyden, Goran. 1997. Civil society, social capital, and development: Dissection of a complex discourse. *Studies in Comparative International Development* 32(1):3–30.

Inglehart, Ronald. 1997. *Modernization and postmodernization: Cultural, economic, and political change in 43 societies*. Princeton, NJ: Princeton University Press.

Isham, Jonathan. 2002. The effects of social capital on fertilizer adoption: Evidence from rural Tanzania. *Journal of African Economies* 11(1):39–60.

Isham, Jonathan, and Daniel Kaufmann. 1999. The forgotten rationale for policy reform: The productivity of investment projects. *Quarterly Journal of Economics* 114(1):149–184.

Isham, Jonathan, Tom Kelly, and Sunder Ramaswamy. 2002. Social capital and well-being in developing countries: An introduction. In *Social capital and economic development: Well-being in developing countries*, edited by Jonathan Isham, Thomas Kelly, and Sunder Ramaswamy. Northampton, MA: Edward Elgar.

Isham, Jonathan, Deepa Narayan, and Lant Pritchett. 1995. Does participation improve performance? Establishing causality with subjective data. *World Bank Economic Review* 9(2):175–200.

Jacobs, Jane. 1961. *The life and death of great American cities*. New York: Random House.

Keck, Margaret, and Kathryn Sikkink. 1998. *Activists beyond borders: Advocacy networks in international politics*. Ithaca, NY: Cornell University Press.

Klitgaard, Robert. 1990. *Tropical gangsters*. New York: Basic Books.

Knack, Stephen. 2002. Social capital, growth, and poverty: A survey of cross-country evidence. In *The role of social capital in development: An empirical assessment*, edited by Christiaan Grootaert and Thierry van Bastelaer. New York: Cambridge University Press.

Knack, Stephen, and Philip Keefer. 1995. Institutions and economic performance: Cross-country tests using alternative institutional measures. *Economics and Politics* 7(November):207–227.

———. 1997. Does social capital have an economic payoff? A cross-country investigation. *Quarterly Journal of Economics* 112:1251–1288.

Kozel, Valerie, and Barbara Parker. 1998. *Poverty in rural India: The contribution of qualitative research in poverty analysis*. Washington, DC: World Bank. (Processed.)

Krishna, Anirudh. 2002. *Active social capital: Tracing the roots of development and democracy*. New York: Columbia University Press.

Krishna, Anirudh, and Elizabeth Shrader. 1999. *Social capital assessment tool*. Social Capital Initiative, Working Paper No. 22. Washington, DC: World Bank.

Loury, Glen. 1977. A dynamic theory of racial income differences. In *Women, minorities, and employment discrimination*, edited by P.A. Wallace and A. LeMund. Lexington, MA: Lexington Books.

Massey, Douglas. 1998. March of folly: US immigration policy after NAFTA. *American Prospect* 37:22–33.

Massey, Douglas, and Karin Espinosa. 1997. What's driving Mexico-U.S. migration? A theoretical, empirical, and policy analysis. *American Journal of Sociology* 102(4):939–999.

Moore, Mick. 1997. Societies, polities and capitalists in developing countries: A literature survey. *Journal of Development Studies* 33(3): 287–363.

Moser, Caroline. 1996. *Confronting crisis: A comparative study of household responses to poverty and vulnerability in four poor urban communities.* Washington, DC: World Bank.

Narayan, Deepa. 1997. *Voices of the poor: Poverty and social capital in Tanzania.* ESD Monograph No. 17. Washington, DC: The World Bank.

———. 1998. *Social capital survey in Ghana—Preliminary results.* Washington, DC: World Bank. (Processed.)

———. 2002. Bonds and bridges: Social capital and poverty. In *Social capital and economic development: Well-being in developing countries,* edited by Jonathan Isham, Thomas Kelly, and Sunder Ramaswamy. Northampton, MA: Edward Elgar.

Narayan, Deepa, and Michael Cassidy. 1999. *A dimensional approach to measuring social capital: Development and validation of a social capital inventory.* Washington, DC: World Bank. (Processed.)

Narayan, Deepa, and David Nyamwaya. 1996. *Learning from the poor: A participatory poverty assessment in Kenya.* Washington, DC: World Bank.

Narayan, Deepa, Raj Patel, Kai Schafft, Anne Rademacher, and Sarah Koch-Schulte. 2000. *Voices of the poor. Can anyone hear us? Voices from 46 countries.* Washington, DC: World Bank.

Narayan, Deepa, and Lant Pritchett. 1999. Cents and sociability: Household income and social capital in rural Tanzania. *Economic Development and Cultural Change* 47(4):871–897.

Narayan, Deepa, and Talat Shah. 2000. *Gender inequity, poverty and social capital.* Washington, DC: World Bank. (Processed.)

National Commission on Civic Renewal. 1998. *A nation of spectators: How civic disengagement weakens America and what we can do about it.* College Park, MD: National Commission on Civic Renewal.

National Commission on Philanthropy and Civic Renewal. 1998. *National Index of Civic Engagement.* Storrs: University of Connecticut. (Processed.)

North, Douglass C. 1990. *Institutions, institutional change and economic performance.* New York: Cambridge University Press.

Onyx, Jenny, and Paul Bullen. 2000. Measuring social capital in five communities. *Journal of Applied Behavioral Science* 36(1):23–42.

Ostrom, Elinor. 1996. Crossing the great divide: Coproduction, synergy, and development. *World Development* 24(6):1073–1087.

Platteau, Jean-Philippe. 1994. Behind the market stage where real societies exist (parts I & II). *Journal of Development Studies* 30:533–577, 753–817.

Portes, Alejandro, ed. 1995. *The economic sociology of immigration: Essays on networks, ethnicity, and entrepreneurship.* New York: Russell Sage Foundation.

———. 1997. Neoliberalism and the sociology of development. *Population and Development Review* 23(2):229–259.

———. 1998. Social capital: Its origins and applications in contemporary sociology. *Annual Review of Sociology* 24:1–24.

Portes, Alejandro, and Patricia Landolt. 1996. The downside of social capital. *American Prospect* 26(May–June):18–21, 94.

Portes, Alejandro, and Julia Sensenbrenner. 1993. Embeddedness and immigration: Notes on the social determinants of economic action. *American Journal of Sociology* 98(6):1320–1350.

Posner, Daniel. 2004. Measuring ethnic fractionalization in Africa. *American Journal of Political Science* 48(4):849–863.

Putnam, Robert. 1993a. *Making democracy work: Civic traditions in modern Italy.* Princeton, NJ: Princeton University Press.

———. 1993b. The prosperous community: Social capital and public life. *American Prospect* 4(13):27–40.

———. 1995. Tuning in, tuning out: The strange disappearance of social capital in America. *PS: Political Science and Politics* (December 1):664–683.

———. 2000. *Bowling alone: Civic disengagement in America.* New York: Simon & Schuster.

Rist, Gilbert. 1997. *The history of development: From Western origins to global faith.* London: Zed Books.

Rodrik, Dani. 1999a. Where did all the growth go? External shocks, social conflict, and growth collapses. *Journal of Economic Growth* 4(4):385–412.

———. 1999b. *Making openness work.* Baltimore: Johns Hopkins University Press.

Rose, Richard. 1998. *Getting things done in an anti-modern society: Social capital networks in Russia.* Social Capital Initiative, Working Paper No. 8. Washington, DC: World Bank.

Rubio, Mauricio. 1997. Perverse social capital—Some evidence from Colombia. *Journal of Economic Issues* 31(3):805–816.

Sanders, Jimmy M., and Victor Nee. 1996. Immigrant self-employment: The family as social capital and the value of human capital. *American Sociological Review* 61:231–249.

Schafft, Kai, and David Brown. 2000. Social capital and grassroots development: The case of Roma self-governance in Hungary. *Social Problems* 47(2):201–219.

Serageldin, Ismail, and Christiaan Grootaert. 2000. Defining social capital: An integrating view. In *Social capital: A multifaceted perspective,* edited by Partha Dasgupta and Ismail Serageldin. Washington, DC: World Bank.

Simmel, Georg. 1971 [1908]. Group expansion and the development of individuality. In *Georg Simmel: On individuality and social forms,* edited by Donald Levine Chicago: University of Chicago Press.

Skocpol, Theda. 1995. *Protecting soldiers and mothers: The political origins of social policy in the United States.* Cambridge, MA: Harvard University Press.

———. 1996. Unraveling from above. *American Prospect* 25:20–25.

Tarrow, Sidney. 1995. Bridging the quantitative-qualitative divide in political science. *American Political Science Review* 89(2):471–474.

Temple, Jonathan. 1998. Initial conditions, social capital, and growth in Africa. *Journal of African Economies* 7(3):309–347.

Temple, Jonathan, and Paul Johnson. 1998. Social capability and economic growth. *Quarterly Journal of Economics* 113(3):965–990.

Tendler, Judith. 1997. *Good government in the tropics*. Baltimore: Johns Hopkins University Press.

Unger, Danny. 1998. *Building social capital in Thailand: Fibers, finance, and infrastructure*. New York: Cambridge University Press.

United Nations. 1951. *Measures for the economic development of underdeveloped countries*. New York: United Nations, Department of Social and Economic Affairs.

Uphoff, Norman. 1992. *Learning from Gal Oya: Possibilities for participatory development and post-Newtonian social science*. Ithaca, NY: Cornell University Press.

Van Bastelaer, Thierry. 1999. *Does social capital facilitate the poor's access to credit? A review of the microeconomic literature*. Social Capital Initiative, Working Paper No. 8. Washington, DC: World Bank.

Van Dijk, Meine Pieter, and Roberta Rabellotti. 1997. *Enterprise clusters and networks in developing countries*. London: Frank Cass.

Varshney, Ashutosh. 2002. *Ethnic conflict and civic life: Hindus and Muslims in India*. New Haven, CT: Yale University Press.

White, T. Anderson, and Glenn Smucker. 1998. Social capital and governance in Haiti: Traditions and trends. In *The challenges of poverty reduction*. Report No. 17242-HA. Washington, DC: World Bank, Chapter 9.

Wilson, William Julius. 1987. *The truly disadvantaged*. Chicago: University of Chicago Press.

———. 1996. *When work disappears: The world of the new urban poor*. New York: Knopf.

Woolcock, Michael. 1998. Social capital and economic development: Toward a theoretical synthesis and policy framework. *Theory and Society* 27(2):151–208.

———. 1999a. Learning from failures in microfinance: What unsuccessful cases tell us about *how* group-based programs work. *American Journal of Economics and Sociology* 58(1):17–42.

———. 1999b. Managing risk, shocks, and opportunities in developing economies: The role of social capital. In *Dimensions of Development*, edited by Gustav Ranis. New Haven, CT: Yale Center for International and Area Studies.

World Bank. 1989. *Staff appraisal report, Rwanda, agricultural services project*. Report No. 7599-RW, May 8. Agricultural Operations Division, South-Central and Indian Ocean Department, Africa Region.

———. 1998. *Assessing aid: What works, what doesn't, and why*. New York: Oxford University Press.

———. 2000. *World development report 2000/01: Attacking poverty*. New York: Oxford University Press

———. 2003. *World development report 2004: Making services work for poor people* New York: Oxford University Press.

World Development. 1996. Special issue on social capital, 24(6).

Zhou, Min, and Carl L. Bankston. 1994. Social capital and the adaptation of the second generation: The case of Vietnamese youth in New Orleans. *International Migration Review* 28 (4):821–845.

CHAPTER THREE

SCENES FROM A MARRIAGE: WORLD BANK ECONOMISTS AND SOCIAL CAPITAL

Jeffrey Hammer
Lant Pritchett

Introduction

This chapter traces World Bank economists' relationship with social capital over the period from roughly 1993 (the publication date of Robert Putnam's *Making Democracy Work*) to 2004. At the outset we must warn that we trace our relationship with and stance toward social capital in a personal and idiosyncratic way, though with the hope that our experience is at least in some ways reflective of that of other World Bank economists. The alternative—to speak with authoritative pretense about the intellectual evolution of the abstract consciousness of a collective called "World Bank economists"—would distort the reality: There are as many views by economists toward social capital as there are economists.[1]

We trace this relationship in three steps, paralleling the course of a romantic relationship. The first section outlines why economists, who stereotypically are more likely to attempt to impose their research program[2] than to borrow from other disciplines, would be susceptible to the charms of a notion such as "social capital," which emerged in the middle 1990s. We argue that this flirtation with social capital was the result of the confluence of three intellectual streams. Within the discipline the research program for studying arm's-length transactions (either through the market or via government) was proceeding apace, but the most promising economic approach for studying non–arm's-length transactions—dynamic game theory—had failed to pan out. Dynamic game theory as a positive behavioral model for studying repeated interactions among known individuals proved much less powerful than most had hoped. At the same time, evidence acceptable to economists indicated that the purely individualistic models, which did not take into account the possibility of cooperation, did not capture the variety of actual situations in which cooperation did emerge and was sustained. Finally, from a World Bank perspective, operational experience repeatedly demonstrated the necessity of taking into account the realities of implementation for those types of projects that required ongoing local cooperation.

The second section documents the rocky stage of the relationship, following the first blush of infatuation. Although something like "social capital" is attractive, there have been many complaints about what "social capital" is, exactly. First, the words *social capital* are not conceptually apt in any sense. Second, the metaphor of "social capital" has been expected to bear too much analytical weight and easily became overextended.

The third section shows that despite the complaints about social capital, what is called for is not a divorce between economists and "social capital" but rather a recognition that the relationship of economists with the array of concepts under the big "social capital" umbrella is productive, but a great deal of work is required to make the relationship work. This section provides an analytical framework that illustrates the range of situations in which a notion like social capital can prove useful. It argues that the tools of economists have been honed to evaluate "arm's-length" transactions in markets or government policies, but that they have neglected the critical role of groups and non–arm's-length transactions, which have proved important in a variety of domains, including information diffusion, enforcement of contracts, cooperation in natural resources, and monitoring the performance of local governments.

Why Economists Were Susceptible to the Charms of Social Capital

The influence of social capital on World Bank economists had three origins. One purely theoretical factor was the dissolution of the field's previous marriage to game theory, once dynamic game theory had proven itself nearly barren. A second impetus was the emergence of concerns within the empirical literature on various types of cooperative behavior. A third force was operational, emerging from experience with the implementation of projects, particularly those in the rural water sector.

Disappointment with Game Theory

Crucial to understanding the flirtation of economics with social capital is the discipline's disappointment with its previous mad crush: game theory. In many ways, the attraction of social capital was a rebound affair. Understanding this requires a few paragraphs of background.[3]

The standard analytical tools of economics are particularly strong in the case of "arm's-length" relationships. The key claim of modern economics is that the interactions of a large number of individual agents, no one of which has a "social" agenda or a "social" relationship of any kind with any other agent, produce "social" outcomes that are surprisingly benign.[4] That is, to the proposition that ensuring the enormous array of complex activities necessary for "social" life (from house building to food delivery into cities to music composition) amounts to "everyone doing whatever they want," most non-economists would counter that this would, in fact, produce absolute chaos. That (models of) this very process produce a stable equilibrium is a bit surprising. That (models of) this process can be shown to possess desirable properties such as Pareto efficiency is quite surprising indeed.[5]

But economists recognized early on that the assumption that producers and consumers act as if their actions have no impact on any other actor (because they are limited relative to a relevant set of interactions or "market") was a poor one where it was not, in fact, empirically true. In particular, where two large firms dominate a market, it is the case that increased production by one firm will lead to a lower price for both firms; hence each firm's choice of actions affects the other firm. The tools that arose to model these types of strategic interactions between agents, which are not arm's length and impersonal, led to the development of game theory.

Far and away the most famous illustration of game theory is the "Prisoner's Dilemma." Two prisoners who have participated in a crime are caught separately, and with no possibility of communication between them they are given the choice either to confess (including implicating their partner) or not confess. The payoffs to the prisoners are symmetric. It is assumed that if neither confesses, the outcome is quite good; if one confesses and the other doesn't, there is a severe penalty for the one who does not confess; whereas if both confess, the penalties for the two prisoners are worse than if neither confesses, but better than if one does not confess but his partner in crime does. With this particular structure the predicted outcome (the unique Nash equilibrium) is that both prisoners confess. The reasoning for each prisoner is simple: If my partner does not confess, then the best action for me is to confess (since the penalty is lighter); if my partner does confess, the best outcome for me is still to confess (since if I am alone in not confessing, I get a particularly severe penalty). The reason this is such a famous model is that it captures a situation in which there is a potential for gains from cooperation and yet the prediction is that self-interested behavior will prevent cooperation.

The immediate response is that this model does not capture the reality of repeated interactions: What if these prisoners knew they were going to face this same situation repeatedly? This led to the emergence of dynamic game theory—models of situations in which agents' actions affect each other and the same (or a known) set of agents interact repeatedly. But if the "Prisoner's Dilemma" is played repeatedly for a fixed number of periods, the predicted outcome is the same—both prisoners confess every period. Again, the reasoning is simple: In the last period, confessing is the best outcome no matter what one's partner in crime does and no matter what has happened before; and since both are going to confess in the last period, then in the next-to-last period the rationale for confessing is the same, so cooperation unravels.

However, the sense that dynamic game theory was the way forward for the "normal science" of economics in modeling strategic interactions and non–arm's-length interactions became seriously unglued in the following three ways, leaving economists' relationship with game theory in a rocky state.

The first breach was one of the fundamental results in game theory, the Folk Theorem (Fudenberg and Maskin 1986). As with any complex mathematical result, any verbal summary of the Folk Theorem is not precise; but basically the Folk Theorem proved that in an infinitely repeated game where the players' discount rates are low enough, there are a very large number of possible equilibrium strategies. The Folk Theorem predicted that just about any sequence of actions can be an equilibrium for any individual player and, as one of our MIT professors put it, "'anything can happen' is not a particularly useful positive model." This was a substantial blow to the practical use of dynamic game theory since, in order to be useful as a positive model, it would have to predict which of the many possible equilibria would emerge.[6]

Notably, this was the second time game theory had first attracted and then disappointed economists. The first was some 40 years earlier, after the path-breaking work of Von Neumann and Morgenstern (1953) failed to generate many successful applications in economics until its resurgence more than a generation later. This shows that the fundamental fact of life that game theory attempted to describe—that economic actors frequently know themselves to be interdependent with particular other actors—has been recognized as an essential feature of economic behavior for a long time. It also shows that economists repeatedly feel compelled to return to game theory because of its fit with other familiar analytical tools, regardless of how frustrated it leaves us.

How is this relevant to social capital? Our conjecture is that one of the reasons economists were susceptible to the notion of social capital was that the research program at the time had no compelling way of examining small-group, non–arm's-length (personalized, repeated) transactions. No economist could rule out that a social *something* was important for outcomes if this *something* affected the relationships of players of repeated games that determined which of the many possible equilibria emerged; it was at least plausible that "high social capital" would produce cooperative equilibria while "low social capital" would produce noncooperative (and Pareto-dominated) equilibria.

Empirical Examples of Cooperation

The second blow to dynamic game theory as the primary research tool for small-group interactions was the emergence of several influential lines of research that demonstrated the limitations of either dynamic game theory (in which agents did take interactions into account) or a purely self-interested approach to small-group interactions.

An important step toward a "social capital" approach was publication in 1984 of Robert Axelrod's book *The Evolution of Cooperation*, which used actual tournaments with repeated Prisoner's Dilemma trials to produce two striking "empirical" findings. The key finding was that the very simple strategy of "tit for tat" was the winner in a Prisoner's Dilemma tournament. That is, although "always confess" was the unique Nash equilibrium of the repeated Prisoner's Dilemma exercise, and although with N periods there was a huge array of possible strategies,[7] in an actual tournament in which Prisoner's Dilemma strategies played against each other via computer, the winner was the simplest possible "tit for tat" strategy: Begin by cooperating in the first period, and then in each subsequent period do what the opponent did in the previous period. If your partner confessed in period $N - 1$, then confess in period N; if your partner did not confess in period $N - 1$, then do not confess in period N.[8]

The second key finding of Axelrod's book is that the absolute and relative returns to various repeated Prisoner's Dilemma strategies depends on the populations of other strategies in the tournament. Suppose we imagine a population of K individuals, each of whom has a strategy—say "tit for tat" or "always confess" or "always cooperate" or "cooperate first, then always confess after the first defection" (keeping in mind that, somewhat perversely, the framing of the story about prisoners is such that confession is the "noncooperative" or "antisocial" behavior). Then imagine a round of the game in which plays consist of random interactions among individuals, and after a certain number of plays scores are tabulated and the lowest-ranking X individuals in that round are eliminated from the population. Then another round is played. Obviously, the composition of the population among individuals with various strategies will evolve. Moreover, populations with various strategies will have high absolute outcomes; for instance, a population of all "tit for tat" will be characterized by a large amount of cooperation.[9]

The general point here is that once it has been demonstrated that, even in an analytical setup in which noncooperation is a powerful temptation, stable populations can emerge that are more cooperative and hence have higher overall well-being. It is not a major leap to conclude that "norms" for behavior could produce cooperative behavior that is stable, both individually and socially, or to call a bias toward a cooperative norm in a given collection of individuals "social *something.*"

Elinor Ostrom's *Governing the Commons* (1990) is another work that prepared economists for receptivity to social capital. In this now-classic work, she showed that the "tragedy of the commons" (Hardin 1968)—the overuse and depletion of a common pool resource (e.g. groundwater, fishing grounds, forest)—was, while possible, not at all inevitable. She gives several examples in which common pool resources have been successfully managed on a sustainable basis without (and even perhaps in spite of) government intervention. Indeed, one of her examples is a system of irrigation that has been maintained for centuries. Of course, she shows that not all common pool resources are successfully managed and gives indications of the types of geographic and social conditions in which a cooperative outcome is more likely than the "tragedy of the commons." Many of these potential determinants of cooperation—such as repeated small-group interactions of relatively homogeneous producers—could be described as "social *something*."

A third empirical phenomenon was the resurgence of micro-credit and other forms of group-based lending/borrowing, and academic attention to such, exemplified by the flamboyant promotion of the Grameen Bank. Again, the experience suggested that *some* characteristic of the social relationships between individuals could determine whether or not some groups could sustain such lending (and identify those situations in which other forms, such as rotating savings and credit associations, or ROSCAs, would emerge spontaneously).

Bank Operational Experience

The precursors of the receptivity of World Bank economists to a notion like "social capital" were based not entirely on intellectual and academic developments, but also on practical experience within the World Bank with project implementation.

The Wapenhans Report, an internal review of levels of failure in World Bank projects deemed unacceptably high, was critical of many dimensions of then-prevailing Bank practices in project preparation. For instance, the report was critical of a "board approval" culture in which staff were rewarded for the presentation of attractive project *designs* to the World Bank's board, with relatively little attention paid to whether those designs were actually implemented. Another key element of the Wapenhans Report was its emphasis on the fact that project design was entirely dependent on government agencies and was disconnected from social realities on the ground.

We regard the Wapenhans Report as creating receptivity to the "social capital" concept for operationally minded World Bank economists. First, the change of focus to project implementation rather than design was the beginning of a long—and ongoing—shift in attention from the "what" to the "how." That is, the "economic" cost-benefit analysis that was part of the project preparation process, enshrined in manuals published by international organizations such as the OECD (Little and Mirrlees 1974) and UNIDO (Sen et al. 1972), had been almost completely focused on which projects (and which types of projects) should be financed and on the valuation problems of attributing the appropriate economic (not financial) prices to project inputs and outputs when markets were distorted. The existence of the implementation apparatus necessary to make the project happen (and enable it to reach the efficiency frontier)—indeed, the motivation of real people to make sure the project was done at all—was simply assumed at the outset.

Second, the Wapenhans Report emphasized the failures of eliciting the ongoing cooperation of the intended "beneficiaries" in project operations and maintenance. The report called for substantially greater social analysis of projects.

The operational experience of a variety of donors (including the World Bank) with the rural water supply sector was perhaps the paradigm case of the old approach to development and was a primary factor in making economists' mindsets more receptive to a concept like social capital. Caricaturing stances, we can describe the mindset behind early water supply projects as driven by the "needs is the problem / least-cost solutions are the technical solution / civil service bureaucracies as implementers" paradigm (see Pritchett and Woolcock 2004). That is, water was defined as a "need," so it was deemed unnecessary to analyze the varying "demands" of individuals for water; the way to address the need for water (given limited resources) was to create a least-cost technocratic solution, and then rely on a civil service bureaucracy to implement it (e.g., assign water engineers to create wells/taps). As of the early 1990s there was a broad consensus that this approach was not working, since bureaucracies could create assets that they did not have the capability to maintain (e.g., they lacked the capacity to keep the created water supply assets in working order). Since communities and individuals had not been engaged in the process of creating the water supply systems, they had little stake in maintaining them (or paying for their maintenance). This led to the emphasis on "participation" of local communities in the process of water supply— from design to construction to maintenance.

The engagement of communities in projects quickly led to the realization that "communities" were not at all common. In fact, they differed in nearly every respect—from geographic dispersion to depth of social ties (from strong communalism to deep internal antagonisms) to the "capacity" for project participation. When water supply projects were redesigned to engage with communities rather than being implemented strictly by bureaucracies, it was expected that this would result in "strong" communities being more adept at creating and maintaining water supply than "weak" communities. Thinking through what made a geographically defined "community" strong or weak in its capacity to implement water supply projects led easily to a notion of "social *something* "as a measure of capacity for collective action.

End of the Beginning

Why were World Bank economists, widely (and perhaps correctly) regarded as arrogant about their discipline and expertise, susceptible to a notion outside their existing disciplinary research program? We conjecture the confluence of three forces. First, the strategy for modeling non–arm's-length transactions via the techniques of dynamic game theory failed to produce a compelling and useful positive behavioral model, though the real-life problem posed by the research strategy was clear. Second, empirical evidence was accumulating that there existed a wide range of outcomes in situations of potential "market failure" that could lead to noncooperative behavior; the "tragedy of the commons" was a theoretical, not empirical, inevitability, since in some (but not all) instances sustained cooperation did emerge. Finally, the operational experience with project implementation in the World Bank (particularly in the water sector) was raising questions about the need for greater engagement of "communities" in project implementation, which in turn led to questions of what constitutes a "community" and what is the capacity of a "community." These three forces together did not suggest that the traditional tools of economic analysis were irrelevant, but they did suggest that there was a *range of phenomena* for which *non–arm's-length* transactions were potentially important in determining outcomes, and that characterization of the personalized relationships among individuals or norms of behavior could lead to positive or negative outcomes.

As one of us (Pritchett) was working on the *World Development Report 1994* on Infrastructure, this intrigue with the role of social *something* and project outcomes led to engagement in research on the determinants of the success or failure of rural water supply projects with Jonathan Isham and Deepa Narayan (a non-economist social scientist at the World Bank). This research demonstrated (to Pritchett's satisfaction) that participation was an empirically important determinant of project success[10] (Isham et al. 1995). This left open the question of what factor(s) beyond project design might account for why some communities participate and others do not—certainly some "social *something*" might increase the community's propensity to cooperate and to participate in collective action projects (such as water supply) and hence improve outcomes.

This led to a second round of collaboration with the same authors on social phenomena using data from a multipurpose household survey in Tanzania on a variety of "social capital"–like variables related to trust, norms, and associational life (participation in community, religious, and other social activities). Analysis of the data provided compelling evidence of a strong association between measures of what could plausibly be called "social capital" (see Narayan and Pritchett 1999) at the village level and village-level outcomes.[11] In fact, in this particular data set the estimated impact on incomes of our measure of "social capital" was something of an embarrassment of riches, as it suggested that social capital had a large impact compared with well-known determinants of household income, such as land and education.

Thus, relatively quickly after "social capital" was (re)popularized by Putnam's (1993) work on the role of associational life in the efficacy of government services in Italy, there was receptivity among economists in the World Bank and a growing body of empirical work acceptable to economists demonstrating plausible empirical links between a social *something* (that could not unreasonably be called "social capital") and outcomes of interest, such as project success, information diffusion, and incomes.

Social Capital: Resisting the Temptations of All Imperialists

Every relationship begins with unrealistic expectations, and economists quickly developed a rocky relationship with "social capital." The previous section explained the evolution of the relationship between economists and social relations, emphasizing the positive elements. However, there are downsides to the construct of social capital in furthering this relationship. As with many successful innovations, there is a temptation to expand the analysis far beyond its original successes and to move too quickly to generalizations that are unsupported and prove to be unsupportable. The two parts of this section lay out arguments against overextending the notion of "social capital." The first is partly semantic—but in an ongoing "discourse" semantics are important—but it also highlights some very clear differences in the way economists might frame the problem if social relations were discussed as a form of "capital." The second subsection reexamines the domain of problems to which social relations (no longer capital) may be expected to apply. The final subsection presents empirical evidence about the ambiguities of "social capital" from a study in Indonesia.

Why "Social Capital" Is Not a Useful Aggregate

In summary, there is *something* about attention to social relations that needs to be incorporated into economic analysis. And since the word sounds familiar to economists, why not call the social phenomenon that improves outcomes "social capital" by analogy with the many other "capitals"? Although we do believe social phenomena are important, we do not believe an aggregate called "social capital" is analytically or empirically useful. There are reasons to resist the use of the word *capital* merely as a mechanism to borrow "prestige" from a science, if only because it risks distorting the process of inquiry. We note two reasons here.

First, "capital" is always an accumulation of investments. Investments are the sacrifice in time or money in the short term needed to bring about a stream of future benefits, and as such "capital" is the (properly valued) stock of accumulated investment flows. One major extension of the term *capital* that has gained currency in recent years applies to education (and, by analogy, to health) where the deferral of consumption that comes from going to school instead of working (a sacrifice of time and money in the short run) leads to greater income in the future. In this case, human capital— the accumulated earning capacity—was indeed capital in a real sense. In applying the concept to social relations, this notion of "investment" is never very prominent. Indeed, social capital usually sounds more like a natural (or at least preexisting) resource, and not capital at all.

One major difficulty with regarding "social capital" as capital is that the "capital" may be created inadvertently, as a positive externality of some other activity, rather than with the intent of improving the stock of capital. That is, it may well be that if people gather weekly for religious services, this connection creates or reinforces social relationships among these individuals that can later constitute a stock that is productive in creating a capacity for collective action (e.g., responding to a crisis or cooperating over natural resources). However, even if participation in religious services does create a "capital-like *something*" that increases the likelihood of positive outcomes in some dimension, people do not attend religious services *because* of this impact. That is, people attend law school *principally* to become lawyers, with the intent of increasing their income via the "human capital" law school creates, so this fits the "current sacrifice to create future gain" notion of capital quite well. But if people attend religious services *because* they have metaphysical beliefs, then even if this creates some increased social capacity, it does not fit the "current sacrifice to create future gain" component of the notion of capital.

The second problem with "social capital" as capital is that individual investments need to be aggregated in some way into a "stock" of something that yields a flow of services. The aggregation is the tricky part. The best way to approach the problem of creating a meaningful aggregate called *social capital* is to examine the conditions under which one might believe that a linear weighted aggregate of different types of objects (e.g., cars, pumps, buildings, hoes) that are not measured in the same units and are owned by L different households, firms, or individuals could be meaningfully called "physical capital." A linear aggregate of physical capital in a village of L individuals with N possible objects would have to use some set of weights w:

$$K = \sum_{l=1}^{L} \sum_{n=1}^{N} w_{n,l} * T_{n,l} \tag{1}$$

Could it be the case that there is some aggregate objective function, say profits (Π), such that the impact on profits of an increase in this linear aggregate across items and individuals is exactly the same no matter what caused the increase (whether it was trucks or plows)? In order for this to be true,

$$\partial\Pi\big/\partial K_{n,l} = \left(\partial\Pi\big/\partial K\right) * \left(\partial K\big/\partial K_{n,l}\right) \quad \forall n, l \tag{2}$$

Why would this condition for aggregation ever be true? The first-order conditions for profit maximization for each of the l atomistic producers (that is, competitive in both factor and product markets) with a production function for output Q as a function of N capital inputs with prices $p_{k_i} > p_{k_n}$ are

$$\lambda = \frac{p_q * \partial Q\big/\partial K_{i,l}}{p_{k_i}} = \frac{p_q * \partial Q\big/\partial K_{j,l}}{p_{k_j}} \quad \forall i, j, l \tag{3}$$

That is, the marginal value product (output price times marginal product per dollar of capital input) should be equalized across all inputs. Therefore, if one creates a capital aggregate with prices for each of the capital goods as the weights for each of the l producers, then combining (2) and (3) gives

$$\frac{\partial\Pi\big/\partial K_{n,l}}{\partial K\big/\partial K_{n,l}} = \frac{p_q * \partial Q\big/\partial K_{i,l}}{p_{k_i}} = \lambda = \left(\partial\Pi\big/\partial K\right) \quad \forall n, l$$

The point of this is not to persuade the reader that existing aggregate measures of physical capital are the least bit reliable. Rather, it is to demonstrate that there exist some conditions in which aggregation *theoretically* could be exact, and that theory itself specifies the weights one would use in aggregating. These conditions are only rarely met even for the simplest aggregations of capital goods. But the analogous conditions for *social* capital can *never* be met.

Let us review briefly the conditions for aggregation of physical "capital" and show how none of these conditions are, or can be, met *in principle* for aggregates of social capital, in the sense of aggregating from household characteristics (which could be either attributes—norms, values, beliefs—or actions—participation in social activities, membership in organizations). First, there has to be a single market price for each good (both outputs and capital goods) faced by all producers over which the aggregation is being made. This implies *tradability* of the good, which requires alienability and transferability across households and mobility in space, neither of which is true for household social characteristics. The social relationships created through associational activity are neither fully transferable across households nor mobile across space (households cannot take relationships with them). That is, if one is trying to aggregate tractors and pumps to estimate "farm capital," it must be the case that farmers can exchange tractors and pumps; the tractor and pump are owned by farmers such that the marginal products are equalized across farmers.[12]

Second, all of the households must have the same *objective function in a common metric,* such as profit maximization. With social capital, people's social behaviors are determined by a variety of considerations, of which household profit maximization in terms of money units is just one, and often not the most important. That is, any aggregate of "capital" is defined only with respect to some particular objective function. With physical capital the aggregate is "profits," which itself requires that one can aggregate distinct physical activities into a common metric. To stick with the "farm capital" analogy: If there are two agricultural products, say corn and grapes, and if there are multiple inputs, it will not be the case that the *physical* marginal products of different types of capital inputs will be equalized across the two outputs. This implies that if people are participating in social activities for a variety of different reasons without a common objective in a common metric, then even if all these different activities contribute to improving social capacity, the contribution of each activity to social capacity cannot, even in principle, be equalized across activities in a way necessary to allow aggregation.

Third, the household objective function and private incentives have to capture the aggregate incentives, or else private behavior will not lead to conditions in which aggregation is meaningful. That is, suppose there are network effects in production such that one additional person joining the network raises the productivity of all existing members of the network;

then prices, which are based on private decisions, will not provide the right weights for aggregation.[13] With social capital there is interest in precisely the benefits to governance of social relationships that are created for other reasons (for example, the impact of religious groups in the spread of information for facilitating collective action). But if this is so, there is no reason to believe that memberships in religious organizations will have the same impact on cooperation and socialization as memberships in political organizations. Moreover, with social dynamics and network effects, the social impact of one household affiliating with an additional group depends on who already belongs to that group. If the household joins a group whose members already have numerous other contacts, the increment to "social connectedness" might be very small. However, if the household is embedded with one social group but joins a group that connects it with another, more densely connected social group, then the addition to social connectedness could be enormous. However, this social benefit may have little or nothing to do with the household's objective in joining either group.

In this sense any aggregate called "social capital" is prematurely reductionist—in the bad sense—in that it presupposes all types of conditions necessary for aggregation, and hence it would be premature to assume homogeneity in impacts both across types of social relations and outcomes. This isn't to say that there do not exist the social phenomena equivalent of tractors, plows, and pumps with respect to some objectives. It is almost certain that the social phenomena thought of as the components of "social capital"—for instance, "trust" or "shared norms"—do, in fact, affect social outcomes. But just as one could believe in the existence of tractors, and that tractors raise the output of corn, without believing that a construct called "farm capital" at any level of aggregation (farm, village, country) was analytically useful or empirically possible, so too one could believe that one type of specific social phenomenon (e.g., sharing an ethnic identity or participating in religious activities) can have real social consequences (e.g., increasing information flows, making cooperative behavior more likely) across a range of dimensions without believing that "social capital" is meaningful.

At this juncture it is better to stick to the measurement of specifics and reporting of empirical results about specifics rather than attempt to generalize about "social capital" and what creates it and what its productivity is. That is, one can ask the empirical question of whether information is transmitted more rapidly in social situations where individuals share an ethnic identity, or whether women who share a religion are more likely to repay group credit, or whether villages with less income inequality are more likely to cooperate in solid waste disposal, without ever using the words *social capital*.

Resisting the Expansion of "Social" Domains

The second element of economists' rocky relationship with "social capital" was the debate between "modernists," "anti-modernists," and "neo-modernists." Personally, we are big proponents of functional and effective *formal* institutions as a key component of development. That is, while informal mechanisms are a key reality of development and in particular fulfill a large range of functions when formal-sector institutions are weak, we are at heart "neo-modernists" and believe that *in the long run* arm's-length transactions through both markets and governments will be responsible for a larger and larger range and volume of transactions as the costs of formal intermediation become lower, and that, by and large, this is a good thing. That said, we are not "modernists" in the sense of having an uncritical assumption of "development" as a linear evolution of formal institutions into common isomorphic structures. But neither are we "anti-modernists" who subscribe to a "small is beautiful" approach to development, nor do we believe that one can entirely dismiss the evolution from informal, personal modes of cooperation and decision making to more rules-based organizations and institutions.

Three examples of the difference between a short- or medium-run emphasis on social capital and the long-run reliance on formal institutions will suffice. First, in no developed country are "micro-credit"–type transactions a major component of financial-sector transactions. This is at least in part because as mechanisms for the extension of loans through formal-sector institutions become lower in cost, one could reasonably expect formal mechanisms to replace informal ones. Crudely put, it is not unreasonable to expect that for financing consumer durables and short-run consumption smoothing, more and more people will rely on credit cards and fewer and fewer on socially based repayment mechanisms.

Second, while families are far and away the most important component of support for the elderly in developing countries, in every developed country formal old-age pension and "social security" programs have expanded as the costs of intermediation have declined, thereby reducing the role of "social capital" in old-age support.

Third, many current anti-poverty programs in developing countries are promoting the formation of groups for undertaking commercial, for-profit activities. While this is quite plausibly a "social capital"–intensive solution (given the weakness of market mechanisms and of the poor in interacting with existing formal market organizations), there is little reason to believe that various forms of "social" organization of economic activity will replace existing legal forms of ownership (e.g., proprietors, partnerships, corporations). Where "informal" mechanisms do exist in richer countries—for example, in immigrant communities that have a hard time gaining a toehold in established markets due to a lack of a credit history or collateral—even these whither away with time.

This contrast between rich and poor countries with developed and undeveloped capital markets, respectively, was brought home to us recently when we visited self-help groups in West Bengal, India, with a team composed of people from several countries. A member of a group asked, "What kind of women's self-help groups are there in your countries, and how are they supported by government?" The correct answer (to a first approximation), of course, was "There are no such things" and (again to a first-order approximation) "There is no role for such things."

Moreover, as the modern state involves the exercise of compulsion, we are neo-modernists in the sense that the exercise of compulsion should be "arm's length" in a very deep sense. That is, while "social" modes of enforcement are important in a variety of informal activities (e.g., social pressure on loan repayment in group-based lending), we think that the evolution of formal controls over the state—the sole legitimate agent for wielding police and judicial powers—is important and cannot and should not be handled "socially."

Economists are also made nervous by an "anti-modern" take in that "social capital" is an important phenomenon that can lead to better outcomes *in those domains* in which some form of "social" intervention is necessary. This in itself does not create a presumption for the expansion of "social"-intensive decision making over any other type. Take the case of schooling. There have been many instances in which "communities" were empowered to form their own schools, with financial support from government (e.g., the EDUCO program in El Salvador). Quality-wise, it has been demonstrated that these forms of community ownership and school management can compete successfully with formal government schools. However, this does not create any presumption that "community" forms of school ownership should be preferred over other types of ownership and management of schools (e.g., not-for-profit or for-profit schools) and other mechanisms of ensuring parental empowerment with regard to school quality. The fact that greater parental involvement in the management of schools can lead to improved performance compared with the existing government schools entails no presumption that the policy framework should privilege "socially intensive" modes of school management over a variety of other alternatives—at least not without substantial proof or reason that entails an analytic beyond social capital.

Third, there is no question that collective action has positive and negative consequences, and the net effect depends to a large extent on the scope of action of the group. Mancur Olson's (1965) work on collective action suggested that stable societies in which greater degrees of cooperation could emerge would have increasingly worsening economic performance. Why? The answer goes back to the father of economics, Adam Smith, and his views on at least one dimension of social capital, namely the sociability of people with common economic interests: "Rarely do people of the same occupation gather together, even if only

for merriment, that it does not end in some plot to defraud the public."
While "social" relations may be the solution to a problem in the "small"
sense—that is, bilaterally or for relations just between the members of the
group—whether or not they are solutions to the larger issue of benefiting
society as a whole is an open question. The formation of cartels referred to
by Smith is the standard conflict between these aims, and the whole of
antitrust regulation is the protection of society at large from these particular social relations. Moreover, if the decision is to allocate a single, indivisible good, then the increased "social capital" of groups binding together
can have no positive effect. Breaking up an indivisible item cannot do
anyone any good. Hence, to a large extent, whether one adopts the positive versus negative views of social capital (say Olson versus Putnam)
depends on whether one views the social capital as devoted to the resolution of an existing market failure (Putnam and the role of social capital in
governance) or to the creation of market failures for others (Olson). This
caution against overexpansion of the domain of the "social" extends to
making "social" decisions out of a range of economic activities.

In short, the existence of "social capital" as a capacity for collective
action does not imply that all, or even many, decisions *should be* made
socially (i.e., by conscious cooperation). Those that should, should, and
those that should not, should not. The theory of "social capital" as a positive theory of capacity for collective action does not itself entail a normative view about what collective actions are desirable; this question needs
to be decided on other grounds.

Summary and Empirical Stage

These problems of appropriately defining social capital came to the fore in
empirical research in Indonesia by one of the authors (Pritchett) along
with economist Vivi Alatas and sociologist Anna Wetterberg (2003). This
research examined the empirical connections between individuals' perceptions of local governance in a variety of dimensions and their participation in an array of "social" activities. However, because of the social
context of Indonesia, in which the apparatus of local government at the
village level was dominated by authoritarian government (Evers 1999), we
distinguished between individuals' activities that were organized for the
purpose of affecting local government decisions and activities that represented more "spontaneous" social cooperation. We also distinguished the
"private" effects: Did person A's participation in social activities (government or other) affect person A's perception of local governance and
"social" effects? Did person A's participation in social activities affect persons B, C, D, and others who live in the same village as A (conditional on
their own participation)? The results were striking.

First, the "private" and "social" impacts of an individual's participation in local government organizations are strikingly different. While the

results differ across the different measures of local governance, by and large participation in local government organizations appears to have positive private effects but social "crowd-out" effects. For instance, individuals who participated in local government meetings reported that they had a greater "effective voice" in local decision making—a result that is not particularly surprising. But the "effective voice" of others living in the same village was *lower* when other people's participation in local government organizations was higher. This balance of negative and positive effects led to overall effects across a variety of indicators that were (with one exception) either small or negative.

In contrast, participation in other local organizations (e.g., religious activities, women's groups) often had "crowd-in" effects. For instance, the propensity of a household to participate in a protest over something that is wrong in the village increases with a person's participation in social activities. Interestingly, the propensity of other people to participate in protest activities also increases. In this case the *total* village effect is larger than the sum of the private effects, as the social engagement of one individual "crowds in" a variety of indicators of the quality of local governance.

These empirical results emphasize three points about the premature aggregation and extension of the notion of "social capital." First, not surprisingly, it matters what activities people participate in. Second, it matters which outcomes are examined. Third, the private and social effects of social engagement must be distinguished. A relationship between a village-level aggregate of social engagement across an array of associational activities and some village-level indicator would miss all of this detail.

Public Economics and Social Relations

We have outlined the reasons why relationships between people, other than through market transactions or through anonymous government actions, should appeal to economists and also why the concept of "social capital" does not quite capture what we would like it to. What *do* we see as the scope of study of social groups in economic terms and the contribution that such an analysis can make to development policy? Can we incorporate face-to-face social relationships in economic analysis and show how this can help in designing policy? Yes, but in line with our bias that these relationships are not always necessary to a well-functioning economy, we would also like to show how they are limited to particular functions or are an explicitly temporary solution until more formal relationships develop.

One way of approaching this is considerably easier and more in line with simple, standard economics than another go at game theory. Such relationships can be embedded into the standard framework of policy analysis provided by applied welfare economics, the branch of the discipline also known as "public economics." This results in a very specific set of steps for policy analysis.

The first step in any economic policy analysis is usually to identify one or more of a small set of specific "market failures" that characterize the sector or set of markets of interest. It is not necessary to review these concepts here, but their essence is that anonymous, arm's-length market relationships cannot be relied upon to solve every material problem of society—that there are, in particular, certain collective problems they cannot address adequately.[14] This can be for reasons of "efficiency," or the way that goods are made or the types of goods that are made could be improved (i.e., someone could be made better off without making anyone else worse off). It can also be for reasons of "equity"; even if the market is efficient as previously defined, it may not be fair relative to widely held beliefs about distributive justice. A person who is made worse off by policy might be very much richer than one who benefits (say, by a forced transfer from the first to the second via taxes), and we as a society might judge this to be a good result. Either of these "failures" provides an a priori reason for government intervention.

The second step is to identify the appropriate *instrument* for a third party to a transaction—almost always assumed to be a government—to use to restore the "efficiency" compromised by the market failure or to achieve a better distribution of goods or income. There is a crucial unstated assumption to this analysis—namely that there exists a government that wants to solve these problems and that has the ability to do so. Government activity is another type of "arm's-length" relationship, where a formal, anonymous set of rules guides the solution to the purely technical problem of fixing markets. Another way of saying this is that government is assumed to want to maximize social welfare and has the ability to overcome the market failures that prevent this from happening spontaneously.

Criticisms of this assumption have generated several strands of literature and research, such as "social choice theory," which sees governments as made up of people having motives other than the maximization of social welfare, such as maximizing their own welfare or their chances of reelection. But independent of any particular characterization, anyone associated with public policy can see that there are "government failures" or, at least, government actions that, by omission or commission, do not conform to this unstated assumption. We will return to ways in which the assumption can fail, but we start with the consequences first.

If, for any reason, the government is not in a position to perform the functions that public finance theory assumes that it does, people are stuck. They are left with the original, collective problem that neither markets nor governments can solve. When formal institutional arrangements fail, people have to solve their collective action problems themselves.

The realization that collective goods may sometimes need to be handled by a self-conscious group of people (those who know they are in a group and need to act cooperatively[15]) leads to a variety of questions, both positive and normative—indeed, enough to call for an entire research agenda. When will such groups provide solutions that are "better" than those of either markets or governments? What characteristics of the problems, the groups, or specific obstacles might be expected to lead to an advantage of social agreements over states and markets?

More important, perhaps, are the normative issues that would guide policy. Is there anything an outsider (a government or an organization from civil society) can do to help the groups reach such solutions? We have ruled out by assumption the government's imposing the solutions directly, but are there better or worse ways of delegating to communities decision-making authority and of facilitating their attempts to find their own solutions?

On positive issues, one major category of circumstances in which groups are likely to have a distinct advantage over markets or governments involves information. Economic theory since the early 1980s has made great strides in illuminating the problems inherent in imperfect information and their effect on economic efficiency. Not all imperfect information constitutes a problem, but there are certain circumstances when detailed knowledge of the characteristics of the parties is necessary for an efficient transaction. Most of the problems arise under conditions of asymmetric information, and there are certain markets—insurance and credit in particular—that are very sensitive to this kind of failure. Further, government programs to replace insurance and credit markets are often subject to the same constraints as the markets that they would ordinarily be expected to fix.

For example, some kinds of risks are very difficult to insure against because the ease of registering false claims makes the supply of insurance services untenable. An example is insurance against disabilities that are not easily observable. There are standard insurance policies against the loss of a limb (which is easily verified) but for the loss of cognitive ability following a head injury, considerably more proof, often involving litigation, is needed. Public programs have precisely the same difficulty identifying eligible recipients of disability insurance. The rates of disability range widely in countries in the developed world and are closely related to the amount of benefits received.

The common difficulty that these programs have is making fine distinctions between the circumstances of individuals that only people who are closely associated with them can make. In these cases, communities may be able to take care of their most vulnerable members—for example, widows with no surviving children (family, of course, being the main non-market social relation that generally accepts responsibility for people in need). Neither the market (through life insurance) nor government programs administered by any but the most competent and compassionate bureaucracies could identify isolated people and their essential needs in a way that avoids fraudulent claims.

Credit markets can also malfunction due to asymmetric information. Without government, adverse selection and moral hazard on the part of borrowers, in combination with the response of potential lenders, can lead to under-provision and misallocation in the credit market in the absence of competent and technically demanding regulatory instruments. With government, bankruptcy laws and deposit insurance can induce excessive risk taking unless they too are designed and implemented with the same kind of sophisticated regulation. In the absence of high-quality markets and regulators, what communities can offer is a much finer appraisal of borrowers' creditworthiness[16] due to a much more detailed knowledge of their character.

They can also provide another service, namely "peer monitoring" of the use of borrowed funds. Neighbors can see what kinds of productive investments are being made by a borrower and can judge if a good-faith effort is being made to bring these investments to fruition. Less benignly, they can apply extra-market pressure on borrowers to encourage such an effort. These are some of the reasons for the general success (in repayment terms at least) of micro-credit schemes. This success is greatly enhanced by the social relations among the borrowing groups, apparently among women in particular.

Credit and insurance are areas where social relations can substitute for essential failures by markets and governments. There is a range of other circumstances where, under the assumption that the government rather than the market will take on particular responsibilities (for some reason—market failure, fairness, or by common consensus in the polity), communities may be enlisted to help in the formulation and implementation of government initiatives. The *World Development Report 2004* (World Bank 2003) applies this idea to the delivery of services, emphasizing the role of "accountability" as the essential ingredient for good performance.

This report, titled "Making Services Work for Poor People," identifies two distinct, crucial roles for social relations where accountability may be compromised. One is ensuring that policy decisions reflect the interests of poor people (politics or "voice"). The second, based on the assumption that policymakers do indeed have the interests of poor people in mind, is improving their ability to translate this intention to benefit the poor into good service. Can they make the direct providers of, say, health, education, water, sanitation, and other infrastructure services accountable either to policymakers or, more fundamentally if indirectly, to the people themselves?

On the second issue—assuming a benevolent government—communities can perform several tasks that are unavailable to government. First, some services are discretionary (meaning that the direct provider of the service must make complex decisions that cannot be specified in full detail beforehand—what a doctor does in the privacy of the clinic, how a teacher deals with a particularly tricky concept or difficult student) and transaction intensive (these things happen all the time, every day, and cannot be constantly monitored by supervisors) (see Pritchett and Woolcock 2004). In these cases, the client—either an individual or a group of users of specific services—is in a much better position to monitor quality than is possible with regular supervision through ordinary hierarchies. Attendance of the provider at clinics and schools is a good example. Again, the issue is information; people who are most interested in the service can help the state "see" better (Scott 1998).

There are two mechanisms that parents in schools or patients in clinics can use to enforce the accountability of providers. One does not rely on social interactions, and one certainly does. The first uses client choice and the competition among providers that this choice elicits to discipline providers and keep them accountable. This could include the use of vouchers for school, primary health care, or safe water or their equivalent through payments to providers that depend on the number of customers. In the British National Health Service general practitioners are paid through a "capitation" system and are compensated according to the number of people who choose to sign up with them; the mechanism does not have to rely on explicit payment. These techniques simply mimic a market, and there is nothing "social" about them.

Where competition is not possible, however, collective action on the part of users of the services may be needed. There is unlikely to be more than one primary school in a small village, for example, and no real competition in the market will emerge. User groups such as parents' associations, educational committees dominated by parents, or other such school management committees that have the right to hire and fire teachers provide a direct form of accountability. Even if there is no scope for competition *in* the market, there can be competition *for* the market. That is, while there will only be one school operating at a time, the contract for the school can be decided on a regular (annual or otherwise) basis by the school committee. These self-conscious groups can be a great help in allowing the state to "see" more effectively, helping it to carry out its responsibilities by delegating authority to communities—that is, people who interact face to face.

Finally, in those policies where identifying beneficiaries of anti-poverty programs leads to better targeting of available funds and less leakage to groups not considered eligible, the precision of information regarding who is "deserving" and who is not is likely to be greater among members of communities compared with any formal administrative mechanism. Other mechanisms for targeting may be better than either, and there may be good reason to prefer universal services to targeted ones, but if policy calls for separating people on the basis of detailed characteristics, communities will probably have the advantage over bureaucracies.

While social relations can be used instrumentally by governments to get better results, they can also be a useful check on governments themselves. The other accountability relationship highlighted in the 2004 report is the "voice" relation, which refers to the ability of people (particularly poor people) to have their interests reflected in public policy; this involves allocations across different services, not just the more effective implementation of whatever services are chosen. Poor people's individual voices are weak, and banding together can certainly give these people's voices more weight, particularly in democracies.

The public policy implications of a government's attempts to improve the first type of accountability, from providers to the intentions of policy-makers, include delegating responsibility for running a particular program—what in the World Bank would be considered a single-purpose Community Driven Development project. This leads to greater technical efficiency from a pre-determined program. The policy implications of the second type of accountability are to encourage broader decision-making authority among community groups, with the choice of project left open. These correspond to Social Investment Fund projects, where communities take on the role of government by allocating investments across sectors. Whether this is encouraged by government (leading to the odd paradox of government mobilizing people to influence itself) or by NGOs outside of, but helping, the community (which is less paradoxical), the "voice" of the poor can be made louder. Both types of accountability are strengthened by these means.[17]

Social Failures?

So far, we have carved out a role for "social" relations, that is, face-to-face transactions and agreements, rather than "arm's-length" relations of markets and states, in the context of standard public economics. We have a clear nomenclature for "market failures" that require some kind of collective action. We have several general concepts of "government failures" that explain why some of these collective actions are not handled well by the state. Might there be an analogous set of "social failures" that circumscribe the role that self-conscious social groups can or should play? Yes, there appear to be several. A positive analysis has to deal with two basic facts. First, there are some pretty obvious social pathologies that characterize all societies but perhaps interfere with economic progress more in poorer countries than in rich ones. Second, there is a clear tendency for these social solutions to whither away as societies get richer and find more efficient ways of handling their collective problems.

We are currently working on South Asia, where the existence of social pathologies is hard to avoid. Exclusion of particular groups on religious, caste-based, or gender grounds is a harsh fact of life in the subcontinent.

In fact, the combination of discrimination among the majority of people (personal animosity) and the power of the state can be deadly. Illustrations are communal conflict in Gujarat (and elsewhere) in India and the treatment of African-Americans in the Southern United States until the federal government stepped in.[18]

Further, while some societies have found beneficent means of dealing with people with special needs, some have exacerbated what would otherwise be a minor disability through the imposition of additional burdensome taboos. The tension between respecting traditional values and ensuring that women have full property rights is also palpable.

More subtly, the institution of sharecropping is an example of social (not friendly, necessarily, but social nonetheless in the sense of non-anonymous) relations substituting for market relations less benignly. For a long time economists considered sharecropping obviously inefficient[19] (in addition to being socially ugly). Economists do not like to see the persistence of something that is obviously inefficient, and the analysis of sharecropping spawned a small industry of papers explaining why it wasn't efficient after all. The main features of the solutions proposed include the value of "interlinked" transactions between landlord and tenant, in which their personal interaction substituted for problems in related markets such as credit or insurance (and the observability of labor inputs). This is a "social" solution to an economic problem, but not such a great one. Indeed, one argument is that the main value of land reform in Kerala (a state of India) was the replacement of these "social" relationships with a much more benign market.

Finally, the truth of the matter is that, in the long run, many of the roles we have been discussing for social groups wither away as technology (in both the narrow sense of electronic equipment and in terms of innovations in organizational structure and management technique) develops. One of the key factors that both require social interactions and make them difficult is the size of the transactions costs of having to deal with large numbers of people to achieve consensus or, at least, some measure of agreement. Poor people have lots of things they can do with their time besides attending meetings on every collective action issue they face, and they would just as soon delegate this responsibility to (i.e., free-ride on) someone or something else, such as a legitimate government. Some of these collective problems are national in scope, but many are local, and the government we expect to take on the load is at the local level.

An example of social relations giving way to markets is the transition of water user associations to commercial water companies. When the cost of metering (necessary for efficient pricing) is large relative to the value of the water metered, communal cooperative agreements on water sharing will improve efficiency. As either the cost of metering (the transactions cost of the market mechanism) falls or the value of crops rises (resulting, by the way, in richer farmers), markets evolve that cost the farmers money but save them time in meetings.

Social relations giving way to government (particularly local government) services is more common. Sanitation (removing solid waste and excreta) and other activities with large externalities may be handled by community consensus. Eventually, though, they are usually handled by local government. Regular maintenance of water systems may benefit from voluntary user groups, but when major (expensive) repairs become necessary, the larger resources of (non-voluntary, tax-based) governments are a better option.

Romanticizing social relations has other risks for long-term improvements in the quality of life. It is not just that formal relationships are more efficient than social ones. If that were the case, we might just expect them to be replaced spontaneously and, in the case of markets, that is probably what happens.[20] But there is a real risk that the development of local governments can actually be undermined by the creation of separate, parallel bodies.

Conclusion

Our view is that the brief infatuation of some economists at the World Bank with "social capital" is over. But the relationship with social phenomena captured in the notion of social capital is not over; rather, it has just moved to a new level, where the complexities of incorporating social phenomena into what were formerly exclusively "economic" analyses is just beginning a long and potentially very fruitful marriage.

For instance, the *World Development Report 2004* is suffused with the notion of social capital, but the words *social capital* are almost nowhere to be seen. That is, the report emphasized the key role of accountabilities of service providers to clients/citizens in the effective delivery of services, and thus the key roles of empowerment, voice (both of the poor and of citizens vis-à-vis the state more generally), capacity for collective action, and local/community control over services and service providers. To a large extent the report was devoted to undoing the "seeing like a state" problems identified by Scott (1998), where individuals were perceived as passive recipients of government-delivered services, and as re-engaging with the complex social realities involved in the delivery of "discretionary and transaction-intensive" services.

Though "social capital" has been enormously productive conceptually and has had a tremendous influence on the way economists approach many issues, perhaps folding up the big umbrella called "social capital," which is blocking the view of the starry sky, would allow for a clearer view of the diverse array of important social phenomena that determine outcomes in many contexts that call for collective action.

Notes

1. Perhaps more; as Winston Churchill famously complained, "If I ask two economists a question I get two answers, unless one of them is Lord Keynes, in which case I get three." It is also our sense that there was relatively little collaboration during the period 1993–2004 among those World Bank economists working on social capital. These economists collaborated in different ways with people doing work within the Social Development division or with social capital researchers outside the Bank far more than they did with each other. This helps explain the different lines of analysis and approaches to social capital in the work of these economists (e.g., in addition to our work see Knack and Keefer 1997; Grootaert 1999; Collier 2002; Knack 2002; and Schiff 2004).

2. The notion of a "research program" draws on the Kuhnian notion of "normal science" within an existing disciplinarian paradigm; that is, a "research program" is the collection of activities geared to making progress in expanding the frontiers of knowledge *within the conceptual frame of a particular approach* and *with a particular method.*

3. Rao (2005) has provided a similar tracing of the links with a more positive emphasis on cooperative game theory.

4. By "modern" economics we mean the intellectual tradition from Adam Smith to the "marginalists" (particularly Marshall), to the "general equilibrium" proofs of Debreu and Arrow and Hahn, to today. The claims about the properties of models have been made mathematical and precise. The question of how well these claims about models map to claims about anything external to those models is open.

5. Economists' models of general equilibrium were an early example of what are now referred to as "emergent" properties of complex systems in which the interactions of a large number of constituent parts produce a collective outcome that is not a property of any of those parts. Perhaps the best examples are human consciousness (produced by the interactions of billions of individual cells, no one of which possesses consciousness) and collective insects (in which simple algorithms involving individual insects produce complex collective behaviors of the "hive").

6. There was a flourishing of attempts to reduce the number of equilibria by introducing criteria that could eliminate some of them, but this was not a very attractive research program because (1) the criteria used were implausible as behavioral criteria, and/or (2) the range of equilibria was still very large.

7. Note that a strategy is not just a specification of an action in each period, but a specification of the action in each of N periods, contingent on the action of the other agent in each of the previous periods.

8. What is particularly striking about this is that, not only is the winning strategy *not* "always confess" (which is the unique Nash equilibrium), but it is not even the sophisticated strategy of cooperating for a while and then confessing (to get the benefits of cooperation for a while and then "cheat" on cooperation to get the big payoff) and that the "punishment" strategy is so forgiving

(one period of cooperation, i.e., not confessing, by the partner restores cooperation) and so simple.

9. It is impossible to capture the richness of the analysis of the evolution of populations, and hence we make no attempt here to convey the many findings.

10. As an aside, one thing that attracted Pritchett's interest as a *research* economist was that the data on the degree of project participation was generated by independent coding of the subjective assessment of the degree of participation by two researchers. Methodologically, this allowed the deployment of econometric techniques that could deal with the problem of "halo effects" and assess the intersubjective reliability and cardinality of the measures of subjective phenomena.

11. Again, what attracted Pritchett, as a *research* economist, to this particular data was that the survey on "social capital" variables was carried out in the same villages, but different households, as a survey taken a year earlier that measured household incomes. *Methodologically,* this was an enormous boon, as the first reaction of any economist when told of a statistical association between income and measures of social capital is that this is a *personal* effect; people with higher incomes are more likely to participate in associational life, trust each other, and so on. Therefore, to be able to show that the measured "social capital" of one group of households was associated with the incomes of a completely different set of individuals in the same village was an important methodological advantage.

12. This problem of nontradability is a problem for aggregates of human capital as well. While one farmer can sell another farmer a pump if conditions or relative prices or land ownership changes to keep marginal products equalized, people cannot sell their human capital, so the conditions for aggregation from physical units to value units will be violated.

13. Another example is a set of capital goods that have different pollution properties. If these costs are external to the household, then an aggregate of capital for predicting aggregate profits will not necessarily be a good one for predicting pollution.

14. "Collective problems" in this case refers to problems or choices that must be made by more than one person at a time. The production and sale of a car, for example, involves thousands of different people, but in market transactions they don't really have to know each other.

15. This is in contrast to markets and government institutions that have the means of coordinating the actions of a group but are not "self-conscious," perhaps because the members of the group do not know the other people involved or because, in any case, this knowledge is irrelevant.

16. *Credit* being derived from the Latin *credere,* "to believe" or "to trust," as in "credible."

17. An example of increased "voice" from such projects is the experience in northeast Brazil, where, once a village had decided to build a school as part of the Sao Joao project, several representatives from the community went to Brasilia, camped out in front of the Ministry of Education office, and demanded that a teacher be posted to it. This belies the common stereotype of the fatalistic northeastern peasant.

18. Indeed, the relations between different levels of government in countering such problems is a broad topic in and of itself, which we leave for future work.
19. Since sharecropping means that producers get only a fraction of their output, they should tend to supply less-than-efficient levels of effort and output.
20. However, some commentators have expressed concern that micro-credit programs might interfere with the development of real, scalable credit markets.

References

Alatas, Vivi, Lant Pritchett, and Anna Wetterberg. 2003. *Voice lessons: Local government organizations, social organizations, and the quality of local governance.* Policy Research Working Paper No. 2981. Washington, DC: World Bank.

Axelrod, Robert. 1984. *The evolution of cooperation.* New York: Basic Books.

Collier, Paul. 2002. Social capital and poverty: A microeconomic perspective. In *The role of social capital in development: An empirical assessment,* edited by Christiaan Grootaert and Thierry Van Bastelaer. New York: Cambridge University Press, pp. 19–41.

Evers, Pieter. 1999. *Village governments and their communities.* Local Level Institutions Study, working paper. Jakarta: World Bank and BAPPENAS.

Fudenberg, Drew, and Eric Maskin. 1986. The Folk Theorem in repeated games with discounting or incomplete information. *Econometrica* 54(3):533–554.

Grootaert, Christiaan. 1999. *Social capital, household welfare and poverty in Indonesia.* Local Level Institutions Working Paper No. 6. Washington, DC: World Bank.

Hardin, Garrett. 1968. The tragedy of the commons. *Science* 162:1243–1248.

Isham, Jonathan, Deepa Narayan, and Lant Pritchett. 1995. Does participation improve performance? Establishing causality with subjective data. *World Bank Economic Review* 9(2):75–200.

Knack, Stephen. 2002. Social capital, growth, and poverty: A survey. In *The role of social capital in development: An empirical assessment,* edited by Christiaan Grootaert and Thierry Van Bastelaer. New York: Cambridge University Press, pp. 42–82.

Knack, Stephen, and Philip Keefer. 1997. Does social capital have an economic payoff? A cross-country investigation. *Quarterly Journal of Economics* 112(4):1251–1288.

Little, I.M.D., and James Mirrlees. 1974. *Project appraisal and planning in developing countries.* London. Heinemann Educational Books.

Narayan, Deepa, and Lant Pritchett. 1999. Cents and sociability: Household income and social capital in rural Tanzania. *Economic Development and Cultural Change* 47(4):871–897.

Olson, Mancur. 1965. *The logic of collective action: Public goods and the theory of groups.* Cambridge, MA: Harvard University Press.

Ostrom, Elinor. 1990. *Governing the commons: The evolution of institutions for collective action.* New York: Cambridge University Press.

Pritchett, Lant, and Michael Woolcock. 2004. Solutions when *the* solution is the problem: Arraying the disarray in development. *World Development* 32(2):191–212.

Putnam, Robert. 1993. *Making democracy work: Civic traditions in modern Italy.* Princeton, NJ: Princeton University Press.

Rao, Vijayendra. 2005. *Symbolic public goods and the coordination of collective action: A comparison of local development in India and Indonesia.* Policy Research Working Paper No. 3685. Washington, DC: World Bank.

Schiff, Maurice. 2004. Labor mobility, trade and social capital. *Review of International Economics* 12(4):630–643.

Scott, James. 1998. *Seeing like a state: How certain schemes to improve the human condition have failed.* New Haven, CT: Yale University Press.

Sen, Amartya, Partha Dasgupta, and Stephen Marglin. 1972. *Guidelines for project evaluation.* New York: UNIDO.

Von Neumann, John, and Oscar Morgenstern. 1953. *Theory of games and economic behavior.* Princeton, NJ: Princeton University Press.

World Bank. 2003. *World Development Report 2004: Making services work for poor people.* New York: Oxford University Press.

CHAPTER FOUR

ENTHUSIASTS, TACTICIANS, AND SKEPTICS
Social Capital and the Structures of Power[1]

Michael Edwards

On a good day in my old job at the World Bank, I would be asked to define civil society by any number of skeptical colleagues—a notoriously slippery task in the best of times, though at least it showed they were interested. On a bad day, they would ask me an even trickier question—what is social capital?—but worst of all was the inevitable sequel: what's the difference between social capital and civil society? Before I had reached the end of the first paragraph of my long-winded explanation, the questioner would have disappeared around the corner and gone back to the "real work" of lending billions of dollars to recalcitrant governments. Like pinning the tail on the proverbial donkey, defining these terms is difficult to do (or at least to agree on), and while the definitions themselves may be somewhat academic, the debates that surround them are anything but. In the World Bank, as in all bureaucracies, this year's theory will be next year's policy, and policy has a real impact on ordinary peoples' lives—for good or for ill. The appearance of social capital as an important theme in the 2000–2001 World Development Report on poverty (World Bank 2001) is a good case in point. Since this is an increasingly important entry in the international development lexicon, how can we relate theory to practice in the social capital debate in more rigorous and responsible ways?

Generally speaking, people want to live in a world of peace, prosperity, and social justice, though they may differ on how best to reach these lofty goals. Intuitively, we know that improvements in the human condition require us to tackle three types of problems in an integrated way: inadequacies in the polity, inequalities in society, and inefficiencies in the economy. Solutions in each of these areas both facilitate and depend on progress in each of the others, but conventional social science—and the politics that social science informs—have dealt with these problems in relative isolation. Not surprisingly, such an approach rarely achieves the desired results, because the most important problems have interrelated causes and effects: Poverty and social exclusion, for example, have their roots in gender and race, culture and values, inequalities in political voice, and the shape of economic institutions, as well as in the distribution of productive assets and opportunities. If there *is* a secret to success, it is most likely to reside in the relationships between interventions in these different areas of life. Social capital, as well as civil society (in some definitions), are important concepts here, because, although they are the latest examples of our tendency to look for easy answers, they also offer the promise of an integrated theory and praxis of social, economic, and political change. As I want to show in this chapter, serious obstacles stand in the way of fulfilling this potential, but if we can overcome these difficulties, we should be able to both advance our understanding of the forces that oppress so many people across the world and increase our ability to foster lasting improvements in their lives. In this sense, the stakes are very high.

The Rise and Rise of Social Capital

Although the concepts of social capital and civil society have a rich intellectual history, it is only since the mid-1990s that they have come to prominence in the decision maker's world. There are a number of reasons for this, but the most important is the recognition that states and markets are but two components of an essential trilogy of principles: Society matters, social institutions count, and citizens make a crucial difference to the health of the polity and to economic success. Post–Cold War, civil society (the realm of citizen action) and social capital (a convenient shorthand for the norms and institutions that make societies work) have been accepted as key components of the development equation—even as "magic bullets" that will correct successive generations of state and market failure.

Beyond this level of generalization, however, there is much disagreement on the meaning and application of these terms. Before going any further, therefore, it is important to define how they are used in the argument that follows. Social capital and civil society each have an analytic and a normative dimension (Woolcock 1998; Krishna and Uphoff 1999; Woolcock and Narayan Chapter 2, this volume). Analytic or structural definitions stress the importance of *forms*—social organizations, contacts, and networks—or, in the case of civil society, the "third sector"—more broadly, the arena in which citizens come together to advance their common interests. Cognitive definitions stress the importance of *norms*: social values and attributes such as trust, cooperation, and reciprocity that are assumed to bring about a certain kind of society defined as "civil." As one moves from the analytic to the normative, the more complex the argument and, for some at least, the less convincing the rubric of "capital" or "sectors" of society becomes.

The most interesting question is not whether one of these definitions is "correct," but how forms and norms, the structural and the cognitive, are related to each other in different contexts—including the vexing question of whether civil society produces social capital and vice versa. If we can find the tools to help us understand and operationalize these connections, we should be able to identify more effective policy levers in the fight against poverty. It is this task—connecting forms, norms, contexts, and objectives—that represents the central challenge for social capitalists in the years to come.

Enthusiasts, Tacticians, and Skeptics

The rise of social capital within the World Bank is part of a wider set of changes driven by political and intellectual agendas. At the political level, James Wolfensohn has an intuitive grasp that the Bank's mission is about more than economics, and he has enthusiastically pursued a series of initiatives to incorporate politics, institutional development, and local ownership of the development agenda into the mainstream of Bank operations—notably through the Comprehensive Development Framework (CDF) and the joint World Bank–IMF Poverty Reduction Strategy Papers (PRSP). Before his departure, Joseph Stiglitz (the Bank's former Chief Economist) laid much of the intellectual groundwork for the Wolfensohn revolution, building on his own pioneering work on the economics of information and the role of institutions in development. The theoretical and political advances achieved by this duo have moved the Bank significantly beyond the paradigm of the "Washington Consensus." However, while these concepts may be increasingly popular, they are not subject to increasing consensus, even within a supposedly monolithic institution like the Bank. Indeed, at the deepest level the debate over social capital is less an argument about definitions than a struggle between competing paradigms of development, and a campaign by different groups to legitimize or de-legitimize particular bodies of knowledge and methods in the social sciences.

To tease out these differences, this chapter outlines three distinct but overlapping schools of thought: enthusiasts, tacticians, and skeptics. Although these distinctions are somewhat artificial, there are real and important differences of opinion in the social capital debate that revolve around two sets of questions: first, whether social capital and civil society are dependent or independent variables—that is, "things" that can be factored into models or "by-products" of politics, economic history, culture, and state-building—and second, how these concepts engage with broader structural questions about power and inequality—something that will largely determine their usefulness as weapons in the fight against poverty. Does social capital help those who are disenfranchised to "speak truth to power" by improving their access to formal institutions? This is a useful litmus test of its practical and theoretical value.[2]

The *enthusiasts* are composed of economists and other social scientists in the World Bank's Poverty and Social Development networks, and a range of academics linked to them through the social capital research network (Dasgupta and Serageldin 2000). For them, social capital is the missing ingredient that, by integrating "non-market rationality" into economic models, explains why some countries or communities grow faster than others. At the extreme (where social capital and economic theory combine through regression analysis and statistical modeling), acts of kindness are reduced to "information pooling," and people associate only when collective action is seen to generate a mutual advantage. This is not a very attractive vision of the social world, but it is certainly an improvement on the complete lacuna that existed before. The use of *capital* here is no accident, since economists respond enthusiastically to this particular word even if they ignore other expressions of what is "social" about the phenomena they study.

In the Bank's case this is certainly true, with a plethora of research studies on this topic launched by economists and other social scientists over the last three years. These studies do show that "more social capital" is associated with "better economic performance," at least if the former is defined by membership in social networks and the strength of social institutions, and the latter is measured using conventional measures of income per head and economic growth rates (Grootaert 1999). Indeed, the Bank's research in Indonesia found that membership in local associations had a bigger impact on household welfare than education, especially if this membership was socially heterogeneous and overlapped with membership in other such groups (Grootaert 1999). One or two cross-country studies also suggest that levels of income inequality decline as social capital increases, but this evidence is contentious (Knack and Keefer 1997). Enthusiasts attribute these findings to the positive impact of social capital on the costs of doing business (it's cheaper if we trust each other) and its influence over other factors, such as institutional transparency and accountability, levels of social learning and adaptability in the economy, and access to contacts and information.

These conclusions are fairly noncontroversial, and have been accepted by non-economists for decades. We all know that social networks are crucial to economic success, and that "trust, reciprocity, and reputation" can solve the problems of common or collective action (Ostrom 1991). What is new is the label *capital* and its use in justifying the reduction of complex social phenomena to a series of numbers. Of course, not all economists accept this label. Nobel laureates Kenneth Arrow and Robert Solow explicitly reject the notion of social capital because the things encompassed by this terminology do not share the characteristics of "capital," as conventionally defined (Dasgupta and Serageldin 2000); but there is no doubt that the concept has gained ground among economists precisely because it is couched in such familiar language. This is something that our second group of World Bank pioneers—the *tacticians*—openly welcome. For them (most of whom are other social scientists in various parts of the Bank) social capital is a godsend—a way, at last, of engaging economists in a serious dialogue about the social world, backed up by empirically verifiable hypotheses. For the tacticians, social capital provides a unifying interdisciplinary discourse in which to discuss a range of otherwise disparate concerns (Bebbington et al. 2004). Since economics still reigns supreme, it's better to influence the field from within than to stand on the sidelines throwing intellectual bricks; and in this effort, social capital is probably the best shot we have.

The tacticians know that their strategy is something of a double-edged sword. On the one hand, they accept that much of the enthusiasts' current work is of dubious worth; it is "preliminary," to put it gently, and needs to be continually challenged along the way. On the other hand, they don't want to alienate their newfound colleagues by rocking the boat too much, and so they tend to approach disagreements in a spirit of consensus: Let's do more research and keep on talking; we're sure we'll come to some agreement. This is a very "social" approach, you might say, but one that may end in co-optation if the dialogue is conducted according to someone else's rules. Tacticians understand that the links between social capital and development outcomes are much more complex than the enthusiasts suggest—dependent on history and context, and operating through processes we do not fully understand. They tend to emphasize the indirect avenues for influence between (for example) strong civil society organizations, greater accountability in government, and pro-poor policy choices; or between the *character* of social capital—not just the amount—and the *shape* of economic performance. For tacticians, the most interesting evidence lies in the interactions between social, economic, and political processes, not in notions of social capital divorced from its wider context; and these are points to be addressed in a marriage between different disciplines, not grounds for a divorce. Their hope is that *all* of the social sciences will be transformed as the Trojan horse of social capital makes its way through the citadel of economics—not (in contrast to the rational-choice theorists) by unifying all disciplines under a single economic paradigm, but by creating an intellectual environment in which different disciplines and theoretical perspectives recognize both their comparative advantages and their inherent limitations, and know how and when to reach out to others. Indeed, this would be the rational end point of social capital theory—in emphasizing continuous collaboration—applied to the production and dissemination of knowledge about itself.

For our third group of observers—the *skeptics* (left-leaning academics and activists outside the Bank, and a few hard-line economists and icono-clasts within it)—this is naive in the extreme (Fine 1999). Let's be blunt, they say: What is economically important about social relations is already known from sociology and political science ("the more you have, the more you get"), and what is not known—how to reshape these dynamics in favor of poverty reduction—certainly can't be found through econom-ics, however much it is reformed. For the skeptics, what is important is not more social capital, but socializing the production and distribution of capital in all its forms. Those who cozy up too close to the enthusiasts will be left by the wayside when their disciplines have been trivialized, de-skilled, and turned into another branch of microeconomics. "Social devel-opment is dead . . . Long live social capital!" (Fine 1999: 1). Tacticians see little danger in their use of social capital as a heuristic device, but for the skeptics this is a dangerous game to play. As the historical record shows, the discipline of economics is very adept at incorporating insights from other social sciences without changing its core methods and assumptions.

The skeptics acknowledge that strong social networks and a dense web of civic associations are likely to facilitate certain aspects of economic performance. However, they don't accept that these improvements neces-sarily result in lower levels of poverty, inequality, violence, and social exclusion. What generate progress toward those goals are *particular config-urations* of social capital and other factors acting together, including the nature of the state and the material base of society. These configurations cannot be engineered, subjected to universal prescriptions, or captured by the language and methods of the orthodox economist. For the skeptics, what is notably absent from the social capital debate is any systematic treatment of power and discrimination in society (Tarrow 1996; McClain and Fleming 2000; Edwards and Foley 2001). Although the concept of social capital raises crucial questions about economic performance, these questions cannot be answered by economists alone since they have an explicitly political dimension.

Going further, one might argue (as a skeptic) that what really matters for poverty reduction is not social capital at all, but *social energy*—the will-ingness of human beings to act from their ideals (Hirschman 1984; Uphoff 1992). More social capital may benefit individuals or households, but it is not guaranteed to serve the common interest, or to promote the ability of citizens to lever fundamental changes in the market economy, and the structures of politics and social relations that underpin it. Under what conditions, the skeptics ask, is social capital accumulation likely to be used for less selfish ends as well as individual advancement (Edwards and Sen 2000)?

Do These Differences Matter?

Agreement on definitions is probably impossible, so we should just be clear on what it is we are studying in the social capital debate, and get on with it. Similarly, attempts to defend a normative understanding of social capital soon founder on the reality of ethnic separatism and destructive social networks—better "bowling alone than conspiring together." At another level, however, differences do matter; they determine the questions we ask, the answers we find, and the actions we take as a result. There are real controversies in the social capital debate that have important implications for what we do to address the deep-rooted problems of poverty and inequality. Three seem especially important.

Derivative or Determinant?

As one moves from "forms" to "norms," especially at the aggregate or national level, the number and complexity of the factors acting on social capital formation will obviously increase, and the outcomes will be less controllable. Both tacticians and skeptics accept that social capital is a "contingent" or "mediating" variable—a by-product of politics, state-building, and social structure that is shaped by history and context, and that in turn influences macro-social and economic outcomes. Therefore, economic and social success is a linear result not of "more social capital," but of a much more complex set of interactions that determine whether more social capital translates into particular results. Only when these other conditions are favorable will more social capital translate into generalized reductions in poverty and inequality. This is intuitively obvious from a glance at the United States, where high levels of inequality and violence coexist with a great deal of social capital and a rich (though perhaps declining) associational life, at least for some (Putnam 2000). To take another example, Lebanese society in the 1970s and 1980s was characterized by strong social networks, but they fought each other to a standstill during twenty years of civil war. It is here that the term *capital* is most problematic, for "capital" is a stock—something to be built up, exchanged, and depleted—whereas development is a flow, implying something that has purpose and direction. We accumulate capital, but social enrichment is a matter of behaving differently toward one another, not just adding on more social contacts.

Because the relationship between forms and norms is likely to be context dependent, it is difficult to theorize about this relationship in universal terms. The same norms (such as reciprocity) are subject to different interpretations in different cultures, and some norms (such as trust) hold differential value for people in different circumstances. Trust is not an unalloyed "good," since one person's confidence may be abused by less scrupulous others, especially in societies ridden with inequality, corruption, and exploitation. Generally, poor people do best when they are cautious reciprocators, predisposed to cooperate but unafraid to retaliate when people take advantage of them (Edwards 1999). To be uncritically trusting where power is unequally distributed is a dangerous strategy for social advancement. Therefore, it can be highly misleading to aggregate these qualities at the level of societies as a whole (cf. Fukuyama 1996).

In their various ways, enthusiasts, tacticians, and skeptics are all looking for ways to unlock the "black box" of these complex interactions. What is it that renders some social, economic, and political configurations more successful than others in promoting positive outcomes? This is an important theoretical question, of course, but it also has fundamental implications for what we do as practitioners, donors, and foundations. What forms of social capital should we be looking to promote? Presumably, those that are equally distributed throughout the population and are used to promote the common good, not just individual advancement. What associational characteristics really make the difference? Presumably, an inclusive civil society that practices tolerance and nondiscrimination. What kind of regime does best in fostering these configurations? Presumably, an open, participatory democracy and a state capable of guaranteeing universal rights (Evans 1996). And underlying all these questions is the thorny issue of whether intervention of any sort can lead to predictable outcomes, since the more contingent its construction, the more difficult it will be to ensure that social capital is used for positive ends. Recognizing this fact is one of the keys to successful intervention.

Power and Inequality

High (and rising) levels of inequality pose a double dilemma for the social capitalists. First, they provide a benchmark against which theory and practice must be tested. Does more social capital lead to more equitable economic growth? If not, one would have to question whether the debate is worth so much attention. Second, inequality represents a challenge to the theory itself. Social capital is most likely to be used for unselfish ends when exchange takes place between equals; without a basic level of voice, security, and equality of rights, people generally lack the confidence required to reach out and surrender some of their ambitions to the concerns of others. But real societies (including civil ones) are fractured by inequalities based on gender, race, and class. In these circumstances, does more social capital combat inequality or exacerbate it?

In answering this question, social capital theory makes much of the difference between "strong and weak ties" or "bridging" social capital (connections across groups), "bonding" social capital (connections within groups), and "linking" social capital (connections to other institutions; Woolcock and Narayan Chapter 2, this volume). Bonding may accentuate inequalities since additions of social capital will be used to promote only the interests of the group concerned; bridging will reduce them over time as people dissolve their differences in recognition of the wider common interest. To promote economic development, therefore, societies must move from bonding to bridging, in order to secure a social consensus in favor of structural changes in the economy, and rise above the constant struggle between interest groups that has derailed progress, for example, in sub-Saharan Africa since independence (Granovetter 1973; Woolcock 1998). This is why many Western theorists (and development agencies) distrust primary affiliations such as clans and tribes, and promote cross-cutting business and NGO networks in their programs.

However, such explanations are unsatisfactory. Throughout history, strong primary associations have been essential to social progress; think of the civil rights movement or the value of strong women's groups in the fight against discrimination. Rosa Parks, who defied racial segregation in 1950s Alabama by sitting in a "whites only" section of a Montgomery bus, did not succeed because of "bridging social capital," but because of her personal courage in the fight for equal rights. Notions of the "common interest" seem somewhat fanciful in deeply divided societies, where conflict and struggle have always been essential to the advancement of people on the margins. Conversely, consensus and "partnership" may offer a false promise to the poor and oppressed.

Clearly, at some stage of their struggle, poor people do need to make political alliances with other groups who can push change through, since the weight of their own representation is usually insufficient to secure fundamental pro-poor reforms. In the same vein, primary ties must extend into networks that can mediate the increasing range of social contacts people need to be successful outside the clan, tribe, or village. As economies evolve, the demands of economic exchange grow more complex, and it becomes increasingly difficult for traditional social networks to cope (Granovetter 1973). Much of the insecurity we feel in a globalizing economy comes from the weakness of these mediating structures at a time when labor unions, extended families, and other traditional sources of support are eroding. However, the goal is not to dissolve traditional bonds completely, but to find a better way of balancing the advantages they bring with the benefits of bridging, for both individuals and societies as a whole. Without the security provided by strong in-group ties, bridging may expose people too quickly to environments in which they have little experience, or may benefit the few who can prosper at the expense of the many who are left behind.

Scholars who have theorized about answers to these questions have focused on concepts such as "coupling and decoupling" (Granovetter 1995) and "linking" social capital to explore how bonding and bridging can be successfully combined (World Bank 2001; Woolcock and Narayan Chapter 2, this volume). This line of analysis might lead the World Bank and other agencies to support federations of strong and independent civil society organizations, for example, or help NGOs to bridge the divide between community action and formal state and market institutions. However, such interventions would achieve little without action to address preexisting patterns of inequality in society, a task that social capital by itself is ill equipped to perform. History shows that the degree of economic concentration of wealth in a society is a prime determinant of political voice, the allocation of social capital to different social groups, and the ability of poor people to use the social capital they gain to access material resources such as land, housing, credit, and education (Portes and Landolt 2000). In societies fractured by race, ethnicity, and asset and gender inequalities, therefore, "more social capital" is unlikely to achieve the desired results unless it is targeted at those who are excluded *and* is backed up by state intervention to protect their rights.

For example, women may gain more access to employment through an expanding range of social contacts, but they still need legislation in the areas of equal pay and child care provision to take advantage of these opportunities. Poor people typically feel as disconnected from the structures of political and economic power as from one another, so a strong (democratically accountable) state is just as important as social capital to the eradication of poverty, especially in instituting the reforms necessary to make more space for the construction of social capital among people who are disenfranchised—through support for affirmative action programs and labor market regulation, for example. Interventions of this kind are likely to be crucial in giving poor people enough security to reach out and make connections with others. As Portes and Landolt (2000) conclude, building social capital is not a substitute for addressing material inequalities in society, and only countervailing structures of authority can introduce increasing reciprocity into deeply divided societies. The raw realities of power need to be explicitly acknowledged and addressed in the debate over social capital, so that we can understand what is good and bad about the way social relations are organized and adjust our policy and practice accordingly.

Where Is Social Capital Produced?

Some commentators claim that social capital is produced (solely or primarily) in the arena of civil society, but there seems no obvious reason why civil society should be privileged in this way, in contrast to interactions in families, workplaces, or even people's dealings with their governments. It may be that certain forms of social capital are more likely to be produced in civic associations and networks, but if it is to be credible as an analytic concept, social capital must be something that can be produced in any sphere of human interaction—certain conditions permitting. In its broader sense, social capital applies to norms, rules, and attributes that can be generated across different cultural and institutional milieus.

This is an important issue, since the choice between perspectives determines our likely course of action. Returning to the question of definitions, is the aim just a strong civil society, or a society that is just and civil in all that it does—in how it practices politics, economics, and social policy as a whole? Is the aim more social capital, or "social capitalism"—meaning a less destructive economic model that generates material advances at less cost to ourselves and the world around us? Michael Walzer (1995: 16) answers this question well. He says that "the associational life of civil society is the actual ground where all versions of the good are worked out and tested, but not where they are completed," since completing that task is as much a matter for states and markets as for civic groups and networks. How, therefore, does a strong civil society lead to a society that is strong and civil? How does more social capital promote a capitalism that is more socially beneficial?

This is a complex debate, and—at least for the World Bank—largely uncharted territory. Attention is often focused on the characteristics of civic associations and how they might translate into broader outcomes—for example, the benefits of internally democratic, membership-based associations versus lobbying groups and other intermediaries; or the link between "civic values," organizational structure, and actual performance. The problem is that the empirical evidence examining these links is very cloudy due to the difficulty of predicting a group's moral effects purely on the basis of its formal purpose, organization, or ideology (Rosenblum 1998). Alternatively, we might look for clues in the different roles that civil society plays in development—in service provision, institutional accountability, and social protest—and the implications of different mixes of roles for economic growth and poverty reduction. Again, however, these roles change as economies evolve, just as the most effective mix of public, private, and civic action differs from one context to another. More usefully, we need to consider the actual record of different institutional "ecosystems" in producing different forms of social capital among different social groups—including public-private partnerships of different kinds, new alliances between corporations and NGOs, and experiments with decentralized, participatory democracy and new forms of multilayered, cross-society governance (Evans 1996; Tendler and Freedheim 1994; Edwards 1999). These experiments provide a challenging agenda for further research. What seems certain is that the results we seek are most likely to come from forms of social capital that are co-generated across states, markets, and civil society, from a base that is not captured by the interests of elites.

To summarize, the more rigorous we are in our treatment of the social capital debate, the more we must return to familiar questions of gender and race, state-society relations, and the material bases of social change. And the deeper we delve, the more difficult it becomes to settle on easy answers about what to do, when, and where. This promotes a level of uncertainty that is especially uncomfortable for bureaucracies such as the World Bank. Kenneth Arrow (2000: 5) puts the central question clearly: "Does the market . . . destroy social links that have positive implications for efficiency?" If so (and the answer must be yes), can these problems be addressed through economic prescriptions? If not (and the answer must be no), what are the alternatives, and what can the World Bank do to help explore them?

Is There a Role for Outside Help?

As the skeptics would argue, and as the tacticians largely accept, the most important areas of social capital are also the most contingent and the most difficult to engineer: attributes of trust, tolerance, and nondiscrimination. Conversely, the easiest areas to influence in the short run—such as the number of NGOs and other civic organizations—may not be especially important in the grand scheme of things. Donor agencies such as the World Bank have a natural tendency to focus on the short term and the easily measurable, and therefore to concentrate on the physical infrastructure of civil society and the mechanics of social capital ("forms, not norms"). This may well be a good thing, given the dangers inherent in interfering with such complex interrelationships at a deeper level. The record of foreign aid in this respect is not impressive; there is an abundance of evidence that poorly designed aid programs have eroded social capital rather than promoted it, at least if social capital is measured by trust, social cohesion, and the absence of violence as a means of resolving disputes (Edwards 1999). Russia and the Balkans are not exactly a ringing endorsement of our ham-fisted attempts to re-create a civic culture, especially in societies undergoing great political and economic stress. The dangers here are very real: "picking winners" by preselecting the organizations that donors think are most important (usually urban-based advocacy NGOs and networks of the civic elite), spreading mistrust and rivalry as groups compete for foreign aid, creating a backlash effect when civic groups are identified with foreign interests, and sowing suspicion through the use of nonreciprocal conditions on loans and grants. Rather than building social capital that is embedded in local realities, these are misguided attempts to manipulate its shape in accordance with Western liberal norms.

For the skeptics, "do no harm" may be an attractive mantra, but as the tacticians have recognized, the fact that change must be endogenous doesn't mean that outside help has no role to play—so long as it is sensitive and properly rooted in the local context. In this respect there are at least three key things that development agencies should be doing.

First, they need to understand the realities and complexities of the processes they want to influence. This may seem self-evident, but our understanding of social capital and civil society in non-Western contexts is extremely shallow and is dominated by Western viewpoints and institutions. What do African researchers think about social capital, or scholars in China or Brazil? Probably lots of different things, so let's seek out these views and give them a higher profile in the debate.

Second, they need to understand—and find better ways of supporting—those configurations of social, political, and economic factors that seem to make social capital the handmaiden of broader normative goals, and not just an asset to be captured by elites. There is a huge canvas to be explored here, in state-society relations and new forms of democracy, the shape of civil society and the characteristics of different associations, and the creative potential of new combinations of public, private, and social action. These complex "ecosystems" of institutions and interrelationships are likely to be context dependent, so comparative research by regime type and transition is essential. Under what conditions are different forms of social capital produced and distributed in such a way as to reduce material inequalities and influence norms of behavior so that they are used to promote the common good as well as the interests of individuals? Answering this question requires more research into the social capital–producing effects of different meso-level or mediating structures in different contexts, including families, community foundations, schools and universities, businesses and other market institutions, local governments, federations of civic organizations, churches and other faith-based groups, and the police and the military. As Tony Bebbington[3] has pointed out, "norms and forms" are linked through *practices*, and practices are nurtured in these meso-level institutional settings where people learn how to exercise their political responsibilities (including voting); care for each other; produce, consume, and invest; hold other institutions accountable for their actions; and participate in creating what gives meaning to their lives—forms of business, for example, that compete successfully in markets but distribute profits with a social purpose, forms of social policy that deliver effective child care without placing an unfair burden on women, and forms of politics that can deliver a more democratic set of trade-offs between the interests of different groups (Edwards 1999). The World Bank has documented other examples of innovations that could be extended: helping community groups in rural Indonesia to monitor aid expenditures and reinvent their relationships with government, for example, or promoting new forms of the social safety net in Malawi that empower existing community institutions to extend their skills and capacities into new areas, leading to a positive spill-over effect between economic and social security, the development of social capital, and the reweaving of the fabric of civil society (Grootaert 1999).

Of course, there are no universal answers to any of these questions, but through careful analysis, experimentation, and learning, it is possible to find the virtuous cycles that will link changes in institutions with changes in norms and values, attacking the inequalities that lie at the root of the problem, and rebalancing those "strong and weak ties" along the way. It is through exploring these cycles—when social capital confronts the structures of power—that the greatest gains are likely to be made.

Third, donor agencies need to acknowledge that current systems for disbursing foreign aid are ill suited to the task of nurturing social capital. The fundamental requirement of any cooperative relationship is the willingness to "put one's house in order," and it is impossible to encourage attitudes of trust and reciprocity through a system riddled with the opposite incentives: built-in asymmetries between "donors" and "recipients," layers of conditions and constraints, and continuous changes of dogma and fashion (social capital being the latest example). In theory, the World Bank has already recognized the futility of this approach by switching (along with other donor agencies) to systems in which countries design their own development plans and are accountable across society for their achievements. Paradoxically, this was the logic that drove the Marshall Plan in 1945, but it was forgotten when foreign aid became a weapon of the Cold War and other external agendas. It is possible to view the international system in ways that both produce and make use of social capital at the global level (Edwards 1999). The Comprehensive Development Framework, the World Bank–IMF Poverty Reduction Strategy Papers, and the United Nations Development Assistance Framework are all predicated on the assumption that societies are more likely to defend goals and strategies that they have argued over and negotiated to an agreement. This process of convening, debating, and coalition building is a social capital–producing intervention in itself.

For the Bank and other donors, these changes imply a primary focus on the enabling environment for social capital formation: strengthening the legal, regulatory and fiscal framework for civic groups and public-private partnerships; encouraging a healthy state-society relationship; developing the "paths and meeting grounds" that are essential if people are to make the right connections; and linking small-scale successes with the national conditions that encourage them to spread. These are less intrusive forms of support that allow local actors to determine the way ahead, but with a greater chance that the journey will be inclusive, peaceful, and democratic. Promoting transparency (in budgeting, for example) and access to information is vital at all levels. Providing special help to those left out of these processes is also crucial—not just fostering social capital in general, but fostering it among the disenfranchised in order to redress the balance of power.

This adds up to an ambitious—if not revolutionary—agenda for a traditional lending institution. A skeptic might say that the World Bank therefore has a limited role to play in social capital formation, so what would need to change within the institution to move these strategies to center stage? There is an obvious need to elaborate a model of lending that places social capital at the heart of operations, backed up by concrete incentives to promote good practice. But that won't happen until the intellectual battle has been won, and that prospect is still some years away. In the meantime, priority should go to an intensive program of cross-disciplinary action and research with country departments designed to address the questions raised in this and other chapters. In turn, this would require a stronger core of expertise in social capital, but dispersed more broadly throughout the Bank; stronger links between those working on social capital and those working on related subjects (such as civil society and governance); and much stronger leadership to drive the agenda through. Paradoxically, all these things require more social capital *within* the World Bank, and that—for this most aggressively competitive and individualistic of institutions—may be the biggest challenge of all. The Bank must learn to collaborate both internally and with others as an equal, for exchange between equals is the raw material of trust, trust is the foundation of cooperation, and cooperation offers the only hope we have of confronting the collective challenges that face us in the twenty-first century.

Conclusions

Neither social capital nor civil society is the solution to the deep-rooted problems of poverty and violence, but there is something fundamentally important about both of them, despite the uncertainties, the gaps in understanding, and the differences and disagreements that arise along the way. In likening civil society to the Indian Ocean, Ramon Daubon of the Kettering Foundation captures the intrinsic value of these concepts well: "Everyone knows where it is, no one cares where it ends and begins, and we know we have to cross it to get from India to Africa." Despite the limitations of their approach, the enthusiasts are welcome on this journey because they take familiar concepts into unfamiliar territory; the skeptics are essential passengers too, since they remind us that there are never any easy answers; but the best pilots are the tacticians, filled with the enthusiasts' fresh determination but savvy to the twists and turns of translating theory into practice along the way. One encouraging sign in the World Bank is the increasing prominence of these tacticians (many of whom are represented in this volume, and whose influence is also apparent in the 2000–2001 World Development Report).

If we understand social capital as the cumulative capacity to work together for common goals, and civil society as the space where these goals are formed and debated, then these two concepts do provide a framework to pursue a different paradigm of development. In pursuing this paradigm, it is best to be a "skeptical tactician" (or should that be a tactical skeptic?), uncovering the truth through rigorous research and critical, public engagement. However, we should remember that there are always preconditions for a successful conversation of this kind—principally voice, security, and equality of rights. Many people—indeed, most people, if we look to the global level—are denied these preconditions by the forces of exclusion. If their claims to conceptual and practical advancement are to be substantiated, these are the forces that social capitalists of all persuasions must help us understand, challenge, and overcome.

Notes

1. Portions of this chapter have been published in "Enthusiasts, Tacticians, and Skeptics: Civil Society and Social Capital," *Kettering Review,* Spring 2000, 18(1):39–59.
2. This test was formulated by Michael Woolcock at seminars on social capital at the World Bank and the Ford Foundation in June 2000.
3. Internal Ford Foundation seminar on social capital in June 2000.

References

Arrow, K.J. 2000. Observations on social capital. In *Social capital: A multifaceted perspective,* edited by P. Dasgupta and I. Serageldin. Washington, DC: World Bank, pp. 3–5.

Bebbington, A., S. Guggenheim, E. Olson, and M. Woolcock. 2004. Exploring social capital debates at the World Bank. *Journal of Development Studies* 40(5):33–64.

Dasgupta, P., and I. Serageldin. 2000. *Social capital: A multifaceted perspective.* Washington, DC: World Bank.

Edwards, B., and M. Foley. 2001. Much ado about social capital. *Contemporary Sociology* 30(3):227–230.

Edwards, M. 1999. *Future positive: International co-operation in the 21st century.* London: Earthscan.

Edwards, M., and G. Sen. 2000. NGOs, social change, and the transformation of human relationships: A 21st century civic agenda. *Third World Quarterly* August (special section).

Evans, P. 1996. Government action, social capital and development: Reviewing the evidence on synergy. *World Development* 24(6):1119–1132.

Fine, B. 1999. The developmental state is dead—Long live social capital? *Development and Change* 30(1):1–19.

Fukuyama, F. 1996. *Trust: The social virtues and the creation of prosperity.* New York: Free Press.

Granovetter, M. 1973. The strength of weak ties. *American Journal of Sociology* 78:1360–1380.

———. 1995. The economic sociology of firms and entrepreneurs. In *The economic sociology of immigration: Essays on networks, ethnicity, and entrepreneurship,* edited by A. Portes. New York: Russell Sage.

Grootaert, C. 1999. *Does social capital help the poor? A synthesis of findings from the local level institutions study in Bolivia, Burkina Faso and Indonesia.* Washington, DC: World Bank, Social Development Department.

Hirschman, A. 1984. *Getting ahead collectively: Grassroots experiences in Latin America.* Oxford: Pergamon Press.

Knack, S., and P. Keefer. 1997. Does social capital have an economic pay-off? A cross country investigation. *Quarterly Journal of Economics* 112:1251–1288.

Krishna, A., and N. Uphoff. 1999. *Mapping and measuring social capital: A conceptual and empirical study of collective action for conserving and developing watersheds in Rajasthan, India.* Social Capital Initiative Working Paper No. 13. Washington, DC: World Bank.

McClain, L., and J. Fleming. 2000. Symposium on legal and constitutional implications of the calls to revive civil society. *Chicago Kent Law Review* 75(2):301–354.

Ostrom, E. 1991. *Governing the commons: The evolution of institutions for collective action.* Cambridge: Cambridge University Press.

Portes, A., and P. Landolt. 2000. Social capital: Promise and pitfalls of its role in development. *Journal of Latin American Studies* 32:529–547.

Putnam, R. 2000. *Bowling alone.* New York: Simon & Schuster.

Rosenblum, N.L. 1998. *Membership and morals: The personal uses of pluralism in America.* Princeton, NJ: Princeton University Press.

Tarrow, S. 1996. Making social science work across space and time: A critical reflection upon Robert Putnam's *Making democracy work. American Political Science Review* 90(2):389–397.

Tendler, J., and S. Freedheim. 1994. Trust in a rent-seeking world: Health and government transformed in Northeast Brazil. *World Development* 22:1771–1791.

Uphoff, N. 1992. *Learning from Gal Oya: Possibilities for participation, development and post-Newtonian social science.* New York: Cornell University Press.

Walzer, M. 1995. The concept of civil society. In *Toward a global civil society,* edited by Michael Walzer. Providence, RI: Berghahn Books.

Woolcock, M. 1998. Social capital and economic development: Toward a theoretical synthesis and policy framework. *Theory and Society* 27(2):151–208.

World Bank. 2001. *World development report 2000–2001: Attacking poverty.* Washington, DC: World Bank.

SECTION TWO

OPERATIONALIZING SOCIAL CAPITAL IDEAS

CHAPTER FIVE

CRISES AND CONTRADICTIONS
Understanding the Origins of a Community Development Project in Indonesia

Scott Guggenheim

It was a brilliantly clear morning in central Sulawesi when the villagers first spied the large pile of lumber. One of the delivery truck drivers stood lazily by the wood, blowing cigarette smoke over his steaming coffee. He had come from Palu, the provincial capital. The gold lettering embroidered on his hat told the villagers that he and the silent man in the neatly pressed green safari suit, also sipping his coffee, worked for the Public Works Department there.

The villagers were curious. Just last year they had gotten funds from the Kecamatan Development Project to build a stone road from their rice fields to the market route, and now here were the materials to repair a bridge. Had the government finally noticed their plight?

"Friend, what is this wood for?"

"It's to build a bridge."

"How much wood is there? What did it cost?"

"That's none of your business. Just be thankful that the government will be building you a bridge."

"But we want to know. This is our new rule here. You have to come to the *balai desa* and tell us about the project. Then you have to post a sign-board so that all of us know how much this bridge costs. If KDP does it, we want you to do it too."

"You are mistaken. KDP is KDP, and it has KDP rules. This is a government project, and we follow our rules. Just be thankful that you are getting a bridge."

The villagers were troubled. That night the village elders met. Some people said they should just accept the wood because the village needed the bridge. But many more villagers were angry. This was now the era of *reformasi*, and people had a right to know about projects in their village.

Early the next morning, even before the first rays of sunlight pierced the dark clouds, the villagers had heaved the wood back onto a large truck owned by the son of the village council head. Two truckloads of villagers and scores of motorcycles joined the procession to the district parliament. When the first parliamentarians arrived for work that morning, they were met by a quiet delegation of villagers standing atop a large pile of wood wrapped in an enormous white cloth.

"What is this?" they asked.

"This is the cloth we use to wrap our dead," the village head replied, "and dead is what this project is. We would rather have no bridge and no wood than go back to the corrupt ways of the New Order. From now on we only want projects that involve us in decisions. If KDP can do it, other projects can do it too."

And with those words, the villagers got back on their trucks and went home.[1]

Introduction

KDP, the Kecamatan Development Project, is the largest community development project ever initiated in Southeast Asia. Covering more than 20,000 villages, the billion-dollar program extends from the northern tip of Sumatra to West Papua/Irian Jaya, three time zones away. KDP is one of the first large development projects funded by the World Bank to draw directly on social theory—in particular, on writings from agrarian studies and comparative history. KDP supports development plans made and approved by communities. By focusing primarily on the process by which local development projects are planned and managed rather than on what gets built, KDP marks a sharp departure from the traditional ways in which large development projects are conceived and carried out.

This chapter is about the genesis of KDP. In keeping with the overall theme of this volume, the chapter primarily looks inward, focusing on the opportunities and constraints that challenge social scientists working within large development bureaucracies. KDP provides a useful way to organize such a discussion. For while there is much to be said for the role played by the World Bank as a forum for testing and provoking critical thinking about international development, what the World Bank actually does is lend very large sums of money to developing countries. Social scientists who think that the Bank must change the way it does development must find a way to change its operations.

The chapter is divided into three sections. The first section describes the project and raises the question of what specific historical factors opened the space for an experiment like KDP. While KDP undeniably draws on a broad range of community development experiences, both in Indonesia and elsewhere, it is also true that the "here" and "now" issues pose an analytical question that is crying out for answers: How could a project that must have been seen as progressive and potentially risky move forward in the large, highly centralized, quasi-military government that was Indonesia in 1998?

The second section gives a brief overview of KDP's ethnographic roots. The purpose of the argument in this section is to show that KDP is substantively different from standard development projects, and that this difference reflects not only changing fashions in development but also the perspective of community-state relationships as viewed through the glasses of an anthropologist rather than those of a development economist, rural planner, or irrigation engineer.

The concluding section draws the case study back to the overarching theme of this book, the question of how the vocabulary of development can be expanded to include the critical insights of social scientists. The argument here is that while the scope for structural alternatives to standard models may be limited, it is not insignificant. Social scientists can play catalytic roles, but they must learn to work within the culture of development institutions. Applied social development must deliver meaningful results in the language and terminology used by decision makers in government and big agencies such as the World Bank. Very few of those people are social scientists.

This study carries with it an internal contradiction that must be acknowledged up front. The author is both informant and analyst. As a project team leader inside the World Bank, I enjoy a special advantage in writing about historical events such as what really happened behind the closed negotiating doors; for most of the closed-door sessions referred to in this chapter, I was sipping tea at the table as the parties argued about terms and conditions. Enough has been written on the virtues and faults of introspective anthropology and the problems that self-reporting poses to any ethnographic account that, for the moment, a word to the wise should suffice to warn readers about the inherent partiality of the discussion that follows.[2]

KDP in Brief[3]

The Indonesian administrative system consists of provinces, districts (*kabupaten*), subdistricts (*kecamatan*), and villages. There are some twenty to fifty villages in a kecamatan; the average Javanese kecamatan will have 50,000 to 75,000 people in it, while a kecamatan in the sparsely populated eastern islands can have as few as 10,000 to 12,000 inhabitants. Although many kecamatans were mapped onto the boundaries of preexisting principalities, off-Java kecamatans are often large enough to contain a number of different cultural groups, particularly in areas of high immigration.

The basic architecture of the Kecamatan Development Project is deceptively simple. It consists of a system to give block grants directly to kecamatan councils, which they can use to fund development plans prepared through a four- to six-month participatory planning process. The funds, which amount to approximately US$60,000–110,000 per kecamatan, can be used for almost anything villagers believe to be a development priority. As in many poor parts of the rural world, villagers tend to place a premium on roads, bridges, and irrigation, but in both theory and practice KDP funds can be used for almost any kind of public good as well as for village-level revolving funds.[4]

The kecamatan councils are themselves something of an odd beast. Formally composed of the elected heads of the village planning group and chaired by the subdistrict head, for many years they were inert, meeting at most once a year. Under KDP they have been revived. Additional, non-voting members are elected by popular approval. All project proponents are also invited to join the meetings, which means that the final gathering for the competition among proposals can be very large.

Each village can submit up to two proposals to the kecamatan council. This always leads to more proposals than there are funds, so the villagers must negotiate among themselves which proposals are the most worthy. KDP rules require that any village group submitting a proposal must send a delegation of at least two women and one man to the kecamatan decision meeting where villagers decide on which proposals will be funded. Negotiations lead to plenty of horse trading among villagers.

Once the kecamatan forum agrees on which proposals merit funding, nobody further up the system can modify the conclusions. Funds are released from the provincial branch of the national treasury directly to a bank account held in the name of all of the villages. They do not go through the different levels of government, though they are recorded in provincial and district budgets. This direct transfer system is not only one of the underappreciated keys to the project's success but also an endless source of frustration for neat and orderly public administration specialists.

Planning is aided by a tiered system of facilitators. In each KDP village, a man and a woman are elected to represent the village within the project. Their main job is to introduce the project to all of the informal as well as formal institutions in the village, which in effect means that they spend large amounts of time in the hamlets rather than the village proper. The next level up is the kecamatan, where a social and a technical facilitator are designated. The social facilitator explains the project's rules, monitors participation, and trains the village facilitators; the technical facilitator helps the villagers assess the quality of their infrastructure and trains them in maintenance. District engineers[5] supervise the quality of physical works, and at the provincial level a management unit conducts training, supervises progress in the field, and acts on complaints received from villages.

For me, some of the most interesting bits of KDP lie in the details of how the project helps (and sometimes hinders) villagers in taking control of how the money gets spent. For example, when villagers decide to buy construction materials, they have to get prices from three different suppliers and announce them at a village meeting. Initially, many villagers do not want to do this; they have their own favorite suppliers where they have bought goods for decades. They are nearly always shocked to find that comparative shopping lowers costs. Villagers also form monitoring teams that, for example, count the contents of delivery trucks as they arrive, to make sure that what suppliers send is what the villagers purchased. They report their checklist back to the village forum. More than a few contractors (and colluding village heads) have been caught delivering less than what their contracts called for, and because it is the villagers' own funds that are being misused, villagers have become increasingly assertive in demanding not just restitution but also punishment for the people who cheat them.

The project has a strong battery of monitoring instruments. Most interesting, given that it was conceived in the waning days of the New Order government, is that the project has the legal obligation to contract independent NGOs in each province, and to provide a blind contract for the Indonesian Association of Independent Journalists to publish stories on how the project is performing in the villages. (The "blind contract" means that the project funds an intermediary NGO to pay for a fixed number of trips to the field, but the project never knows who is going where, nor is there any prior review of what the journalists publish.) So far the journalists have published some 850 articles in regional newspapers, about a third of which deal with corruption or other forms of abuse.

Monitoring also includes kecamatan cross-audits and participatory monitoring by villagers themselves, as well as a number of case studies on special topics, such as women's participation in meetings or how villagers adapt the core design to *adat* (customary) forms of organization. The case studies are summarized in a colorful bimonthly newsletter that goes to all 20,000 villages. During one ten-day trip across Java, I asked all the villagers I met which of the case studies they thought was the most interesting. The hands-down winner was the story of the village head who went to jail for stealing KDP funds from his village.

KDP has evolved over time.[6] In its first years the focus was almost entirely on firming up the planning system, defining roles for the facilitators, and breaking through the government's prohibitions against using loan funds to involve NGOs and independent monitoring in development projects. Its second phase consisted of strengthening village internal capacities by sponsoring broad-based training programs in bookkeeping and procurement, infrastructure assessments, and village-wide development planning. The current installment is concerned with institutionalizing the system by helping the district government pass regulations that promote more democratic village government. These include guidelines on how village heads and councils are elected and recalled, how village development planning happens, consolidating village rights to review development projects proposed for them, and other matters.

KDP also serves as the laboratory for a number of experiments. In 2001 two provinces ran pilot studies on the provision of legal aid services to poor villages; this will now be scaled up to cover five provinces.[7] Another large pilot project linked to KDP works with a group of women's NGOs to help widows in conflict areas, primarily through training, micro-credit, and an impressively innovative use of documentary photography. In Papua the program was unable to recruit sufficient numbers of trained Papuan engineers, so it developed its own two-year training course for more than 200 Papuan students recruited from different rural kecamatans. Recently a competition was held to see which field teams could come up with the most creative ways to actively involve women in village-wide decision meetings (see also Buchori et al. 2002).

The preceding discussion should convince anyone familiar with standard international development projects that KDP is a creative deviant from the norm. And yet KDP is not a small pilot operation tucked away amidst a huge program of dam and airport building. From 2001 to 2003, KDP has accounted for more than half of World Bank lending in Indonesia. Why would a quasi-military government, as was Indonesia's New Order regime in 1998, borrow large amounts of money to bypass its own bureaucracy, assign paralegals to rural villages, and pay independent journalists to publish newspaper stories on development corruption? Why would the World Bank abandon its love of highways and irrigation networks to embrace micro-investments in thousands of impossible-to-manage communities? Perhaps the timing was right.

Indonesian Development in 1998: Three Institutions in Crisis

Indonesia under the Late New Order

Few countries have traversed the path from crown jewel to tarnished paste as rapidly as Indonesia. When I first arrived in Indonesia in 1994, the country was a tribute to the power of the neoclassical development model. Between 1976 and 1993, Indonesia's census figures reported that poverty had dropped from 40.1 percent of the population to less than 15 percent. Between the early 1960s and the late 1980s, average per-capita calorie and protein supplies rose by 45 percent and 50 percent, respectively (Hill 1996). Universal education was ensured by a mass building program that saw 200,000 schools built within five years, and a country whose people had no problem recalling what foods they had eaten during the recurrent famines were suddenly facing the bizarre problem of rising heart attacks rates from too much dietary fat and too little exercise. In 1995 the United Nations crowned President Suharto as a "Hero of Development," a reward he received in the large ranch he maintained in the hills of western Java.

By 1999 all of the praise showered on Indonesia had vanished in the cloud of smoke that rose over the fallen regime. Exposed as the architect of New Order kleptocracy, and accused of the systematic violation of human rights in East Timor, Aceh, Papua, and elsewhere, Suharto today is few people's idea of a "Hero of Development." "Corruption, collusion, and nepotism" has become the catchphrase for a generation of commentators on Indonesian development practice. World Bank reports speak of Indonesia "muddling through," and development in Indonesia today is more concerned with preventing catastrophe than with bounding along the path of sustainable growth.

Despite the current scorn for the achievements of the Indonesian New Order, it is worth reviewing the mechanisms that the government used to obtain those impressive results. The macro story of stability and a secure and predictable investment environment is well known by now, as is the country's welcoming large amounts of foreign investment to help translate its abundant natural resources and large population into productive assets to fuel its development push. But the New Order government's social achievements should not be downplayed. Mass programs to immunize children, build primary schools, and construct economic infrastructure all across the sprawling archipelago contributed enormously to Indonesia's development spurt.[8]

By the mid-1990s, however, it had become clear that not all was well in Indonesia. Suharto's success brought with it problems whose severity was casting a pall across the country even before the May 1998 uprisings that eventually toppled the New Order government. Among analysts of the time, the main concern lay in the fact that although Suharto had successfully institutionalized not just one-party but one-person rule, he had failed to find a way to identify a successor who would be sufficiently competent to run the country and yet not so competent that he would threaten Suharto's own grip on power (Schwarz 2000).

Corruption had always been endemic to Indonesian development. But with the maturity of Suharto's children, corruption attained a new magnitude. Very few of the national industries, banks, commodity-trading companies, or development projects avoided their grasp. But the corruption was not confined to national elites. Subsequent developments were to make shockingly clear the extent to which the entire political system had come to depend on illegal rents.[9]

Commentators, including analysts inside the government, increasingly noted that many people in Indonesia believed that inequality was worsening across the country. Quantitative reviews did not support this perception. Nevertheless, the government's more sensitive political antennae had detected the currents of popular disillusionment. Even before analysts or donors voiced concern over rising inequality, planners in the powerful National Planning Agency (Bappenas) began to prepare a series of targeted programs to reduce poverty.

Just how fragile the New Order had become by the late 1990s is blindingly clear in retrospect, but it was not so obvious at the time. People were not so naive as to think that Indonesia's growth was without its flaws, but the primary concerns were about how to consolidate gains so that Indonesia could successfully make a transition into the company of middle-income nations. To be sure, there were some Cassandras crying that the end of the New Order was nigh, but the common speech in development circles was one of "course corrections" rather than structural reform.

Nevertheless, the government itself perceived a need to shore up its base among the masses. In the middle part of the decade, the government launched a series of poverty reduction programs called the *Inpres Desa Tertinggal* ("program for left-behind villages") (IDT). These were a series of block grants given to poor villages across the country. The brainchild of a professor at the country's largest university (see, e.g., Mubyarto 1996), the IDT program built on Hernando de Soto's (1989) views that the problem of poverty was due not to lack of skills, but to government red tape and insecure property titles. Above all, the Indonesian interpretation of de Soto's assertion was that all these barriers blocked poor people's access to the seed capital they needed to launch their own micro enterprises that would lift their families out of poverty. IDT would provide it.

As the core of a final push in its war on poverty, the New Order government adopted IDT and declared it to be the country's premier national anti-poverty program. Backed by the personal support of Suharto himself, the project was directly managed by the powerful National Planning Agency rather than some technical agency so that the country's top planners and project administrators could make sure that the project was well planned and managed. Approximately $200 million of government money was committed to the first phase of the project, with an assurance of more to follow. The World Bank and the United Nations Development Programme (UNDP) were asked to provide independent monitoring of the project, and the government formed a high-powered IDT Secretariat to make sure that the program would not become too bureaucratic.

Initially supported by academics and NGOs, the program soon soured when it became clear how corrupt the local administration of the program had become. IDT's objectives were laudable and the project's targeting appeared to be reasonable, but the program simply could not be implemented through the government bureaucracy. Large amounts of money went missing; and when the money did reach the village, all too often the village heads preferred to give it to local elites with a track record of using money effectively, rather than poor people, who would be unlikely to pay it back. An ex post statistical evaluation of IDT three years after it was halted found a total net impact on poverty of zero (Molyneaux and Gertler 1999).

Other programs followed suit. Emergency public works to counter the spreading economic crisis became watchwords for corruption and theft, to the point of triggering mass demonstrations outside of the once all-powerful Ministry of Planning. The government was trapped. The consolidation of a rentier bureaucracy had left the government with virtually no way to implement its own programs, even when it genuinely wanted to shore up its base among the increasingly restive population.

The World Bank

If Indonesia was feeling a little shaky as the century drew to a close, the World Bank was facing its own crisis of legitimacy both in the world at large and in the smaller world of Indonesia. As shown by J. Fox and others (see Fox and Brown 1998), the rise of the world environment movement brought into the open a range of difficult questions about the impacts of Big Development that before then had been shrugged off as the necessary costs of growth. Independent scrutiny of several of the biggest development schemes supported by development agencies around the world confirmed that their costs were much higher and their benefits much lower than internal appraisals had suggested.[10]

Involuntary resettlement had proven to be a particularly ugly problem. Following the deeply critical independent review of the Narmada Sardar Sarovar projects in western India (Morse and Berger 1992), the Bank commissioned an internal, Bankwide review of all projects that involved involuntary resettlement to see what measures would be needed to bring Bank-funded operations in line with institutional policy (Cernea and Guggenheim 1994). Although the Bank was funding only a small percentage of the projects that required resettlement, these projects were often the largest and most visible development activities within a country, and they came to symbolize the development mentality as a whole (Rich 1994).

World Bank support for the New Order government had been consistent and strong for nearly thirty years, and it is no surprise that the Bank was closely identified with the New Order's development ideology as a whole. Within Indonesia, activists singled out two projects for special attention: the multi-billion-dollar transmigration programs and a large dam called Kedung Ombo, which displaced more than 35,000 villagers as part of a multipurpose irrigation project for central Java. NGOs rallied around the two projects as illustrations of destructive development. The Bank initially ignored the protests, but over time pressure to acknowledge the problems mounted even as internal doubts grew about what was going on in the two projects and what role the Bank should be playing, as it became clear that too many of the accusations were turning out to be true.

The 1994 Bankwide Review on Involuntary Resettlement highlighted the wide deviations between the World Bank's own resettlement policy and the nature of the projects funded by the Bank in Indonesia (among others). The two biggest systemic problems appeared to be the wide gap between the standards and rules required by the Bank's policies and those used by the Indonesian government; and the fact that within the Bank's operational programs there was virtually nobody who knew the social impact policies well or had a special interest in making sure that they were properly implemented, especially if that would lead to a slowdown in the approval of projects.

Responses to the Bankwide review varied across the World Bank's country departments. In Indonesia the response was to form a small Environment and Social Development Unit that would report directly to the Country Director. The unit's tasks were to oversee the environmental and social aspects of the Bank's portfolio in Indonesia, and to narrow the gap between Bank and government policies. Four people joined the unit; I was one of them.

It soon became clear that this would amount to too little, too late. The resettlement problem was but a symptom of a much bigger problem with the Bank's relationship with Indonesia. Evidence that the "Indonesian miracle" was not all it was cracked up to be was mounting; even the Bank's own managers were starting to raise questions about why rural services in the villages they visited looked so bad when the project reports continued to highlight how well the projects were performing.

Three events in particular brought the rising doubts to a head. The East Asian crisis that began in 1997 not only exposed the fragility of the country's banking system and the systematic looting of the economy that had been going on, but it also witnessed nearly half the country suddenly drop below the poverty line. How could this have happened when report after report had described Indonesia's success in reducing poverty at an unprecedented rate? Suddenly the objectivity of the Bank's analysis and reporting was called into question.

The second event that rattled the Bank was that the crisis revealed just how effectively the fragility and corruption of the country's financial system had been hidden from the Bank and IMF. Bank macroeconomic staff in particular were genuinely shaken; not only did it turn out that the country was effectively bankrupt, having seen its banking system eviscerated of its resources in order to fund the money-losing enterprises of the country's elite, but their most trusted counterparts were either not aware of what was going on or, more likely, too cowed to speak. This ex post realization that the IMF's and Bank's own monitoring and reporting had failed produced a crisis of self-confidence that reverberated all the way to the top floors of Washington (Blustein 2003).

At least as damaging were a series of revelations showing that the Bank was aware of the extent of corruption within Indonesia's development projects. With development agencies no longer protected by government censorship of Indonesian critics and the rationalizing comfort of 7 percent annual growth, civil society groups and political leaders freely criticized the Bank for having willingly aided and abetted the New Order government in looting the country and papering over the facts, all the while claiming to be supervising its projects. Nationalist and reformist politicians in the new government and parliament quickly joined the chorus of criticism. The Bank found itself on the defensive.

That it was the New Order government's own bureaucracy—the Bank's statutory counterparts—that lay at the root of the economic crisis presented the Bank with three major problems. First, the pressure to find ways to prevent a poverty and humanitarian crisis across the collapsing economy—which freakishly coincided with a recurrence of El Niño–related crop failures—was met with a realization that the tools to act either did not exist or were themselves likely to divert much of any aid that was possible. Second, the scale of the popular backlash against the government's chief financier alarmed World Bank management and demoralized the staff. Third, the Bank itself was overexposed on Indonesia's debt, and a debt moratorium by an incoming government would have affected the World Bank's credit rating worldwide. Thus, in mid-1998, the World Bank in Indonesia was facing a crisis of its own.

The Crisis of Leadership in Indonesian Villages

Indonesia's 65,000-plus villages had not escaped the New Order's social transformations. On Java, the "closed corporate peasant community" described by Eric Wolf in the 1950s had ceased to exist (if, indeed, it had ever existed at all—see Wolf 1957, 1986; Koentjaraningrat 1967), replaced by a system of village government defined by the Village Law of 1979 and the implementing regulations that followed (Bebbington et al. 2005).

As with all New Order administrative designs, the two keys to the new Village Law were the standardization of bureaucratic form and the centralization of authority and resources. The new law forced all hamlets[11] to come under the authority of a village. The village head was notionally elected, but his election had to be ratified by the district head, which in effect gave the latter veto power and control over who would be acceptable. Village chiefs, in turn, became the preeminent source of power in the village; they were the statutory heads of the village planning (*Lembaga Ketahan Masyarakat Desa* [LKMD]) and consultative (*Lembaga Musyawarah Desa* [LMD]) councils, while the wife of the village head became the head of the mandatory association of women.

Following the establishment of an administrative structure to bring Indonesia's diverse village organizations within the ambit of state control, the next twenty years saw the systematic weakening or destruction of all alternative sources of social organization. In most areas, government land titling and water user programs replaced traditional forms of land and water management groups. Traditional law was subsumed by the civil code, which, however overwhelmed and ineffective the courts were, could find no space to accommodate traditional dispute resolution mechanisms.[12]

Development programs were active contributors to this state-building project. Virtually all development programs channeled their resources through the village chief or the LKMD, which was itself chaired by the village head. Development programs also naively, and sometimes not so naively, funded the user groups that competed with traditional forms of social organization, and the fact that they brought with them resources and skills as well as government approval offered strong advantages to the people who joined.

Without access to state institutions or development resources, traditional leaders lost much of their space to maneuver. In many areas, particularly off-Java locales, marginalization of traditional leadership actually led to an increase in appeals to "culture"—the importance of exerting authority through magic, tradition, spirituality, and ethnic distinctiveness, since these were the domains that remained open to them. But changing demographics weakened this strategy as the large number of immigrants generated through transmigration and off-Java job creation brought with them populations who simply did not believe in the efficacy of cultural means of control and would not accept culturally based claims to village governance (K. Chandrakirana 2003, personal communication).

Understanding the crisis of village leadership requires understanding that not all of these changes were perceived to be for the worse. Indonesian villages before the New Order were not homogeneous, egalitarian, or solidary. The New Order's changes opened up much-welcomed opportunities for many people on the bottom rungs of the social ladder. Similarly, for all their problems of patronage, poor quality, and mandated participation, the mass construction programs brought broad-based benefits to villagers that paid off in longer life spans and higher incomes. Our field interviews across rural areas suggest that the strategies of opposition embedded in notions of peasant resistance oversimplify perceptions of development in Indonesia. Most villagers saw development as a mixed bag that brought desirable opportunities as well as unwanted risks and controls.

If this mix of regulatory marginalization and economic competition created a crisis among traditional leaders, the government leaders who competed with them rested on foundations that were no less shaky. Lacking a base of popular support within the communities, village chiefs in particular cultivated close ties to the district head both for political support and for the release of development resources and budgets. District heads relied on village leadership to secure political loyalty and to ensure political stability, and the failure to deliver one or the other was the most common grounds for dismissal. Development soon became both the justification and the reward for consolidation of the new political order.

A third factor affecting both traditional and modern leadership was the achievement of universal education. For the first time, children of both the traditional and modern elites could attend school beyond primary levels and, with that education, get reasonably good jobs in Indonesia's rapidly growing cities. Many did.[13] This rural to urban demographic transition dramatically shrank the pool of future village leaders, a point that was repeatedly commented on by reflective villagers when the Bank started its first round of village ethnographies in 1996.

The Roots of a Development Project

It would be nice to be able to write that the design for a billion-dollar, nationwide community development program came from a grand concept that guided the team from the outset. Nice, but it would not be true. If the argument of the first part of this chapter is that the historic conjuncture of crises within the Indonesian government, the World Bank, and village leadership opened the door to what became the Kecamatan Development Project, the argument of this section is that it is largely a matter of historical coincidence that a project such as KDP fell through it.

My version of KDP's history starts with a series of village case studies we began in 1996. Called the Local Level Institutions (LLI) studies, the research program was part of a three-country study to see if the ideas on social capital in the context of Italy presented in Robert Putnam's book *Making Democracy Work* (1993) made sense in the context of developing countries. Was "social capital" a useful way to think about building democratic institutions from the bottom up?

For many of us in the World Bank's Social Development group, the social capital vocabulary served an additional function. It provided a much-needed bridge to the Bank's economists in a way that the traditional vocabulary of social structure, social organization, and the like didn't. While to some extent we all recognized that there was a certain amount of "old wine in new bottles" repackaging going on, the social capital framework also provided an exciting chance to put to the test a number of questions about how social organization pragmatically links with political structure and notions of political leadership. Putnam's notion that a diverse associational life provided the kinds of learning games that can translate well into different kinds of social controls on local governance passed the intuitive test of why all projects in culturally rich Bali seem to work well no matter how much the development experts screw up their designs. And given the rumblings of social change that could be heard off on the Indonesian horizon, the theory gave some direction as to why it makes sense to focus on grassroots organizing and not just national political actions, should the New Order finally be giving way to a more broad-based form of government.

The LLI studies began in 1996, when the luster of the Indonesian development may have been fraying a bit at the edges but, by and large among most Bank staff, the country's star was still shining brightly. Villagers had been the beneficiaries of thirty years of development, and numerous studies had documented the positive changes transforming the countryside as a result. I didn't quite buy into this vision—Indonesian villages didn't look all that different from the peasant villages I'd studied in Latin America—but I was having a hard time making sense of the dissonance between the glowing reports circulating in the development world and what appeared to be somewhat unimpressive results in the field. On the time-honored principle "when in doubt, commission a study," we launched LLI both to provide an empirical assessment of what was really happening in Indonesian villages and to provide a rigorous cross-country test of new thinking on social capital.

The LLI teams selected three provinces as far apart as possible—Nusa Tenggara Timur (NTT) in the east, central Java, and a newly colonized part of Sumatra, the province of Jambi—to carry out a 1,200–household survey and forty-eight village ethnographies on the nature and quality of social capital, community capacities, and village government.[14] Developing the study's methodology required a much closer relationship than the Bank's usual arm's-length relationship with consultants. Ensuring that the researchers would have the space to carry out time-consuming ethnographic research rather than rapid rural appraisals or random, easy-to-quantify surveys required the hands-on involvement of the Bank's core social staff, including repeated visits to the field sites over the course of the study.

All three LLI studies produced the same core findings.[15] The first set of questions looked at local capacity within villages, with "capacity" defined as the ability of the village to solve self-identified problems. Here the studies found that villages carry out nearly the same range and scope of projects as the government and development agencies, and that community-owned projects performed better than projects from the government or from NGOs. Community-owned projects also reflected higher participation of the poor and of women, and significantly greater contributions from the villagers themselves.

The second set of questions compared the morphology of community-owned organizations versus the organizations formed by the government for development purposes. Again there was a high contrast: Community organizations had existed for long periods of time, were multipurpose, and had played a social role beyond their immediate practical purpose. By contrast, development project organizations sprang up for specific project purposes and left behind a litter of organizational shells. Community organizations also included mechanisms that would allow members to challenge leaders and to call for reflective "breaks" should disputes remain unsettled. By contrast, development project organizations did not brook challenges to leadership, and if villagers were directly involved in them at all, it was primarily to carry out the project, not to criticize its founding assumptions. A final structural difference was that while development projects functioned at the level of the villages formed by the 1979 Village Laws, in the villages studied the effective unit of local planning was the much smaller hamlet.

The third set of findings came from looking at organizing capacity from a dynamic perspective: What led to the strengthening or weakening of capacity in communities? Here the studies point to a strong disconnect between community organizing capacities and the government. The government's bottom-up planning system was ineffective—less than 3 percent of the village proposals generated through the mandatory annual development planning process got funding—and there was no evidence that the government ever provided incentives or rewards for the communities that did manage to organize well. Most noticeably, there was apparently an inverse correlation between the presence of a project-based organization and the participation of the poor in that same activity. That is, not only were elites capturing development project organizations, but the very presence of such organizations actively undermined and weakened the organizations that the village poor joined. This finding later received statistical validation (Alatas et al. 2003).

Finally, the studies looked at cases of local development success stories. The patterns were striking. First, in the best cases, government officials from the subdistrict level made a positive difference even on community projects because they could play roles of conflict mediation, coordination, facilitation, and problem solving together with community leaders and village-based extension workers. Second, in both high-capacity and low-capacity villages, effective groups could take advantage of project schemes that provided them with funds, clear accountability rules, and the space to implement their own projects without interference. Third, communities benefited from strong leadership and somebody who could play a facilitating role to share information, invoke dispute resolution procedures, and help villagers find external assistance when it was needed. Finally, there were a number of cases where villagers formed alliances with civil society groups operating at the level of the district.[16] In such cases, outside organizations could provide access to technology or engineering skills, and, more important, they could curb problems of corruption or other abuses of authority.

It is important to be clear about the challenges that LLI raised to the familiar ways of doing community development projects in Indonesia. Standard project designs recognized many though not all of the prob-

lems turned up by the LLI teams, but they treated them as *technical* problems that could be solved with more technical assistance, better fiduciary
controls, and tighter supervision by project managers. By contrast, the LLI
studies suggested that these methods could *never* lead to sufficient
improvement because the root of the problem lay with the fundamental
assumptions being made about projects, about villages, and about the
implementing agencies themselves. What was needed was a radical
departure away from the model of "projects as tools for resource delivery"
and toward a framework where projects provided resources and opportunities, and communities could make their own interpretations and adjustments—that is, away from a construct that sees projects as something that
delivers a particular product and toward a model that sees projects as a
way to trigger and support a process that helps villagers solve self-identified
development problems.

The LLI studies served an additional purpose that sounds like a minor
side benefit but is highly relevant to the purposes of this volume. Whereas
standard World Bank contact with villages is through one-off visits to
supervise the quality of project-funded infrastructure, with the LLI team
there was an entire pool of reasonably well-studied villages that would
reveal a far from ordinary story to visiting World Bank officials. Fortunately, the World Bank's president, James Wolfensohn, had recently
launched his "spend a week in a village" reeducation program for World
Bank staff, so ambitious Washington managers were on the lookout for
opportunities to write movingly eloquent back-to-office reports on how
they had directly experienced the lives of the poor.

I remember the first time I was able to accompany the World Bank's
Country Director—the Bank's top official working on Indonesia—to one
of the LLI villages in central Java. Aside from me, nobody from the Bank
or the government joined the field trip. We had planned to stay for two
days, including overnighting in the house of one of the villagers, where
we would get a debriefing from the field team, who were just finishing up
their interviews.

We arrived toward the end of the rainy season. On one side of the
highway the land was flooded; on the other side it was suffering from
drought. The contractor who built the highway had ignored the design
requirements to build culverts so that water could drain across the barrier
formed by the newly built road. As a result, farmers on both sides of the
road had lost their crops. We next walked to an irrigation drain, where two
farmers were prying open a large iron gate. Our hopes of hearing a song
of thanks for bringing precious irrigation to the fields were dashed when
one of the farmers explained that what they were actually doing was trying to tear down the gates, which had been so poorly hung that they were
causing saltwater intrusions into their fields. (Fortunately, it was a project
funded by the Asian Development Bank). And so it went: Water supply
projects had stopped producing water just weeks after the NGO that pro-

vided them left; a health clinic had no medicine because it was being rented out to a television-watching rental business owned by the village head's family; and a dam safety project's quality was so poor that the engineers overseeing the reservoir re-lining fled under cover of night so that the villagers wouldn't catch them. Stories like these lasted well into the night, with villagers and our young research team laying bare for our visiting director just how different life in the villages was from the descriptions in the reports arriving on her desk.

Other opportunities for Bank managers to contrast the reports with the reality of village life followed. My personal favorite picked up on an LLI finding that one reason (not the only one) why village schools were in such bad shape was that many districts had passed regulations prohibiting village groups from maintaining primary schools and clinics, requiring instead that all maintenance be done by district contractors. After passing through the seventh village studded with collapsed government school buildings that were surrounded by immaculately maintained private houses and gardens, a Bank director (whose professional background was in research on educational economics) who joined us on a long slog through fifteen poor villages in west Java commented that he was starting to get some sense of an emerging pattern. Amusingly enough, the only reply from the Minister of Education, to whom he passed his field report, was that his sample wasn't statistically representative.[17]

Building the Kecamatan Development Project

LLI described the problem of community development primarily as one of changing the development project process. That is, the problem with projects lay not with *what* they did, but with how they did it, whatever "it" was. Top-down needed to change to bottom-up, or, as we phrased it for the internal market, projects needed to respond to community demand, not to agency supply. Turning the findings from forty-eight village studies into a nationwide development project required a giant leap across disciplinary and cultural boundaries, from the world of critical research to the world of projects. Fortunately, there were several stepping-stones along the way.

What always strikes me about KDP is how simple the core design is. Stripped to its essentials, the entire project consists of little more than a disbursement system linked to a facilitated planning and management procedure. Financial records are kept in bare-bones format, and no form in KDP is more than three pages long. (By way of contrast, the standard contract required on development projects is a minimum of eighty pages of densely packed legal language.) Unlike most projects, KDP has virtually no "content," no specification about the kinds of groups that can join the project and the kinds of proposals they can make.[18]

This simplicity is no accident. Indonesia is one of the world's most diverse countries. Virtually any assumption about what the social content of the project should be would prove to be wrong for big swaths of the population. While at the time there was no alternative and several advantages to using the formal administrative system—the kecamatan—as the project's formal management unit, making the project's focus the community planning process itself provides virtually unlimited scope for allowing communities to adjust the project to local conditions.

Since the fall of the New Order government and the subsequent resurgence of regionalism across the country, communities increasingly alter, revise, and improve the way they go about developing proposals. Several provinces have produced their own operational manuals, which typically replace the kecamatan with the *negari*, *mukim*, or *marga* in West Sumatra, Aceh, and North Sumatra, respectively. Kecamatans have also introduced a rich diversity of variants on the core design. Of special interest are their proposals for adding different "wise people" to the village and kecamatan councils, people outside the government whose job is to ensure transparency, mediate disputes, and certify to villagers who could not attend the meeting that their proposal was reviewed fairly.

Why kecamatans? Working in subdistricts rather than further down the system, in villages, or further up the system, in districts, was a critical initial gamble. Kecamatans are one of those "neither fish nor fowl" administrative units that crop up in large rural countries where the formal administrative units are either too big or too small. Districts see the kecamatan as a technical outpost where the district head can post a representative and where managers from some of the line agencies that need to be in regular touch with villages (that is, education, rural extension agents) can supervise their field staff. LLI showed that villagers saw the kecamatan as the last level of government that they could approach, because they could travel back and forth to the kecamatan reasonably easily, and also because the sociological distance between villagers and a kecamatan official was a lot less than the distance they experienced when entering the powerful and intimidating district office complexes.

Kecamatans seemed advantageous for reasons above and beyond their relative accessibility to villagers. Because they were not a fully autonomous unit of government, they had no budget and contracting powers of their own. This meant that the collection of commercial and political interests that maintained a stranglehold over government in the districts was much weaker in the subdistricts. There was also a requirement to "coordinate" village development through a kecamatan council that included all of the village heads, but because the kecamatan had no budget of its own to invest, most of these councils met only once or twice a year. Still, there was a statutory basis for working with councils rather than executive branch administrators. And last, having villagers compete for KDP funds in kecamatan meetings would, we hoped, encourage the kinds of direct negotiations and cooperation that would provide a basis for rebuilding the supra-village horizontal institutions destroyed or neglected by the New Order.

From a project design perspective, the two key stumbling blocks facing the development of a program to support village planning were how to get the money to the villagers without going through the government transfer system, and how to introduce facilitators who were not part of the government bureaucracy. Neither concept was entirely alien to government development planners. For all of their flaws, the poverty programs of the early 1990s had, in fact, worked on the basis of a block grant–like system with each village receiving a flat amount of 20 million rupiahs. Furthermore, the annual national development planning process, though dysfunctional, meant that large numbers of people were already familiar with the idea of development planning. KDP's only apparent twist to this system was that rather than have the plans flow to the center for aggregation and review, the funds to support them would move down the system, directly from the center to the villages.[19]

Contracting consultants outside of the bureaucracy to work in villages was not entirely unprecedented either. A genuinely innovative predecessor of KDP called the Village Infrastructure Project, also assisted by the World Bank, assigned to clusters of villages a consultant engineer who would help them manage small road, bridge, and water supply projects. KDP borrowed quite a bit from this program, particularly the operational manuals and financial management formats, although it again introduced a twist to the idea of the consultants who support villagers by specifying that they should first and foremost be people familiar with general social facilitation, as recommended by the LLI studies, rather than exclusively engineers.[20]

KDP's third building block was in some ways the most problematic. Everyone can agree in principle that promoting transparency in development projects is a great idea; yet the collective wisdom on how best to do this in thousands of rural villages is extremely limited. KDP relies on two kinds of mechanisms, neither of which works perfectly and both of which pose interesting challenges for anyone interested in carrying out a community development project.

The first consists of the internal rules and procedures that promote transparency. At the national level, these can include requirements to publish audit reports, adopt project transparency policies, and release procurement committee reports. Procedures used within villages can also promote transparency; a KDP example is the requirement that all suppliers present their quotes in public meetings, not through sealed bids given to local officials. As the example opening this chapter shows, KDP's requirement to post all financial information on signboards displayed in public places is a sharp departure from practices of the past.

It is important to note that these examples are applications of the formal rules and requirements that any project lays down in its operational manuals; they are not examples of winning the hearts and minds of a constituency eager for more transparency in development. Yet with bureaucracies, the formal rules are key tools: That single instruction from the Ministry of Home Affairs to post project budgets on signboards in public places led to 20,000 villages knowing for the first time just what their daily wage entitlement was for work on a government development project.

The other main mechanism used to promote transparency in KDP is simply to increase the number of nongovernmental actors involved in the project. Rather than invent entirely new "stakeholder fora" or the like, KDP uses the existing administrative institutions of government but requires that communities elect additional representatives at each level whose job is to monitor transactions and report to the community at large. At the national level, the government contracts independent NGOs to monitor each province, and it has also managed a "blind" contract with the Association of Independent Journalists to investigate and publish, without any prior review, stories of KDP performance in the villages.

It is impossible to avoid pausing here for an anecdote. The blind contract with the journalists is actually a legally binding condition of the project, which means that project funds from the World Bank cannot flow without its being followed. Surprising as this is by itself, what is even more surprising is that at the time the condition was written, the Association of Independent Journalists was legally banned by a government all too aware of the threat posed by an independent press. And yet the condition was not a last-minute afterthought slipped into the legal documents without the government's awareness; it was discussed and finalized with a very sophisticated negotiating team that spent two days in detailed review of each clause in the project loan documents. It would be hard to find a clearer example of the contradictions of government policy at the end of the New Order era.

The final building blocks for KDP have been the new or reformulated institutions created by Indonesia's ongoing decentralization program, primarily the ones that provide some checks and balances on the overly powerful and unaccountable executive positions of the New Order. KDP's initial strategy to improve the quality of local governance was simply to increase the involvement and awareness of people who joined the village and kecamatan meetings where decisions about the project were made. Project staff and their World Bank advisers were unconvinced that the new groupings were more than just new platforms for domination by the familiar village and district elites. But the second round of LLI studies in 2000–2001 documented that *reformasi* had triggered unexpected changes in a large number of villages across the country. Many of the old leadership dynasties were out; the new village leaders and councils had been democratically elected and were indeed more responsive to village needs.

Providing support to help the new leaders do their jobs is a constructive intervention that KDP can carry out well provided that it stays flexible enough to match its support with local capacities (Ministry of Home Affairs 2002).

How well has KDP performed? Clearly, it is too soon to make any definitive assessment of KDP's impacts on local governance, nor can KDP effects be convincingly extracted from other events more closely linked to Indonesia's tumultuous political economy. While this is not the place to enumerate all of the project's flaws, it is worth highlighting some of the main problems, particularly the unexpected ones. Nobody expected a highly participatory project implemented through a bureaucracy nurtured on top-down development to be smooth sailing, and many of the initial problems involve various attempts by line agencies and local government to "explain" to the villagers what their best development choices are. Unpunished corruption is also an anticipated but always disconcerting event.[21] The quality of central government management of the project has been erratic, ranging from highly supportive and helpful for solving problems, to causing long delays because of in-house squabbling and inefficiency.

Other problems have been less predictable. We clearly had not appreciated just how effective the New Order restriction on access to villagers had been at preventing the development of a cadre of facilitators skilled at community development. Both the quality of facilitators and the practicality of the training programs provided through the project have been problematic. While there is some exciting innovation taking place in the field, for the most part facilitators see themselves as contractors whose job is to implement project manuals, not to enable local responses to development problems.

How powerful local contractors are is another unanticipated finding. KDP itself can resist most attempts to impose contractors rather than use village labor on projects, but this is only because there is a strong project in place to back the villagers. When local governments adopt their own version of KDP, which many now do because of its local popularity, very first to go are the limits on using contractors. While there are some cases where contractors can bring in machinery and technologies not available to the villagers, by and large contract management remains poor, non-transparent, and resistant to any form of redress for poor-quality work. This continued reliance on contractors does not bode well for the long-term sustainability of KDP.

KDP faces a number of dynamic challenges in coming to grips with decentralization and the revival of traditional (*adat*) institutions. *Adat* varies greatly in its rules and strength, but across the country very few *adat* institutions are especially democratic when it comes to the voices of the poor or openness to the participation of women. In many cases, KDP has found ways to negotiate with leadership so that the program can work within the *adat* umbrella and still remain inclusive, but all such arrangements are ad hoc. It is too soon to tell how many of the new restrictions will become formalized and what opportunities are available to work out more progressive accommodations.[22]

Finally, KDP's record at reaching the very poorest of the poor is at best mixed. The program's approach of negotiating decisions through group meetings carries limits to involving the highly vulnerable. Many of these problems could be overcome with better training for facilitators and a more flexible planning structure that would allow intensive training in small groups. But KDP's design and management structure are too rigid to allow this on a large scale. A pilot program in four provinces run by a strong women's advocacy NGO to help organize widows so they can collectively rejoin group decision making has shown that positive solutions to the problem of subvillage poverty targeting are possible, but without significant changes to its management design, KDP will not be the structure for accomplishing it.

Nevertheless, the anecdotal body of evidence that KDP pries open stuck doors is large and growing. Three domains have been of particular interest. First, the significant participation of women in KDP processes stands out, and this separates KDP from both standard development projects and traditional *adat* decision making. Of course, women's participation in KDP varies from sitting mutely against the back wall of the village meeting hall to equal participation in all parts of the process. Evidence on changes is both quantitative and anecdotal.[23] There are a few cases where all of the women's proposals in a kecamatan are funded and none of the men's are. There are even anecdotal reports of spillovers from KDP to *adat*, such as an unverified case in Nias where the wife of a village chief marched into a community meeting and declared that if she and the other women could co-manage KDP discussions, they could damn well sit in the *adat* councils too. We still do not know if what followed was just a stunned silence or genuine acquiescence, but field staff continue to report a major change in the gender makeup of village meetings.

The second notable domain where change can be seen is in the area of corruption—both its incidence and the tolerance of villagers for it. Infrastructure built through KDP costs significantly less than roads and bridges built by public agencies and traditional projects, even controlling for quality and technical sophistication. While some of KDP's lower costs can be attributed to very high voluntary labor contributions from the villagers, most of the cost savings are due to KDP's use of transparency and social controls. That per-unit costs of KDP construction are so much lower than the costs through public agencies is not going unnoticed by other levels of government, which under the new decentralized administration must worry about fiscal efficiency and delivering goods in time for elections.

But more interesting than the "facts" of corruption are the perceptions of it and an understanding of the triggers that would make villagers act to end it. A Bank-funded study called "Justice for the Poor" documents villagers' willingness to pursue corruption cases in KDP using both informal and formal dispute resolution procedures. Nearly 1,400 cases of financial abuse of different kinds were reported over the project's first three years;[24] in nearly half of them, most or all of the money was recovered. KDP villagers are surprisingly vocal, and as confidence that there will be a response to their complaints grows, villagers file more and more reports of abuses by officials that would have been hushed up in the past.[25]

The third domain is the revival of interest in village and kecamatan meetings tied to issues of governance. Village meetings in Indonesia are usually attended only by a core elite, while the kecamatan forum is in most places close to defunct. But in KDP areas attendance at both levels is usually high, with as many as 60 to 100 people joining the village meetings and 200 to 300 villagers making the trip to the kecamatan decision forum. Having a focal point between villagers and government has a number of immediate benefits. In Java in particular, growing numbers of technical agencies and parliamentarians are attending kecamatan meetings to review programs and meet constituents. Another possible spillover benefit currently being studied by KDP is the apparent pattern in which villages that have gone through kecamatan negotiations are less likely to be subject to the ethnic and religious disputes that have ripped apart large areas of Indonesia's Outer Islands (see Smith 2003).

To what extent these changes carry over into other areas of community decision making will be the true test of KDP's success or failure. KDP's village and kecamatan facilitators are the key actors who can break through the informational monopolies that have constrained village development, but over time their role should become less essential as people assimilate KDP's patterns into routine action. There is some evidence that this is happening, and even more evidence that where it does happen, it will be resisted. KDP's current phase seeks to give the reformed village and kecamatan councils a foundation in the legal structure created by the decentralization laws, but it remains an open question whether they can avoid slipping back into the authoritarian traditions of rural politics.

KDP continues to evolve, and we all continue to learn from its mistakes and many inadequacies. From being an innovative project idea intended to test some hypotheses about social capital in development, KDP is now at risk of being mainstreamed in both Indonesia and the World Bank, with all the rigidities and complacencies that mainstreaming entails. Nor does KDP replace in any way the need for a more fundamental restructuring of state-society relationships in Indonesia. But the project does show that even within the narrow confines of large international organizations, there are ways to do development differently.

Reflection

This chapter has argued that the participation of social researchers in the shaping and management of KDP has made a difference in how the project has developed. The LLI and other ethnographic studies demonstrate that direct support to local organizations is a better starting point for community development projects than working through the official hierarchy. But even the LLI findings would have made little impact without a way to express the language of social research in a vocabulary that can be assimilated by a development institution.[26] The core argument here, which I hope has been made without too much self-justification, is that to have social specialists sitting in the belly of the beast has allowed a translation of ethnographic findings into project designs and mechanisms that would not have happened otherwise.

This discussion has also tried to explain how a project like the Kecamatan Development Program came to exist. Historical developments in Indonesia and the World Bank created a dynamic that opened the door for a national community development program that is at once aimed at transferring resources to poor villages and contributing to the re-working of state-society relationships in Indonesia.

Yet the motivations behind KDP varied among the different players involved, a point that is important. Much modern writing on development emphasizes the importance of "stakeholder ownership" to the success of a project. But the KDP that the government owns is not quite the same KDP as the one supported by the Bank. Senior ministers in government support KDP because it builds large amounts of infrastructure in hard-to-reach areas, because it disburses its funds faster than any other project supported by the World Bank in Indonesia, and because it requires next to no pre-financing from the national treasury. The Bank's management likes it because it provided a way to engage poverty and governance reform at a time when its portfolio of lending to Indonesia had shrunk by 75 percent. Bank staff like it because it is very rewarding to hear villagers openly state that they like a project and that this one is different from development approaches they have encountered previously.

In this section, I would like to reflect on my own role in this process, since I was both team leader for the LLI studies and, until recently, what the World Bank calls a Task Manager—the project head—for the KDP program. Although to talk about oneself in a chapter that purports to present an analysis of a historical case (at least while the author is still alive) is what Indonesians call *malu*, it would be disingenuous for me to pretend that the team leader was just someone I happened to interview in passing!

An understanding of the role that social science discourse has played in the Bank's Indonesia program begins not in Jakarta, but in Washington. There is no question that any of the changes that have taken place in the Indonesia program would not have been possible without the social awareness of Bank president James Wolfensohn. And, as noted earlier, much of the overall impetus to reform the Bank came from the growing criticism of international groups who no longer accepted the Bank's self-perpetuating calculations of the costs and benefits of giant development schemes.

Responses within the Bank to these pressures varied. The World Bank's Indonesia team responded to the criticism of its resettlement management by forming a social and environmental impact unit staffed by four core staff members who reported directly to the Country Director. By contrast, the Bank's India Department, which had received even more criticism for its deviations from World Bank resettlement policy, confined itself to carrying out further internal reviews, with no structural change to its internal team organization.

In Indonesia's case, the decision to form a free-standing social and environmental impact unit meant that there were individuals within the organization who had an immediate interest in opening channels to critical groups in Indonesian civil society—groups who had previously been closed to the idea of contact with the Bank and who were generally bypassed by Bank staff members. My own experience on the Bankwide resettlement review had been a good lesson in the value of external alliances for introducing unpopular changes in the organization (cf. Fox and Brown 1998). Activities undertaken during the group's first years included reviews of NGO operating environments; land policy in traditional communities, parks, and other protected areas; and a series of meetings between Bank president Wolfensohn and leading members of Indonesia's civil society and growing human rights movement.

Reflecting on the KDP experience, there were four specific challenges to the standard project model where familiarity with social science made a direct contribution. The first of these was something that lies at the heart of anthropology: the continuing tradition of ethnographic fieldwork. Ethnography is often treated in the literature as a particularly anthropological methodology, but this to me seems incorrect. It is far more accurately defined as an epistemology, a way of knowing reality that is different from that of the deductive disciplines (see, e.g., Geertz 1971; Wolf 1964). KDP "appropriated" the Local Institutions Study's ethnography not just by using its findings on local capacity, but also by making the core planning question one of how a development project can provide the space for the insider's point of view.

For the case of the World Bank in Indonesia, legitimating ethnography as a style of inquiry was a two-step process. One step required the immersion of trained social researchers in villages for a time sufficient to allow them to unravel at least some of the complicated relationships and histories that underlie individual events. But it was just as important to be able to translate those findings into a language that could be grasped by the Bank and government officials in charge of development. For that, the field visits proved to be key.[27] Field-based research of differing quality and depth has now spread to several other areas of Bank work in Indonesia.[28]

The second specific challenge lies in the explicit focus of KDP on the political institutions of community development. KDP is not about how to help government agencies bring development to villages, nor is it a way to simply give resources to village organizations. The project focuses on the relationship between villagers and the state, and it uses the institutions of both.[29] KDP begins with a focus on both the social capital embedded within local culture and social structure, but over time it increasingly concentrates on moving upward, toward what Woolcock (1998) has called the "linking social capital" that would bind well-grounded community organizations into a healthier relationship with the organizations of a democratic state.

Nevertheless, the social capital vocabulary proved to be too limited. The argument of this chapter is that KDP emerged in a context of institutional crisis, when Indonesia, the World Bank, and community institutions all faced internal contradictions of a kind that the standard development toolkit could not help resolve. The language and concepts of social capital, so useful in inter-village negotiations over how to agree peacefully that one village's project was more important to fund this year than was its neighbor's, could not address the complex question of why anyone would want to do such a thing at all.

The third challenge has been to introduce the idea of historical process to Bank analyses of local politics and local economies. Very few people, for example, realized the extent to which the villages they visited for their projects were the creation of a 1979 law on village structure; still fewer were aware that the lamentable loss of traditional mechanisms for social control was the direct outcome of development interventions meant to improve on them. Today there is much more humility and uncertainty inherent in the Bank's program; people are both conscious of their own mixed history and also well aware that there aren't any simple formulas that can predict where Indonesia will go next.

The fourth, though certainly not the final, challenge is whether a large-scale development project can respond to the problem raised most articulately by James Scott in *Seeing Like a State* (1998). Scott argued that the rising power of modern states and the expansion of bureaucratic modes of development cannot help but "flatten" complex social realities into homogeneous bits that bureaucracies can understand, count, and control. Resistance to this flattening is the root source of the tension between community views of development and what development agencies propose, and it explains why so many programs fail to engage the hearts and minds of their putative beneficiaries.

As noted throughout this analysis, for KDP the jury is still out on whether state-run development projects inherently provoke resistance, which in any case will not be determined by whether one individual project "works" or not. But dealing with this contradiction through the design and management of KDP has certainly made the problem a vivid one. KDP could not function without its operational manual, disbursement system, poverty targeting criteria, and innumerable "coordination teams." Each one of these components flattens villages in the way Scott describes: KDP villages twenty kilometers from Jakarta use the same formats, planning cycle, and facilitator structure as villages in the jungles of Papua.

At the same time, KDP is built on the premise that giving villagers resources, information, and a voice in decision making will also give them some tools to resist the flattening and to negotiate better outcomes for themselves. To my mind, for all of the many insights that Scott's argument generates, the problem itself is somewhat misphrased because it again abstracts "states" and "villages" from a historical context that involves many other players. KDP probably can help level the villagers' playing field in their encounters with the current version of the Indonesian state *if* it is part of a more general process of social change. The most promising political outcome from KDP is not just that the program helps support local forms of organizing, but that in a growing number of cases villagers learn entirely new ways to engage state actors, as the story that opened this chapter showed, and this is also because Indonesia's state actors are going through a historical transformation of their own.

In the end, I think that structural determination of the type built into Scott's and others' arguments probably oversimplifies things a bit too much. Indonesians have a choice. Whether KDP continues to do more for reform than for flattening depends on changes taking place in Indonesia at large. But it also depends on whether the people involved in KDP decide to throw their lines toward other people involved in the reform movement or whether the project remains a generally good way to manage a state-run community development program.

Concluding Remarks

So there you have it, warts and all.[30] KDP's innovations and on-the-ground performance should not be overestimated, and this narrative perhaps does not give full voice to the problems and difficulties that can make project work so frustrating. Corruption; authoritarianism; incompetence; resistance to change, to involving the poor, and to the participation of women—KDP provides almost as many grounds for interpreting the failures of development projects as it does for studying the potential for change.

As we approach the end of this discussion, it might be useful to reca-pitulate the underlying premises, strengths, and weaknesses of the pro-gram, at least from the perspective of community development in a transitional time in Indonesia's history. I hope that two core arguments have stood out in this review. The first is the extent to which KDP is a product of a particular set of histories. KDP came about at least in part because the project concept provided a way out for powerful institutions that were each facing a major crisis of credibility. Reforming community development met a perceived need in each of the institutions involved in formulating the program, and it also provided a way to introduce new notions of process into a development model that had bypassed it. For these very same reasons, we can expect KDP to become obsolete, and indeed, in some areas it is possible to see how KDP could be a step back-ward rather than the beacon of progress it likes to think that it is.[31]

The second argument threaded through this discussion is that a development project like KDP can contribute to a reordering of local political relationships. The New Order's model for development obviated political process as a foundation for programs that require local adapta-tion and ownership. Cast in the language of participation, transparency, and accountability, KDP has been a wager that Indonesia's reform will succeed in moving away from the development authoritarianism of the New Order government toward a model built on representative institu-tions. The tale of the white shroud for the unwanted lumber that began this discussion shows that villagers have their own moral economy of development.[32] Whether and how much stories like these multiply depend on developments far outside the control of KDP or the villagers, but small steps forward matter. KDP's underlying premise has been that villagers learn about democracy by practicing it. The avid interest shown by villagers across Java in the stories about officials who were jailed for stealing KDP funds testifies to their wish to believe that their actions count.

Late in 2002 I was visiting Aceh to see how the ill-fated cessation-of-hostilities agreement would play itself out in that beautiful but battered landscape. It wasn't my first visit there; I'd been to Aceh several times when the project was starting so that I could help the KDP facilitators plot a neutral path between the government and rebels. We always made a point of joining those early village meetings to repeat the message that they and only they could decide how to use their KDP funds. During those first visits I would at times be taken aback (and a bit amused) by the toughness of the questioning. "Why should we believe you?" seemed to be the dominant theme, and indeed, the story of development in these broken villages was an unending tale of broken promises and barely disguised theft.

But now we were sitting on the tiled floor outside of the village mosque drinking young coconut juice and lazily swatting flies as the villagers walked us through their record books and pictures. They still seemed a bit suspicious, as if I were one last hurdle, come to snatch back the money or to tell them that they had done a rotten job designing the stone road that now led from their bright green *sawah* to the town market. But the frowns smoothed into smiles as we talked about how they had decided who would be the village facilitators for KDP, and how the whole village had joined in laying the stones for the road.

I knew one of the old women who was talking from the time of my first visit to this village. She was a tough old crank who would very disconcertingly interrupt conversation to lean over and spit tobacco juice on the ground. The last time we spoke she either had had an exceptionally large plug of juicy tobacco in her mouth or else was even more expressive than the rest of the village as they had listened to us explain that KDP's fate lay entirely in their hands. So I decided to ask her straight out whether she thought KDP had done anything worthwhile or whether it was just more meaningless words and promises. She looked at me for a long, long while before the shadow of a smile cracked her wrinkled face. "Not bad," she said. "Not bad at all."

Notes

1. This story was related by Enurlaela Hasanah.
2. Even though much of this discussion is written in the first person, the analysis, the ethnography, and the project are from the product of a very large number of people, only some of whom can be acknowledged here. Michael Cernea not only survived his mentoring me for many years in the ways of giant bureaucracies, but his writings on social organization as "entry points" for development shaped much of my own thinking. Ben Fisher, now retired, was the founder of the Bank's Social and Environmental Group for Indonesia. Gloria Davis led the three-country Local Level Institutions study. Team leaders for the LLI study were Kamala Chandrakirana, Pieter Evers, Kastorius Sinaga, Leni Dharmawan, Anna Wetterberg, Silvia Werner, Yando Zakaria, and Erwin Fahmi. Anna Wetterberg deserves a special acknowledgment. Ibnu Taufan, Muhammed Roesli, Sentot Satria, Enurlaela Hasanah, Susan Wong, Sri Kuntari, Steven Burgess, Linda Citra, Taufik Rinaldi, Richard Gnagey, Victor Bottini, and Nani Zulminarni are daily contributors to KDP. Herman Haeruman, Tatag Wiranto, Bito Wikantosa, Samsul Widodo, Ayip Muflich, and the late Pramono provided critical insights into how the government sees community development. Thanks for comments on drafts of this paper go to Kamala Chandrakirana, Sarah Cliffe, Leni Dharmawan, Cyprian Fisiy, Enurlaela Hasanah, Richard Manning, Lant Pritchett, and Susan Wong.

3. For a particularly fine summary of KDP that provides many more details on its design and performance, see the first-phase evaluation report, *Kecamatan Development Program Phase One Final Report, 1998–2002*. It is available from the Ministry of Home Affairs, Community Development Agency, in both Indonesian and English.

4. A short negative list excludes items such as paying official salaries, purchasing weapons, planting tobacco, and buying pesticides.

5. "Districts" is the translation of *kabupaten*, which are also called "regencies" in the literature. Indonesian districts are quite large, with as many as two or three million inhabitants, although one million is closer to the norm for Java.

6. A summary of the structural changes to KDP between 1998 and 2003 is provided in the Project Appraisal Document for the Third Kecamatan Development Project, available on the World Bank web site, www.worldbank.org

7. KDP also provides technical assistance for villagers seeking legal redress; by 2002 at least twelve government officials had been fined or jailed for unauthorized uses of KDP funds on the basis of complaints brought by villagers.

8. A key insight into why New Order mass development programs is in Lant Pritchett and Jessica Poppele's poverty report (World Bank 2000), where they argue that the design of the highly centralized New Order development agencies should be compared to that of the equally centralized armed forces. National programs such as school building or immunization campaigns could be delivered through centralized military-like campaigns. Programs requiring local adaptation or close attention to quality rather than quantity were simply beyond the capabilities of organizations designed for mass, standardized delivery.

9. The 2001 Corruption Perception Index (CPI), released by Transparency International in June 2001, ranks Indonesia as eighty-eighth in a survey of ninety-one countries, above only Nigeria and Bangladesh (Transparency International 2001). The survey is a "poll of polls" from various different sources and attempts to measure perceptions of corruption across countries.

10. Within the World Bank, the single biggest impetus was the traumatic events associated with the Narmada River development projects. Public criticism reached such a pitch that the World Bank's then president, Barber Conable, commissioned an independent review chaired by Bradford Morse, a former UNDP administrator. Unfortunately, for the most part the independent review confirmed the criticism, particularly with respect to the poor planning for the 200,000-plus people who would be involuntarily resettled by the project (Morse and Berger 1992). A follow-up internal review of World Bank projects necessitating resettlement, produced by a team led by Michael Cernea and myself (1994), documented the pervasiveness of the resettlement problem and the failure to ensure that people displaced by Bank-financed projects would receive compensation sufficient to restore their lost living standards.

11. "Hamlet" here is the translation of *dusun*, a co-residential spatial unit below the village level. Hamlets are not part of Indonesia's formal public administration.

12. Strictly speaking, traditional *adat* institutions were not banned outright from having a role in local governance; regulations specified that *adat* mechanisms

could play a role in local government only if they contributed to Pancasila, supported national stability, and were guided by the government (see Evers 2000).

13. Between 1976 and 1991 alone, Indonesia's census figures show that the country went from 26 to 45 percent urban.

14. Research was conducted in two districts in each of the three provinces, selected with the objective of pursuing relationships in different local institutional, geophysical, and political contexts. The research was conducted in two phases. The first phase, which occurred prior to KDP, was conducted between 1996 and 1997. It involved a 1,200-household survey and forty-eight village mini-ethnographies on the nature and quality of social capital, community capacities, and village government; this study team also constructed a unique database of more than 800 village development projects classified by type, quality, coverage, and other criteria. The same villages and households were studied in 2001, after the economic crisis and fall of the New Order government. Six-week mini-ethnographies were conducted in five villages, followed by week-long rapid-appraisal exercises in all forty villages and a 1,200-household re-surveying of the original panel. (The follow-up study had one fewer district than the original because of civil unrest and natural disasters in West Timor.)

15. This section draws heavily on the individual team reports: Evers (2001), Chandrakirana (2000), Dharmawan (2002), and Wetterberg (2005). The reports can all be located on the World Bank's Indonesia web site. See also the syntheses in Bebbington et al. (2004, 2005).

16. Political parties were banned from villages by decree, and few NGOs were given the necessary permits or space to work in villages.

17. A follow-up education project in west Java that switched over to direct school grant financing for primary school construction, though far from perfect, achieved an immediate average cost reduction of 40 percent.

18. Building on LLI findings about unrooted project-created shells, however, KDP does specify that groups must have existed for at least a year. The project also includes some positive rules about an earmarked allocation for proposals from women.

19. Yogana Prasta of the World Bank's Jakarta office was the inspired person who with one sharp blow cut through the Gordian knot of Indonesian fiscal transfers to figure this disbursement system out.

20. Other innovative aspects of KDP were slightly more technical in nature and are not relevant to the discussion here. For example, KDP included methods to avoid extensive pre-financing by the government and, in later phases, a unique form of direct procurement of the facilitators. These are described in the project's formal documentation, the project appraisal report, which can be found on the Indonesia page of the World Bank web site, www.worldbank.org.

21. KDP has produced some interesting documentation on corruption and how the project recovers missing funds. See Woodhouse (2005) and the KDP Final Report (Ministry of Home Affairs 2002), both available at www.worldbank.org.

22. For example, before the latest fighting in Aceh, KDP, the NGO forum, and the leaders of *adat* institutions (*mukim*) had formed a working group to identify

opportunities to work together constructively under Aceh's special autonomy rules.

23. A proper evaluation has not yet been conducted of whether increased women's participation in KDP carries over to other cultural domains or whether—and which—villagers simply bracket KDP as something apart from local practice.

24. To give a sense of proportion, there were 55,000 subprojects.

25. An ongoing controlled experiment within KDP is quantifying corruption responses to different *kinds* of social controls by using different methods to increase villager participation; results will be posted on the World Bank and KDP web sites.

26. For example, one sympathetic World Bank economist noted, "An important part I think of the space created within the Bank for KDP was tied to the use of four terms: 'incentives,' 'competition' (between proposals), 'demand-driven' and 'budget transparency' which appealed strongly to an audience of economists within the Bank not normally convinced of pink and fluffy social projects" (personal communication).

27. The signal from the top was important in prying open the door here. J. Wolfensohn's order for managers to visit villages may in some sense sound naive, but it nevertheless made senior managers find the time to do it. Some benefited more from the experience than others, of course.

28. See, for example, S. Teggeman on field studies of corruption and the urban poor, and K. Kaiser on participatory public expenditure reviews in Aceh, for example. These can be found on the Indonesia link of the Bank web site, www.worldbank.org

29. Village-based development is, of course, not the only way to formulate this problem. The KDP model, in fact, largely excludes super-village networks and associations that may be critical institutions operating within villages.

30. For fascinating, in-depth examples of some of the warts, see Woodhouse on corruption (2005) and Zulminarni on the straitjacket of KDP's "project" mentality in her review paper manuscript "Program Pemberdayaan Perempuan Kepala Keluarga" (2003). Both papers are available in draft format on the World Bank web site.

31. KDP's rootedness in Indonesia's historical context also explains why proposals to "replicate" or "scale up" the model should be treated with great caution.

32. Anecdotes abound about how threatening authorities find KDP's disclosure rules. One subdistrict head, for example, actually passed an official regulation banning the public posting of financial information about development projects.

References

Alatas, V., L. Pritchett, and A. Wetterberg. 2003. *Voice lessons: Evidence on organizations, government mandated groups, and governance from Indonesia's local institutions study.* World Bank Policy Research Working Paper No. 2981 (March). Washington, DC: World Bank.

Bebbington, A., L. Dharmawan, E. Farmi, and S. Guggenheim. 2004. Village politics, culture and community driven development: Insights from Indonesia. *Progress in Development Studies* 4(3):187–205.

Bebbington, A., L. Dharmawan, E. Farmi, and S. Guggenheim. 2005. Local capacity, village governance and the political economy of rural development in Indonesia. *World Development* (forthcoming).

Blustein, P. 2003. *The chastening: Inside the crisis that rocked the global financial system and humbled the IMF.* New York: Public Affairs.

Buchori, C., E. Hasanah, and N. Zulminarni. 2002. *Meningkatkan partisipasi aktif perempuan.* Jakarta: World Bank.

Cernea, M., and S. Guggenheim. 1994. *Involuntary resettlement and development: The Bankwide review of projects involving involuntary resettlement, 1896–1993.* Washington, DC: World Bank.

Chandrakirana, K. 2000. Local capacity and its implications for development: The case of Indonesia. Unpublished LLI manuscript, http://www.worldbank.or.id/

De Soto, H. 1989. *The other path.* New York: Harper & Row.

Dharmawan, L. 2002. Village leadership in central Java. Unpublished manuscript, http://www.worldbank.or.id/

Evers, P. 2000. Resourceful villages, powerless communities: Rural government in Indonesia. Unpublished LLI manuscript, http://www.worldbank.or.id/

Fox, J., and D. Brown. 1998. *The struggle for accountability: The World Bank, NGOs and grassroots movements.* Cambridge, MA: MIT Press.

Geertz, C. 1971. *The interpretation of cultures.* New York: Basic Books.

Hill, H. 1996. *The Indonesian economy since 1966: Southeast Asia's emerging giant.* Cambridge: Cambridge University Press.

Ministry of Home Affairs, Community Development Agency. 2002. Kecamatan Development Program: Phase I Final Report 1998–2002. Unpublished. Jakarta, Indonesia.

Molyneaux, J., and P. Gertler. 1999. *Applying a simple method to measure program impact: An evaluation of a large scale micro-credit/poverty alleviation program in Indonesia.* Berkeley: RAND Corporation/University of California Press.

Morse, B., and T. Berger. 1992. *Sardar Sarovar: The report of the independent review.* Vancouver, BC: Resources for the Future.

Mubyarto. 1996. *Ekonomi Rakyat dan Program IDT.* Jogjakarta: Aditya Media Press.

Putnam, R. 1993. *Making democracy work: Civic traditions in modern Italy.* Princeton, NJ: Princeton University Press.

Schwarz, A. 2000. *A nation in waiting: Indonesia's search for stability.* 2nd ed. Boulder, CO: Westview Press.

Scott, J. 1998. *Seeing like a state: How certain schemes to improve the human condition have failed.* New Haven, CT: Yale University Press.

Smith, C. 2003. Conflict and conflict resolution at the local level in Indonesia: Cases from Lampung, central Kalimantan, and east Java. Unpublished manuscript, http://www.worldbank.or.id/

Transparency International. 2001. *Corruption Perception Index 2001.* Berlin: Transparency International.

Wetterberg, A. 2005. *Testing social capital theory with evidence from Indonesia.* Jakarta: World Bank

Wolf, E. 1957. Closed corporate peasant communities of MesoAmerica and central Java. *Southwestern Journal of Anthropology* 13:1–18.

Wolf, E. 1964. *Anthropology*. Englewood Cliffs, NJ: Prentice Hall.

Wolf, E. 1986. The vicissitudes of the closed corporate peasant community. *American Ethnologist* 13:325–329.

Wolf, E. 1999. *Envisioning power: Ideologies of dominance and crisis*. Berkeley: University of California Press.

Woodhouse, A. 2005. *Village corruption in Indonesia: Fighting corruption in the World Bank's Kecamatan Development Program*. Jakarta: World Bank.

Woolcock, Michael. 1998. Social capital and economic development: Toward a theoretical synthesis and policy framework. *Theory and Society* 27(2):151–208.

CHAPTER SIX

SOCIAL CAPITAL AND INDIGENOUS PEOPLES DEVELOPMENT PROGRAMS IN ECUADOR

Jorge E. Uquillas
Martien Van Nieuwkoop[1]

Introduction

The World Bank launched its Indigenous Peoples Development Initiative in Latin America in the early 1990s and has worked ever since to open new and innovative avenues of support for indigenous peoples development. Initial efforts focused on mitigation measures, training and capacity building, and pre-investment operations. Gradually, indigenous peoples development is becoming an integral part of the Bank's loan portfolio.

Ecuador's Indigenous and Afro-Ecuadorian Peoples Development Project was the direct result of this initiative. The local conditions for such a project were right both in terms of the level of organization of indigenous peoples and in terms of the readiness of the government to embark into this uncharted territory. The major national indigenous federations claim that the project was the result of their long struggle for recognition of the rights of indigenous peoples, including the right to a fairer share of fiscal resources.

The project is the first stand-alone investment operation financed by the World Bank that focuses exclusively on indigenous peoples and other ethnic minorities. It marks the first time that Ecuador has borrowed resources specifically for investments to benefit poor indigenous and Afro-Ecuadorian populations, channeling resources directly through indigenous organizations, with a minimal role of the government. It also is the first occasion that indigenous federations and the Ecuadorian government have joined forces in an effort to put into practice the vision of "development with identity," or "ethnodevelopment." This vision builds on the positive qualities of indigenous cultures and societies—such as their sense of ethnic identity, close attachment to ancestral land, and capacity to mobilize labor, capital, and other resources for the attainment of shared goals—to promote local employment and growth. It is an effort to build social capital as an asset of the poor, while at the same time working directly with that asset.

This is a complex project, involving an arduous preparation and implementation process that illustrates some of the difficulties in taking the social capital argument seriously. The project has revealed that strengthening existing organizations is not easy, that building coalitions and alliances takes a great deal of time, and that these alliances are often fragile and short-lived. Nonetheless, this project has become a flagship for other initiatives aimed at fostering community-based approaches that emphasize the notion of poor people having assets, as opposed to only deficits (World Bank 2001). That said, the Bank is still building its base of knowledge and experience in this field. This chapter distills lessons from the preparation and implementation of the project.

The Indigenous and Afro-Ecuadorian Peoples Development Project invests in local capacity building; small-scale, demand-driven rural sub-projects; land tenure regularization; cultural heritage activities; and institutional strengthening of the Council for the Development of the Nationalities and Peoples of Ecuador (*Consejo Desarrollo de las Nacionalidades y Pueblos del Ecuador*, or CODENPE). The total project budget is US$50 million: US$25 million from the World Bank, US$15 million from the International Fund for Agricultural Development, and US$10 million from the Ecuadorian government and from beneficiary communities and organizations. The project began preparation in early 1995, was approved in early 1998, and became effective in September 1998. Implementation was completed in April 2003. A second phase was prepared during 2003–2004 and was expected to become effective in 2005. However, on August, 31, 2005, the World Bank was notified by the government of Ecuador that it will not pursue the loan contract because indigenous organizations did not want the second phase financed by an external loan.[2]

The chapter proceeds as follows. The first section discusses the contexts into which the project fed. These contexts relate to the emergence of indigenous organizations in Ecuador (the second section), the policy environment in Ecuador (the third section), and the policy environment within the World Bank (the fourth section). The fifth section discusses the specific political economic and institutional conditions that made this project possible, and the sixth discusses how it operationalized its conceptual framework, particularly those parts relating to organizational strengthening. The final section contains concluding comments.

The Emergence of Indigenous Peoples as Political Actors in Ecuador

Socioeconomic Profile

Indigenous peoples and Afro-Ecuadorians are important segments of Ecuador's multicultural society. They differ from the mainstream Hispanic (white and mixed, or mestizo) population both in their degree of economic deprivation, their high level of social capital (particularly among indigenous peoples), and their cultural and social characteristics.

Indigenous and Afro-Ecuadorian peoples together represent almost 20 percent of the population, although estimates vary widely.[3] There are thirteen officially designated non-Hispanic ethnic groups or nationalities in Ecuador.[4] The largest nationality comprises the highland Quichua speakers (also known as the Runa), who constitute more than 90 percent of Ecuador's indigenous peoples. However, the Quichua, or Runa, themselves are culturally diverse, as demonstrated by the contrasts between subgroups such as the Otavalo and Saraguro, or the Chibuleo and Cañari peoples.

By the early 1990s 35 percent of Ecuador's population lived in poverty and another 17 percent were highly vulnerable to poverty.[5] Overall, the relationship between poverty, household characteristics, and social indicators varies considerably both across and within regions. Urban poverty is associated with low educational achievement, employment in the informal sector, rented housing rather than home ownership, and low rates of participation in the labor force by women. Rural poverty is associated with lack of education, little access to land, a low degree of market integration, and lack of employment in the vibrant nonfarm rural sector (World Bank 1995). Many indigenous people have moved to urban areas and in some cases have become assimilated into the dominant mestizo society. However, in rural areas they have tended to maintain their distinct identity. Ecuador's rural population of indigenous peoples and Afro-Ecuadorians is concentrated in 288 of the country's 966 *parroquias* (parishes, the smallest division in the country). This segment of the Ecuadorian population, comprising more than 1.5 million people, is associated with the country's highest indices of poverty, measured in terms of both income and unsatisfied basic needs (Tables 6.1 and 6.2). In *parroquias* with an indigenous majority, the poverty rate (including those highly vulnerable to poverty) is approximately 85 percent. This is 14 percentage points higher than the rural average, and 32 percentage points higher than the national average.

Table 6.1   Percentage of Children under 18 Years of Age Belonging to Households with Income below the Poverty Line (US$28 per month), 2002

Indigenous	79
Afro-Ecuadorian	68
White/mestizo	61
Female head	66
Male head	62
Coast	64
Highlands	60
Amazonia	70
Urban	52
Rural	79

Source: SIISE (2001)

Table 6.2   Illiteracy Rates (Proportion of the Population Age 15 and Over), 1999

Sector	Female	Male	Total
Country	13	9	11
Urban	7	4	6
Rural	23	15	19
Indigenous	53	31	43

Source: SIISE (2001)

Levels of Social Organization

In general, indigenous peoples in Ecuador suffer from economic deprivation but are well endowed in social capital (for example, organization, solidarity patterns, and shared social and cultural values). They are well organized at the grassroots, regional, and national levels. Their form of organization varies. In some cases they are principally organized along the lines of political parties and labor unions, in others by religious affiliation, and in still others directly by ethnic affiliation. This diversity of origins and organization has caused friction among regional and national federations, particularly after the 1998 Constitution elevated the legitimacy of ethnic-based organizations. However, the peoples all are part of a vibrant social process that is contributing to the revitalization of indigenous identity and leading to the formulation of new perspectives on development.

Organizations based on ethnic lines were recognized during the Incan Empire. The conquistadores tried to dismantle and destroy these organizations, and during colonial times community-based organizations were used by the Spaniards to wring taxes and labor from the indigenous population. However, the organizations persisted, and in the period following Ecuador's independence they were known as *parcialidades indígenas*. With approval of the *Ley de Organización y Régimen Comunal* in 1937, many organizations were formally recognized and became known as *comunas*. The 1964 *Ley de Reforma Agraria*, as well as reforms in 1973, specifically recognized the *comunas* as an element of Ecuadorian society.[6] Originally *comunas* were managed and held land resources jointly, but in recent years there has been a trend toward individual land ownership. However, the contributing of labor for community enterprises (*mingas*) is still common, especially for small-scale infrastructure projects.

There are about 2,500 grassroots indigenous organizations (communes, centers, and cooperatives) at the community level. By 1998 these, in turn, had engendered about 250 second-tier organizations (*organizaciones de segundo grado*, or OSGs). The OSGs may be considered associations, unions, or federations, and frequently are affiliated with provincial, regional, and national organizations. Many of the OSGs were created or promoted initially by activist church groups and sympathetic NGOs (Carroll 2002).[7]

The first effort was the building of community-level organizations, which in turn organized into higher-tier associations or local and regional federations in a pyramidal structure, ending with the formation of national federations. Illustrative of this trend is the case of the Shuar, who in the early 1960s organized at the community level as "centers" and then formed second-tier organizations called "associations," and these in turn led to the creation of the Shuar Federation. The Shuar Federation joined other ethnic federations in the eastern lowlands to form the Confederation of Amazonian Indigenous Peoples of Ecuador (*Confederación de Nacionalidades Indígenas de la Amazonia Ecuatoriana*, or CONFENIAE), which in turn joined forces with highland and coastal federations and organized the National Council of Ecuador's Indigenous Peoples (*Confederacíon de Nacionalidades Indígenas de Ecuador*, or CONAIE).[8]

In a long and arduous process over about four decades, indigenous organizations have become more complex and have also broadened their agenda. They still take measures to strengthen their own social organizations and to secure land for those communities that lack access to it. Yet their struggle has led them to question the basic political structure of the country and the development model being implemented. Currently, they advocate a peaceful transformation of the country, with the elimination of corruption at the highest levels; maintenance of state control of key national/strategic assets such as energy, oil, and communications; and provision of greater voice to social organizations representing the poor.

Indigenous organizations have become stronger and are increasingly recognized as significant actors in Ecuadorian development and politics. In the 1980s, while Latin America as a whole suffered a regression, indigenous peoples strengthened their social capital. In the 1990s they have advanced further and participated successfully in local, regional, and national politics (Cameron 2001). As a result, in the new millennium there have been several indigenous legislators in the National Congress, one of whom was the first indigenous woman to hold the office of Vice President of the Congress. After the May 2002 elections, the Pachacutik Indigenous Movement and its allies gained control of twenty-six municipalities (twelve headed by indigenous mayors) and increased indigenous representation in the municipal councils (*consejos cantonales*) and parish councils (*juntas parroquiales*). They have built on the experience of Guamote, a municipal government controlled by indigenous peoples since 1992, which has evolved into a model of indigenous governance (*poderes locales*) (for details, see Bebbington and Carroll 2000: 12–18). Guamote has been able to coordinate actions among its local indigenous federations, to establish a municipal government under indigenous control as well as a local development committee, and to create its unique version of an indigenous law-making body, the Indigenous Parliament (see also Bebbington and Perreault 1999; Torres 2001).

On top of the preceding gains, in January 2003 Colonel Lucio Gutierrez was elected President of the Republic thanks to an alliance of the Pachacutik Indigenous Movement and other center-left political parties. As a consequence, several indigenous leaders have participated in high-level offices, including ministerial-level posts.[9]

The Public Policy Environment in Ecuador

Indigenous Peoples Policies

State policy regarding indigenous peoples has not been clearly defined and has numerous ambiguities, but certain general trends may be distinguished. Since the creation of Ecuador in 1830, attempts have been made to integrate indigenous peoples into general society by promoting acculturation. However, at times certain forms of social exclusion have persisted, such as limitations on indigenous collective property, citizenship rights (for example, by denying illiterate persons the right to vote or be elected), land ownership, and the right to maintain their own form of government.

Since the 1980s there has been a gradual shift toward greater openness to the interests and demands of indigenous peoples. Although agrarian legislation has many gaps, significant progress has been made in acknowledging indigenous land rights. Bilingual education has been legitimized, with autonomous management by indigenous organizations (Selverston-Scher 2001). Opportunities have been created for the establishment and legal recognition of second- and third-tier organizations, from community associations to provincial federations to regional and national organizations. The 1998 National Constitution states that the country is multicultural and recognizes a broad array of collective rights for those self-identified as indigenous peoples and nationalities, clarifying previously recognized rights to ancestral lands and separate forms of cultural identity and self-governance, including the establishment of indigenous "jurisdictions" in areas of their domain. Moreover, the inclusion of indigenous people in national society in the context of cultural diversity is increasingly becoming a reality.

Rural Development Policies

Historically, development interventions in Ecuador have been top-down, designed and implemented by government and intermediary nongovernmental organizations (NGOs). The assumption was that the design and implementation of projects had to be done by formally trained technicians, that is, development experts. Local knowledge and capacity was thus neglected and treated as useless or nonrelevant for change. The "transfer of technology" concept pervaded both governmental and nongovernmental organizations (Uquillas 1993).

In tune with the interests of international organizations, Ecuador's state-led approaches included a wide array of models. In the 1960s the community development approach became fashionable, supported by the United Nations' International Labor Organization (ILO) and the national government under the famous Andean Mission. In the 1970s approaches to rural development were more ambitious, among them the integrated rural development and regional development projects, which were usually associated with agrarian reform and/or irrigation schemes. Some areas of Ecuador, such as Guamote, Jipijapa, and Salcedo, have been the objects of consecutive regional or rural development projects. The beneficiaries were again rural people, either those who participated in land distribution or those who benefited from new irrigation sources. The objective was usually to transform whole regions, converting them into models of development to be replicated in similarly endowed areas. Local people, as beneficiaries, often had little involvement in the preparation of the proposed projects.

Other projects that used the same approach were the agricultural development projects, characterized by the "transfer of technology" mentality, whereby knowledge about new varieties of plants and animals and the use of agricultural inputs (chemical fertilizers and pesticides) was the domain of university-trained scientists. Poor farmers, in contrast, were supposed to exchange their old-fashioned/backward technology for the new. Most of these projects promoted better varieties of wheat and maize and improved animal husbandry. In the same period, NGOs appeared as intermediary organizations between the state and the population. They were either providing technical assistance to rural people or advocating local people's rights. Although participatory approaches were increasingly used, they were usually limited to the sharing of information and consultations, with little feedback to local people.

The application of these new development approaches, aiming at achieving a better distribution of land, water resources, and agricultural production knowledge, had a strong impact in rural areas. Indigenous peoples in particular benefited greatly from these efforts. The new development projects helped indigenous peoples organize, first to obtain land titles and then to administer large water irrigation schemes or to work on agricultural development projects. With the oil boom of the 1970s, Ecuadorian peasants enjoyed greater access to improved seeds, fertilizers, and methods of pest control, inputs that had long been denied them.

The infusion of financial resources and technology had a great impact on indigenous people's capacities, assets, and organization. However, not all of the impacts were positive. Along with the emphasis on new knowledge and technology came a disregard for the value of traditional knowledge. New commodities were introduced, and traditional varieties of crops were gradually replaced by the new hybrids. Old cultural patterns of production and consumption were labeled as backward and tended to disappear.[10] In addition, some development initiatives such as the opening of roads in the coastal and Amazon lowlands had deleterious effects on native peoples and their environment. Their lands and forests were threatened, as were the indigenous peoples themselves and their cultures.

The new trend viewed physical assets as more important than cultural assets (World Bank 2000). The transformation favored the appearance of new, development-oriented social organizations commanded by young people, many of whom had been trained by the Catholic and Protestant churches (Partridge and Uquillas 1996). The role of traditional authorities became negligible. The new organizations emphasized sociopolitical aims and, besides the objective of building social capital, had as their main goal to compete for physical assets, especially the land rights of their people, as a basic condition for cultural survival and development.

The World Bank and Indigenous Peoples

In the early 1990s the World Bank's approach to indigenous peoples in Latin America was oriented primarily toward fulfilling the conditions of its Operational Directive 4.20 on Indigenous Peoples. This policy stresses the need for the informed participation of indigenous peoples and the minimization, avoidance, or compensation of any adverse effects on indigenous peoples by development interventions financed by the Bank. Particular efforts were directed toward securing the land tenure rights of indigenous peoples in those projects that threatened their territories, particularly large infrastructure projects (Wali and Davis 1992). This approach resulted in the preparation of Indigenous Peoples Development Plans or specific components of project documents addressing indigenous peoples issues. In actual practice, compliance with the Bank's indigenous peoples policy was gradual since the institution needed to build capacity to implement and monitor its own policies (Partridge and Uquillas 1996: 243–246; World Bank 2003). Nevertheless, there was important advocacy on indigenous issues from certain parts of the Bank, including the implementation of a pioneer study on Indigenous Peoples and Poverty in Latin America (Psacharopoulos and Patrinos 1994).

Operationally, the Bank worked under the assumption that its development and poverty reduction interventions would reach all of the poor, regardless of ethnicity or gender. It was only in the 1990s that the Bank's Latin American Region began to consider alternative approaches to indigenous peoples development. The Indigenous Peoples Initiative took shape in the context of the United Nations' declaration of the Decade of Indigenous Peoples Development and after a September 1993 meeting of several agencies to discuss strategy for increasing the social capital of indigenous organizations via capacity-building efforts.[11]

The source of funds for this initiative, the Institutional Development Fund, required a basic cooperation agreement between indigenous organizations and government agencies in charge of indigenous affairs. In 1994 in Ecuador, as in other countries where this program has functioned (see Uquillas and Aparicio 2000), these requirements led to a mode of cooperation between the main national indigenous organizations that had coalesced around the so-called Committee of the Decade of Indigenous Peoples (*Comité del Decenio*) and the former National Secretariat of Indigenous and Ethnic Minorities (*Secretaría Nacional de Asuntos Indígenas y Minorías Étnicas*, or SENAIME), the predecessor of CODENPE.

This capacity-building program became the entry point for Bank operations with indigenous peoples. Both indigenous peoples and government agencies saw the benefit of this collaboration and started thinking about follow-up actions both in the areas of building social capital as well as in the areas of targeted intervention aimed at reducing poverty and promoting development with cultural identity or development from the vision of the beneficiary ethnic groups themselves.

Thus, the concept of ethnodevelopment, formulated during the 1970s by Latin American social scientists and by UNESCO, was used within the Latin America Region of the World Bank (Partridge and Uquillas 1996). At a broader level, the institution began to discuss the concept of social capital and to sponsor research, including some case studies in the Andean countries (see, e.g., Sandoval et al. 1998). The focus on indigenous peoples and their social and cultural assets undoubtedly influenced the discussion of social capital (Davis and Patrinos 1996). When the Indigenous and Afro-Ecuadorian Peoples Development Project began implementation in 1998, the concept had gained acceptance among the local Ecuadorian technical staff of the project, who started redefining project components in terms of different types of capital: social (organizational strengthening), human (education, training), environmental (land and water), and financial and physical (investments, assets). Aware of the interest in the concept of social capital within the Bank, the task team started using this concept in its discussions of the project.

Past advocacy stressed indigenous people's rights and the need to end their social exclusion (to bring them out of poverty and marginalization). It was relatively successful in attracting attention to their plight, yet it pitted indigenous peoples against the rest of the poor and downtrodden, who were often more numerous. The language of social capital, on the other hand, emphasized not deficits but assets. It focused on the positive aspects of social groups, and helped highlight that, beyond needs, indigenous peoples have a tremendous capacity for improving their conditions of existence.

Interface Between Ecuador and the World Bank

Conditions Favoring Collaboration

By the mid-1990s a combination of favorable factors led to the preparation of the Indigenous and Afro-Ecuadorian Peoples Development Project (*Proyecto de Desarrollo de los Pueblos Indígenas y Afroecuatorianos*, or PRODEPINE)—the first World Bank operation focusing exclusively on ethnic minorities.

First, indigenous peoples' level of organization and capacity for social mobilization had grown substantially. In 1990, as a demonstration of their newfound power, indigenous peoples marched from Puyo, in the eastern lowlands, to Quito to push their demands for recognition of collective title to the lands they occupied. In 1992 indigenous and black organizations joined forces and formed the *Coordinadora Agraria* (Agrarian Coordinating Commission) to pressure the government to revise its recently approved Agrarian Law. After the United Nations declared 1995–2004 the International Decade of the World's Indigenous People, calling for the formation of joint government and indigenous peoples committees, the *Coordinadora Agraria* was transformed into the Committee of the Decade (*Comité del Decenio*), with a mandate to propose and respond to proposals for development activities for member organizations.

Second, in 1994 the government of Ecuador (GoE) created SENAIME and appointed an indigenous entrepreneur as its first secretary. Immediately thereafter, Ecuador initiated a series of contacts with donors to request support for SENAIME and its proposed operations to benefit indigenous peoples and Afro-Ecuadorians. The GoE conveyed its interest in this matter quite strongly to the World Bank through direct contacts between the President of Ecuador and the Vice President of the Bank's

Latin America and the Caribbean Regional Office, a visit by the secretary of SENAIME to the Bank's headquarters in Washington, and other means.

Third, partly in anticipation of the International Decade of the World's Indigenous People, in 1993 the World Bank began its own Indigenous Peoples Development Initiative, hiring more social science staff, organizing workshops to discuss alternatives for indigenous peoples, and designing pre-investment operations, in particular a technical training program for indigenous peoples in Latin America. Thus, the institution was relatively well positioned to respond to requests such as that from Ecuador.

Fourth, the existence of a strong ethnicity-poverty relationship documented by a country-specific Poverty Assessment (World Bank 1995) stressed the need for a targeted poverty intervention focusing on Ecuador's indigenous and Afro-Ecuadorian population. The fact that other rural development projects experienced difficulties reaching out to this population further emphasized the need for a new approach.

However, moving from these favorable conditions to the final form assumed by PRODEPINE involved much negotiation, conflict resolution, and alliance building. The concerns within indigenous organizations are discussed in the next section; however, there was also a need for negotiation and alliance building within the Bank and the GoE. While Bank technical staff, particularly those working in rural and social development sectors, tended to support this initiative, other project advisors and country economists were not in favor of targeting indigenous peoples. They argued that these groups were already being served by existing projects such as Ecuador's Social Investment Fund and that, in any case, targeting indigenous peoples would create conflicts with other sectors of the poor population. Ultimately, an alliance of social and rural development specialists, plus the Ecuador country representative and some division chiefs in Environment and Rural Development, persuaded Bank skeptics that targeting ethnicity within a rural development context was necessary and that it made sense financially to invest in indigenous and Afro-Ecuadorian peoples. The task team argued that targeting was not new in the Bank and that, given the quantitatively demonstrated fact that indigenous peoples were among the poorest of the poor in Latin America (Psacharopoulos and Patrinos 1994; World Bank 1995), it was sensible to direct resources at this sector of the population. In addition, the great assets of indigenous peoples, which lie mostly in social capital but also in physical capital (usually communal landholdings in tropical forests and other important ecological regions of the country), were brought to the attention of decision makers in the Bank.

Alliances also had to be strengthened or formed at the governmental level in Ecuador. Although SENAIME, a government agency attached to the presidency, had requested Bank support for the GoE, other key public agencies—such as the National Planning and Coordinating Secretariat, the Ministry of Agriculture, the Land Development Institute (*Instituto*

Nacional de Desarrollo Agrario, or INDA), and the National Forestry and Natural Resources Institute (*Instituto Ecuatoriano Forestal y de Areas Naturales,* or INEFAN)—had to be brought on board.

Overall the building of internal coalitions was a way of building social capital—first, in the relationships among indigenous organizations, particularly the national federations in the *Comité del Decenio;* second, in the relationships linking indigenous organizations and government at the local and national levels; third, in the relationships linking the project team to other constituencies in the Bank; and, finally, in the relationships between indigenous organizations, the GoE, and the Bank. Such alliance building required a deep knowledge of the social and political realities of the country, and was facilitated by the fact that one of the authors of this study had a long working relationship with government agencies, NGOs, and indigenous peoples in Ecuador and thus had his own network of contacts and a high degree of credibility. The importance of personal trust and a proper political approach cannot be underestimated; without it indigenous federations would have exhibited stronger resistance to the idea of collaborating with the GoE in a Bank-financed project.

Dilemmas of Indigenous Participation

From the very beginning of project preparation the Bank committed itself to three basic objectives: (1) alleviating poverty by targeting resources at the poorest sectors of the population; (2) promoting participatory processes to ensure that project design responds to grassroots demands, thus building social capital and trust; and (3) maintaining close coordination between governmental and nongovernmental organizations to increase project efficiency.

When the government requested World Bank assistance in identifying an operation focusing on indigenous peoples, the Bank asked for advice from its technical staff with expertise on indigenous peoples issues. They recommended making contact with the national indigenous organizations and initiating a gradual, fully participatory approach in order to create the minimal conditions for success. Nevertheless, indigenous organizations had reservations about working with either the government or the Bank. There were various antecedents for this. In the early 1990s the GoE had attempted to pass an agrarian law facilitating the breakup of communal lands in order to create a more open land market. Indigenous federations had formed the *Coordinadora Agraria* to join forces and oppose the passing of the law. Also during the early 1990s, CONAIE—which turned out to be a particularly tough negotiator—had organized well-attended popular marches to put forward claims for indigenous rights. In addition, indigenous leaders had not completely accepted SENAIME and were concerned about co-optation activities that could divide their organizations. Indigenous organizations also had grievances against the World

Bank, particularly for its support of neoliberal reforms, which they opposed. Given this history of confrontation and distrust in relationships among government, indigenous organizations, and the Bank, it was clear that a substantial change of mindsets was required before the two sides could engage in constructive dialogue (even though such dialogue was mutually desirable). To overcome the initial distrust, the project concept document addressed the historical demands of indigenous organizations, namely access to land, strengthening of social organizations, and rural investments.[12] The Bank team also argued that indigenous peoples had the right to public investments and that one of the best ways to secure funds was through internationally financed projects.

In addition to the distrust among actors, it became clear that although the national indigenous organizations had come together in the *Comité del Decenio*, they were not particularly well linked and did not necessarily speak with one voice. In fact, there was a fair degree of rivalry and continuous jockeying for the best position at the negotiating table. The role of the Bank's task team as honest broker and intermediary to assist the stakeholders in defining common ground for joint action turned out to be crucial at this stage of the project preparation process and later, during implementation.

It took several months to secure a formal commitment from the indigenous organizations to participate in the project. At first the government suggested the creation of a consultative group in which indigenous organizations would be represented, but with a minority status. This model of participation was rejected by the indigenous organizations. Instead, they proposed a model in which they had a direct relationship with the Bank, and administered project preparation and implementation themselves, without the participation of the government. Because the World Bank's charter mandates that it work with national governments, neither the Bank nor the government could accept this model. Further negotiations led to a co-administration model in which a Managing Committee (*Comité de Gestión*) would make decisions with equal representation by government and indigenous peoples. The government would be represented by three delegates from SENAIME, and indigenous organizations by three representatives selected by the *Comité del Decenio*. In addition, the parties agreed to create a Technical Unit (*Unidad Técnica*) to support the work of the *Comité de Gestión*. The coordinator of the former was also a member of the latter.[13] This helped ensure a strong link between decision making and implementation. Because the coordinator was selected from a list of three candidates provided by the indigenous and Afro-Ecuadorian organizations, in effect they gained an extra representative on the *Comité de Gestión*. Figure 6.1 provides an overview of the agreed-on institutional structure.

During project implementation SENAIME was replaced by the National Development Planning Council for Indigenous and Afro-Ecuadorian

Figure 6.1   Project Institutional Structure During Preparation Process

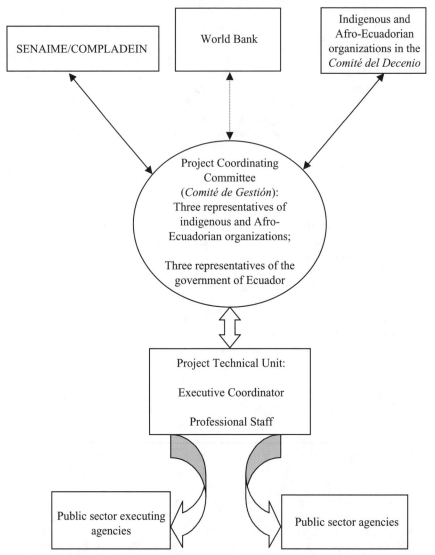

Project Institutional Structure during Preparation Process

Peoples (*Consejo Nacional de Planificación de Desarrollo de los Pueblos Indíge-nas y Negros*, or CONPLADEIN), whose board included all the national indigenous federations plus a representative of the Afro-Ecuadorian peoples. After just a year of operation—and reflecting constitutional changes in 1998 that gave far greater recognition to indigenous nationalities—

CONPLADEIN was replaced by CODENPE. This body includes only representation of peoples and nationalities, that is, organizations with an ethnic orientation, leaving out those organizations that have a social class orientation (peasant federations). Indeed, the project has faced strong pressures from the Secretary-General of CODENPE not only to adjust to new constitutional principles but also to take into consideration the new leading role of CONAIE. During negotiations between the GoE and CONAIE in 1999, PRODEPINE was an important part of the agenda. CONAIE pushed for greater say in the project's implementation by advocating the appointment of CONAIE-affiliated professionals in the project senior management team. Meanwhile, the other indigenous-peasant and Afro-Ecuadorian federations saw this as a means of excluding them from the project's benefits, and they pressured the GoE and the Bank to keep the project open to the participation of all types of organizations. This changing institutional reality meant that the Bank's task team had to redouble its efforts to maintain old alliances and to promote social and institutional arrangements to ensure the project's inclusive approach and the conditions for a successful implementation.

The relative autonomy of the project has also been strongly questioned by CODENPE. The council has argued that, being the government counterpart, it should have greater control over the procurement and disbursement process and that PRODEPINE should be an instrument for the advancement of central government policies on indigenous peoples. The project, with Bank support, resisted these efforts under the argument that the institutional makeup of the project was the result of a consensual agreement among the national indigenous federations and the government that took three years to obtain. Project agreements, having international legal standing, reflect this institutional setup. More important, if the project is to succeed, it must be relatively free of political interference from national governments and from indigenous federations. PRODEPINE directors maintained that they were obliged to implement the project and annual operating plans, as agreed between the GoE and the World Bank. The World Bank supported their position, but after the presidency intervened in favor of CODENPE, it reluctantly accepted the dismissal of the Executive Director, which was followed by the resignation of the Technical Director in June 2000.

Conflict Resolution Mechanisms

The project's high degree of autonomy provided an opportunity to create a "business culture" conducive to a productive working environment. The subject of business culture was discussed explicitly at various stages during project preparation. Key notions about the appropriate elements of the business culture were even included in an aide-mémoire signed by the various parties. The discussions resulted in an agreement that the project's working environment would be based on several factors, including (1) a high degree of tolerance and respect; (2) direct, frank, and transparent communication focused on issues rather than persons; (3) a drive for high-quality results; and (4) willingness to learn from mistakes and to accept constructive feedback. This provided a code of conduct for people who, until recently, had never worked together. The usefulness of this exercise was reflected in the fact that on various occasions people made reference to the written principles. Agreeing on these principles early in the process definitely helped to shape a positive work environment and contributed to an atmosphere of cooperation and mutual trust.

The mechanisms and processes that were employed in the project to deal with conflicts and differences indirectly contributed to fostering more constructive relationships among the indigenous organizations themselves, as well as between indigenous organizations and the government. A case in point is that when CONPLADEIN was established in March 1997, its organizational structure reflected that of the *Comité de Gestión,* as agreed in November 1995. Since all the indigenous organizations were interested in having the project hire professionals affiliated with their particular group, considerable efforts were made to set objective personnel selection procedures and to ensure that they were clear to all stakeholders. Terms of reference, qualifications, and selection criteria for each position financed under the project were agreed on from the beginning. To acknowledge and validate the goal of having indigenous professionals employed in the project, knowledge of indigenous languages was included as one of the selection criteria for positions for which a pool of qualified indigenous professionals was available. For specialized positions in which there were expected to be very few, if any, qualified indigenous candidates, the language requirement was replaced by a stipulation that the candidate have relevant experience working with indigenous organizations.

The Bank went to great lengths to ensure that all parties complied fully with what they had agreed to on paper. This was necessary because of the significant pressure to appoint consultants and divide training budgets according to quotas put forward by indigenous organizations. Though it risked being labeled bureaucratic by insisting that the rules be observed, the Bank in doing so established a solid reputation as a guarantor of due process for all stakeholders. Given the limited trust among the stakeholders, this role was highly appreciated, and probably was one of the most valuable aspects of the Bank's role in the preparation process.

Building Broad Alliances

Second- and Third-Tier Indigenous Organizations: The Executing Agencies

While the national-level indigenous organizations were legitimate representatives of the project's intended beneficiary population, it was recognized that their particular strength lay in the political and public policy arena. Given the project's orientation toward generating direct benefits for indigenous communities, it adopted a strategy of also working directly with second-tier indigenous organizations, which are usually based in small urban or rural towns accessible to their community-level member organizations. Since second-tier organizations have a closer relationship with indigenous communities, they are in a better position to know local needs and demands, are inclined to focus on providing services to their members rather than merely representing them politically, and they generally have a more pragmatic agenda. During implementation, executing agencies not only included second-tier organizations but also some third-tier organizations and even a few municipalities where indigenous mayors and councilors had been elected recently.

This strategy of making the project known at the regional level, including the second-tier organizations in project preparation, and aligning project design to the pragmatic agenda, created a substantial "pull" effect, with second-tier organizations speaking in favor of the project at relevant meetings and fora. Because the credibility of the national indigenous organizations depends to a large extent on effective linkages with their bases, the opinions of second-tier organizations tend to be taken into account by national leaders. Reaching out to the second-tier organizations created a more deeply rooted base of support for the project, and reduced its risk of being subject to politically motivated decisions by a few indigenous leaders.

International Fund for Agricultural Development
Because the project was the first of its kind, the Bank recognized that it did not have a comparative advantage in all areas covered by the project. In this context, the International Fund for Agricultural Development (IFAD) proved to be an appropriate co-financing partner.

First, IFAD had two ongoing rural development projects—one in the province of Cañar and another in Saraguro—that already involved working closely with indigenous organizations at the local and regional levels. Learning from IFAD's experience in those projects, whether positive or negative, could benefit the preparation of the Bank-supported project. Second, IFAD had a strong interest in starting a rural development project targeting Afro-Ecuadorians in the coastal province of Esmeraldas. Third, IFAD's experience in financing rural credit programs complemented the Bank's experience in financing matching-grant funds. This enabled the project to establish an integrated program of rural investments that could respond to a wide range of demands from indigenous communities, including those with a public-good or a private-good nature. Fourth, IFAD's more flexible stand on financing land purchases complemented the Bank's in-house financing possibilities and widened the range of options for financing land regularization and conflict resolution programs.

Fifth, combining the Bank loan with lower-interest IFAD resources offered a more attractive financial package and lessened the chance that the government would lose interest in the project even if macroeconomic conditions deteriorated.

Inter-American Foundation
Another attractive partner was the Inter-American Foundation (IAF), which was experienced in financing and implementing small-scale initiatives in cooperation with Ecuadorian indigenous organizations. The IAF had a long and successful history in this field and had established a wide reputation and excellent relations with the indigenous movement in Ecuador. The Bank project provided a good opportunity to build on those experiences and successes, especially since the IAF was scaling down its programs at the time. The IAF was enlisted to serve as a peer reviewer during project preparation.

This arrangement provided a vehicle for the IAF to increase the scope of the model it had developed. Second, with the IAF as part of the team, the project had access to relevant information that was required for the design of some key aspects of the project, particularly with respect to participatory planning and local capacity building. Third, IAF officials became effective spokespeople for the project and provided an excellent alternative channel of communication with indigenous organizations. Indigenous organizations with doubts about the Bank's intentions during the preparation process could express these doubts to the IAF officials whom they had worked with and trusted for a long time.

Continuity of the Task Team

During the five years between preparation and implementation, the Bank task team remained substantially the same. It included experts in agricultural economics, rural sociology, and agriculture, among other fields. This interdisciplinary team had a shared belief that the project represented a unique experience that required a long-term commitment in order to succeed.

This continuity paid off in several ways. First, given the sensitivity of the relationship between the indigenous organizations and the government, especially in the early stages, the task team played an important intermediary role that required a fair amount of trust that could only be built up over time. Second, the various indigenous organizations did not always have a common strategy, and on occasion pursued their own separate agendas. Continuity allowed the task team to understand and appreciate these different agendas, and to move project preparation forward while taking these agendas into account. Third, continuity enabled the team to build a track record as an objective mediator. It consistently proposed solutions based on three basic principles: (1) inclusiveness, or ensuring that the solution to a certain problem allowed all stakeholders to continue to participate; (2) technical orientation, or keeping political issues from interfering at the operational level; and (3) clear formulation of rules or codes of conduct.

Operationalizing the Project Focus on Social Capital

Targeting Ethnicity and Poverty

One of the first challenges of the project was to identify the indigenous peoples and Afro-Ecuadorians who were the intended beneficiaries. The two principal questions were whether the mestizo population living in the same areas would be part of the project's target population, and how to settle the politically contentious issue of defining who is indigenous.

To tackle these questions, the project adopted an approach that combined quantitative methods and geographical location with the notion of self-identification and community affiliation with second-tier organizations. Census information on indigenous and Afro-Ecuadorian population at the *parroquia* level was crossed with data on poverty (an index of unsatisfied basic needs) to obtain figures on level of poverty by ethnicity. Additional information was gathered in the field, particularly self-identification of communities as either indigenous or Afro-Ecuadorian, and membership in a second-tier indigenous organization. This information was then represented in an indigenous poverty map.

The quantitative analysis gave an idea of which *parroquias* had a majority indigenous or Afro-Ecuadorian population and which ones had a significant minority presence of these groups. Once the makeup of the *parroquias* was known, second-tier indigenous organizations operating there could be identified. The project would then form an alliance with these organizations for implementation purposes, and would thereby accept the membership eligibility criteria of the organization as the basis for targeting the intended beneficiary population in that particular *parroquia*. Depending on these locally defined criteria, the project would include the mestizo population to the extent that they were members of the second-tier organizations. Through this analysis the project targeted about 815,000 people who were members of indigenous and Afro-Ecuadorian communities in rural areas, and around 180 second-tier organizations operating in the 288 *parroquias* in which indigenous and Afro-Ecuadorian populations are concentrated. It is through these organizations (generally grouping contiguous communities) that the project defined its annual operational plans and implemented agreed-upon activities.[14]

Conceptual Framework

Social exclusion, economic deprivation, and political marginalization are commonly perceived as the predominant characteristics of Ecuador's indigenous peoples. But, as they often remind outsiders, indigenous peoples are also characterized by strong positive attributes, particularly their high level of social capital. Much of this social capital is manifest at the level of the traditional community through informal networks of reciprocity and is strongly survival oriented. The challenge is to mobilize or build on this type of relationship for development purposes, as well as to develop more formal organizations that may require different types of collective action and hierarchies.

Besides language and a sense of unique ethnic identity, the distinctive features of indigenous peoples include solidarity and social unity (reflected in strong social organizations), a well-defined geographical concentration and attachment to ancestral lands, a rich cultural patrimony, and a set of customs and practices different from those of Ecuador's national society (cf. Salomon 1981), which bears a strong Western influence. There are also some negative traits embedded in indigenous culture, such as political and religious factionalism and particular forms of gender inequality. Nevertheless, the project aimed to mobilize social capital, based on these characteristics, as a platform for ethnodevelopment following the conceptual framework presented in Figure 6.2.

The ultimate aim of the project is to generate results and impacts that directly benefit indigenous and Afro-Ecuadorian communities in Ecuador. To achieve this, the project finances investments to improve the stock of human capital, financial and physical capital, and environmental capital at the disposal of these communities. In the process, it expects to build social capital in at least three different ways. First, where there is already considerable social capital, the other forms of capital can complement it effectively (e.g., strengthen preexisting water users associations). Second, where social capital is limited, these additional resources, which in most cases are not individual goods, will promote collective management and solidarity among members.[15] Third, if the preexisting social capital in traditional indigenous communities is different from and not necessarily connected with the type needed in modern administrative/economic and even social infrastructure management, the project will stimulate the gradual extension of the original social capital into new fields, levels, or types of cooperation (for example, women's solidarity credit associations, which have no equivalent in traditional Andean communities).

To ensure the appropriate use of these various types of capital, the project relies on participatory planning as a mechanism to facilitate an effective demand-driven approach, and self-management as a tool to retain a strong sense of project ownership on the part of indigenous and Afro-Ecuadorian organizations. The configuration of investments in vari-

Figure 6.2 Conceptual Framework for Operationalizing Social Capital

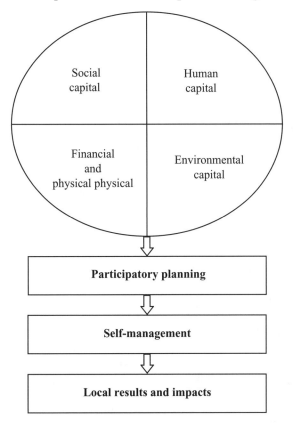

ous types of capital coupled with the focus on participatory planning and self-management as the basic principles for the project's operational procedures form the conceptual framework of the project.

Despite the strong desire of most organizations for self-managed control of the development process, there are great differences in available institutional capacity among these organizations. Some have a long history of providing services to their member communities, while others lack basic knowledge of financial self-management. With recognition of this wide variation in institutional capacity, it became clear that the project could not use a blueprint approach to initiate partnerships with these organizations as project-implementing agents. A standard level of supervision might be interpreted by one organization as the absolute minimum level of operational support required, while another might consider it as representing excessive micro-management.

To tailor the relationship between second-tier organization and the project, PRODEPINE developed an index of organizational capacity.[16] This index combines indicators grouped under four categories: management capacity, organizational culture, human capital, and financial capital (Ramón 2001). An aggregate index of organizational capacity was calculated, and this determines the nature of partnership with the project in terms of operational responsibilities and local capacity-building support activities.

The index was applied to most known second- and third-tier organizations in the Amazon. Three categories of potential partnerships are distinguishable.[17] The first category includes second-tier organizations that have ample institutional capacity to be effective partners in the full range of activities supported by the project. Most support provided by the project for this type of organization is demand driven, while controls tend to be of an ex post nature.

The second category includes organizations with limited institutional capacity. The project enters into agreements with these organizations for the design and implementation of subprojects if there is a willingness on their part to participate in training programs supported by the project. The project also maintains a ceiling of $25,000 instead of the usual $90,000 for subprojects implemented by organizations in this category. Project personnel maintain close relations with these organizations to provide support on a regular basis. Controls exercised by the project for this category tend to be more ex ante in nature.

The third category includes organizations that apparently have no institutional capacity whatsoever. The project enters into agreements with these organizations if they associate themselves with an NGO in a formal alliance. The underlying idea is that the NGO has a local presence and is in a position to provide support on an almost continuous basis—something the project cannot do. Most of the capacity-building efforts supported by the project focus on the second category of organizations, though organizations move between categories depending on performance.

The project also supports a range of activities specifically aimed at improving the institutional capacity of second-tier organizations, particularly those in the second and third categories. These activities include support for building management capacity and technical capacity with special emphasis on project preparation and management. The project also helps organizations obtain legal status if necessary. To emphasize ethnodevelopment, the project supports activities that strengthen the identity and cultural patrimony of indigenous and Afro-Ecuadorian communities and their organizations.

Capital Accumulation

To make project investments in human, environmental, financial, and physical capital more effective, social capital must be taken into consideration in the orientation and design of these investments.

Human Capital

To increase the available pool of indigenous professionals in both quantitative and qualitative terms in the long run, the project has entered into agreements with twenty-seven universities and colleges that provide formal high school and college education to indigenous students supported by the project. The project also supports students in disciplines that are particularly relevant to the modus operandi of the second-tier organizations, including community development, anthropology, and communications. Potential candidates for project support are proposed by second-tier organizations and subsequently selected by the project based on previous educational achievements. To increase the probability that students who have completed their education remain in their respective communities and organizations, the formal education program puts a heavy emphasis on distance learning. The presence of indigenous students in the predominantly white/mestizo university is already changing attitudes.

In addition to formal training programs, the project supports short courses for professionals working in executing agencies. Courses encompass a wide range of topics, most related to participatory planning, project administration and management, procurement, and technical issues. Learning by doing is a key element of these courses, and for this reason they are organized in close association with the program of small-scale investments financed by the project. The project also offers a limited number of internships in its regional offices. These internships provide an opportunity for young indigenous professionals to obtain exposure to the operational aspects of the project's rural investment program that could be useful for their work in second-tier organizations.

By the end of 2002, 1,080 high school students (of whom 335 graduated) and 850 college students (of whom 67 graduated) had received fellowships from the project; 77 individuals had taken courses in irrigation, soil conservation, agroforestry, and other topics; and 496 young men and women had benefited from an internship program in agro-ecology (World Bank 2002).

Environmental Capital

The project supports a land titling and regularization program in collaboration with the *Instituto Nacional de Desarrollo Agrario* (INDA). Given the sensitivity surrounding land property rights, the execution of this program is in the hands not of government officials but of locally trained paralegals of indigenous and Afro-Ecuadorian communities. In collaboration with

CARE, the project has supported a training program aimed at the formation of about 100 paralegals and the establishment of a professional network for these individuals. Given their local background and knowledge
of participating communities and organizations, paralegals are in a much
better position than outside government officials to facilitate the resolution of land conflicts. The cooperation agreement between the project and
INDA explicitly recognizes the integration of paralegals into INDA's operational procedures for land titling and regularization.

Currently, about 122,685 hectares (ha) of land have been titled for 71
grassroots organizations, and 97,312 ha are being processed. In addition,
160 paralegals have finished their training program. Furthermore, 458
community irrigation systems have been studied, corresponding to 2,647
km and 37,194 users (World Bank 2002).

Financial and Physical Capital
The project finances a substantive program of small-scale rural investments identified through a participatory planning process at the community level. Investments with a public goods character are financed through
matching grants. Investments with a private goods character are financed
on a credit basis. The use of traditional collective labor (*minga*) is accepted
as the counterpart contribution of the communities for financing particular rural investments. Community enterprises are also financed under the
project. These enterprises are typically small-scale agribusiness ventures
owned by the community and operated by community members. After
covering all relevant costs, including salaries of personnel, overall profits
are plowed back into the communities and invested in social infrastructure (for example, a school or health clinic). While these agribusiness ventures might be seen as private firms that should be financed with credit,
indigenous communities view them as public ventures, since the communities own them and the profits are used to finance public goods. The
project accepts the latter definition, and so community enterprises are
financed on a matching grant basis.

By the fourth year of implementation, PRODEPINE has supported
the preparation of 210 local development plans, 1,918 subproject proposals, and 830 pre-investment studies. It has also financed 654 small investment operations at over US$12 million, plus an estimated US$4.5 million
community contribution. As a special activity targeting indigenous
women, 547 community banks have been created that benefit 14,022
members (World Bank 2002).

Self-Management, Participation, and Cultural Identity

Project beneficiaries and their organizations are involved in the strategic
management of the project through a Consultative Committee (*Comité
Consultivo*) formed within CODENPE. The Consultative Committee

includes representatives from CODENPE and delegates from the main indigenous and Afro-Ecuadorian organizations. The committee reviews and approves the project's Annual Operational Plans, and discusses progress reports submitted by the Project Technical Unit.

The Project Technical Unit is responsible for coordinating implementation of the Annual Operational Plans approved by the National Council. A three-person management team heads the unit: an executive director, a technical coordinator, and a financial-administrative coordinator. The composition of the Project Technical Unit mirrors the project's design and areas of operation. Requiring knowledge of indigenous languages and experience working with indigenous or Afro-Ecuadorian organizations among the selection criteria encourages hiring of indigenous and Afro-Ecuadorian professionals. This approach has worked well, creating a unit staffed by qualified and culturally diverse professionals, including mestizos.

Because the project's success will be measured largely in terms of concrete results at the community level, the vast majority of professionals in the Technical Unit work in regional offices. This enables them to be closer to the second-tier indigenous organizations, through which most project activities are implemented. Over time, the project has worked in close partnership with about 250 of these indigenous and Afro-Ecuadorian membership organizations. As a first step, second-tier organizations decide with their member communities on a local development plan that provides an overall perspective and tool to prioritize project activities in a particular area. Once a plan is defined, these organizations prepare and implement small-scale investments, not exceeding US$90,000 per sub-project, that benefit their member communities.

Second-tier organizations also provide input in the elaboration of the project's Annual Operational Plan for a particular region, further contributing to the demand-driven nature of the project. An additional benefit of operating in a decentralized fashion with most of the operational decision making authority shifted to the regional level, is that once the Annual Operational Plan is approved, the project operates relatively independently from the political arena. This independence of operation is enhanced by the fact that small-scale investments are financed with loan funds and counterpart contributions from the communities only, avoiding reliance on government counterpart funds.

Recognizing self-management as a crucial element of community development implies that project activities by definition should be demand driven. The project relies on participatory planning to foster this. The process is designed to facilitate the effective involvement of community and grassroots organizations in their own development. More specifically, participatory planning in the context of the project (1) contributes to the decentralization of decision making, (2) stimulates grassroots participation in local planning and demand generation, (3) helps rural communities formulate development strategies and investment plans, and (4) increases investment sustainability by intensifying stakeholders' commitment in the execution and supervision of rural investments. The methodology involves the organization of community and district workshops over the course of several weeks. At the workshops, project field promoters and second-tier organizations help the communities to carry out a participatory diagnostic and to formulate a development strategy. Workshop participants are community delegates, representatives from development organizations, and interested individuals. After each workshop, time is allotted for the community delegates to return and inform the community of the workshop proceedings and to receive community feedback. Because in some communities decisions are made by consensus, this process can be lengthy.

The project also includes features intended to sustain and strengthen indigenous and Afro-Ecuadorian cultures. For instance, as part of the institutional strengthening efforts geared toward CODENPE, the project supports a team of professionals who, among other duties, review and assess the potential impact of new legislation on the indigenous and Afro-Ecuadorian population and propose changes in case there are anticipated adverse impacts. As part of the land tenure regularization efforts supported by the project, an attempt is made to clarify the concept of ancestral rights in more concrete terms, with the aim of strengthening land rights of indigenous and Afro-Ecuadorian communities in forestry and protected areas.

Conclusion

PRODEPINE is part of a new breed of poverty-targeted interventions of the World Bank. It is also part of an experimental initiative, started in 1993 in Latin America, designed to build pro-poor forms of social capital and promote indigenous development. The project represents an effort to operationalize new and old concepts (ethnodevelopment, social and human capital, community-driven development) to address old realities. It is an effort to mobilize local resources and to direct new ones to the poorest segment of the population, who will manage them in accordance with their own vision of what their problems and solutions are.

The project is unique because it is the Bank's first stand-alone operation exclusively targeting indigenous and Afro-Ecuadorian peoples, and also because of its highly participatory nature—from inception, through preparation, and into the implementation phase. The operation's most distinctive feature, however, is its approach to organizational strengthening by building on positive qualities of indigenous cultures and societies—their sense of ethnic identity, cultural values, solidarity and social cohesion, close attachment to ancestral land, and capacity to mobilize labor, capital, and other resources to attain shared goals.

Several design features of this project seem particularly relevant for other operations of this kind. First, the design should reflect the capacity of indigenous peoples and ethnic or racial minorities to mobilize social capital and should include efforts to consolidate and strengthen this capacity, including its cultural dimensions. Second, the design should incorporate a range of complementary inputs, including the formation and strengthening of human, environmental, and physical and financial capital. The specification of interventions in these fields should take into account how they interact with and complement existing forms of social capital. Third, to ensure relevance of the activities financed under the project, its investments should reflect priorities established in local development plans elaborated in a participatory fashion. Fourth, to ensure ownership and ultimately the sustainability of the investments financed under the project, the institutionalizing of self-management should be the guiding principle for project implementation.

The Bank's major investment in this project lies in building alliances among poor people in Ecuador and between these people and other social sectors. Indigenous peoples are increasingly cognizant that the financial investment will bear fruit only if those alliances remain and become stronger. If they are weakened and, as a consequence, the links among the different groups break, then the domination by the white/mestizo society will continue unabated, as will social exclusion and poverty. Thanks to their organizations and capacity to mobilize alliances, indigenous peoples have become important social actors in local, regional, and national politics. They are at the forefront of social movements advocating change in Ecuador. To continue playing that role and to achieve their ultimate goals, they will need to maintain their social cohesion and demonstrate true leadership capabilities.

Experience from the project indicates that the formation and consolidation of these alliances is not an easy task, since indigenous and Afro-Ecuadorian grassroots organizations represent different political orientations and ideologies. The challenge is to isolate, to the extent possible, development efforts supported by the project from political interference and manipulation by government, national indigenous organizations, and other external actors. This requires an explicit commitment from all stakeholders involved to the technical focus of the project, the use of professional criteria in the selection of its personnel, and the recognition of social inclusion as the driving principle for the project's participatory framework. Sustaining this commitment is greatly aided by two aspects of project organization: first, the existence at the strategic level of a decision-making and conflict resolution mechanism in which representatives of key project stakeholders are all able to participate; and second, the presence of a third party—in this case the stable Bank task team—to act as a broker, constantly reminding all involved of the project's agreed-upon core principles, and to play a significant role in consolidating the alliances that form the foundation of the project.

Notes

1. The authors are grateful to Anthony Bebbington, Thomas Carroll, and Shelton Davis for their valuable comments and suggestions with regard to previous drafts of this work.

2. The government's letter responded to a specific request made by CONAIE. Other indigenous or Afro-Ecuadorian organizations did not agree with this position. In any case, the fact is that the enabling conditions for a successful project, referred to elsewhere in this chapter, were no longer present. Among other things, the coalition of indigenous organizations had dissolved, increasing oil revenues apparently made an external loan for indigenous development less critical, and CONAIE's leadership had radicalized its stand and decided to oppose a Bank-financed project.

3. Indigenous peoples organizations often give higher estimates (about 40 percent of the total population), while Ecuador's Integrated Social Development Indicators (Sistema Integrado de Indicadores Sociales del Ecuador 2003) puts the figure closer to 10 percent on the basis of census data.

4. Indigenous peoples in Ecuador prefer to be designated as "nationalities" or "peoples" rather than "ethnic groups." The first two terms imply that a group has standing as a nation and a broad range of rights as established in United Nations instruments and the International Labor Organization's Convention 169. Non-Hispanic nationalities in Ecuador include the Runa or Quichua, Shuar, Huao, Siona, Secoya, Cofán, Huancavilcas, Manteños, Punaes, Chachi, Epera, Tsáchilas, Awa, and Ecuador's black population.

5. The 1998 financial crisis, and its aftermath, have aggravated poverty. As of 1999, 55 percent of the population lived in poverty (40 percent of the urban population and 76 percent of the rural population).

6. The agrarian reform process stimulated the organization of indigenous peoples so as to facilitate their access to land being redistributed or to recognize their ancestral possession of land.

7. The African-descendant population in Ecuador is characterized by less formal organization than the indigenous population. Organization for most Afro-Ecuadorians occurs primarily at the community or grassroots level (commune, compound, cooperative, committee, and peasant union), and only recently have they begun to form more complex organizations. The main features of grassroots organizations are a sense of belonging, a recognizable territoriality, certain forms of self-government, and calendars of celebrations. Grassroots organizations are formed more through real or ascribed family networks than as community societies.

8. For discussions of federations see Bebbington et al. (1992, 1993), and Carroll (2002).

9. Nina Pacari became the new Minister of Foreign Relations and Luis Macas the Minister of Agriculture.

10. See Uquillas (1993) for a case study of Ecuador's Amazon region.

11. These included the Inter-American Development Bank (IDB), the International Fund for Agricultural Development (IFAD), the Fund for the Development of Indigenous Peoples of Latin America (Fondo Indígena), the Pan American Health Organizations (PAHO), and others.

12. The need to strengthen the government's ability to formulate indigenous people's policies was not a demand coming from the indigenous organizations, but it was eventually accepted by them as a necessary part of a project that had a government agency as counterpart.

13. The *Comité del Decenio* sent a letter to the World Bank and to the government of Ecuador stating its formal commitment to collaborate in the project. In the final analysis, indigenous and Afro-Ecuadoran organizations became the majority bloc in the committee, since the coordinator of the Technical Unit was the secretary and a voting member of the *Comité de Gestión*.

14. The target population exhibits great cultural diversity, especially among indigenous peoples. The most numerous among the indigenous peoples are the Quichua speakers (or Runa) in the Sierra. They may be further divided by area of ethnic predominance into subgroups, including the Otavalo, Carangui, Cayambi, and Quito in the northern region, and the Panzaleo, Puruha, Cañari, Salasaca, and Saraguro in the south-central region. The next largest group are the peoples of the Amazon region, including the Shuar, Achuar, and Runa or Quichua speakers of the lowlands, and the Huaorani, Cofán, and Siona-Secoya. In the coastal region are found the Awá, Emberá, Tsachila, and Chachi, and other peoples such as the Huancavilca, Manteño, and Puna, who have lost their language but retain strong indigenous cultural features. Afro-Ecuadorians live in both coastal and highland areas, though there is not as much diversity between subgroups as there is between the indigenous subgroups.

15. John Durston (1998), who has worked in Guatemala, argues that the native communities have latent social capital that has been disrupted and repressed during the civil strife in that country, but that now, with a combination of physical and financial investments and organizational assistance, can be restored and built up in an atmosphere of trust.

16. This work ties in with initiatives in this area launched by the Social Development Family of the World Bank, under the "Social Capital Initiative," underwritten by the Danish Trust Fund. The PRODEPINE index was developed in dialogue with researchers of an Andean study on campesino federations (see Bebbington and Carroll 2000; Carroll 2002).

17. The universe of OSGs was divided into three groups: (1) those with scores above 81 (out of a maximum of 116), accounting for 27 percent of the total; (2) those with scores between 50 and 80, representing 55 percent; and (3) those with scores below 50, for 18 percent. The main purpose of this exercise was to determine which OSGs could and which could not manage project resources (see Ramón 2001).

References

Bebbington, A., and T. Carroll. 2000. *Induced social capital and federations of the rural poor.* Social Capital Initiative Working Paper No. 19. Washington, DC: World Bank.

Bebbington, A., H. Carrasco, L. Peralvo, G. Ramón, V.H. Torres, and J. Trujillo. 1992. *Los actores de una decada ganada: Tribus, comunidades y campesinos en la modernidad.* Quito: Abya Yala.

Bebbington, A., H. Carrasco, L. Peralvo, G. Ramón, V.H. Torres, and J. Trujillo. 1993. Fragile lands, fragile organizations: Indian organizations and the politics of sustainability in Ecuador. *Transactions of the Institute of British Geographers* 18(2):179–196.

Bebbington, A., and T. Perreault. 1999. Social capital, development and access to resources in highland Ecuador. *Economic Geography* 75(4):395–418.

Cameron, J. 2001. Local democracy in rural Latin America: Lessons from Ecuador. Paper prepared for the Latin American Studies Association Meetings, Washington, DC, September 6–8.

Carroll, T., ed. 2002. *Construyendo capacidades colectivas: Fortalecimiento organizativo de las federaciones campesinas-indígenas en la Sierra Ecuatoriana.* Quito.

Davis, S., and H. Patrinos. 1996. Investing in Latin America's indigenous peoples: The human and social capital dimensions. In *Indigenous peoples production and trade.* TemaNord, p. 6980.

Durston, J. 1998. Building social capital in rural communities—where it does not exist. Paper prepared for the Conference of the Latin American Studies Association.

Partridge, W., and J. Uquillas, with K. Jones-Schwartz. 1996. Including the excluded: Ethnodevelopment in Latin America. In *Poverty and inequality,* edited by S. Burki, S. Aiyer, and R. Homes. Washington, DC: World Bank, pp. 229–252.

Psacharopoulos, G., and H. Patrinos, eds. 1994. *Indigenous peoples and poverty in Latin America: An empirical analysis.* Washington, DC: World Bank.

Ramón, G. 2001. El índice de capacidad institucional de las OSGs en el Ecuador. In *El capital social en los Andes,* edited by A. Bebbington and V.H. Torres. Quito: Abya Yala.

Salomon, F. 1981. The weavers of Otavalo. In *Ethnicity in modern Ecuador,* edited by N. Whitten. Urbana: University of Illinois Press, pp. 420–449.

Sandoval, G., et al. 1998. *Estudio sobre las instituciones locales en Bolivia.* Local Level Institutions Working Paper No. 3. Washington, DC: World Bank.

Selverston-Scher, M. 2001. *Ethnopolitics in Ecuador: Indigenous rights and the strengthening of democracy.* Miami, FL: North-South Center Press.

Sistema Integrado de Indicadores Sociales del Ecuador. 2001, 2003. www.ssise.gov.ec.

Torres, V.H. 2001. Los municipios son agentes del cambio social? Reflexiones en torno al capital social y desarrollo local en Ecuador. In *El capital social en los Andes,* edited by A. Bebbington and V.H.Torres. Quito: Abya Yala.

Uquillas, J. 1993. *Research and extension practice and rural people's agroforestry knowledge in Ecuadorian Amazonia: Rural people's knowledge, agricultural research and extension practice.* Latin American Papers. IIED Research Series 1:4.

Uquillas, J., and T. Aparicio. 2000. *Strengthening indigenous organizations: The World Bank's indigenous capacity building program in Latin America.* Latin American and Caribbean Region Sustainable Development Working Paper No. 10. Washington, DC: World Bank.

Wali, A., and S. Davis. 1992. *Protecting Amerindian lands: A review of World Bank experience with indigenous land regularization programs in Lowland South America.* Latin American and the Caribbean Technical Department, Report No. 19, Environment Division. Washington, DC: World Bank.

World Bank. 1995. *Ecuador poverty assessment.* Washington, DC: World Bank.

———. 2000. *Culture counts: Financing resources, and the economics of culture in sustainable development.* Washington, DC: World Bank.

———. 2001. *World development report 2000–2001: Attacking poverty.* Washington, DC: World Bank.

———. 2003. *Implementation of Operational Directive 4.20 on indigenous peoples: An evaluation of results.* OED Report No. 25754. Washington, DC: World Bank.

———. 2002. *Implementation completion report: Ecuador's indigenous and Afro-ecuadoran peoples development project.* Washington, DC: World Bank.

CHAPTER SEVEN

SOCIAL CAPITAL IN THE OPERATIONS AND IMPACTS OF SOCIAL INVESTMENT FUNDS

Julie Van Domelen

Introduction

Social investment funds, or "social funds" (SFs), are a type of development intervention that has gained in popularity since their inception in the late 1980s. Social funds are agencies or programs that channel funds in the form of community grants for small-scale development projects that are identified, prepared, and implemented by local actors, such as community groups, local governments, and NGOs. Social funds typically finance some mixture of socioeconomic infrastructure (e.g., schools, health centers, water supply systems, roads), productive investments (e.g., micro-finance and income-generating projects), social services (e.g., nutrition campaigns, literacy programs, youth training, support to the elderly and disabled), and capacity-building programs (training for community-based organizations, NGOs, and local governments).

Because social funds operate at the community level, they have been at the forefront of the World Bank's efforts to operationalize concepts and development practices around social capital. This paper analyzes how, why, and the extent to which social capital became relevant to the operations of social funds. The first section provides an overview of the evolution of social funds and basic design principles. The second section traces the entry of social capital concepts into the discourse of social funds and the main effects of this on operations. The final section reflects on some of the remaining challenges in operationalizing the concept of social capital as applied to social funds and other community-driven programs.

Social Funds

A New Way of Doing Business

The first social fund was established in Bolivia in 1987. Bolivia's Emergency Social Fund was designed to provide temporary employment and stabilization of social services during a time of economic crisis and adjustment. Since that date, the World Bank has committed about US$3.5 billion to social funds through June 2000, covering ninety-eight projects in fifty-seven countries (see Table 7.1). Additional financing from other multilateral sources (US$630 million), bilateral assistance (US$2.1 billion),

Table 7.1   Expansion Path of World Bank Financing of Social Funds, by Year of World Bank Loan Board Approval and Region

	Latin America and Caribbean	Africa	Eastern Europe and Central Asia	East and South Asia	Middle East and North Africa
1987	Bolivia				
1989		Sao Tome			
1991	Haiti, Honduras	Zambia		Sri Lanka	Egypt
1992	Guatemala, Guyana, Nicaragua	Rwanda			
1993	Peru	Burundi, Comoros, Madagascar	Albania		
1994	Ecuador				
1995	Argentina	Angola	Armenia	Cambodia	
1996	Jamaica	Ethiopia, Eritrea, Malawi	Bosnia and Herzegovina		Algeria
1997	Belize		Georgia, Tajikistan		West Bank and Gaza, Yemen
1998		Benin, Mali, Zimbabwe	Bulgaria	Philippines, Thailand	
1999	Panama, St Lucia	Ghana, Lesotho, Togo	Kosovo, Moldova, Romania, Togo	Pakistan	
2000 and after	Colombia	Senegal, Sierra Leone, Tanzania, Uganda	Ukraine, Uzbekistan	Bangladesh, East Timor, Laos	Lebanon

and local support (US$1.6 billion from governments and community contributions) brings the total to about US$8 billion.[1] Although significant in terms of the number of countries, social funds still account for only a small percentage of World Bank support—about 2 percent of total disbursements and 9 percent of specific poverty-targeted interventions in recent years (World Bank 2002). While social funds represent a new approach, they have yet to represent a major shift in resources.

A key factor in explaining the rapid expansion of the social fund model was that it presented a new way of doing business for the World Bank and developing-country governments that filled a niche:

- *Speed in crises*. Social funds initially gained a reputation for their speed and efficiency, and thus for being particularly useful in responding to crises. Social funds tended to disburse funds quickly, due in part to simplified procedures, in part to good management and operational autonomy, and in part to the approach itself, which harnessed a wide range of available implementation capacity.

- *Streamlined and simplified procedures*. Most of the World Bank's internal procedures for investment projects were developed to respond to large-scale infrastructure programs. Social funds were one of the first significant efforts at financing small-scale projects, usually on the order of US$20,000–$50,000. Such implementation required the development of streamlined procedures for disbursement and procurement that addressed many of the constraints and rigidities that can hinder implementation (Jorgensen et al. 1992; Gopal and Marc 1994).

- *Choice and direct access to communities*. Social funds were one of the only avenues that allowed communities to decide not only whether they were going to participate, but also what kinds of investments they wanted. At the time, this was a relatively untested concept for both the World Bank and developing-country governments, where most public investments were determined by central departments of sectoral ministries, in terms of both the type of investment and location.

- *Wide range of local implementation capacity*. Social funds financed NGOs and community groups. This dovetailed with the growing call for the participation of civil society in World Bank projects. This link with community-based organizations and the participation discussion in the Bank was significant in setting the stage for later discussions around social capital.

- *Links to poverty—the evolving mandate of the Bank*. One of the main observations about social funds was their ability to reach underserved regions and communities in ways that other programs could not.

Social funds offered the World Bank and other donors what were per-ceived as efficient channels for investment in direct poverty alleviation at the community level. This filled a gap between macroeconomic policies supported through structural adjustment lending and sectoral investment programs that often had longer-term institutional reform and develop-ment objectives. The projects received positive evaluations and were con-sidered successful. This allowed for a level of acceptance of the model that furthered its expansion.

Building a Community of Practice

Another key factor in the model's expansion was the social capital created between World Bank and developing-country practitioners. Very early on, an informal community of practice emerged around social funds.[2] People on both the Bank and developing-country sides were highly committed and exchanged information frequently. This allowed for rapid dissemina-tion of tools and experiences.

It is worth noting that this was done from the bottom up; there were no formal World Bank policy papers on social funds, no directives that they be set up in every country, no lending targets, no overall strategy. The design and development of social funds was driven almost exclusively by frontline operational staff. Originally, a handful of staff working on social funds met informally in "brown bag lunches" or organized study tours that brought in both World Bank staff and representatives from develop-ing countries to understand how funds operated in the field. At the social fund level, it was not uncommon for the Bolivia social fund, or the Zambia social fund, to receive a steady stream of visiting delegations. Indeed, the expansion path of the early social funds was tied to key people, both within the Bank and through direct government-to-government contacts. Social fund staff had largely been recruited from the private and NGO sectors, and several moved into consulting on the establishment of social funds in other countries. These ties and contacts helped the experience to leapfrog between regions quickly.

As more and more social funds were created, these exchanges became more formal. In 1997 the first International Conference on Social Funds was convened in Washington, with over 200 delegates. At the same time, social funds were linking directly with each other through a series of regional networks, initiated in the Latin American and Caribbean Region as a form of spontaneous South-to-South cooperation. Other regional networks in Africa, the Middle East and North Africa, and Eastern Europe began in the late 1990s, with support for some exchanges and seminars provided by the World Bank Institute.

Expanding Objectives and Mandates

The objective of many of the early social funds, as was the case in Bolivia, was to create an agile, temporary mechanism to assist a country during an economic crisis. As the model expanded and evolved, social funds began to be put to use in addressing the more medium- and long-term needs of the poor. The basic mechanism of grant financing to small-scale projects was "generic" enough, and, given the successful track record of the institutions themselves, governments and donors have continued to adapt the programs to evolving country needs.

Most social funds are now viewed as more permanent components of a country's poverty alleviation strategy. Today, objectives of social funds include providing compensation to the poor during times of crisis, improving access of the poor to basic social services and productive assets, strengthening the capacity of local governments and community-based organizations, and, more recently, social capital creation in marginal areas and populations.

With this expanding agenda, most funds juggle multiple objectives. All social funds involve some combination of the following broad poverty alleviation objectives.

They enable a *quick response to crises*, typical of the early stages of funds established during economic adjustment periods (Bolivia, Honduras, Egypt), to address the employment situation in transition economies (Bulgaria), to respond to financial crises (Thailand), or as part of an emergency reconstruction effort in countries afflicted by internal strife (Rwanda, Angola, Sierra Leone) or natural disaster (Honduras and Nicaragua after Hurricane Mitch).

Social funds *increase access of the poor to basic social services and productive assets*. This objective is shared by most social funds, with some focusing more on basic social services (Bolivia currently; also Jamaica, Zambia, Armenia, Moldova, Nicaragua, Belize, Ethiopia, Madagascar, etc.) and others adding a significant degree of support to productive investments such as micro-enterprise development (Chile, Egypt, Albania, Yemen, etc.).

A growing number of funds have collateral objectives that look beyond the immediate benefits of jobs, infrastructure, and services and seek to *improve the underlying institutional capacity of poor communities*. These efforts are typically directed at strengthening local government (e.g., Bolivia, Nicaragua, Honduras, Zambia), developing the capacity of NGOs and community-based organizations (West Bank and Gaza, Pakistan, Argentina, Chile), and/or strengthening the social capital of poor communities (e.g., Romania, Zambia, Thailand, Argentina, Chile, Moldova).

As social funds' objectives have evolved and looked more to the longer term, so have their desired impacts. For most social funds, the initial preoccupation was with quick disbursements and performance indicators that focused on the volume of outputs (number of temporary jobs created, kilometers of roads upgraded, classrooms constructed/ repaired, children vaccinated, number of micro-loans, etc.). With the shift to greater concern over the long-run impacts of these community investments, greater attention has been placed on issues of sustainability and improvements in the welfare of poor households, including reduction in infant mortality, increased school attendance, improved prenatal care, reduced time spent collecting water, and so forth.

In addition, social funds are increasingly looking to the potential broader effects on local institutions and the very social fabric of poor communities. It is more and more common to find among a social fund's development objectives the intention to leave behind not just a new water supply system or health center, but a community more able to address its needs and solve local problems. This call to put social funds to the purpose of building social capital was explicitly acknowledged in the conclusions of the first International Conference on Social Funds, held in Washington in 1997, which recommended that social funds support the development of social capital through the involvement of NGOs in the design, not only in the implementation, of subprojects, the training of community-based organization staff, and facilitation of the open selection of subprojects based on the needs of women (Bigio 1997).

The Critics Weigh In

The expansion of social funds has not been without controversy. The main criticisms fall in three areas:

- *"Not enough jobs; not a good safety net."* Some of the early criticisms of social funds stemmed from their insertion in strategies designed to mitigate the social costs of economic adjustment processes. The overall level of job creation was not commensurate with the amount of unemployment in needy countries, and the social costs of economic adjustment programs had to be addressed through the redesign of adjustment policies themselves rather than by focusing on compensatory measures (Lustig 1997; Stewart 1995).
- *"Distorts the public sector."* The main criticism from the public sector management viewpoint both within and outside the World Bank has been that social funds set up "enclaves of excellence" that do little to reform existing government institutions. Because of their popularity, there is a fear that they may divert resources and attention from the reform of sectoral ministries (Tendler 2000). There is the additional challenge of ensuring that recurrent cost financing is available in government budgets.

- *"Not 'true' community development."* A more recent critique has focused on how social funds work with communities. Here the argument is that communities and community development are complex. Allowing access to funds can end with elite capture of benefits given existing power relationships in poor communities (Platteau 2002; Rao and Ibanez 2005). Worse, it can weaken a community's ability to bootstrap their way out of poverty (Ellerman 2001). True community development is not just a matter of improving the accessibility and quality of services; it is building more egalitarian, participatory, and transparent social relations.[3] This process can be distorted by the incentives that the transfer of funds creates. Effective community development, it is argued, requires long-term interventions by external facilitators and trainers (Platteau 2002).

How Social Funds Work

To understand the relevance of social capital to social funds, it is necessary to understand the basic design and operating procedures of these agencies. Operations are meant to be "demand driven." Project proposals should come from the community—as opposed to central planners and technocrats—and local organizations should have a major role in the execution and eventual operation and maintenance of these investments.

Even with different objectives, most social funds follow a similar pattern of operation. This is an outcome of the basic similarity of social funds: They are second-tier agencies that finance many small-scale projects. Social funds do not execute, but only promote, appraise, and supervise, the implementation of investments by other parties, be they local governments, local offices of line ministries, NGOs, or community-based organizations. Social funds offer fixed-term financing, usually grant based, but do not engage in financing longer-term operations and maintenance.

All social funds define a "menu" of eligible projects (or a "negative list" of noneligible interventions) and determine which local agencies and organizations may apply for funding, in line with the general needs of the country, the overall objectives of the social fund, and the roles and responsibilities of other agencies and programs in the country. Social fund operations are typically organized along a "project cycle" that includes

- Promotion/identification of a specific investment
- Technical preparation
- Ex ante appraisal
- Approval and contracting of the project
- Execution
- Monitoring and supervision

No two social funds are alike, and there is a great deal of diversity in how the project cycle is organized and who does what, which depend on the objectives of the fund and the country context. Table 7.2 illustrates the variation in social fund project cycles. When social funds adopt operating procedures that are more participatory and embedded more deeply in the community (toward the right-hand side of the matrix), the underlying social capital of the community becomes more important in program design and impact. Social funds with a greater focus on short-term job creation or emergency reconstruction, for example, usually place less emphasis on community participation, with project cycles that correspond more to the left-hand side of the matrix.

The design of the project cycle not only varies between countries; it is also often adapted over time to reflect the evolving objectives of the fund. For example, the social fund in Bolivia at the outset allowed project proposals from a wide variety of agencies (line ministries, NGOs, local governments, and community-based organizations). In the aftermath of fiscal decentralization in the country, all social fund proposals must now come directly from local government investment plans. In Zambia a similar process of integration with local governments is under way. In the past, the Zambia social fund largely financed micro-projects managed directly by community project committees. To support the decentralization process, it has opened a window of grants to be managed by local governments, and has involved local governments and district officers to a greater extent in the planning and execution of the community projects.

Social Funds and Social Capital

How Social Capital Entered the Social Funds Discourse

Social capital was not explicitly discussed in the early days of social fund development. These programs were meant to be temporary, and studies did not address longer-term impacts. Most were initiated in crisis situations, with a premium on showing results quickly. The main impacts sought were temporary employment creation and increased access to basic social services. Attention was focused on the machinery—the "how to"—which was subject to adaptation as more and more countries began to establish social funds.

By the late 1990s this had changed. A small but growing number of social funds had explicit objectives that could be considered related to social capital creation. Community dynamics and associative behavior had a more prominent place in the design of social fund operations. In addition, the research community had begun to look for ways to measure the phenomenon of social capital in relation to social fund interventions. Several key factors were behind this evolution.

Table 7.2   Social Fund Project Cycles

	Specific Social Fund Operating Procedures		
Stage in Project Cycle	**Lesser Relevance of Social Capital**	⇒ ⇒ ⇒ ⇒	**Higher Relevance of Social Capital**
Determination of eligible sponsoring agencies	Only formal intermediaries may apply (NGO, LG, LM)	More informal CBOs may apply	Only community project committees may apply
Identification of community needs and projects	Intermediaries identify projects (NGO, LG, LM)	Ad hoc local discussions to identify needs	Formal community assembly and democratic selection of priorities
Appraisal/approval	Social fund central board approves projects; appraisal only looks at technical aspects	Social fund approves projects, including social assessment in appraisal criteria	Local development committees approve projects; social assessment included in appraisal process
Contracting	Social fund selects contractor	Intermediaries (NGO, LG, LM, CBO) select contractor	CBOs/CPCs "contract" themselves directly (self-help)
Financing	No community contribution required or solicited	Community contribution encouraged and accounted for in microproject financing	Mandatory community contribution up front
Execution	Social fund controls finances, disbursing directly to contractor based on work completed	Payments made through intermediaries (LG, NGO, LM)	All project funds managed directly by CBOs/CPCs
Supervision	Social fund contracts external supervisor	Some supervision functions delegated to intermediaries (LG, LM)	Community organizations given responsibility for supervising
Operations and maintenance	Local agencies (LG, NGO, LM) fully responsible for all aspects of operations and maintenance	Shared responsibility for operations and maintenance between community groups and local agencies (LG, LM)	Community organizations responsible for operations and maintenance

NGO, nongovernmental organization; LG, local government; LM, line ministry; CBO, community-based organization; CPC, community project committee

Evidence from the Field
The most powerful indication of the linkage between social capital and social funds came from direct observations from the field—due largely to the systematic use of beneficiary assessments. Beneficiary assessments (BAs) were developed by the World Bank in the late 1980s as a tool to elicit direct feedback from citizens.[4] Because social funds were demand driven, there was a need to receive feedback directly from that source of demand on how the program was operating. Thus, beneficiary assessments were seen as essential tools for social fund managers to obtain quick feedback in order to improve and adjust program design, particularly the aspects related to community participation. The extensive use of beneficiary assessments was due to a combination of good fit with social fund operating principles and the personal convictions and contacts of the Bank staff involved early on. One of the first beneficiary assessments done in the context of a World Bank project was for the Emergency Social Investment Fund, carried out by Lawrence Salmen, who has been the leading advocate for and expert on beneficiary assessments at the Bank. With the establishment of this precedent, other social funds quickly picked up on this tool, and it became a standard part of monitoring.

By querying aspects of participation and community dynamics, beneficiary assessments began to identify two important links between social funds and social capital (see Box 7.1)—first, that community dynamics surrounding participation in a social fund micro-project was directly related to the preexisting forms and patterns of social and power relations in the community; and second, the action of organizing and implementing a micro-project might have certain spillover benefits that relate to social capital. Here, the potential impacts on social capital were expressed in terms of a number of manifestations, including increased perceptions of trust, greater willingness and interest in entering into mutually beneficial collective action, greater levels of optimism and self-confidence about the community, changes in the number and civic engagement of community-based organizations, and improved organizational skills (see Box 7.2).

Input from Participation and Social Capital "Thinkers"
Social fund practitioners needed terms and concepts to help them describe the dynamics that they were observing at the community level. Originally, this description was couched in terms of participation, the lexicon of the day. During the early and mid-1990s the need for participation of citizens and community groups in development projects was gaining a voice within the World Bank and within project design in particular. Social funds experience informed some of the first efforts to draw lessons learned from participatory techniques and projects at the World Bank. The hallmark *World Bank Participation Sourcebook* (World Bank 1996) drew from background work on social funds and participation (Marc and Schmidt 1995). The broader concept of social capital and its relevance to

> **Box 7.1   A Villager's Perception of the Moldova Social Fund's Influence on Social Capital**
>
> "Before the fund was created, there was capital and community in villages, but until then they [the government] lacked trust in our capacities. Only later on, when they understood that we can design for ourselves, did it become important. The community organized themselves, so that they could then follow [Moldova Social Investment Fund] procedures. The community talked about the needs of the community—those were very big. We chose to first rehabilitate the school. So what we understood was important was not the physical rehabilitation, but the rehabilitation of the human side of the school. The people of the village were involved from the very beginning in deciding what to do until the last minute when the project was finalized. We had difficult situations with procedures not followed exactly, but the community helped out and finally they got the skills of being able to obtain what they wanted. We got the school rehabilitated, but more important is the creation of a community development organization that will work on other needs, too."—*Valentine Odobescu, school principal, Village of Recesti, Soroca County, Moldova (at the Second International Conference on Social Funds, June 2000, Washington, D.C.)*

development had yet to be clearly or forcefully articulated during the initial years of social fund development.

As the conceptual and research basis around social capital began to receive attention in the World Bank, the term entered the language of social fund operations. Social capital concepts helped enrich the way local dynamics were perceived, and it was a shorthand way of describing some of the observed spillover effects that extended beyond the immediate benefits of access to basic services and infrastructure.

One of the first applications of the term "social capital" in relation to social funds came when two of the principal World Bank researchers on social capital, Deepa Narayan and Katrinka Ebbe, carried out a review of social funds (Narayan and Ebbe 1997) with the objective of "improving their effectiveness by becoming more demand oriented and focused on fostering community participation and building local organizational capacity." This building of local organizational capacity is where the explicit link with social capital was made, because, as the authors posited, "local organizational capacity building involved fostering the ability of groups of people, especially the poor, to work together, trust one another, and organize their efforts to mobilize resources, solve problems resolve conflicts and network with other groups in order to leverage resources and achieve shared goals." The authors found that social funds were evolving toward what they termed a community-driven development

---

Box 7.2   Examples of Beneficiary Assessment Findings

Participation is dependent on pre-existing relationships and social organization:

- In Ecuador, the higher level of community participation observed in the pre-investment stage in water supply projects was explained, in almost all cases, by the presence of a local neighborhood association responsible for organizing and mobilizing beneficiaries (Desarrollo y Autogestión 1995).
- In Zambia, 86 percent of communities studied had undertaken self-help activities in the past, and 40 percent of micro-projects used existing community organizations, mainly PTA committees, to spearhead the implementation. Existing tribal leadership also played a key role in mobilizing the community for action. (Rural Development Studies Bureau 1993)
- In Armenia, the most active implementing agencies and beneficiaries were those that in the past had shown a high degree of involvement in community initiatives. In all communities, a high degree of participation in a micro-project correlated with a high degree of overall community participation. (Development Programs, Ltd. 1997)
- In Argentina, 60 percent of members of the local project committees had no prior experience in other community organizations before joining the committee. Of those with previous participation experience, three-quarters were elected to representative positions on the local project committees, whereas less than half of those with no previous experience were elected to such positions. (FOPAR 1999)

The experience of participation can, in turn, affect the propensity for mutually beneficial collective actions:

- In Moldova, many communities have subsequently established formal beneficiary associations that have gone on to receive other grants. A few have registered as NGOs. (OPINA, 2001)
- In Chile, according to interviews of community members after the conclusion of a project, three-quarters had more trust in the organizations in the community, and greater trust in their leaders and neighbors, and 82 percent said they were more able to solve their own problems.(Centro de Estudios de la Realidad Contemporanea 1999).
- In Peru, 25 percent of households reported that the group formed by the FONCODES project has continued working on other local initiatives (Instituto Apoyo 1995).

- In Argentina, 97 percent of those interviewed felt that the local group formed to prepare and implement the project should continue functioning. Two-thirds of group members believed that the group would keep meeting, with a wide difference between rural areas (86 percent) and urban areas (58 percent). Reasons cited for continuing to meet were to initiate new projects, and to conclude or to improve an ongoing project. For those groups that no longer continued to meet, the principal reason for not continuing was internal conflict between members, followed by lack of motivation and lack of time. (FOPAR 1999)
- Greater levels of trust and cooperation were noted in several social fund evaluations, for example, in Moldova, Zambia, Malawi, and Chile.

approach, but progress was uneven and could be improved with greater attention to participation aspects.

Entry of New Countries with Different Characteristics and Objectives

Another key factor was the expansion of the social fund model to very different country contexts. The challenges of rebuilding the social fabric in post-communist Eastern Europe, bringing marginal and excluded groups and communities into development in Argentina, and promoting peaceful demobilization and reconstruction in post-conflict countries helped draw in considerations about social capital. Here, the major difference was that social capital became an end in itself rather than a means.

The issue of generating local organizational capacity where none or little exists has been a primary issue in the countries of the former Soviet Union and Eastern Europe. In 1998 the government of Romania launched the Romanian Social Development Fund. The RSDF was among the first social funds to explicitly place the creation of social capital among its objectives. The Bank-government preparation team diagnosis was that the country had a low level of social capital as a result of the systematic destruction of civil society and of private property. Values and norms such as trust, transparency, reciprocity, and participation had been undermined. This was reflected in people's passivity, and their inability to articulate needs or to participate at the community level in activities of common interest. The Project Appraisal Document stated that the most important policy supported by the program would be the development of social capital at the community level by strengthening local organizational capacity.[5] The second policy supported by the RSDF would be poverty alleviation at the community level. Through its demand-driven and participatory approach, the RSDF would increase people's ability to trust each other and cooperate in mobilizing resources and solving problems (World Bank 1998).

The situation in post-conflict settings, such as Uganda, calls for investments that contribute to maintaining peace. In the five subregions constituting the north, development had been stifled by both local and international cross-border conflicts as well as inter- and intra-tribal conflicts (World Bank 2002). The traditional community safety-net systems and social fabric had been greatly disrupted and weakened by the armed conflict and displacements. As a result, people had "lost the motivation and confidence, let alone the energy to play roles in the development process." This led to the establishment of the Northern Uganda Social Action Fund (NUSAF) to channel grants to communities. The Project Appraisal Document is clear about the importance of social capital to its objectives: Social capital is viewed as

> a powerful entry point to address poverty. . . . Peace building initiatives by the traditional leaders supported by civic organizations constitute the lynch-pin for survival in the insecure areas by enhancing integration and social cohesion among the displaced and vulnerable. The organizational integrity of these institutions enables them to influence local government structures to deliver services to the needy and to promote positive synergies between the state and civil society in support of the poor. (World Bank 2002)

A middle-income country, Argentina has relatively good coverage of basic social infrastructure but faces challenges of high income inequality, social exclusion, and pockets of structural poverty. In 1995 Argentina's Secretariat for Social Development launched a new program aimed at building capacity of poor communities to better manage the process to improve their welfare. The Participatory Social Investment Fund (*Fondo Participativo de Inversión Social*, or FOPAR) was designed to provide technical assistance and financial resources to the poorest communities to support training of community leaders in: addressing social problems and in building organizations; strengthening of community-based organizations; promotion of community development (for communities with no previous organizational experience to assist them in mobilizing, identifying their needs, and formulating a project); and financing of community services and micro-finance. All funds were channeled through newly formed *nucleos de beneficiarios* designed to elicit broad citizen participation and development of capacity among groups that had largely been excluded from decision making—primarily women, youth, and, in selected areas, indigenous groups (World Bank 1995).

Operationalizing Social Capital Concepts

The "operationalization" of social capital is typically viewed in terms of how the community interacts with the social fund at each stage in the project cycle. Specific social capital concepts took shape in three areas: (1) building in participation mechanisms, (2) creating community capacity through learning by doing, and (3) investing directly in social capital formation.

Participation: What For and How?

The concept of how local associations participate in identifying, implementing, and sustaining small-scale investments has changed significantly over time. The first social funds considered "demand driven" simply to mean that the fund did not determine investments; others came to the fund with proposals. Most were based on the principle of first come, first served. What happened within a community to determine what would be requested or who would be involved was beyond the purview of the fund. The fund would engage in promotion activities, via the general media or orientation sessions with NGO networks or local officials. The community itself was considered a black box: Provided with an incentive and adequate information, it would self-organize (or rely on existing intermediaries such as associations and local governments) to access program resources.

This assumption proved valid. Social funds were flooded with demand. In almost every case, this demand far outstripped available resources. Program objectives in terms of number of projects or communities reached could be easily met without any further efforts in capacity building. This was true even of the poorer areas. And beneficiary assessments consistently revealed that citizens were satisfied with the investments made.

So why improve participation? First and foremost, the Achilles' heel of social funds was their lack of continued financing for operations and maintenance. Since social fund financing was finite, it exposed social funds to a great deal of skepticism about the sustainability of their investments, particularly against the poor track record in this respect of development projects in general. While social funds established explicit coordination mechanisms with sectoral ministries, which committed in writing to staffing health posts with nurses and drugs, or schools with teacher and books, it was considered a significant risk that neither the central nor local governments would provide for sufficient maintenance. Here, the worldwide NGO experience was instructive in terms of mobilizing community action around operations and maintenance of social infrastructure. The general mantra of the day was that effective participation increased the sense of ownership, which in turn generated a postive dynamic toward using and maintaining these services (World Bank 1996). As social funds became more concerned with the long-term impacts and hence the sustainability of the community investments, participation became essential.

Another driver of increased attention to participation was the move to direct community management of social fund resources. Social funds were one of the first World Bank projects to transfer funds to community groups to be managed directly (De Silva 2000). Almost half of all social funds now use this mechanism, whereby community project committees are wholly responsible for selecting contractors or NGOs, setting up a bank account, receiving funds, and accounting for the use of those funds to the community and the social fund. When community groups manage resources, this raises demands on participation. It requires more than attendance at meetings; it requires organizational capacity, and this involves rules of the game for setting up or nominating those organizations and training in terms of how those organizations will function.

Finally, understandings of what it means to be "demand driven" have changed. Most social funds have moved from "first come, first served" to the facilitated selection of community priorities using some form of participatory mechanisms. So having once been interpreted as "proposals come from the community," "demand driven" is now often taken to mean that project proposals are identified in an open, participatory, and egalitarian way by a fully informed citizenry, and reflect the top priority of the majority of community members (World Bank 2002). This "raising of the bar" requires more intensive participation mechanisms, including community facilitation by external agents and strengthened participatory planning processes through local governments.

Investing in Capacity Building via Learning by Doing

The actual process of managing an investment project is viewed as an essential element in organizational strengthening. This contrasts with approaches to community capacity building that focus on training alone, and include no investment resources or local management of funds. The social fund "learning by doing" approach may be more compelling than just supporting broad organizational training to communities.

One perspective on this comes from Argentina, where there is experience with financing stand-alone training interventions, as well as infrastructure and other investment projects that come with training (both technical and administrative). An in-depth assessment of projects in two peri-urban areas in northern Argentina found

> The reality is that it is very difficult for these communities that are so oriented to concrete actions, so in need of many basic needs and/or so used to being "given" things—it is difficult for them to realize the value of organization for its own merits. . . . In a comparison of projects to train community leaders versus community development projects with an infrastructure component, the latter clearly display more stable attendance by community members at training ses-

sions, more enthusiasm, and greater acceptance by the beneficiaries. (Benencia 1997)

The overall emphasis has been on strengthening community organizations around investments to improve living conditions, rather than addressing power relations explicitly within communities. There is very little discussion of or differentiation between bonding and bridging types of social capital. The general assumption seems to be that strengthening local organizations, giving them a role in local development, and linking them to other agencies, even if it is only the central social fund, works on both aspects of social capital simultaneously.

Investing Directly in Social Capital

One effect of adopting explicit goals with respect to strengthening social capital is that it has broadened the traditional menu of eligible investments. From a narrower focus on basic needs-type investments (e.g., schools, water supply, health services), social funds with social capital objectives have expanded their menus. As examples, the following microprojects in Argentina were oriented directly toward increasing the social capital of the community while addressing basic needs:

- *Training for volunteer fire protection services in Garza.* The project provides training to a group of twenty, mainly youth, in the techniques of firefighting. Training is provided by the nonprofit School for Voluntary Fire-Fighters. At the end of the training, the group formed their own nonprofit community organization. They have received donations from other NGOs and direct community support. These volunteers have established relations with other sectors of civil society in the region and province.
- *Community radio communications in rural Santiago del Estero.* The project supports the establishment of a community radio network linking ten communities in a rural zone. The project includes training in the use of radio equipment and in basic community organization. Radio links combat rural isolation and link dispersed communities.
- *Community center in Los Blancos.* The project was managed by a rural farmers' group and financed the construction of a community center to be used for community meetings, training, and support to the organization. The project has helped link NGOs and governmental programs working in the area with the farmers' organization.

Similarly, the Northern Uganda social fund finances peace meetings and negotiations between clans or tribes; intertribal dialogue, including visits to other districts; and counseling and psychosocial support to returnees, ex-abductees, and the receiving communities.

Outstanding Issues and Future Directions

The integration of social capital concepts into social fund operations is not without its limitations, including a number of conceptual issues that practitioners will need to address in the evolution of these mechanisms.

Work with Existing Organizations or Form New Ones?

One of the main decisions in the design of a social fund is whether to allow for the creation of ad hoc local project committees to manage local investments, or restrict participation to preexisting local organizations, or some combination of the two. Table 7.3 highlights some of the main advantages and disadvantages of each option.

There is seldom clear, and often conflicting, guidance from the social capital theorists. To build on the stock of local social capital, social fund administrators are instructed that it is usually advisable to work through existing organizations.[6] However, this may do little to increase the density of social organization, which is one of the main performance indicators used to measure social capital creation. In addition, it can leave out vulnerable and excluded groups and exacerbate existing inequalities. The standard answer to this is to use existing groups and somehow make their membership and operating procedures more inclusive, but there has been little acknowledgment that there may be an essential contradiction here and that external social engineering is not without its own dangers and limitations.

In practice, the dichotomy between preexisting organizations and local project committees is not so clear. In the Argentina experience,

> when promotion begins in a community, there exists a structure of social relations [that is] reflected in the level of organization. This structure is a result of the internal dynamics of a community and the actions of distinct institutions, such as the state, churches, political parties, NGOs, etc. In this sense, the constitution of a local project group takes place over a base of a particular social configuration already existing in a community. (FOPAR 1999)

Because this derives from the existing framework, these newly created local project committees are not necessarily incompatible with the approach of strengthening the existing social capital of the community.

Moreover, it is not clear that the continuity of specific organizations is an ultimate goal. Even where the group is not based on an existing organization or ceases to function after a specific intervention is accomplished, its lack of permanency may not mean that it has no long-term impact on social capital. The skills and experience of the community members may well be put to service in other areas of social networks. As other researchers have found, as goals are met, such organizations may disappear and

Table 7.3   Issues in Working with Existing Organizations versus Creating New Ones

	Working through Existing Organizations	**Creation of Local Project Committees**
Advantages	• Builds on existing social capital • Potential for longer-term impact on local organizational capacity • Existing organizations may best express community priorities and needs • Existing organization have established linkages within the community and often with external actors	• Allows program to operate in areas with little local organizational capacity or presence • Promotes participation by those previously excluded (by choice or social norm) • May increase program efficiency and transparency • Can introduce new social norms (democratic selection of members, local accountability)
Disadvantages	• Local organizations may not exist • Local organizations may not match with area of program interventions • Perpetuation of local inequalities: Local organizations may promote elite capture and exclude marginal/vulnerable groups • Country framework may discourage spontaneous civil society formation (restrictive registration laws, political oppression)	• May create leadership conflicts with existing organizations • Organizational structure not designed to be permanent (although many continue with activities) • Can undermine existing social norms (role of traditional leadership may change)

then reappear in other forms to solve other problems (Narayan and Ebbe 1997).

How to Address Potential Negative Effects?

There is evidence that in a small number of communities, the introduction of participatory mechanisms and the demands of collective action have caused tensions and a potential weakening of social capital.[7] For social fund managers, communities without the requisite motivation or capacity to participate, or communities with high levels of conflict and internal fission present a real challenge. In such communities, not only are the chances for successful local management of investments reduced, but there is a danger of exacerbating conflicts and causing further divisions.

What Role for Local Governments?

Most discussion on the interactions between social funds and social capital focuses on the level of civil society organizations and networks. However, there is a growing subset of social funds whose main objective is to strengthen local governments and the decentralization process (e.g., in Bolivia, Nicaragua, Honduras). These funds tend to work less closely with civil society. Most or all of the projects are identified, designed, and managed by local governments. Technical assistance and training is focused on improving local government capacity to manage investments. There is little mention of social capital in the context of these programs.

As social funds, and community-driven development (CDD) programs in general,[8] move closer to supporting decentralization processes, there is a question of how, and if, social capital will remain a primary interest. A study on social funds and decentralization cautioned that social funds that work directly with community-based organizations may undermine the prerogatives of local government (Parker and Serrano 2000). However, the study also reinforced the idea that social funds can act positively on local government by making it more responsive to civil society by virtue of the procedures for micro-project identification and implementation. Here we might expect a positive effect on social capital by bringing local government closer to the people and holding it more accountable. Closer and more accountable local government is likely to be more responsive to local needs and more involved in the solution of community problems—which in turn may generate greater trust on the part of civil society. Closer governments also tend to encourage community-wide participatory initiatives, such as the formation of groups and associations, providing an "enabling environment" for social capital to flourish. These links between local governments and social capital have been little explored to date.

Social Capital and Dynamic Individuals

The effectiveness of community leaders goes a long way toward explaining degrees of community passivity or assertiveness. Interviews and evaluation at the community level have consistently turned up examples of this.[9] In Chile the most important exogenous factors in determining the positive impact and sustainability of projects had to do with the characteristics of the beneficiaries, particularly the degree of entrepreneurial spirit, preexisting leadership, and previous experience with social projects (CIEPLAN and CyS 1996). In Argentina the election of representatives in the project committees reflected the broader role of certain individuals in the civic life of a community: 94 percent of those with previous experience in community organizations had held a leadership position in those other organizations. In Armenia one-third of communities had respondents who said they chose not to get involved in order to avoid stepping on the prerogatives of a strong leader (FOPAR 1999). In Malawi poor leadership was seen as a handicap. Communities without effective leaders could not unite for joint action to meet local counterpart requirements, as indicated in the following beneficiary assessment comments referring to two rural communities in Malawi;

> [I]n one case, Chivala, a rural growth center was quoted as an example of a village which is now totally transformed, all because of a dynamic, able chief who commands respect and mobilizes citizens for development action. In Matandani, for example, poor leadership was voiced as a handicap and communities could not unite for joint action to meet requirements for local contributions. (Malawi Institute of Management, 1997)

The interplay between these leaders and the formation and capacity of local groups and organizations has been inadequately explored in the social capital literature. There are several operational issues facing program designers: Can communities with many social networks but weak leaders participate as effectively? Are the capacity of leadership and the existence of social networks positively correlated? How should a program address issues of strong local leaders when those leaders display exclusionary behavior? Can leadership substitute for denser social organizations, or, conversely, can greater levels of social capital improve program performance in communities with low education bases and weak leadership?

How to Measure Impacts?

If strengthening social capital is to be an objective for which governments are willing to devote scarce resources, impacts need to be measurable. The issue of social capital measurement is relatively new, and there appear to be as many measures of social capital as there are researchers. The usual approaches to measuring social capital appear to take two paths: (1) an emphasis on the number and density of associational behavior, that is, the number of groups, the level of group membership, and so on; and (2) levels of overall trust and civic engagement.

However, some of the simplest and easiest-to-capture variables, such as the number of local organizations or associations, may be the least appropriate to use as measures of program performance. For example, the absolute number of groups does not differentiate by type, size, or internal cohesion or effectiveness of the group. Using this as a measure can introduce perverse program effects, where the formation of community groups is valued above improving the performance of existing groups. Other, more subjective measures, such as perceived levels of trust, are affected by many factors both inside the community as well as external factors, making it exceedingly difficult to isolate program effects. It is unlikely that any one measure will be sufficient to truly capture the multidimensional nature of social capital.

Social fund managers must overcome these limitations if they are to be able to assess the impacts of their interventions on community social capital. To date, most analysis has rested on qualitative information gathered at the community level. This is usually done in the context of evaluating social fund performance more broadly, so questions pertaining to the effects of and on social capital are typically few and only loosely formulated around any analytical framework.

Constructing useful measures of social capital for social funds is at the top of the future research agenda. Any framework for evaluation will need to be carried out over a period of time, and preferably institutionalized within a social fund's monitoring and evaluation system. Periodic in-depth focus group interviews and community case studies should be combined with more objective information collected from communities (either sample based or census based, depending on resources) as part of the ex ante and ex post evaluation process of the specific social fund.

Conclusions

With over US$8 billion in investments so far in about sixty developing countries, social funds have been one way in which governments, with the support of donor agencies, have attempted to reach poor communities with investments to improve their well-being. Concepts of social capital have given social fund administrators a richer understanding of community dynamics and a greater focus on community organizational capacity as a basis for sustaining social fund investments. A focus on social capital as an outcome has expanded the basic mandate of a handful of social funds. In turn, greater weight has been placed on social capital concepts by linking them directly to investments for poverty reduction—rather than treating them as just a set of interesting theories about how communities function.

However, the fit is imperfect. There is much speculation about whether social funds are the best (or even a valid) way to support social capital strengthening. On the other hand, social fund performance is ultimately judged by poverty impacts, not on its effectiveness in building trust and social cohesion. The links between social capital and poverty alleviation at the community level are often not obvious or direct, compared with reductions in infant mortality or increases in school enrollments through provision of basic infrastructure and services. This adds to the difficulty of justifying loans of millions of dollars for social capital strengthening.

There has been a rapidly expanding universe of adaptations and "close cousins" to social funds, including demand-driven rural investment funds, indigenous development funds, community poverty reduction programs, demand-driven community water supply programs, and the like. They are often supported by different departments in the World Bank as the basic practice of funding community grants proliferates. In the early 2000s, the Bank's efforts to integrate these experiences into a more coherent strategy and body of practice under the umbrella of community-driven development was initiated (Dongier et al. 2002).

The future positioning of social funds (and of social capital) will depend greatly on the evolution of the broader debate on community-driven development. To a certain extent, the community-driven model is here to stay. This has been clearly enunciated by senior World Bank management. In the words of President Wolfenshon at the Second International Conference on Social Funds in 2000,

> If you have got problems of poverty, do not try and make the decisions in Washington or London or Paris or in some UN agency or at the World Bank. Trust the people to know what they need. Engage people so that they become owners and drivers of development. . . . And if you give them the chance to be participants, you can usually be sure of several things: First, that the money is not wasted; secondly that they own the project; thirdly, as you know, that they contribute between five and 20 percent to the projects; and fourthly, if they do the project, that it will be there when you go back ten years from now." (Levine 2000)

As social fund approaches aim at longer-term community impacts, and as understanding of the characteristics and potential importance of social capital grows, the ability of both social funds and social capital to shape community-driven development theory and practice will broaden.

Notes

1. These amounts include only social investment funds financed by the World Bank and identified under the Bank's Social Protection Department. Excluded are funds that are either government funded (Chile, Mexico) or are funded by other multilateral organizations without World Bank participation (e.g., Dominican Republic); also not included are the expanding universe of social fund–type projects managed by other World Bank departments, for example, the Rural Development Network.

2. As the World Bank sought to formalize the experience of communities of practice into Thematic Groups under its Knowledge Management Strategy in

the late 1990s, the social funds community was looked to as a very effective example of knowledge sharing among peers.

3. Rao and Ibanez (2005: 833) capture this view in their study of the Jamaica Social Investment Fund:

> The JSIF does seem to have had a social impact—trust has increased, and people from JSIF communities are more likely now to be able to work with strangers in making community-based decisions. However, the JSIF process does not seem to have been very democratic, with community leaders dominating decision-making. The data suggest that JSIF may have strengthened the hand of community leaders. When leaders are benevolent this could be a good thing, but if they are corrupt then this could result in bad outcomes. In these communities—overall—they seem to have been leaders who had the best interests of the community at heart. While it seems that respondents are for the most part happy with the project and with JSIF, and that JSIF has built good feelings within the community, it is not clear that the JSIF process has democratized decision making, any more than other processes present in Jamaica.

4. According to Salmen (2002: 1–2),

> Beneficiary assessment is a tool for managers who wish to improve the quality of development operations. This is an approach to information gathering which assesses the value of an activity as it is perceived by its principal users. The approach is qualitative in that it attempts to derive understanding from shared experience as well as observation, and gives primacy to the centrality of the other person's point of view. As the Bank and others engaged in development activities seek to do their work better, one key indicator will need to be how the ultimate customer, or intended beneficiary, assesses the value of this work, project or policy, as it affects his or her life. . . . One particular area of Bank activity where beneficiary assessment has shown itself to be a useful tool is in the design, implementation and evaluation of Social Funds.

5. Setting social capital as an explicit objective of investment was questioned in some of the internal reviews. Discussions centered on whether enough was known about impacts on poverty and the relative newness of the concept as a direct objective of a development program.

6. Narayan, Deepa, "Designing Community-Based Development," ESSD Discussion Note 17. In contrast, an evaluation of social funds by the World Bank's Operations Evaluations Department was critical of social funds as "users rather than producers" of social capital because they built on existing institutions to develop collective capacity (Rawlings et al. 2004).

7. In a 1996 evaluation of the impact of FOSIS (*Fondo de Solidaridad e Inversión Social*) projects in Chile, 60 percent of projects had a positive impact on the communities, 12 percent had no discernible impact (neither positive or nega-

tive), 8 percent had mixed results, 14 percent did not have enough evidence to determine impact, and 6 percent were judged to have had a negative impact on the communities. When the nature of the negative impact was probed, the study found that "these negative impacts are seen either in situations where there has been a weakening of the social organization—generation of community conflicts and breaking of pre-existing social relations, or in the weakening of the community in a psycho-social sense (frustration, dismotivation, lack of trust vis a vis the external intervention), or in the worsening of material conditions (indebtedness, unproductive investments, etc.)" (CIEPLAN and CyS 1996). This potential for generating conflict and undermining self-help initiative was also described in one of the beneficiary assessments of the Zambia social fund (Milimo 1994), where three distinct pictures emerged of the possible impact on community organization and the spirit of self-help. The first pertains to projects where there is no impact, positive or negative, on community organizations and on the spirit of self-help. This usually occurs when the community is not at all involved in the implementation of the project. The second picture emerging is that of a community whose cohesion and organization has been greatly enhanced by the social fund micro-project. A third picture emerges in micro-projects that unintentionally cause divisions in the community and kill the spirit of self-help. For example, Henry Kapata's Parent-Teacher Association caused divisions within the community when they decided to hire skilled labor from only one village. The excluded villages felt alienated.

8. The importance of local governments to CDD programs is clearly enunciated in the World Bank's guidance to member countries. The *Poverty Reduction Strategy Sourcebook*, for example, states,

> Regardless of the mode of CDD intervention (CBO partnerships with local government, private support organizations, central government, or central funds), local governments can be critical to the success and sustainability of CDD. Local governments are often well positioned to facilitate coordination across communities and allocate resources. When local governments interact with communities and informal groups in a participatory way, it is possible to achieve economies of scale in producing and providing goods and services that could not be achieved by CBOs operating independently. Furthermore, in many cases, local governments are needed to support operation and maintenance of services, and for continuing funding of community groups. (World Bank 2002)

9. See Owen and Van Domelen (1998). This was echoed in a more recent social fund evaluation (Carvalho et al. 2002) that highlighted the role of "prime movers" (for example, local leaders) who were critical in the mobilization of support and preparation of a successful subproject proposal." This observation is consistent with findings on other community-driven development programs. For example, an evaluation of the Aga Khan Rural Support Program found that strong leadership seemed to be one of the most important

factors in the capacity of the community organizations studied (Narayan and Ebbe 1997).

References

Benencia, R. 1997. Los proyectos ejecutados por el FOPAR en barrios perifericos de Posadas y Salta. Buenos Aires: Department of Monitoring and Evaluation, Participatory Social Investment Fund (FOPAR), June.

Bigio, Anthony, ed. 1997. *Social funds and reaching the poor: Experiences and future directions*. Proceedings from the International Workshop on Social Funds, May 27–30, World Bank, Washington.

Carvalho, Soniya, Gillian Perkins, and Howard White. 2002. Social funds, sustainability and institutional development impacts: Findings from an OED review. *Journal of International Development* 14(5):611–625.

Centro de Estudios de la Realidad Contemporanea—CERC-UAHC. 1999. Informe Final de Evaluacion de Impacto en Dos Territorias FOSIS: Malleco Norte y Cachapoal. Universidad Academia de Humanismo Cristiano. Santiago, Chile Mayo.

CIEPLAN and CyS. 1996. *Evaluation and redesign of programs*. Institutional Strengthening Project of FOSIS. Santiago, January.

Desarrollo y Autogestión. 1995. *Evaluación de beneficiarios y procesos del FISE*. Quito.

De Silva, Samantha 2000. *Community-based contracting: A review of stakeholder experience*. Washington, DC: World Bank, Social Protection Department.

Development Programs, Ltd. 1997. *Report of the Armenia Social Investment Fund Project impact assessment study*. Yerevan.

Dongier, Philippe, Julie Van Domelen, Elinor Ostrom, Andrea Ryan Risvi, Wendy Wakeman, Anthony Bebbington, Sabina Alkire, Talib Esmail, and Margaret Polski. 2002. Community driven development. In *PRSP Sourcebook*, PREM ed. Washington, DC: World Bank, pp. 303–331.

Ellerman, David. 2001. *Helping people help themselves: Towards a theory of autonomy-compatible help*. Washington, DC: World Bank, Operations Evaluation Department, October.

FOPAR. 1999. *The intervention of FOPAR and the development of social capital: The case of the department of Ledesma, Province of Jujuy*. Buenos Aires.

Gopal, G., and A. Marc. 1994. *World Bank–financed projects with community participation: Procurement and disbursement issues*. World Bank Discussion Paper No. 265 (November). Washington, DC: World Bank.

Insituto Apoyo. 1995. *Evaluacion ex-post del desempeno de FONCODES—1994*. Lima: APOYO.

Jorgensen, Steen, Margaret Grosh, and Mark Schacter, eds. 1992. *Bolivia's answer to poverty, economic crisis and adjustment: The emergency social fund*. Washington, DC: World Bank, Regional and Sectoral Studies.

Levine, Antony, ed. 2000. *Social funds: Accomplishments and aspirations*. Proceedings of the Second International Conference on Social Funds, June 5–7, World Bank.

Lustig, Nora. 1997. *The safety nets which are not safety nets: Social investment funds in Latin America*. Note prepared for the Conference on "Governance, Poverty Eradication, and Social Policy," November 12–13. Washington, DC: Inter-American Development Bank.

Malawi Institute of Management. 1997. *Beneficiary Assessment, 1991 (BA-1)*. Malawi Social Action Fund, April.

Marc, Alexander, and Mary Schmidt. 1995. *Participation and social funds*. Participation Series, Environment Department, Paper No. 4. Washington, DC: World Bank.

Milimo, John 1994. *Beneficiary Assessment Phase III*. Lusaka: University of Zambia, Participatory Assessment Group, April.

Narayan, Deepa, and Katrinka Ebbe. 1997. *Design of social funds: Participation, demand orientation and local organizational capacity*. World Bank Discussion Paper No. 375. Washington, DC: World Bank.

Owen, Daniel, and Julie Van Domelen. 1998. *Getting an earful: A review of beneficiary assessments of social funds*. Social Protection Discussion Paper (December). Washington, DC: World Bank.

Parker, Andrew, and Rodrigo Serrano. 2000. *Promoting good local governance through social funds and decentralization*. Social Protection Discussion Paper 0022 (September). Washington, DC: World Bank.

Platteau, Jean-Philippe. 2002. Rushing to help the poor through participation may be self-defeating. Mimeograph. Belgium: Centre for Research on the Economics of Development (CRED), Faculty of Economics, July.

Rawlings, Laura, Lynne Sherburne-Benz, and Julie Van Domelen. 2004. *Evaluating social funds: A cross-country study of community investments*. Washington, DC: World Bank.

Rao, Vijayendra, and Ana Maria Ibanez. 2005. The social impact of social funds in Jamaica: A "participatory economic" analysis of participation, targeting and collective action in community driven development. *Journal of Development Studies* 41(5):788–838.

Rural Development Studies Bureau. 1993. *Report on the beneficiary assessment study—Phase 1*. Lusaka: University of Zambia, March.

Salmen, Laurence. 2002. *Beneficiary assessment: An approach described*. Social Development Paper No. 10 (August). Washington, DC: World Bank.

Stewart, Francis. 1995. *Adjustment and poverty*. London: Routledge.

Tendler, Judith. 2000. Why are social funds so popular? In *Local dynamics in an era of globalization*, edited by Shahid Yusuf, Weiping Wu, and Simon J. Evenett. New York: Oxford University Press.

World Bank. 1995. *Staff Appraisal Report: Argentina Social Protection Project*. Report No: 14832-AR. Washington, DC: World Bank, Human Resources Operations Division, Country Department I, Latin America and Caribbean Region.

World Bank. 1996. *The World Bank Participation Sourcebook*. Washington, DC: World Bank, Environmentally Sustainable Development Department.

World Bank. 1998. *Project Appraisal Document: Romania Social Development Fund*. Report No: 17379-RO. Washington, DC: World Bank, Human Development Sector Unit, Bulgaria and Romania Country Unit, Europe and Central Asia Regional Office.

World Bank. 2002. *Project Appraisal Document: Northern Uganda Social Action Fund.* Report No. 23885-UG. Washington, DC: World Bank, Human Development 1, Country Department 4, Africa Regional Office.

SECTION THREE

EVALUATING OPERATIONS THROUGH A SOCIAL CAPITAL LENS

CHAPTER EIGHT

ENABLING SOCIAL CAPITAL?
Lessons from World Bank Rural Development Projects in Mexico and the Philippines

Jonathan Fox
John Gershman

Introduction[1]

The concept of social capital has followed a contested trajectory in the debate over how to describe poor people's social resources. Some frame social capital in terms of a broader, comprehensive theory of how the barriers to collective action can be overcome. Others see it as a descriptive term whose main value is in facilitating communication about collective action across disciplinary boundaries. Critics see it as yet another example of the increasing domination of mainstream economics over other intellectual traditions. In the international development field, this debate reached a high point with the World Bank's use of the social capital concept in its 2000/2001 World Development Report. Both advocates and skeptics see the concept as closely associated with the World Bank's recent endorsement of poor people's empowerment, though they come to different conclusions about whether it is possible for the institution to encourage the process.[2] Rather than focus on the contested impact of the concept itself, this chapter adds to the debate by focusing on actual practices of the World Bank, assessing the degree to which the Bank's new-style projects actually contribute to the "enabling environment" that most would agree is key to permitting poor people to consolidate their own representative organizations.

The idea of enabling environments refers to the institutional context that either facilitates or blocks the collective action that is critical to providing leverage and voice to under-represented people. This includes political, social, and economic institutions; inequalities in power and wealth and varied forms of social capital (as outlined in Chapter 2). This study is concerned specifically with the interaction between nation-state development agencies influenced by World Bank projects on the one hand, and representative organizations of the rural poor on the other. The case studies detail how the design and implementation of these develop-ment projects either facilitate, obstruct, or destroy processes of pro-poor social capital accumulation.

Few would disagree with the claim that the World Bank, through its projects, can make or break poor people's social capital. Indeed, the nega-tive impacts of specific Bank projects are well known and persistent, in spite of the frequent claim that the lessons of the past have been learned (e.g., Clark et al. 2003). In principle, however, the Bank's extensive array of social and environmental policy reforms do enable positive contributions to "social capital accumulation" as well, under specified conditions.[3] A focus on these policies is relevant because they constitute a critical con-ceptual and empirical bridge between official institutional discourse (see Chapter 1) and actual practices.

The Bank's most relevant reform policies are of essentially two types: "safeguards" and "good practices." The former are of the "first do no harm" variety and include policies on environmental assessment, indige-nous peoples, and resettlement; they are supposed to be mandatory.[4] The "good practices" policies, which are merely recommended, advocate, for example, good governance, gender equality, collaboration with NGOs, and informed participation by beneficiaries of World Bank–funded projects.[5] If implemented, both kinds of policies could contribute to an enabling environment that facilitates poor people's collective action. The empirical question that follows is when, where, and whether these poli-cies are implemented. The process of translating policies into institutional practice has been quite uneven so far, with significant variation occurring among countries and across sectors within countries.

This chapter examines the ways in which the policy process affects horizontal social capital on the ground, and how this policy process is in turn influenced by intersectoral social capital that bridges social and insti-tutional divides. The processes are analyzed here by assessing the degree to which World Bank projects contribute to enabling institutional environ-ments for both of these kinds of social capital, based on comparative field studies of "post-reform" rural development projects.[6]

Overview

This study suggests that the most direct impact of "post-reform" World Bank projects on social capital development depends on whether or not the projects contribute to an *enabling environment*. This term refers to a political and economic environment that facilitates the strengthening of representative poor people's organizations. The case studies confirmed the hypothesis that this process depends on the convergence of three sets of actors. Projects must (1) at the international level, be supported by specific World Bank actors willing to invest their political as well as economic capital on promoting pro–collective action institutional changes; (2) at the governmental level, be designed to support agencies that are *already* controlled by policymakers who favor balanced partnerships with broad-based social organizations; and (3) also target sectors and regions where pro-participation civil society actors already have some capacity to take advantage of institutional openings. If any of these three pro-reform actors are not involved in the project process, reform implementation is likely to fall short.[7] The basic point is quite straightforward: Putting pro-participation reforms into practice requires balanced, multisectoral coalitions in order to offset the inevitable opposition. The project cases reviewed here assess these three sets of actors in terms of their relative strengths and the relationships between them.

Drawing on Woolcock and Narayan's conceptual framework in Chapter 2, three different kinds of social capital are involved:

- *Horizontal social capital.* Local, horizontal social capital constitutes the basic building block for grassroots action. This kind of social capital is difficult for policymakers to create where it is absent, but easy for Bank-funded projects to destroy where it is present (most directly, through large-infrastructure projects).
- *Horizontally and vertically scaled-up social capital.* When local horizontal groups form ties with other base groups to form networks and federations, the vertical and horizontal ties between them may be weaker than intragroup ties, but they play a critical role in terms of generating bargaining power vis-à-vis other actors. This kind of social capital is more susceptible to consolidation in response to the institutional environment, including freedom of association and participatory policy innovations.
- *Intersectoral social capital.* In order for national and international policymakers to promote institutional innovations that encourage grassroots social capital, intersectoral social capital between diverse coalition partners between pro-reform actors across institutional boundaries is needed.[8]

This study focuses on the scaled-up and intersectoral dimensions of social capital. World Bank and national policymakers often promote social capital among themselves; the question here is whether they extend their efforts to build coalitions with existing poor people's organizations.

The research strategy combined cross-national/cross-regional and subnational comparisons. The field research generated a detailed data set on the institutional dynamics of ten post-reform rural anti-poverty and "green" projects, six of which are discussed here.[9] The project cases were chosen from two large Bank borrowers, the Philippines and Mexico, with one rural development project, one natural resource management project, and one rural finance project in each country. Both countries have significant "stocks" of poor peoples' social capital in the form of membership-based, networked, and scaled-up rural economic development organizations, as well as diverse experiences of state-society synergy that has encouraged social capital consolidation in the past (Fox 1996; Borras 1999). While the two countries had different political regimes during the period under study, the key variables in the proposed explanation of "pro–social capital" outcomes do not depend on national regime type. Common to the two states were a major World Bank role in the national development policy process, a heterogeneous state apparatus that included both pro- and anti-reform factions, and a diverse but relatively consolidated civil society, including organized rural social organizations. These shared contextual variables allow a research focus on variation between and within projects.

To focus analysis on those cases where at least partial reform was *possible*, the project cases were chosen based on two criteria. First, they were designed under the mandate of the World Bank's social and environmental policy reforms, and thus purportedly aim to combine targeted support for pro-poor economic development with sustainable resource management. Second, all the projects were implemented in sectors or regions where some degree of consolidated social capital already existed, in the form of broad-based rural grassroots organizations and experienced development NGOs. Projects varied in terms of the government agency supported (politically as well as economically) by a World Bank loan. This led to variation in terms of the second variable in the hypothesis. In both countries, for example, the environment ministries were dominated by pro–social capital policymakers while those in charge of rural financial projects were not. In terms of the third variable, the regions targeted ranged from those with consolidated, broad-based organizations of the rural poor to areas where dense social capital was lacking.

Case research focused on both the design and implementation phases of each project. World Bank evaluators agree that "quality at entry" (referring to "entry into the loan portfolio") is closely associated with the quality of project outcomes. The design process for investment projects, especially in socially and environmentally sensitive areas, usually takes several years, creating a rich track record for research and analysis. The World Bank reforms that guide the project design process include its environmental assessment policy (1989, revised in 1991), its public information disclosure policy (1994), and its indigenous peoples policy (1982, revised in 1991). All three policies were designed to promote informed participation by key stakeholders in the design as well as the implementation of projects, among others.

Each project design process was analyzed in terms of the degree and the nature of implementation of each of the World Bank's ostensibly mandatory "pro–social capital" policy reforms. To operationalize the study of reform policy compliance, the assessment was based on a series of measurable indicators drawn from the official policies themselves. In the case of environmental assessment, for example, the key indicators involve the process, nature, timing, and impact of the pre-loan project impact assessment.[10] In the case of the public information policy, indicators of implementation include the quality of the public project summary (Public Information Document, or PID), the point in the project design process when it was made public, and the language in which it was published and channeled for public dissemination. While the project summary is the single most important public document mandated by the new information policy, this study also assesses the degree to which other relevant policy information was shared with key stakeholders (such as the operational manuals and guidelines for Bank-funded government programs). The indigenous peoples policy is relevant because all the projects under study affect large numbers of indigenous communities.[11] This policy's key provision is the ostensibly obligatory mandate to permit the "informed participation" of affected indigenous peoples at all stages of the policy process, including the design phase. At least 10.5 percent of Mexico's population is indigenous, and at least 8 percent of the Philippine population are ethnic minorities.[12] They are among the poorest of the poor in both countries and therefore should be among the principal beneficiaries of targeted rural anti-poverty projects. In both countries, indigenous people also inhabit most of the biodiversity hotspots, many of which are targeted for support by World Bank projects.

Indicators of Institutional Preconditions for Informed Participation by Social Actors

This study focuses on only some of the institutional changes that contribute to an enabling environment for social capital.[13] The first three indicators detailed below highlight the fundamental role of opportunities for informed public participation. The fourth indicator assesses whether intersectoral coalitions emerged to promote these institutional changes. Each project was rated zero, low, medium, or high on each indicator.

- *Public participation in the project design process.* To what degree did the project design process involve informed participation by a pluralistic range of organized low-income people, especially indigenous people's and rural women's groups? If consultative meetings were held, but the input was ignored, this would be considered a low level of public participation. Medium to high levels involved some degree of public impact on the policy process, such as the creation of power-sharing bodies to allocate resources to subprojects.

- *Timely public access to information in the implementation.* Did organized beneficiaries have timely access to the basic project documents, in their languages, at an early stage of the implementation process? If only the minimum official requirement of English-language Bank documents available upon request to Washington was met, then for the purposes of assessing the institutional environment for grassroots action, such projects would be ranked "zero." If such documents were available only in English but within the country, the ranking would be "low." If the key project information was publicly available in the main local language, perhaps through a government agency operating manual, then the ranking would be "medium." If the government or the Bank made a systematic effort to translate and disseminate not only the basic documents but also ongoing project implementation information, such as regular progress reports, the rating would be "high."

- *Institutional mechanisms for state-society power sharing in resource allocation.* Did the project include institutional mechanisms for the sharing of power over resource allocation between the state and representative civil society organizations, especially indigenous people's and women's groups? If so, to what degree were such institutions actually created in practice, and were they inclusive of the full range of existing poor people's socioeconomic organizations in the specific region or sector?

This indicator is disaggregated in terms of both national and local-regional levels, where state-society power sharing is more likely to be permitted. If multiple anti-poverty resource allocation bodies were created, did their decision-making processes vary, and if so, how and why? If power-sharing bodies included the relevant social organizations but lacked actual authority over resource allocation, their contribution to the environment for social capital consolidation would still be considered "low to medium," since their existence might allow future efforts toward their gaining authority over the process. If, however, at most a small minority of regional councils were even partially inclusive, such a project would rank "zero to low" in terms of power sharing. If a substantial minority of project councils were inclusive and actually had some authority, such a project would rank "medium." If a majority were both inclusive and had authority, the project would rank "medium to high" or "high." In the case of diverse regional outcomes, a project could be ranked "low to high."

- *Intersectoral coalition building.* Did international and national policy-makers make efforts to reach out to form pro–poor people's social capital partnerships—with each other or with civil society stakeholders? Note that this is a very specific kind of intersectoral partnership, in contrast to other kinds, such as partnerships between Bank and government officials not interested in engaging with civil society organizations. This study assesses the degree to which Bank, government, and civil society actors came together for the specific purpose of making the policy environment more conducive to public transparency and pluralistic state-society power sharing over resource allocation. Timid, erratic efforts to form coalitions would be rated "zero to low." Discrete, selective, but nontrivial efforts would be rated "medium." More sustained, broader coalition-building efforts would be rated "medium to high" or "high." Did Bank and/or government policymakers actually develop practical strategies and invest their own political capital to offset resistance from anti-participation factions embedded in both the Bank and the state?

Case Analysis

The official goals of each project are summarized in Table 8.1, based on their "founding" operational documents.[14] All the projects explicitly stress the official intention to target benefits to the rural poor, and/or to protect their immediate environment. Several add the explicit goal of supporting poor people's organizations, but the majority do not. The findings are based on the review of the official documents, as well as extensive field interviews with World Bank staff, national and local government officials, and representatives of grassroots stakeholder organizations.

The World Bank and Social Capital Formation in Rural Mexico[15]

The World Bank reoriented its Mexican lending portfolio during the first half of the 1990s, shifting from its 1980s focus on structural adjustment toward allocating significant investments to anti-poverty and environmental projects.[16] Though this shift in lending priorities turned out to be temporary, it brought a broad range of Mexican rural development policies in the 1990s under the scope of the World Bank's social and environmental policies. Notably, the targeted anti-poverty efforts involved millions of indigenous people, yet in very few cases were the Bank's indigenous peoples policy and its implications for social capital taken into account.[17] During this period, most of the World Bank's rural portfolio in Mexico ignored the potential contribution of poor people's social capital to anti-poverty efforts.

**Table 8.1   Official Goals of Six Post–World Bank Reform
Rural Development Projects**

Project (Loan Date)	Official Goals (Social Capital–Related)
Mexico	
Rural Financial Markets (1995)	"To augment the participation of rural entrepreneurs in rural financial markets, especially of the poor . . . [and] to demonstrate that it is possible to supply financial services to small and micro-entrepreneurs in small rural localities—in a sustainable manner" (World Bank/Global Environment Facility 1995c: 3)
Community Forestry (1997)	"Designed to empower the communities and *ejidos* in their decision-making as to the nature, extent and timing of the training and technical assistance on sustainable forestry management they would receive" (World Bank/Global Environment Facility 1997a: 21)
Rural Development in Marginal Areas (1997)	"Improve the well-being and income of smallholder in about 24 targeted marginal areas . . . fostering community socio-economic development, organization, and participation" (World Bank/ Global Environment Facility 1997b: 2)
Philippines	
Protected Areas (1994)	"Provide program support for the development, conservation and management of resources with 10 priority sites under the Government's National Integrated Protected Area System" (World Bank/Global Environment Facility 1994: 16)
Second Rural Finance (1995)	"Expand . . . commercial credit to agriculture and rural development . . . and . . . enhance the policy framework of the rural financial sector by . . . [financing] private sector investments in the rural areas, . . . strengthening [the Land Bank, and] upgrading the operating capacity of rural cooperatives [and] participating financial institutions" (World Bank/Global Environment Facility 1995b: 15)
Agrarian Reform Communities (1996)	"Provide support services for agrarian reform beneficiaries through institutional development of membership organizations, agricultural enterprise development and rural infrastructure" (World Bank/Global Environment Facility 1996: 20)

Note: Each statement quotes the official project document (formerly called the Staff Appraisal Report, more recently called the Project Appraisal Document). Since all of these loans were signed after 1994, they are subject to the information disclosure policy and are therefore available at the World Bank's Public Information Center.

Rural Financial Markets

This project was designed after a Bank-funded study made the "remarkable" discovery that rural financial markets in Mexico do not work equitably or efficiently (World Bank/Global Environment Facility 1995b). The study surveyed families in three regions about rural financial markets but did not focus on the actual operations of existing poor people's financial organizations, such as the numerous savings clubs and small farmers' credit unions. The project design nevertheless assumed that only large private commercial banks had the potential to provide efficient financial services to the rural poor. The project combined technical assistance, designed to support those policymakers favoring the withdrawal of the small amount of remaining public sector farm credit, with a pilot project to subsidize those private banks willing to experiment with low-cost banking systems appropriate for rural areas. Only the technical assistance part of the project (with less than 10 percent of the budget) could conceivably have reached NGOs or social organizations, but they received at most a small fraction of this small fraction.

The project's design phase involved considerable debate with one of the Mexican peasant movement's networks of regional economic organizations, the Mexican Association of Social Sector Credit Unions (*Asociacion Mexicana de Uniones de Credito del Sector Social,* or AMUCSS). AMUCSS raised concerns with the Bank and the Treasury Ministry about the rejection of their point of view, and cited Bank policies mandating consultations with indigenous peoples (AMUCSS affiliates in Oaxaca and Chiapas are broad-based indigenous credit co-ops). The Bank's response suggested that its field surveys on rural financial markets "went beyond the World Bank participatory guidelines." However, the surveys dealt only with how financial markets worked, and did not ask for views regarding a range of possible solutions. The Bank's written reply also asserted that the proposal to hire local individuals to staff the proposed experimental rural branches of financial intermediaries would count as indigenous people's participation and somehow guarantee accountability and responsiveness. The Bank response also noted that AMUCSS affiliates had attended a Bank–Treasury Ministry seminar, and they had therefore been "consulted."[18]

AMUCSS represented 35,000 smallholders. Its strategy was not confrontational, nor was it associated with the political opposition. Though autonomous from the government, it was led by a member of the peasant wing of the ruling party. AMUCSS's views were rejected because World Bank and counterpart Treasury Ministry officials considered all credit unions to be fatally flawed. Indeed, the government's weak institutional framework did permit corruption at several major credit unions, but mainly urban ones. The Bank-sponsored study did not examine those credit unions linked to producer unions, to see whether, in spite of financial weaknesses, they might have created compensatory pro-accountability structures and embodied considerable accumulated social capital. Indeed, some of the credit unions' main structural flaws were shared by Mexico's private banks (such as permitting owners to lend to themselves). Nevertheless, the private commercial banks were seen as the solution to the problem of rural financial market failures. In practice, Mexico's private banks were resistant to inducement by the project's offer of subsidies. This was not surprising, given the systemic problems and short-term orientation of most Mexican private banks. After three years few funds were disbursed, and the project was later canceled.[19]

On balance, this project contributed nothing to enable social capital formation or consolidation. Indeed, project proponents would have preferred to liquidate poor people's existing financial organizations rather than attempt to, for example, restructure them to harness their accumulated social capital. Because there was some serious debate with social organizations during the project's design phase, one could rank that as zero to low participation, but during the implementation phase the project rated zero.

Community Forestry
Mexico is unique in that 70 to 80 percent of its forest resources are in community-based landholdings (World Bank/Global Environment Facility 1997a: 1). Over the last two decades Mexico's forest policy has shifted from promoting corporate and state firm exploitation of these resources to encouraging community-based self-management, in addition to promoting corporate forest plantations. These different policy priorities coexisted uneasily within the government. In this context, this project takes sides: Its goal is "to empower the communities and *ejidos* in their decision making" regarding access to technical assistance (World Bank/Global Environment Facility 1997a: 21).

This project was designed in response to the prior failure of an earlier World Bank forest project and is an instructive case of "social learning" in the Bank, the state, and civil society (Brown 1998). The predecessor project focused on subsidizing logging roads on indigenous lands in northern Mexico, without taking into account the environmental or social costs.[20] The Mexico–United States cross-border coalition that challenged the project in 1991 was empowered by the NAFTA debate. In addition, indigenous rights advocates within the Mexican government shared critical information about the then-secret project with NGOs, reflecting a discreet state-society partnership.[21] The external pressure shone a spotlight on the project's inadequate environmental and social assessments, empowering Bank staff to suspend it in 1991. According to the official Bank retrospective, administrative problems and the "mounting public criticism of the operation" led the government to perceive the project as "problematic," lose interest, and eventually cancel the balance of the loan (World Bank/Global Environment Facility 1995d: iii). This was the first

Mexican World Bank project to be canceled in part due to civil society concerns.

Bank staff then convened a collaborative sectoral analysis with the Mexican government and invited some of Mexico's most socially and environmentally concerned nongovernmental forest policy experts. This produced an overview study that provided the conceptual framework for the participatory project design process that followed (World Bank/Global Environment Facility 1995a). Collaboration between pro-reform Bank staff, Mexican Environment Ministry policymakers, Mexican forest policy researchers, and NGOs also led to a series of participatory workshops with community-based indigenous timber enterprises (Martínez et al. 1995a, b). The project that emerged was targeted geographically at the state of Oaxaca, which included many of Mexico's most consolidated, community-based indigenous economic enterprises, many with years of experience managing their own timber resources. The project was designed to bolster access to diverse forest management services and to increase the quality, environmental sensitivity, and accountability of those service providers.

Project implementation included regular consultations and information sharing with a wide range of stakeholders, resulting in the building of partnerships between project managers within the Environment Ministry, forest management NGOs, and community forestry organizations. The project faced opposition from the Treasury Ministry, which blocked and then slowed allocation of most counterpart funds.[22] Less public but at least as significant was the quiet resistance from traditional foresters within the Environment Ministry who did not share the project goal of encouraging forester accountability to community organizations.[23] It was difficult for Environment Ministry managers to be accountable to their civil society partners when they had few funds with which to operate the project, but the intersectoral relationships were sufficiently strong to survive this test. Indeed, World Bank project staff have been consistently supportive of their Mexican project manager colleagues in internal debates with Treasury Ministry and other Environment Ministry officials.[24] These challenges to the implementation process suggest that the combination of broad-based horizontal social capital with diversified intersectoral social capital is necessary but not sufficient. These coalitions must also mobilize their *political capital* to offset opposition that is inherent in the process of encouraging the empowerment of poor peoples' organizations.

Overall, this project ranked medium to high during the design phase, not only because of the inclusionary consultation process, but also because this process had an impact on the actual design of the project. The implementation of the project involved high degrees of public access to information in Spanish, at both the national and regional levels, as well as medium levels of power sharing with community forestry organizations in the resource allocation process in the targeted state of Oaxaca.

Rural Development in Marginal Areas

This project emerged from the recognition by a World Bank institutional development specialist that more participatory, targeted approaches were needed to reach low-income, indigenous small producers in Mexico. The project's first Bank manager invested in building "bridging" intersectoral social capital, making the effort to meet relevant NGO leaders and to learn about the actual functioning of Mexican institutions, and even commissioned the first-ever Spanish translation of a Bank PID (1995). The project design process was, at the time, the most participatory ever for a World Bank project in Mexico, including studies and consultations from a wide range of relevant viewpoints (Velásquez 1996). Oaxacan public interest groups and indigenous producer organizations strongly recommended that the project allocate its resources through participatory councils that would include regional organizations. These councils, in their view, needed a significant degree of autonomy from government agencies in order to avoid problems previously experienced with "power-sharing" bodies that either excluded the larger, more autonomous organizations or lacked real decision-making power.

The early phase of the project design process reflected institutional learning, both from Bank projects that had limited results and from earlier Mexican government programs that had shown some promise in terms of building balanced relationships with indigenous producer organizations. The project design drew lessons from the National Indigenous Institute's experience with regional producer councils.[25]

The project design was constrained by the decision to shift the project's location from the Social Development Ministry to the Agriculture Ministry (which prioritized productive projects but lacked any track record of balanced power sharing with autonomous indigenous producer organizations). The process was also weakened by high turnover among Bank Task Managers, who either lacked authority (one was a temporary consultant) or did not prioritize participatory approaches. In addition, the project's geographical coverage was expanded far beyond the original focus on three regions within Oaxaca where conditions for balanced state-society relations were most promising. The Huasteca region, which covers parts of three states, was also included, benefiting three additional ruling-party governors.[26] Both intersectoral and scaled-up horizontal social capital were lacking in most of that region. The final version of the project retained the general idea of the regional councils, but design changes significantly weakened their potential for power sharing with autonomous producer organizations by giving unsympathetic government agencies veto power (Subsecretaría de Desarrollo Rural 1998).

In spite of the moderately participatory early project design process, the final design produced very weak pro–social capital provisions. This does not mean, however, that project outcomes were predetermined. Mexican rural development programs have sometimes followed more participatory paths than observers had first predicted. In past experiences, however, the degree to which programs could "outgrow" their initial constraints depended heavily on the capacity of social organizations to respond to small openings for participation within the system, and on the capacity of pro–power sharing policymakers to gain actual control over program implementation (Fox 1992). In the case of this program, the implementation experience shows that many autonomous social organizations did consistently *try* to participate, but they did not manage to find policymakers willing to invest in building partnerships. At the federal level, the program was assigned to a department of the Agriculture Ministry that was managed by a nominally sympathetic undersecretary, but one whose views were not shared either by his key operational subordinates or by the four state governments directly involved in managing the regional councils. The state governments varied only in their degree of hostility to partnerships with autonomous organizations.[27]

As program implementation proceeded, policymakers began to subdivide the original regional councils into smaller, subregional councils. This measure was intended to strengthen the hand of those state and federal government officials who opposed power sharing, and it worked. The program had ten distinct regional or subregional decision making processes in its six original regions by August 1999. Of those ten regions or subregions, one lacked any participatory mechanism whatsoever (Mixe Bajo–Cuenca), two involved only incipient inclusion (Huasteca Veracruzana and Huasteca Hidalguense), three involved some combination of incipient and partial inclusion (Mixe Alto, Mazateca Alta, San Luis Potosí–Plains), three involved partial inclusion (Mazateca Baja, Mixe Bajo–Istmo, and Huasteca San Luis Potosí–Sierra), and only one council could be considered fully inclusionary (Cuicatlán)—and it was soon dismantled. This exceptional case, in which all of the representative producer organizations in the region were involved, warrants further discussion. Not coincidentally, rural civil society in this region had an unusually high degree of organizational and social cohesion, with all the representative organizations unified under a single umbrella group, the *Unión de Ejidos y Comunidades Cuicatecas.*

Cuicatlán's regional indigenous producer organization had extensive experience participating in and directly managing other government rural development programs (Fox 1994). Though autonomous in practice, this organization was actively affiliated with the ruling party, and therefore was less likely than more overtly autonomous groups to be excluded from a government program. Though it appeared that all of the conditions for successful participation and the construction of intersectoral social capital were in place, project authorities decided unilaterally to dissolve their regional council in favor of creating three new "micro-regional" councils. A statewide network of regional councils emerged in an attempt to sustain participation in the program, but state and federal program authorities succeeded in dismantling it.[28]

Overall, this project ranked medium during the project design phase because of its unusually significant degree of public consultation in one of the states involved. This process had only modest impacts on actual project design, and few information access and power-sharing reforms were carried out during the implementation phase.

The Bank and Social Capital Formation in the Philippines

The World Bank's portfolio in the Philippines was dominated by structural and sectoral adjustment programs in the early to mid-1980s. Following the fall of the Marcos dictatorship in 1986, World Bank lending gradually expanded its support for infrastructure, social development, rural development, and natural resource management projects throughout the 1990s. This shift in lending priorities incorporated a whole new set of rural development policies and programs under the auspices of the Bank's operational policies. The impact of World Bank–funded infrastructure projects on indigenous peoples had been a key political issue in the Philippines (and at the Bank) in the 1970s and 1980s, but had not translated into steps to promote the participation of indigenous people's organizations when they were putative beneficiaries of other kinds of projects. In this period the World Bank's natural resource management and rural development portfolio took a very uneven approach to poor people's social capital with respect to poverty alleviation, both across sectors and across geographic regions. At best, poor people's organizations were seen as potential instruments for project implementation, but they were largely ignored when it came to project design.

Integrated Protected Areas

The Integrated Protected Areas System (IPAS) project was originally identified by a World Bank–funded environmental sector review that targeted biodiversity conservation as a critical weakness in the Philippine natural resource management sector. This project was funded by a $20 million grant under the Global Environment Facility (GEF) managed by Bank staff under the same reform policies as for a regular Bank-funded loan project. The project initially identified ten Protected Areas (PAs) in biodiversity "hot spots" but subsequently reduced its focus to nine sites. Unlike previous conservation efforts, the project aimed at encouraging community participation in the protection of natural resources and also addressed livelihood concerns by providing land tenure security and local development investments. This project was featured in the Bank's *Participation Sourcebook* (Wiens 1996).

The design phase included some consultation with potentially affected communities. One indigenous community rejected participation, and the site was changed. Consultations with membership-based civil society organizations in the site areas were not extensive, though some NGOs were actively involved. Scientists drafted management plans for each site, but with virtually no participation on the part of local groups. As the World Bank Task Manager noted, during the design phase he "hadn't paid much attention to the participatory aspect of the project. I assumed that, because it was being done by local NGOs, participation would take care of itself. I was soon to learn that this was not the case" (Wiens 1996: 103).

At the national level, the project was co-implemented by the Department of Environment and Natural Resources (DENR) and a consortium of environment and development NGOs. At the PA sites, the key implementing actors were the park superintendent, an employee of the DENR and typically a forester, and the host NGO, typically a consortium of local NGOs (or local chapters of national NGOs). The project ran into difficulties in its first three years as the result of design problems, poor national-level management (from both the DENR and NGO sides), and rapid turnover of project managers. These problems limited the prospects for building strong state manager–civil society social capital.[29] New staffing on the NGO side in the beginning of 1998 along with the longer tenure of a DENR manager, the project's mid-term review, and a new, more pro-reform task team leader on the Bank side all combined to enable a project re-design.

The project's original emphasis on site protection over community participation resulted in an attack on the PA residents' livelihood activities prior to the investment of the development funds. A combined grant–revolving credit fund constituted roughly 50 percent of the total donor-provided project funds, yet it was nearly three years into the project before livelihood guidelines were completed and communities were able to access the funds. Part of this delay was due to poor management on the NGO consortium side, and part was due to a debate over the terms of how to invest the livelihood funds.[30]

Involvement by representatives of the PA communities in project implementation was uneven across the nine sites. In six of the PAs there were some preexisting consolidated peoples' organizations and/or the indigenous communities were either fairly cohesive or settled. Also, there were existing local NGOs that led on-site implementation. In three sites social groups were effectively nonexistent or very weak, and the indigenous communities lacked cohesion or were nomadic. The local NGOs were weak. While no original project documents were ever translated into local languages during the design phase, information access under project implementation improved, with Protected Area management plans and livelihood project guidelines eventually translated into relevant local languages. All nine sites organized some kind of community-based committees involved in site protection and patrolling forest and coastal resources.

The key local decision-making body was the Protected Area Management Board (PAMB), which was chaired by the park superintendent and included government and nongovernmental representatives, including a representative of the indigenous communities living in the PA. Of the nine sites, seven included indigenous communities and one was almost entirely indigenous. All sites had provision for NGO and private organization (PO) membership on the PAMBs, although the extent of actual representation and participation on the boards ranged from low in areas where there was little preexisting social capital (three sites) to more significant in areas with consolidated social organizations. Civil society was weak in these three regions due to their history of repression and political clientelism.

Meetings of many of the boards were often conducted in English, a language spoken only by those with relatively high levels of formal education. This made effective participation by some indigenous groups very difficult. In one site, the "indigenous" representative was a non-indigenous official from the former government agency responsible for state-indigenous relations. There were no allowances made, however, for the variation in preexisting social capital in terms of the length of time for which resources for community organizing were available.

The criteria for accessing livelihood funds were transparent, and in the case of smaller investments, the decision-making process was participatory, varying to some degree because of uneven local NGO capacity. For larger proposals, decisions were made nationally by the DENR-NGO Integrated Protected Areas Fund Board, which handled policy for overall financing of the PAs. There was virtually no representation of directly affected communities at the national level.

Indigenous communities' participation was limited by the government's failure to provide the land tenure provisions necessary to recognize their resource claims. In some sites there was significant local elite opposition to recognizing the ancestral land claims of the indigenous communities living in the area. In four cases, however, indigenous groups were stronger and had more external allies (both governmental and nongovernmental). One lesson of this is that local politics and alliances—themselves also products of the historical geographies of political activism—have great influence on the extent to which a Bank-funded project affects scaled-up and intersectoral social capital formation.

Overall, this project ranked low to medium in terms of grassroots participation in project design, low to medium in terms of national-level public information access, and high in terms of local-regional information access, though with local variation. In terms of power sharing over local-regional resource allocation, the project ranks low to medium nationally and ranges from low to high across diverse PAs (see further discussion of regional diversity below). The project did involve significant "social capital building" between pro-participation actors in the World Bank, the DENR and NGOs, making important mid-course corrections possible in project implementation.

Agrarian Reform Communities Development

The Agrarian Reform Communities Development Project (ARCDP) was designed to provide support services and infrastructure for 100 Agrarian Reform Communities (ARCs) composed of agrarian reform beneficiaries. Based on a participatory planning process, each ARC was supposed to create a development plan that identified and prioritized subprojects (mostly infrastructure). Project sites were chosen in provinces where other donors were not operating, but were not chosen specifically in areas where there were strong community-based organizations (CBOs) and/or strong NGOs with proven track records in community organizing.

Community investment planning involved government officials and CBO leaders, including *barangay* (village) consultation workshops, household surveys, and focus group discussions (the latter done by farmer leaders). The strength of this process depended on the facilitator, the strength of existing POs, and the openness of local government officials. The final plan was produced in English. There was uneven attention to the gender composition of the group, and the farming systems plan rarely incorporated information on the gender division of labor. The plans developed through this process were also supposed to be incorporated into *barangay* and municipal development plans, to ensure local government counterpart funding. This proved to be a major obstacle to project implementation, for example, when newly elected officials refused to utilize the development plan drafted under his or her predecessor.

The institutional development components focused almost entirely on building the creditworthiness of cooperatives in each *barangay* of the ARC, and within this, there was an emphasis on the need to develop appropriate "cooperative values" by the members. The project was weakened by its almost exclusive focus on the cooperatives, to the exclusion of other social organizations. Many of the cooperatives were weak, were dependent on the government, and lacked basic capacities in planning and financial management. Many were unable to act as financial intermediaries because of arrears to the Land Bank from previous credit programs. In the exceptional cases where the local Department of Agriculture and project staff had community organizing experience, their efforts led to greater autonomy for the community-based organizations. In one paradigmatic case, however, the local development facilitator (working for the department) described her role as "caring for [the project beneficiaries] as you would care for children."[31]

Each subproject was supposed to be monitored by joint government–People's Organization Village implementation teams, which included village government and co-op representatives. In the case of construction projects, there were widespread reports that this system worked to hold private contractors accountable. Numerous comparisons were made (in cases of road rehabilitation) with the lack of accountability and poor quality of roads constructed under the Department of Public Works and Highways in previous projects.[32]

This project ranked zero to low for its design phase, medium in terms of national public information access, and high for information access at the local and regional level. Power sharing for subprojects reached low to medium levels. Some degree of synergy was created between implementing agency staff, local governments, NGOs, and grassroots organizations in the design of the *barangay* development plans and the monitoring of the construction of the rural infrastructure components.

Second Rural Finance Project

The Second Rural Finance Project (1995–1999) provided funds to the government's leading rural development lender, the Land Bank, which would in turn make funds available to rural financial institutions to lend for agricultural, agro-industrial, and rural projects. This investment was a response to the decline in formal lending to the agricultural sector. Agricultural loans as a percentage of total loans had dropped from 8.0 percent to 4.1 percent from 1983 to 1992 (World Bank 1995b: 6).

In addition to the project funds allocated for financial intermediation, the Land Bank was to invest $1.5 million in counterpart resources in institutional strengthening, including rural cooperatives. Many had been established in either the late 1970s or late 1980s, in periods that coincided with targeted credit programs for farmer cooperatives. These programs had been managed by the Land Bank. Many cooperatives were in arrears. Through early 1998, two-thirds of total project loans (in value terms) were released through commercial banks, with an average loan amount of 9.3 million pesos, although a larger number of loans were released to rural banks.[33] No funds were loaned to cooperatives.

The strengthening of rural cooperatives would have contributed to strengthening poor people's social capital, especially if it included training for cooperative leaders. In this sense, the Second Rural Finance Project was an advance over the First Rural Finance Project, which had not disbursed its funds earmarked for cooperatives. The program charged interest rates that were higher than the other preexisting Land Bank lending windows to farmer cooperatives.[34] The Second Rural Financial Project emphasized capacity building through the training program in order to enable farmer cooperatives to access credit at market rates.

Under the terms of the Second Rural Finance Project, the Land Bank revised its accreditation criteria for cooperatives in 1997, reinforcing an ongoing decline in their number. The number of cooperatives accredited by the Land Bank fell by 50 percent, from 8,165 in 1993 to 4,035 in 1998.[35] This project's impact on poor people's social capital is hard to determine because it included no systematic monitoring and evaluation framework to help the Land Bank evaluate the impact of its cooperative strengthening efforts. The Land Bank collected data only on the numbers of training program participants. The program did not collect data (or focus on) the role of women in those cooperatives. The Land Bank tracked the numbers of accredited cooperatives and whether they were upgraded or downgraded on an annual basis, but that data was not systematically fed into the operations of the Land Bank to evaluate the impact of training programs.[36] The main thrust of the cooperative strengthening program was to encourage mergers of weaker cooperatives into stronger ones. According to Land Bank staff, the most common explanation for the failure of rural cooperatives was that "the rural poor just don't have the right values," which is why there was a major emphasis on "values formation" in their cooperative training program. The Land Bank refused to release copies of its Institutional Strengthening Action Plan, claiming, "It is confidential because it is part of our strategic plan. If it fell into the wrong hands. . . ."[37]

This project ranked zero in terms of participation during design, and low for public information access. Since no mechanisms were created for power sharing over resource allocation for subprojects, it ranked zero on both counts. This project made virtually no contribution to the policy environment for community-based rural financial organizations.

Empirical and Conceptual Findings

Varied Bargaining Power Among Pro-Reform Actors Drives Varied Social Capital Outcomes

The outcomes were very uneven across both sectors and regions. While most projects did not systematically put pro-participation discourse into practice, two of the six projects did take significant strides in that direction. The two projects (Marginal Areas in Mexico and the Protected Areas program in the Philippines) where regional variation was studied in greater depth also revealed that even in some of the more promising cases, a wide range of different local-regional outcomes was the norm (Fox and Gresham 2000; Fox 2003).

The patterns of variation showed that projects in which funds were directed to implementing agencies that were already under the control of pro–social capital policymakers performed better than those projects whose funds were not. In three of the ten cases originally studied (Protected Areas and Agrarian Reform Communities in Philippines, and Community Forestry in Mexico), the projects directed funds to agencies led by (though not exclusively composed of) relatively powerful pro-participation managers (and also operational NGOs in the Protected Areas case). These were the same three projects where pro–social capital Bank staff played more influential roles, specifically investing their political capital to build coalitions with reformists within both the state and civil society.

In all the projects that actually underwent implementation, the key institutional obstacles/opportunities were located in powerful state-society coalitions that opposed power sharing with poor people's organization's, particularly indigenous people's groups. These coalitions were found to be well entrenched in provincial governments but were also embedded within the national agencies led by pro-participation reformists. Regional variation within projects was due to two main factors: cross-regional variation in the strength of scaled-up social capital within civil society, and cross-regional variation in mid-level program managers' attitudes toward autonomous organizations. The mixed cross-regional results—even in two quite promising projects—were in part the result of policymakers' "underinvestment" in promoting more enabling national and subnational institutional environments in the face of predictable opposition.

Ethnic and Gender Dimensions of Social Capital Remain Under-Recognized

Little evidence emerged of policy attention to either the ethnic or gender dimensions of social capital accumulation (one project was mildly gender sensitive in the Philippines, and one in each country took ethnic differences seriously into account). In the Philippines, the Integrated Protected Areas project paid some specific attention to the delineation of indigenous people's ancestral domain claims. The Agrarian Reform Communities project was the only one that paid any attention to the gendered dimension of social capital accumulation. In that project, monitoring indicators included data on women's membership and leadership roles in the cooperatives. But in the overall design stage and community planning stage, no particular attention was paid to building the social capital of poor women.

In Mexico, none of the projects studied was influenced by gender perspectives. Indeed, in at least one case in Oaxaca, organized rural women engaged in militant direct action to press for their right to be included in the program.[38] In terms of ethnicity, in Mexico only the Community Forestry project promoted partnerships that systematically respected the autonomy of Mexico's many and diverse indigenous producer organizations. In contrast, the once-promising Rural Development in Marginal Areas project either excluded or bypassed the most consolidated autonomous indigenous producer organizations in most of its areas of operation, according to diverse field reports. Federal officials blamed state government counterparts for these problems, but the entire project design was based precisely on reinforcing state officials' leverage over resource allocation.

Intersectoral Trust Is a Resource for Reform That Requires Investment

There is some confusion in the social capital literature over whether trust is an *element* of social capital, built into its definition ("norms and relationships"), a factor that *encourages* social capital, or the *result* of social capital. For this reason, the definition of social capital used here does not incorporate norms, and is limited to relationships. Conflating norms and networks under the same conceptual umbrella makes it difficult to understand causal flows: Is trust generated by relationships, or do relationships generate trust? The process is often reciprocal, but it may also be path dependent, which suggests that it matters whether the chicken or the egg comes first.

Levels of trust reflect previous experiences with relationships. For example, where trust is initially lacking, relationships must be built that can justify trust. This is clearly an issue for those attempting to build intersectoral social capital under less-than-democratic conditions, where, based on past experience, state actors are not widely perceived as pluralistic or motivated by the public interest. From the point of view of autonomous membership organizations, the reaction to the *promise* of participatory inclusion in the policy process is often one of "rational wariness." As a result, efforts to create enabling environments for intersectoral partnerships face a problem of strategic interaction. Pro-participation policymakers often start out relatively weak, in terms of their limited leverage over the rest of the state apparatus, so they need social actors to mobilize in support of their efforts. Yet those social actors may be quite skeptical. This is where the subjective factor of trust becomes relevant: For a mutually reinforcing coalition to emerge, each potential partner must make an investment with a high degree of uncertainty regarding the commitment, capacity, and intentions of every other potential partner.

The Rural Development in Marginal Areas experience in Mexico revealed the central role of trust in building intersectoral social capital. Here was a case that began with an unusual degree of communication and trust between the initial World Bank Project Manager and key social organizations and NGOs in the relatively densely organized state of Oaxaca. After the key Bank Manager was transferred and the project design process rejected key civil society recommendations for resource allocation power-sharing decision-making processes, years went by before the project itself was launched. Even after the loan was signed, funding flows at best trickled—leaving the regional councils to "dry up," as one federal Agriculture Ministry official put it.[39] In short, the intersectoral social capital that had accumulated during project preparation was consumed rather than invested.

This experience suggests a possibly generalizable dynamic, a *vicious circle of unmet expectations* that might describe why some participatory projects start off well but then veer off track. To understand this pattern, one needs to start by assessing the strategic calculus of the key subjects of the development process. Broad-based, autonomous producer organizations that have emerged in less-than-democratic environments may choose not to invest their scarce human resources and political capital by getting involved in ostensibly participatory development programs because they expect little or no return to their organization's investment. Based on their extensive past experiences with rural development programs, producer organizations are often relatively well informed about which kinds of government programs are likely to respect their autonomy and to deliver what they promise. Leaders who are accountable to their base will be especially sensitive to the risks associated with raising their members' expectations about the possible benefits from investing organizational resources in a government program. That is, organization leaders' time and credibility are also scarce resources, and they will be understandably wary about risking members' trust in them. This "rational wariness" underscores that it is critical for government and Bank officials to take tangible measures designed specifically to generate trust, and to make only commitments that they can comply with.

If, because of this rational wariness, only few broad-based organizations choose to participate in the government program, then the perverse effect will be that pro-participation officials in the government and the Bank will lack the organized constituency they would need to offset likely opposition to social participation. As a result, program managers will be unlikely to be able to deliver on their promises to the few organizations that do choose to participate, further eroding intersectoral social capital. At the same time, those organizations that decide not to participate will see their rational wariness to have been vindicated, in turn raising the minimum threshold that policymakers will need to establish credibility and trust in the future.

This schematic vicious circle describes the Marginal Areas experience in Oaxaca from 1995 to 1999. The largest and most influential of the state's autonomous producer organizations, such as the Oaxaca State Network of Coffee Organizations, chose not to invest further resources after the delayed and watered-down project design process eroded incipient intersectoral social capital. Those organizations that stuck with the participation process ended up feeling that their investment in participation had been wasted. National policymakers repeated their pro-participation promises, but they remained unable to prevent state and federal operational officials from breaking those promises. The broader process of decentralization strengthened the capacity of anti-participation state-level officials to ignore federal-level reformers.[40]

In contrast, the capacity of the Community Forestry project to open up space was the result of the intersectoral social capital that had been built up between state, Bank, and civil society participants, in the face of opposition within the state. The more general proposition here is that intersectoral trust is a resource for policy reform that requires investment to generate and may in turn need to be invested to sustain partnerships.

Unpack the State to Identify Obstacles and Opportunities for Reform

The original study focused on the three-way relationship between the Bank, the implementing government agency, and civil society. The field results suggest two important modifications of this schematic triangular relationship, both involving further "unpacking" of the state (both horizontally and vertically). At the national level, the cases highlight the important role played by the national financial intermediaries between the Bank and the national states (the Treasury Ministry in Mexico and departments of Budget and Management and Finance in the Philippines). In both countries, the national legislatures lack effective oversight over much of the executive's resource allocation, which reinforces the autonomy of the national financial authorities. They retain considerable leverage over all projects because they are responsible for the actual disbursements of government counterpart funds. Even if the finance ministries are not the implementing agencies, they can still act to inhibit or promote the enabling environments for social capital accumulation. In the Philippine cases, the role of the Budget and Finance ministries was important because they chose an austerity strategy that weakened the capacity of government agencies. Across-the-board 25 percent cuts in government counterpart funds undermined the ability of pro-reform government staff to pursue field operations because those were the first activities to be cut. In the Agrarian Reform Communities and Protected Areas cases, this meant that sectoral department project staff were unable to provide training for field staff, to supervise local-level staff, or to pursue enforcement operations against encroachments on indigenous lands. In the case of the Protected Areas project, the NGO partner consortium actually funded some of the government staff activities (suggesting unusually high levels of intersectoral social capital).

In Mexico, the Finance Ministry systematically undermined the Community Forestry project by withholding counterpart funds. This project was the only exception to the dominant trend insofar as sectoral policymakers and social actors sustained a consolidated pro-reform alliance. Even here, World Bank staff allies who had been critical to the project's birth and launching lost most of their leverage even over the Treasury Ministry, once the project moved into the implementation phase.[41] The Mexican Treasury Ministry systematically micro-managed Environment Ministry budget plans, and retained more than sufficient autonomy to resist entreaties from Bank staff. From a Treasury point of view, these projects were marginal to the main Bank-state policy agenda and were not seriously backed up by higher-level Bank managers.

The second way in which the national state needs to be institutionally "unpacked" in order to realize prospects for encouraging social capital consolidation involves decentralization. This is the "vertical" dimension, in which state and local governments are gaining increasing responsibility and autonomy for the implementation of national social and environmental policies. Local and/or provincial governments played important roles in two of the three Philippines projects and in one of the Mexican cases, but in none of the cases did decentralization fulfill its widely hailed promise of bringing the government closer to the people. Indeed, in those cases where notable pro–social capital initiatives were documented, they consistently came from national agencies dominated by reformist policymakers. The challenges of local democratization and capacity building were greater than policymakers had assumed.[42]

The World Bank and Social Capital

What do these findings imply for the relationship between discussions of social capital inside the World Bank and project practice? First, how ideas—and specifically how a *pro-poor* social capital agenda—translate into practice depends greatly on specific linkages between Bank staff and national governments. Homogeneity cannot be assumed. In these cases, it was the *variation* in commitment to pro–social capital reforms within the Bank and nation-states that explained the variation in enabling environments.

Second, getting ideas into project design is not, per se, sufficient. There is no unidirectional arrow between the design and implementation phases. Projects can begin as participatory and then erode, as state actors unwilling to share power with civil society capture them (as in the case of the Marginal Areas project). Therefore, project design should not be assumed to guarantee momentum. Similarly, a mid-term review, plus a new in-country Bank Project Manager, enabled the IPAS project to strengthen its participatory dimension. Since efforts to derail participatory initiatives are to be expected, continuous monitoring, plus checks and balances, are essential to identify and offset those threats. This suggests that pro-participation projects require significant, early investments of resources to encourage independent civil society–based monitoring mechanisms and to facilitate more sustained, bottom-up supervision before opponents of participation gain the upper hand. The often rapid turnover among Bank Project Managers also underscores the limits of focusing only on project design, since staff change may be associated with a loss of whatever pro-reform intersectoral social capital had been generated during the design phase.

Conversely, projects without much participation in the design phase can sometimes improve their contribution to an enabling institutional environment, as in the case of the Philippine Agrarian Reform Communities project, where new national policymakers encouraged more participatory partnerships. While the institutional dynamics of project loans are usually quite path dependent, these examples suggest that if new Bank or borrowing-country implementing agency staff come into a project after the design stage, a willingness to invest in new intersectoral social capital can create new room for maneuvering.

Third, pro–social capital strategies must identify and work to weaken, sidestep, or neutralize the inevitable opposition from the beginning, by launching the "virtuous circles" that can change the balance of power. Otherwise, pro-participation forces will lose the initiative and be obliged to focus on rearguard, defensive battles. Bank staff and national policymakers in favor of such changes are often in relatively tenuous positions within their respective institutions, and they therefore need each other. Pro-participation Bank staff can help their national counterparts to overcome their isolation by providing venues for them to come together, share experiences and information, and build the kind of esprit de corps that both the regional bosses and macroeconomic technocrats have. In other words, enabling environments themselves need enabling environments.

Notes

1. Field research was funded by the Pacific Basin Research Center of the Soka University of America, with additional research grants from the University of California's Institute for Global Conflict and Cooperation and UC MEXUS. The authors are also very grateful for institutional and intellectual support from two public interest research centers, Trasparencia (Oaxaca, Mexico) and the Institute for Popular Democracy (Manila, Philippines). John Gershman also acknowledges the research assistance of Francisco Lara and the Guava Consulting staff. Parts of this chapter draw in substantially revised and updated form on J. Fox and J. Gershman (2000), "The World Bank and Social Capital: Lessons from Ten Rural Development Projects in the Philippines and Mexico" (*Policy Sciences* 33: 399–419).

2. See Bebbington et al. (Chapter 1, this volume), Bebbington et al. (2004), and Edwards (Chapter 4, this volume). See also Grootaert (1997). Critics argue that the concept has the effect of depoliticizing development by embedding social capital in a discourse that excludes or obscures relations of power, domination, and inequality. See Harriss and DeRenzio (1997), Harriss (2001), and Fine (2001). Some analysts counter with a more politicized deployment of the concept. See, for example, Evans (1997) and Fox (1996), among others. See also Krishna (2002) and Moore (2004).

3. The World Bank being a large, complex institution cross-cut by multiple pressures and factions, it is not surprising that different branches can do contradictory things. For a political analysis of the Bank's social and environmental reforms, see Fox and Brown (1998).

4. The safeguard policies are bolstered by a relatively autonomous investigative body, the Inspection Panel, which produces reports that have sometimes had significant impacts. See Clark et al. (2003).

5. The complete list of Bank policies is in its operations manual, which is accessible at www.worldbank.org.

6. The research results then can speak to social capital skeptics because the central issue remains the enabling environment for the accumulation of social resources for collective action, whether that is understood as social capital or social *capacity*. See, for example, Smith and Kulynych (2002).

7. This hypothesis was generated from previous field research on the World Bank's anti-poverty projects (Fox and Aranda 1996) and sustainable development policy reforms (Fox and Brown 1998). The approach is compatible with the Operations Evaluation Department findings on NGO collaboration with the World Bank, which also highlights both enabling environments and intersectoral relationships (Gibbs et al. 1999). There are two principal differences, however. First, this study focuses on membership organizations while the OED analysis dealt mainly with NGOs. Second, while the OED study refers to a general notion of "close working relationships" (Gibbs et al. 1999: 15ff), this study attempts to develop more precise indicators of such relationships, and of the specific policies that facilitate them. For the OED study, close intersectoral relationships are a cause of positive development outcomes. This study, in contrast, treats such relationships as the result of compliance with key Bank mandates and participatory project goals.

8. See Brown (1991) and Brown and Ashman (1996), among others.

9. For discussion of all ten, see Fox and Gershman (2000).

10. Relevant questions include whether or not the assessment was completed early enough to influence the project design; the degree to which the assessment actually influenced the eventual project design; the degree to which the assessment process included consideration of alternative investment possibilities, as mandated by the policy; as well as the degree and nature of public consultation with stakeholders in the assessment process.

11. For background on the Bank's indigenous peoples policy, see Gray (1998) and Thorne (1998).

12. On the Philippines estimates, see Anti-Slavery Society (1983). For Mexico, see Serrano Carreto (2003).

13. The degree of respect for human rights, though in many ways more important than the indicators discussed here, was not a main focus because it was not primarily determined by the World Bank and the specific government agencies involved.

14. For more details, see the initial project documents, accessible through the World Bank's web site as a result of the post-1994 information disclosure policy reform. For hard copies, see the Bank's Infoshop.

15. For a more detailed analysis of six World Bank rural development projects in Mexico, with additional citations, see Fox (2003).

16. World Bank lending commitments for anti-poverty and environmental projects totaled only 8 percent of lending to Mexico during the 1986–1990 period, rising to more than 45 percent of new lending during 1991–1995, then

falling back to 16 percent during the 1996–2000 period. For details on this portfolio shift, see Fox and Aranda (1996) and Fox (2000).

17. For an institutional analysis of the "social capital impact" of the Bank's rural portfolio at the time, see Fox (1997).

18. See Cruz (1995); the exchange of letters between AMUCSS's elected leadership and President Wolfensohn of the World Bank, May 23, 1996; and the reply from Task Manager Rodrigo Chaves, September 27, 1996 (also sent in Spanish translation).

19. Interviews with Mexican Finance Ministry, May 1999.

20. For details on the critique from US and Mexican public interest groups, see Lowerre (1994).

21. Interview with former Mexican government policymaker involved with the project, Mexico City, May 1999.

22. See the project implementation progress report (Subsecretaría de Recursos Naturales 1998) and Oaxaca press coverage, which highlighted the Treasury Ministry's opposition (Bermúdez 1999b).

23. Interviews with Oaxaca-based forest NGOs and program managers, May 1999.

24. Interviews with World Bank and Environment Ministry officials, August 1998 and May 1999.

25. See Fox (1994) for analysis of these regional councils. See Fox (1992) for a discussion of the first important Mexican experience with representative, power-sharing regional councils in the case of targeted rural consumer food subsidies. Both sets of councils still function as state-society power-sharing bodies, though they lack consistent government support.

26. The predominantly indigenous Huasteca region is northwest of Mexico City, where the states of San Luis Potosí, Veracruz, and Hidalgo meet. This region has long been highly conflictive, and only San Luis Potosí has consolidated, broad-based autonomous producer organizations.

27. This assessment is based on extensive interviews with two key federal program officials in May 1999; field visits and detailed interviews with social organization participants from five of Oaxaca's six councils in April, May, and August 1999; the government's own commissioned evaluation of implementation in Oaxaca (Sánchez et al. 1998); Rangel's (1999) detailed evaluation of the San Luis Potosí experience; and August 1999 interviews with independent policy analysts based in Veracruz. See also the press accounts in Bermúdez Santiago (1999a) and the producer organization testimonies reported in workshop minutes (Trasparencia 1998, 1999).

28. Interviews with the leaders of the *Union de Ejidos y Comunidades de Ciucatlán,* Cuicatlán, Oaxaca, April 1999. During 1999–2000 the Oaxacan regional councils networked and proposed specific ways to improve project implementation (see Coordinadora 2000). The state government then managed to disarticulate the network and subdivided most of the regional councils.

29. On the DENR side, there were five project directors up to the mid-term review of the project in June 1998. For the NGOs, the rate of turnover for technical assistance personnel (who provide much of the legal support for indigenous land claims and technical training for host NGO staff and

participating community-based organizations) was 70 percent in the first half of the project. IPAS's monitoring and evaluation framework was completed only a few months before the project's mid-term review in June 1998 (and after the initial program management team were fired).

30. Under the original project design, the funds were to be made available as either grants or market-rate loans, repayment of which would constitute the basis for a revolving fund for the broader Protected Areas program of the Philippine government. As a result of the economic crisis, those market rates would have been in the 25–30 percent range, unsustainable for the vast majority of potential beneficiaries. Initially the NGOs proposed lending at subsidized interest rates, a stance the Bank opposed on the grounds of Bank policy as well as the poor track record of repayment for subsidized credit in the Philippines. This meant that the majority of funds would be made available as grants, a position that the NGOs were comfortable with. The DENR was not, however, because it was depending on the repayments of the loans to fund PA operations, having failed to increase the Philippine government budget allocations for PA operations.

31. Interview with Department of Agrarian Reform (DAR) Development Facilitator, Bondoc Peninsula, Quezon II.

32. Field interviews (April–June 1999).

33. Wholesale Lending Department, Countryside Loan Fund Release by Region and project through March 31, 1998.

34. Project Completion Report for Rural Finance Project 1 (loan 3356-PH), Countryside Loan Fund Unit, Land Bank of the Philippines, p. 10.

35. This Land Bank data was provided by its Wholesale Lending Department, June 1999.

36. Interview with Land Bank Vice-President Jun Climaco, June 9, 1999; and Land Bank Director Jaime Tadeo, June 1, 1999.

37. Interview with Land Bank Vice-President Jun Climaco June 9, 1999.

38. In one extreme case in Mexico's Rural Development in Marginal Areas project, one rural peasant women's organization that was excluded from access to the program because of gender bias responded by holding Agriculture Ministry officials hostage in their offices for three days (interviews with organization leaders, Tuxtepec, Oaxaca, April 1999).

39. Interview, Mexico City, April 1999.

40. The key problem of trust as a "missing link" in the process of building intersectoral social capital was underscored by the PDRAM program's operations in Chiapas. Here, federal program officials sent powerful signals that undermined possibilities of building trust with the state's many and diverse autonomous indigenous producer organizations. The federal program focused its attention on the key zones of conflict in the state, the Altos and Cañadas regions. To carry out its operations, the program subcontracted its core outreach and training activities to a private consulting firm that is very closely associated with one of the national government's most influential counterinsurgency strategists. As a result, this social program was reported in the national press as having been directly incorporated into the government's military strategy (Henríquez 1999).

41. Interview, Environment Ministry officials, May 1999.
42. For further discussion of the contradictions of decentralization and anti-poverty projects in Mexico, see Fox and Aranda (1996) and Fox (2002, 2003).

References

Anti-Slavery Society. 1983. *The Philippines: Authoritarian government, multinationals and ancestral lands.* London: Anti-Slavery Society.

Bebbington, Anthony, Scott Guggenheim, Elizabeth Olson, and Michael Woolcock. 2004. Exploring social capital debates at the World Bank. *Journal of Development Studies* 40(5):33–64.

Bermúdez Santiago, Rafael. 1999a. Desconocen indigenas el destino de 47 mmd otorgados por el BM al combate a la pobreza. *La Hora*, April 9 (Oaxaca).

Bermúdez Santiago, Rafael. 1999b. La SCHP se perfila como un obstáculo para el desarrollo forestal de Oaxaca. *La Hora*, April 26 (Oaxaca).

Borras, Saturnino, Jr. 1999. *The Bibingka strategy in land reform implementation.* Quezon City, Philippines: Institute for Popular Democracy.

Brown, L. David. 1991. Bridging organizations and sustainable development. *Human Relations* 44(8).

Brown, L. David. 1998. Social learning in South-North coalitions: Constructing knowledge systems across social chasms. *IDR Reports* 14(1).

Brown, L. David, and Darcy Ashman. 1996. Participation, social capital and intersectoral problem-solving. *World Development* 19(1).

Clark, Dana, Jonathan Fox, and Kay Treakle, eds. *Demanding accountability: Civil society claims and the World Bank inspection panel.* Lanham, MD: Rowman and Littlefield.

Coordinadora Estatal de los Consejos para el Desarrollo Regional Sustentable en Zonas Rurales Marginadas de Oaxaca (CRSs). 2000. Por un desarrollo regional sustentable, construido corresponsable y participativamente, entre las comunidades en cada región y organismos gubernamentales coordinados. Propuesta para el Segundo Encuentro Nacional de CDRSs, October 26-27.

Cruz, Isabel. 1995. La integración e las uniones de credito del sector social al sistema financiero Mexicano. Paper presented at the Latin American Studies Association, Washington, DC, September 28–30.

Evans, Peter, ed. *Government action and social capital: State-society synergy in development.* Berkeley: University of California, Research Series/International and Area Studies.

Fine, Ben. 2001. *Social capital versus social theory: Political economy and social science at the turn of the millennium.* New York: Routledge.

Fox, Jonathan. 1992. *The politics of food in Mexico.* Ithaca, NY: Cornell University Press.

Fox, Jonathan. 1994. Targeting the poorest: The role of the National Indigenous Institute in Mexico's National Solidarity Program. In *Transforming state-society relations in Mexico: The national solidarity strategy,* edited by Wayne Cornelius, Ann Craig, and Jonathan Fox. La Jolla, CA: UCSD, Center for U.S.-Mexican Studies.

Fox, Jonathan. 1996. How does civil society thicken? The political construction of social capital in rural Mexico. *World Development* 24(6), June.

Fox, Jonathan. 1997. The World Bank and social capital: Contesting the concept in practice. *Journal of International Development* 9(7), November/December.

Fox, Jonathan. 2000. Los flujos y reflujos de préstamos sociales y ambientales del Banco Mundial en México. In *Las nuevas fronteras del siglo XXI: Dimensiones culturales, políticas y socioeconómicas de las relaciones Mexico–Estados Unidos,* edited by Alejandro Alvarez Béjar, Norma Klahn, Federico Manchon, and Pedro Castillo. Mexico City: UNAM/La Jornada Ediciones.

Fox, Jonathan. 2002. La relación recíproca entre la participación ciudadana y la rendición de cuentas: La experiencia de los Fondos Municipales en el México rural. *Política y Gobierno* 9(1), January.

Fox, Jonathan. 2003. De la teoría a la práctica del capital social: El Banco Mundial en el campo mexicano. *Foro Internacional* 43(2), April–June.

Fox, Jonathan, and Josefina Aranda. 1996. *Decentralization and rural development in Mexico: Community participation in Oaxaca's municipal funds.* La Jolla: University of California–San Diego, Center for U.S.-Mexican Studies.

Fox, Jonathan, and L. David Brown, eds. 1998. *The struggle for accountability: The World Bank, NGOs, and grassroots movements.* Cambridge, MA: MIT Press.

Fox, Jonathan, and John Gresham. 2000. The World Bank and social capital: Lessons from ten rural development projects in Mexico and the Philippines. *Policy Sciences* 33(3, 4).

Gibbs, Cristopher, Claudio Fumo, and Thomas Kuby. 1999. *Nongovernmental organizations in World Bank–supported projects.* Washington, DC: World Bank, Operations Evaluation Department.

Gray, Andrew. 1998. Development policy–development protest: The World Bank, indigenous peoples and NGOs. In *The struggle for accountability: The World Bank, NGOs and grassroots movements,* edited by Jonathan Fox and L. David Brown. Cambridge, MA: MIT Press.

Grootaert, Christian. 1997. "Social capital": The missing link? In *Expanding the measure of wealth: Indicators of environmentally sustainable development.* Environmentally Sustainable Development Studies and Monographs Series No. 17. Washington, DC: World Bank.

Harriss, John. 2001. *Depoliticizing development: The World Bank and social capital.* London: Stylus.

Harris, John, and Paolo DeRenzio. 1997. An introductory bibliographic essay. *Journal of International Development* 9(7).

Krishna, Anirudh. 2002. *Active social capital: Tracing the roots of development and democracy.* New York: Columbia University Press.

Lowerre, Richard. 1994. Update to "Evaluation of the Forest Development Project of the World Bank in the Sierra Madre Occidental in Chihuahua and Durango, Mexico." Austin: Texas Center for Policy Studies, May.

Martínez, Juan, et al. 1995a. Memoria: Primer Taller de la Zona Norte—Programa de Capacitación para el Desarrollo de los Pueblos Indígenas Forestales de Mexico del 20 a 30 de Marzo, 1995. Mexico: Comunidad Indígena Nvo. San Juan Paragaricutiro/World Bank Institutional Development Fund.

Martínez, Juan, et al. 1995b. Memoria: Segundo Taller de la Zona Sur—Programa de Capacitación para el Desarrollo de los Pueblos Indígenas Forestales de Mexico del 20 a 30 de Agosto, 1995—UZACHI—UCFAS. Mexico: Comunidad Indígena Nvo. San Juan Paragaricutiro/World Bank Institutional Development Fund.

Moore, Mick. 2004. Making sense—and use—of "social capital." *Governance and Development Review* 25, January.

Rangel, Gabriela. 1999. El sentido de la participación social en el proyecto de desarollo rural en areas marginadas o del enredado mundo de los proyectos del desarrollo rural en Mexico. Undergraduate thesis. Mexico City: Escuela Nacional de Antropología e Historia, April.

Sánchez López, Sergio, et al. 1998. Evaluación general del program de desarrollo sustentable en las regiones Mixe, Mazateca y Cuicateca del Estado de Oaxaca, 1997. Oaxaca: Gobierno del Estado de Oaxaca, Secretaría de Agricultura, Ganadería y Desarrollo Rural & Jubileo.

Serrano Carreto, Enrique, Arnulfo Embriz Osorio, and Patricia Fernández Ham, eds. 2003. *Indicadores socioeconómicos de los pueblos indígenas, 2002.* Mexico: INI/PNUD/PNUD at www.ini.gob.mx.

Smith, Stephen Samuel, and Jessica Kulynych. 2002. It may be social, but why is it capital? The social construction of social capital and the politics of language. *Politics and Society* 30(1):149–186.

Subsecretaría de Desarrollo Rural. 1998. *Manual de Procedimientos de Operación: Programa de Desarrollo Productivo Sostenible en Zonas Rurales Marginadas.* Mexico City: Secretaría de Agricultura, Ganadería y Desarrollo Rural.

Subsecretaría de Recursos Naturales. 1998. *Proyecto de Conservación y Manejo Sustentable de Recursos Forestales en Mexico: Informe 1998.* Mexico City: Secretaría de Medio Ambiente y Recursos Naturales.

Thorne, Eva. 1998. The politics of policy compliance: The World Bank and the social dimensions of development. Ph.D. dissertation. Massachusetts Institute of Technology, Political Science Department.

Trasparencia. 1998. Seguimiento al programa de desarrollo productivo en zonas rurales marginadas del Estado de Veracruz. Unpublished manuscript, Mexico City.

Trasparencia. 1999. Intercambio de experiencias sobre el proyecto "Desarollo Rural en Areas Marginadas: Oaxaca de Juárez, 18–19 de Febrero, 1999" Oaxaca: Trasparencia.

Velásquez, María Cristina. 1996. Proyecto "Desarrollo Sostenible en Zonas Rurales Marginadas" (Banco Mundial): Aciertos y desaciertos para promover la participación en las etapas de identificación y prepapración del proyecto en Oaxaca. Unpublished manuscript. Oaxaca: Trasparencia, August.

Wiens, Thomas. 1996. Philippines: Integrated protected areas project in Environment Department. In *The World Bank participation sourcebook.* Washington, DC: World Bank.

World Bank/Global Environment Facility. 1994. *Republic of the Philippines: Conservation of Priority Protected Areas project.* Washington, DC: World Bank, Staff Appraisal Report No. 11309-PH, April.

World Bank/Global Environment Facility. 1995a. *Mexico resource conservation and forest sector review*. Washington, DC: World Bank, Report No. 13114-ME, March 31.

World Bank/Global Environment Facility. 1995b. *Second Rural Finance Project*. Washington, DC: World Bank, Staff Appraisal Report No. 13116-PH, August 16.

World Bank/Global Environment Facility. 1995c. *Mexico rural financial markets*. Washington, DC: World Bank, Report No. 14599-ME, August 25.

World Bank/Global Environment Facility. 1995d. *Implementation completion report: Mexico forest development project*. Washington, DC: World Bank, Report No. 14625, June 2.

World Bank/Global Environment Facility. 1996. *Philippines agrarian reform communities development project*. Washington, DC: World Bank, Staff Appraisal Report No. 15624-PH, October 24.

World Bank/Global Environment Facility. 1997a. *Mexico community forestry project*. Washington, DC: World Bank, Staff Appraisal Report No. 16134-ME, January 21.

World Bank/Global Environment Facility. 1997b. *Mexico rural development in marginal areas project*. Washington, DC: World Bank, Project Appraisal Report No. 17263-ME, December 23.

CHAPTER NINE

SOCIAL CAPITAL FROM SERICULTURE?
Actors, Markets, and Power in a Multi-Agency Project in Bangladesh

David Lewis
M. Shameen Siddiqi

This chapter examines a multi-agency project funded by the World Bank in Bangladesh, focusing on the involvement of two of the participating NGOs with their grassroots producer groups, or *samitis*. Although the NGOs can be seen as building social capital through their formation and support of these groups, our fieldwork revealed a more complex relationship. NGO producer groups of this kind in Bangladesh do form a foundation for income generation activities and social solidarity, but these groups were also found to be characterized by a dependence on the NGOs for technological assistance, access to markets (often restricted to the NGOs as buyers), and overall leadership and motivation. The element of patronage and dependence found in these NGO–*samiti* relationships caused problems for the project in a dispute over whether the groups should become more market-based sericultural "producer groups"—an approach favored by the World Bank and the Bangladesh Silk Foundation (and to some extent by the groups themselves) or whether they should remain multipurpose, closely linked NGO *samitis* (the view of the NGOs, which have resisted suggested changes). In this sense, the project has been able to make only limited gains in the attempt to break from a long history of top-down, external control within the struggling sericulture subsector in Bangladesh.

Introduction

Development projects increasingly involve a wide range of organizational actors and relationships. This chapter examines a recent case study of the Silk Project, a multi-agency project funded by the World

Bank in Bangladesh that aimed to increase incomes and build empowerment. Although the project apparently contributed to improved livelihoods of low-income women in some important respects, it also
generated a set of problems that affected its performance in relation to
sustainability and empowerment objectives. The chapter analyzes key
areas of the project activities against the wider backdrop of power, structure, and social networks in which such projects are embedded.[1] Though
the concept of social capital did not form an explicit part of the rationale
for this project, an analysis of project practices, inter-organizational relationships, and cultural tensions of the Silk Project may be instructive in
helping us reflect in general terms on the World Bank's overall approach
to working with local "organizations of the poor" within a project setting
in Bangladesh. Such an analysis may also be helpful in examining the usefulness of the concept of social capital as a way of understanding processes of empowerment and poverty reduction.

Such projects are inevitably complex in their operating structures, in
the diverse objectives of the different organizational actors involved, and
in the various intended and unintended outcomes that emerge (Lewis
1998). The sericulture project in question achieved certain positive results
in terms of poverty reduction—as various evaluation reports show—but
there were also a distinctive set of problems and failures. The strengths
and weaknesses in the performance of the project can be attributed to
both "internal" and "external" factors. One set of explanations follows
from the wider structural and historical factors related to public efforts to
intervene in the sericulture subsector in Bangladesh and from the overall
context of political struggles between government and international
donors over public sector restructuring and reform. Other explanations
concern intra- and inter-organizational relationships among the project
partners themselves (such as multiple and conflicting actor objectives
about project aims and activities) and a set of tensions about balancing
income and empowerment aims and claims.

One of the distinctive features of the institutional landscape in
Bangladesh is the large and relatively well-developed nongovernmental
organization (NGO) sector. NGOs are, in practice, the key partners with
the government and the World Bank within this project. Unlike the situation in some other parts of the world where NGOs operate, NGOs in
Bangladesh tend not to work with preexisting grassroots people's organizations, or—in the World Bank's term—"organizations of the poor,"
which, for a wide range of historical and political reasons, are very limited
in scale and capacity in rural areas. Instead, Bangladeshi NGOs have
opted to form their own community-level groups across the country.
These grassroots groups are known locally as *samitis*, and they can be
characterized analytically as a form of "induced social capital" (Bebbington and Carroll 2000). Although many NGOs plan in theory to exit at the
appropriate time and leave self-sustaining federated *samiti* group struc-

tures behind, this has only rarely taken place to date, and in cases where it has happened, the autonomy and sustainability of the *samitis* has been somewhat limited. Within some NGO *samitis*, the emphasis is on a range of services, self-help initiatives, and proactive discussion about issues that are of importance to the poor, but as Devine (2003) points out, there is evidence that many *samitis* are, in practice, mainly "collection meetings" concerned with gathering loan repayments from the credit programs that now tend to dominate the agendas of many NGOs.[2]

The concern of this chapter is the usefulness of the concept of social capital in relation to understanding the story of the Silk Project. Although the original research project analyzed a wide range of project actors in detail, the primary emphasis in this chapter is the role of NGOs in the project, whose *samitis* play a central role in structuring the ways in which sericulture production activities are supposed to create spaces for low-income women to pursue income generation activities and empowerment opportunities.[3] Yet these *samitis* are located within a set of social relationships in which there is intense competition for scare resources—competition between the individual members of the *samitis*, between *samiti* members and leaders, and between *samitis* and their NGOs, respectively as clients and patrons. In the context of wider debates about social capital, the apparent conflicts over the exact role and purpose of the grassroots *samiti* groups in the Silk Project and the nature of the overall relationship among these groups, the NGOs, and the market illustrate a number of tensions that highlight the difficulties of any straightforward process of social capital "strengthening" in support of income generation and empowerment objectives within the project framework.

Two sets of observations in relation to the social capital debate emerged in this study. First, the *samitis* we encountered in our research do not fit easily into "standard" definitions of social capital as horizontally structured, trust-based sets of relationships or units in Putnam's (1993) sense. There are certainly elements of these norms of trust and reciprocity, but the NGO *samiti* groups are also simultaneously characterized by vertical patron-client relationships, both internally in relations between members and leaders and externally in the *samitis'* relationships with NGOs. The second observation is that although there may be truth in the depoliticizing critiques of social capital (e.g., Harriss and de Renzio1997; Harriss 2002), it is interesting to note that the formation of social capital in these cases—however imperfect in relation to the ideal type—also plays a role in "de-marketizing" project processes. This is because the NGOs are usually anxious to preserve their relationship with their *samitis* (for a variety of reasons) and to guard them from the broader market-based business thrust favored by the World Bank in the Silk Project. Whether these relationships contribute to income generation and empowerment objectives by providing producers with a degree of economic security and protection from a volatile or potentially hostile market,[4] or whether such vertical relationships and ties ultimately disempower the poor because they restrict market-based economic forms of empowerment is a critical question.[5] The question cannot be answered conclusively by our data, and to some extent the answer depends on the personal priorities and viewpoint of the observer.

The Sericulture Sector in Bangladesh

Silk production in Bengal has a long history, and for many centuries it was a major agro-industry. Rural households that specialized in this area of work produced silk yarn for local weavers, who then produced textiles for local sale and for export. Changing market conditions during the last century led to a massive decline in the industry. According to the World Bank, advances in technology brought mechanization that dramatically reduced production costs, and imported washable silks that improved the durability of finished garments emerged at the same time. Silk quality in Bangladesh slowly declined due to lack of investment in production and increasing pressure from imports. There have been a series of governmental and nongovernmental efforts since the 1970s in Bangladesh to revive the industry (Van Schendel 1995). According to this viewpoint, the production of silk is well suited to a labor-abundant economy since it is highly employment oriented rather than capital intensive. However, it is highly skilled work that requires the careful rearing by hand of silkworm larvae and the management of delicate silkworm cocoons (Sinha 1990).

These efforts to revive sericulture in the Indian subcontinent provide an opportunity to study "long-term development in Third World conditions" since they represent an encounter between "the secure confidence of hereditary experts" and "the bearers of technical improvements" within planned development efforts (Charsley 1982). Writing about the success of sericulture in South India, Charsley argues that this has been achieved through "the realistic adjustment to local circumstances achieved by its practitioners, on the one hand, and on the other, major technical innovation achieved by research and the development of systems" (68).

Results in Bangladesh have been less successful. The Bangladesh Sericulture Board (BSB) was created as a coordinating body in 1977 and began to initiate development programs for the silk subsector. Mulberry acreage grew from 500 ha in the early 1970s to 3,000 ha in the late 1980s, but this was still less than a quarter of the figure for neighboring West Bengal. In the 1980s Bangladesh was producing 460 tons of cocoons and 30 tons of raw silk per year, but this was still less than 5 percent of West Bengal's output (Van Schendel 1995).

At the time of Van Schendel's study, the primary source of international support to sericulture in Bangladesh had been, since 1978, the Swiss government, but according to Van Schendel, the results had been disappointing: A large bureaucracy had been created (with a thousand people in the BSB alone, "many of them poorly trained, poorly motivated for the work they were supposed to do, or frustrated"); extension efforts intended to spread silk production beyond the Rajshahi area had met with little success;[6] and there had been considerable spending on "scientific research" that yielded few results, in the sense that most producers continued to use low-yield mulberry varieties and traditional silkworm varieties. Furthermore, the BSB depressed prices for sericulture producers because it was the monopoly buyer of cocoons. It was also the view of the Task Manager for the project at the World Bank that, by the 1990s, the Swiss had tired of working with the mainstream public institutions of sericulture development, with little achieved in the way of productivity increase and poverty reduction.[7]

Under this system, silk production was akin to a "putting-out" industry. Producers received silkworm eggs from the BSB, reared them, and then sold the cocoons to the Rajshahi Silk Factory: "Neither transaction took place in an open market. Silk producers were not allowed to buy silkworm eggs or mulberry saplings from any other source nor could they sell their cocoons to any other buyers" (Van Schendel 1995: 119). There were no written contracts, and producers were generally poor households in search of a little extra income. The "silk bureaucrats" sometimes used violence to prevent private sale of cocoons. Continuing losses at the factory and by the BSB did not reduce the government and donor flow of funds into sericulture, but on the contrary, were used as an argument for more resources to overcome "the technological backwardness of the producers."

Although proto-NGOs such as the Salvation Army had sericulture projects in the subcontinent as early as 1915, modern NGOs became involved in the Bangladesh sericulture sector beginning in the late 1970s. NGO efforts have centered on the creation of "nontraditional" silk producers—driven by the idea that sericulture could provide a new source of income for poor and marginal households needing to supplement low incomes from marginal agriculture or laboring.[8] However, according to Van Schendel (1995: 86), "Their dispersed and uncoordinated projects could not effect a breakthrough in silk production on the national level." Some NGOs have been relatively optimistic about sericulture, such as the Bangladesh Rural Advancement Committee (BRAC), which sees substantial benefits for the status of women and has invested in technical innovation for sericulture as part of its income generation programs (Lovell 1992). On the other hand, Proshika—another large Bangladeshi NGO—concluded in 1993 that its rearing projects "were still to contribute significantly" to the income generation efforts of the poor. The reasons given were the poor quality and timeliness of eggs from BSB, weak follow-up by extension staff, inadequate facilities for drying, and poor transportation to the weighing center.

The result of this history is—according to Van Schendel—a continuing tendency among government and development agencies to see silk as an unrealized source of potential for income generation, economic growth, and exports in Bangladesh. The government therefore has seen a need to spend more on "technology and administration" and has tended to see "uneducated" or "ignorant" producers as the main source of the sector's problems. There has been little or no interest by silk officials in "the view from below," and there has been a history of top-down implementation, poor extension, and weak policies (1995: 181). Van Schendel argues that the history of silk production in Bengal is characterized by a tradition of "authoritarian developmentalism." In one sense, the World Bank Silk Project can therefore be seen simply as the latest in a long line of more or less top-down attempts to reinvigorate the silk subsector in Bangladesh. However, as we shall see, elements of the project design also sought to challenge this tradition, since the central role accorded to NGOs and their grassroots groups in the project design was an attempt to build more of a "bottom-up" perspective. We turn now from the sericulture subsector to the World Bank project itself.

The Project in Theory

This section examines the rationale of the project based on a reading of relevant World Bank documents and on interviews with the World Bank and NGO staff of participating agencies.[9]

Some international donors and NGOs still perceive that the sericulture sector in Bangladesh has the potential to provide improved livelihoods for the poor. According to the World Bank, by the mid-1990s average sericulture productivity and output from silkworm rearing and cocoon processing in Bangladesh was "much lower" than the averages for India, southwest China, and Thailand, despite similarities of agro-climatic conditions. The reasons for this disparity, states the Bank, include the government's continuing monopoly over silkworm egg production and the lack of new research in support of revitalizing the subsector, both of which factors have prevented the introduction of improved varieties. Those presenting this argument see a reduction in the public sector role in sericulture in Bangladesh as a means for unlocking significant economic potential for the country.

As we have seen, NGOs have long worked with sericulture as an income generation activity with their locally formed beneficiary groups. Despite the difficulties resulting from sericulture's technical complexity, high risk, and unfavorable economic climate, many NGOs see persevering with sericulture as worthwhile because—at least in theory—it offers potentially high rates of return for poor households, and it involves both male and female members of the household in relatively light, skilled work. At the moment, though, the NGOs effectively subsidize silk production. This is happening in part because there continue to be donor funds available for sericulture initiatives, on the basis of the success of sericulture elsewhere in the region and the argument that it is an underutilized and potentially productive subsector for Bangladesh.[10] Another reason for continuing is that many NGOs are now seeking to generate additional institutional income that can contribute to their own sustainability as the availability of donor funding to NGOs declines. The production and sale of silk products both in Bangladesh and internationally are seen by some of these NGOs as part of a potential resource mobilization strategy.

The Silk Project was approved with a US$11.35 million IDA credit by the World Bank in November 1997 and was a five-year project intended to revitalize silk production in Bangladesh.[11] The aim was to improve the quality and value of silk production so that the incomes of poor rural women, who form the bulk of small-scale silk producers, would be increased along with the value of silk exports on the world market. A key element of the project was support to the government's efforts to restructure the parastatal BSB and its technical wing, the Bangladesh Sericulture Research and Training Institute (BSRTI). This "restructuring" would involve abandoning the BSB's commercial activities—aside from continuing to manage a small number of grainages—and instead focusing BSB on the technical matters of research, extension and training, and working together with the BSF. In addition to the restructuring process, the project set a number of ambitious production and income targets. Annual domestic silk output, which was twenty-nine tons in 1994–1995, was expected to rise to thirty-six tons by 2002. Exports of silk products were expected to increase by at least 30 percent from their current levels by the end of project. The income of rearers was expected to triple over the project period, and employment in all areas of silk production was to increase.

As we have seen, the development objectives of the Silk Project were, foremost, to increase the incomes of small-scale silk producers through improved technology and to create institutional and policy improvements designed to encourage sustainable development of the silk sector; and, second, to address the institutional, economic, and technical constraints that are affecting silk development in Bangladesh. There were also important empowerment objectives to the project. Since around 80 percent of small-scale silk producers are women, the project has been expected to have a positive impact on the empowerment of women, helping them not only to become financially self-sufficient, but also to become established entrepreneurs. This was to be achieved through the participation of a group of large and small local NGOs, which would be supported by a newly created, private Bangladesh Silk Foundation (BSF) to strengthen the NGOs' sericulture work with their *samitis*. The basic operation of the project is set out in Figure 9.1.

Figure 9.1   A Simplified Outline of the Sericulture Project

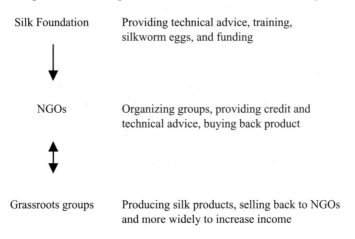

Silk Foundation	Providing technical advice, training, silkworm eggs, and funding
NGOs	Organizing groups, providing credit and technical advice, buying back product
Grassroots groups	Producing silk products, selling back to NGOs and more widely to increase income

The BSF was established in 1997 as an autonomous not-for-profit company owned by the government, and it is designed to respond with technical assistance to demands from sericulture clients brought "up" to it through the NGOs. The foundation is in theory supporting and advising the NGOs, which are directly fostering improved sericulture as an income generation strategy for *samiti* members. The foundation has indeed been active in providing some training and inputs, but in practice, the links between the BSF and the NGOs were found to be rather one-way, which is why the arrow in the figure is unidirectional. The NGOs' involvement with their members runs very deep, and it is common to find that they provide training, inputs, credit, and arrangements for the buyback of produce from the *samitis*. Finally, the *samitis* themselves are grassroots groups, organized by the NGOs with elected leaders. These tend to be multipurpose groups that help structure participation in other NGO activities beyond sericulture, activities such as functional literacy work and health education.

The Project in Practice

Within a few years of the project's inception, it became clear that despite many micro-level gains, the macro-level objectives of the project were not going to be achieved due to political resistance within the project's wider institutional context.

In November 2001, there was an internal Project Implementation Review Mission that reported to the IDA management. There were three basic findings in this document, summarized in a cover letter from Frederick T. Temple, Country Director, to the Secretary, Ministry of Textiles (19 December 2001): (1) the project's development indicators were judged "broadly achievable" in terms of outcomes such as increases in silkworm rearing productivity, raw silk output, rearers' daily income, and employment generation, with the BSF "continuing to perform well," now that it was successfully operating "an expanding extension service through NGOs" and supplying 20 percent of the demand for silkworm eggs; (2) the BSF would not become financially self-sustaining by the end of the project and would require continued financial support from government after project completion—earlier expectations had proved to be "overly optimistic"; (3) however, overall project implementation "has been rated unsatisfactory because of the continued failure of MOT [Ministry of Textiles] to implement the restructuring of the BSB/BSRTI." This part of the project was canceled and the US$4.4 million was canceled from the credit in order to allow the government and IDA to focus on the BSF component of the project.

At the micro level, the project thus performed well in some respects. An evaluation report (Bentvelsen and Hena 2001) found that poor rural women had, on average, increased their cocoon production due to the better-quality silkworm eggs available, leading to increased yields. However, there were wide variations in production level and therefore income. The status of women involved in silkworm rearing had improved due to the knowledge, skills, and income they gained from the project, which helped them gain respect, self-confidence, and more mobility. The report found that the project was arguably successful in (1) setting up the Silk Foundation as a participatory alternative to the old BSB for producers and NGOs; (2) bringing modest improvements to the livelihoods of poor, female, nontraditional silk producers; and (3) building links between NGOs involved in sericulture and other actors in the silk subsector.

Despite this, the report also found that the women tended to remain "more dependent on NGOs than would be necessary." The review recommended—among other things—that the BSF consider "whether and under which conditions sericulture can be economically and financially sustainable, without depending on subsidies" and that the NGOs improve the transparency of cocoon pricing in order to make rearers more aware of costs and benefits in sericulture, and pay more attention to "graduating" beneficiaries toward reduced dependence on NGO services. The review also concluded that the formation of producers' associations was not viable under present conditions and required NGO support and homogeneous membership. There were also significant problems related to important macro-level factors. The first was the reluctance of the government of Bangladesh to undertake the agreed-upon institutional reforms in relation to the BSB and the BSRTI. The second was the continuing importation of higher-quality cheap silk, both legally and illegally, into Bangladesh.

Selected Findings from the Fieldwork

During the research, we learned a great deal from our face-to-face discussions with NGO group members, who were articulate about their experiences with sericulture and their interactions with the NGOs. One of the surprising issues that emerged from our research "on the ground" was the nature of the relationships between group members and their NGOs, relationships that were characterized by higher-than-expected levels of paternalism and quite low levels of trust, as the following extracts from our conversations illustrate.

One important area in which this paternalism was manifested was in the high level of control by the NGOs of the production process and the marketing of sericulture products generated by the *samitis*. There were complaints from *samiti* members that the NGOs practiced a form of "tied" market transaction in their dealing with the groups, preventing the *samitis* from taking produce to sell in the market to the highest bidder or going to other NGOs active in sericulture to compare the prices paid. Each NGO was effectively subsidizing its producers and was unwilling to forgo recouping its "investment." As one group member observed,

> Because we take the eggs from the NGO, the condition is that we must give them what we produce. Even if another organization gives a higher price, we cannot sell our *gutis* [silkworm cocoons] to them.

These tied transactions are a feature of wider rural society in Bangladesh, where markets are frequently imperfect and transactions of many kinds are permeated by patron-client relationships (Wood 1981; Lewis 1991), but we did not expect to find such relations reproduced to such an extent within development NGO activities. What is also distinctive here is the high degree of continuity with the earlier history and tradition of top-down control of producers in the sericulture subsector, as observed by Van Schendel (1995) and discussed earlier.

Related to this, the *samitis* are subject to various forms of dependency on the NGOs. First, the producer groups feel a strong sense of dependence on the NGO for technical support and inputs. There is a low level of trust, in part created by a perceived lack of responsiveness on the part of NGOs to producers' requests for improved sericulture technologies and infrastructure. The leader of one group remarked,

> One of the biggest problems is that we don't have a separate shed for rearing silkworms. The NGO had promised us the money to build a shed and to bring in electricity, but then they didn't provide it. Now the NGO tells us we won't get the cash. Nor will we now get payment for tree planting work beyond just one year, even though this was first promised for a longer term.

Though the producers say they have shown a readiness to learn new skills and techniques, and most are committed to sericulture, some nevertheless point out the continuing technical challenge they face in producing high-quality *guti* with the limited scope for sustainability that exists beyond the life of the project.[12] When asked whether or not the group of rearers could continue in the future without the support of the NGO, one person pointed out,

> It's not as simple as just saying we'll continue. We will need appropriate skills and technical know-how. For example, when the silkworm is sleeping, someone cannot unknowingly dump mulberry leaves on them—if you do, all the silkworms will die. If it goes to sleep at 2 o'clock, the rearer has to know exactly when it will wake up, and check from time to time.

The discussions that we held with *samiti* group members suggested that these groups' relationships with their NGOs were more similar to those between patrons and clients than to the more evenly balanced partnerships described as the ideal by NGO staff. Aside from the implications of these limitations for building a cohesive and empowering relationship between organizations of the poor and organizations for the poor (to return to the language of the Bank), such tensions, as we shall see, can also produce negative implications for building economic sustainability.

Although there are problems in the relationships between the *samitis* and the NGOs, there are also tensions within the *samitis* themselves, particularly between group leaders and members. It is a challenge for NGOs and members to maintain the coherence of these groups, which can quickly become fragmented as a result of conflict brought about by intra-group factors, such as conflicts over resources or personality clashes, or developed through wider social tensions related to roles and identities in the broader community. One group was explicitly pessimistic about the ability of *samiti* leaders to continue to run their groups without the explicit support of the parent NGO:

> No, not really, if the NGO is not there, the *samitis* won't work . . . if the people from the organization are not there, having only money will not be enough. The root of a tree is very important. If the NGO is not there, it will be hopeless.

Another *samiti* showed tensions as group members became distrustful of the benefits that the group leader received from the NGO when she responded to incentives to collect loan repayments.[13]

At the root of many of these problems are both structural and cultural factors. At a structural level, as we have seen, patron-clientelism is a dominant form of relationship in Bangladesh, where there are high levels of social hierarchy both within community relationships and within institutions such as the state. These relationships are further reproduced within many NGOs, as Wood (1997) has argued, and between the NGOs and their grassroots groups. There is an emerging critique of NGOs as "the new patrons" as it becomes clear that, rather than offering a comprehensive challenge to such deep-rooted structural relationships, NGOs are all too easily fitted into those relationships—sometimes with changed local power dynamics, but at other times merely reinforcing them. McGregor (1989a and b), Karim (2001), and Devine (2003) have drawn attention to different aspects of these processes in relation to NGOs. At a cultural level, we have already seen the ways in which tensions have emerged between the income generation or market-related aims of the project and its empowerment or social development objectives.

One of the key areas of disagreement between the World Bank/Silk Foundation and the NGOs was the Bank's view that the NGOs should gradually encourage their groups to move toward an independent business model as relatively autonomous "producer groups" or associations. This would mean reconstituting these "organizations of the poor" as dedicated sericulture "producer associations" with the autonomy to specialize in sericulture and sell their produce on the wider market to whoever offered the best price. This idea was completely opposed by the NGOs, who saw it as both unrealistic and contrary to their wider group-building agenda. First, it was perceived as a "top-down" idea that had clearly come from the WB/BSF, and it ran counter to the NGOs' own approaches to organizing, which were based on the development of multipurpose *samitis*. The nontraditional silk producers were mostly drawn from existing NGO *samitis*, which are used as the basis for a wide range of income generation, education, and credit purposes. This made the wisdom of creating specialized silk producer groups rather questionable. In the words of one NGO manager, "Our groups are not sericulture groups or apiculture groups or fishing groups or anything else, they are formed for the development of the members as people." Second, the NGOs wished to discourage their grassroots groups from moving into the wider market and still expected them to both buy inputs and sell the majority of their produce to them. This was couched in terms of "protecting" the producers from market competition, but it may also be linked to the NGOs' need to make sericulture profitable for the NGOs themselves. Third, the fear of trade unionism is strong among the NGOs in their reluctance to allow producers to form autonomous associations, and one large NGO had the experience in 1979 of closing its silk factory for this reason.[14] Fourth, NGOs argued in this disagreement with the World Bank and the Silk Foundation that the producers were still thinly spread (with one or two in each *samiti*), making it logistically impossible to organize these people into groups.

It also became clear that there was tension around the business aims of sericulture. The tension was between the need to build a sustainable, viable enterprise with the beneficiaries of the program and the more "political" vision of supporting the poor that was implicit in the views of the staff. For example, one NGO field staff member with the Organization for Empowerment said that because his NGO was about "development, not profit," he felt very much at ease in the organization. In discussions, staff emphasized the social welfare aims of the NGO and said that they saw themselves "as development workers, not managers." This NGO also had the unusual policy of "graduating" group members from an initial dependent ("target") to a more independent ("non-target") status as they become more self-reliant. For example, in the credit program certain forms of assistance—such as help with basic shelter—may be given in the form of grants; later, the individual—if he or she improves his or her condition—becomes ineligible for such forms of welfare-based support and becomes part of a credit program that aims to recover its costs. This is designed to reduce the dependence of *samiti* groups on the NGO over time. This contrasted with the Welfare for Women approach, which had a stronger tradition of bringing its group members under its overall protection in a more "top-down" manner.

Conclusions

Actor Perspectives on the Project: Fragmented Meanings

As might be expected, the incentives and relationships that structure the sericulture project "on the ground" look somewhat different from the ways the original project documents set out the project's planned functioning. In practice, the perspectives of each of the participating actors are different, or at least each participant develops a different *emphasis* in its view of "what the project is about."

For the World Bank, the project is as much a part of its drive to encourage public sector restructuring as it is an instrument that contributes to poverty reduction and empowerment objectives. Its view of NGOs is still a mainly functional one, emphasizing the NGOs' capacity to "deliver" resources to the poor. The Bank's vision of the NGOs' role in the project seeks to combine their function as organizations engaged in broad empowerment of the poor with a strong emphasis on their ability to foster market-driven results, even though there is a cultural tension around these issues within many NGOs. Such a view places more emphasis on the NGOs' private, service delivery character than on their wider social, political, or charitable objectives. NGOs are strongly seen as organizations that can strengthen the technical and business aspects of sericulture production and marketing. During our fieldwork, it became quite clear that the Bank was ambivalent about the motivations and the capacities of the NGOs—though there was a very wide diversity of views among different

Bank staff on NGOs and, indeed, about the project itself. From our discussions with Bank staff, it seems logical to assume that although the Bank was aware of the difficulties likely to be encountered with this project, the wider political imperatives of public-sector restructuring and the priorities to "move money" took precedence over the details of operationalizing an empowerment strategy.

For the NGOs, participation in the sericulture project is linked partly to a genuine belief that sericulture can form one element in a wider portfolio of income generation activities for their group members. But it is also part of an agenda that seeks opportunities for funding to support wider work with their groups, including credit provision, literacy work, and a range of other activities not directly related to sericulture. At the same time, the Silk Foundation is interested in pursuing its new organizational mandate, which is to support production within a private-sector reorientation of the sericulture subsector by contributing to improved technologies development, training, and extension to NGOs and other organizations, including commercial companies. But since the Silk Foundation is supposed to be self-financing once the project has ended, it has become increasingly concerned with the need to secure further funding and legitimacy for itself. Finally, for the members of the NGOs' *samiti* groups, participation in sericulture is seen partly as an aspect of the struggle for employment and livelihood and partly as an element of the support that they negotiate from their NGOs within a long-term, ongoing relationship with a range of external patrons. For example, we sometimes found clear tensions between group leaders and relatively passive and even resentful group members, as well as clientelistic vertical linkages between NGO staff and group leaders.

"Cultural" Tensions in Relation to Project Purposes

The fieldwork data collected from these different project actors reveal the high level of internal complexity of the project as compared with the rather functional logic set out in the project design. A tension or conflict exists among the cultures of business, of "helping the poor," and of "empowering the poor," but such conflicts remain veiled and obscured within various forms of "neutral" project language. Indeed, there are quite fluid perspectives within these different agencies. For example, the issue about whether or not NGOs should focus more on commercial, charitable, or empowerment activities varies between different NGOs and between different staff members within the same organization. At the same time, the ways in which NGOs manage relationships with their organizations of the poor may not be at all straightforward. On the one hand, they speak of empowerment and increasing autonomy, but at the same time they may seek to control the levels of autonomy that these groups are provided, whether in terms of their freedom to take commercial decisions and participate in the market, the amount of information and transparency they are "allowed" in the course of their sericulture work, or their ability to develop more autonomous decision making about their overall direction. Within the wider framework of power and relationships, the logic of social capital as a form of horizontal solidarity and trust can be reproduced only very weakly, if at all. For example, though the debate about the "producer groups" resulted in a stand-off that was in the end acceptable to both the World Bank and the NGOs (who could publicly remain committed to their different viewpoints), the *samiti* members themselves were unable to influence the debate or take matters into their own hands to advance themselves economically. Only one *samiti* was found to have taken this route, based on the sympathetic support of one or two junior NGO field staff. Though one critique of the idea of social capital relates to its tendency to depoliticize development, it may be the case that certain forms of social capital can also serve to "de-marketize" forms of empowerment that may be open to the poor.

Social Capital from Sericulture?

Can the Bangladesh model of "social capital" embodied in the initial assumptions and the subsequent outcomes of the silk project ever lead to genuine empowerment outcomes? There is reason to be pessimistic here because the NGOs involved in the project find themselves unable in any real sense to "set their *samitis* free" for three main reasons. The first is that the NGOs in a sense need their *samitis* to legitimize themselves, since the groups demonstrate to funders and to the government that the NGO is engaged in meaningful poverty reduction work. At the same time, the NGOs remain strongly tied to these groups because of the nature of the patron-client relationship that binds them to their groups, as a result both of conscious strategy and of wider social norms that lead both sides to frame much of their relationship in this way. Finally, there is a market logic in the NGOs' need to pursue a strategy for institutional sustainability, which encourages keeping hold of as much of the economic value produced by sericulture activities as possible.

The construction or strengthening of social capital in the form of grassroots "organizations of the poor" as part of initiatives such as the Silk Project may be achieved in a formal sense through the incorporation of NGOs and their groups into such projects. However, the lens of social capital does not in the end tell us as much as we may need to know about the wider relationships of power, culture, and structure that contribute to or constrain both income generation and empowerment objectives. For example, the anthropologist Angela Cheater (2000: 7) has written of the "mystifying rhetoric of empowerment" that can unhelpfully blur the distinction between the language of empowerment claims and meaningful changes in the control of resources. She discusses the ways in which empowerment processes that are *mediated*—in our case by NGOs—can all too easily result in people who are dissatisfied with their resultant state of partial empowerment, brought about by the uncertain rules and meanings that have been mostly constructed and handed down from above. *Samiti* members in the Silk Project are in this frustrated state—since they are both partially empowered and simultaneously constrained by the rules and meanings of empowerment that have been negotiated within the project. Though the concept of social capital may help draw attention to the importance of relationships, networks, and resources, it does not take us far in understanding the subtleties of the negotiations, contests, and struggles—both "successful" and "unsuccessful"—that may take place. Long's (2001) understanding of power as "an outcome of complex struggles and negotiations over authority, status, reputation and resources [that] necessitates the enrolment of networks of actors and constituencies" (71) would provide a richer set of insights into the workings of the Silk Project.

Notes

1. This paper draws on research undertaken as part of the "Organisational cultures and spaces for empowerment" research project, which undertook qualitative project case studies in three countries during 2000–2002, focusing on the role of organizational culture as an influence on multi-agency project performance. A more detailed discussion of the concepts and assumptions that inform the original research project can be found in Lewis et al. (2003). A more detailed report from the research is provided in Lewis and Siddiqi (2002).

2. One of the main themes in the research literature on NGOs in Bangladesh is what might be termed the "de-radicalization thesis"—the idea that many NGOs had their origins among left-leaning activists who were influenced by activist traditions such as the work of Paolo Freire and the Bangladesh Rural Advancement Committee's (BRAC) influential analysis of structural inequalities in the rural power structure (written up as "The Net" in 1986), but that this radicalism gradually dissipated—through a combination of local elite resistance and foreign donor pressures for sustainability—toward the ubiquitous micro-credit agenda that forms the bulk of most NGOs activities these days (cf. Hashemi and Hasan 1999; Devine 2003).

3. Two of the nine participating NGOs were selected for fieldwork. These two NGOs were small local NGOs rather than the better-known NGOs such as BRAC or Proshika, which also participate in the Silk Project. Despite broad similarity in their approaches to working with grassroots groups, one NGO (Welfare for Women) operated in a more charitable, paternalistic style while the other (Organization for Empowerment) worked nominally within a Freirean empowerment and development tradition. The names of the organizations studied have been changed to preserve anonymity.

4. One illustration of this practice could be helping to embed group members in a Polanyian sense in order to reduce their vulnerability.

5. The definition of social capital developed by Lin (2001: 19) as "investment in social relations with expected returns in the marketplace" raises the question as to *who*—in the case we discuss here—is actually doing the "investing." Is it the group members who wish to participate more fully in the market but are prevented from doing so, or is it the NGO, which is arguably using the *samiti* groups to protect its own investment in the marketplace through the sale of silk products, but is doing so outside of the control of the groups themselves?

6. The Rajshahi district in Bangladesh remains famous for its silk and is the traditional center of silk production.

7. Telephone interview with the Task Manager for the project, World Bank, Dhaka, 3 April 2002.

8. There are now two different sets of sericulture producers in Bangladesh. One group is composed of the "traditional" household rearers, reelers, and weavers who have worked with silk for generations and who are highly skilled but who increasingly lack up-to-date technologies. Most of these people do not have access to NGO services. The other group are "nontraditional" sericulture producers who have been established and trained by NGOs and who are predominantly female, supported by male household members, and organized into groups by the NGO to receive credit and undertake a range of joint activities. Income from sericulture supplements other household income. Due to lack of skills, shortage of mulberry leaves, and low-quality inputs, average cropping levels remain low.

9. In the field, our study was based mainly on semi-structured interviews with a range of staff from NGOs, the World Bank, and the Silk Foundation who were involved in the silk project. Focus group discussions were also held with a sample of NGO field staff and with *samiti* group members.

10. The underutilization argument is perhaps similar to the argument made with respect to the aquaculture sector in Bangladesh, but in aquaculture such views are overly optimistic because they ignore or downplay important social and political constraints (Lewis 1998).

11. The formal name of the project is the Bangladesh Silk Development Pilot Project.

12. The NGOs and the BSF are effectively subsidizing the silk sector in the hope that it can once again become productive and profitable. Since nontraditional silk producers usually do not have access to their own mulberry supplies, NGOs see supporting investment in local mulberry plantations as necessary. Some NGOs say that planting mulberry trees on *khas* (unowned land that is distributed by the government to the landless) or jointly purchased land (as opposed to roadside mulberry) would form a sound basis for strengthening the viability of any future attempt to build producer associations. However, in the case of *khas* land, it is often difficult in practice to prevent land earmarked for redistribution from being occupied by more powerful local interests.

13. This example is perhaps reminiscent of the powerful disciplinary regimes of NGOs identified by Fernando (1997). His research in Bangladesh highlighted

the perception by users that NGOs were less flexible in their dealings with the poor than were "traditional" patrons and moneylenders.

14. Trade unions in Bangladesh are widely regarded by NGOs not as fellow "civil society organizations," but as predators strongly characterized by patron-client relationships and penetrated by party politics.

References

Bebbington, A.J., and T.F. Carroll. 2000. *Induced social capital and federations of the rural poor.* Social Capital Initiative Working Paper No. 19. Washington, DC: World Bank.

Bentvelsen, K., and H. Hena. 2001. *Beneficiary assessment mission report.* The Hague: Femconsult, May.

Charsley, S.R. 1982. *Culture and sericulture: Social anthropology and development in a South Indian livestock industry.* London: Academic Press.

Cheater, A. 1999. Power in the postmodern era. In *The anthropology of power: Empowerment and disempowerment in changing structures.* London: Routledge, pp. 1–12.

Devine, J. 2003. The paradox of sustainability: Reflections on NGOs in Bangladesh. *Annals of the American Academy of Political and Social Science* 590:227–242.

Fernando, J.L. 1997. Non-governmental organisations, micro-credit and empowerment of women. *Annals of the American Academy of Political and Social Science* 554:150–177.

Harriss, J. 2002. *Depoliticizing development: The World Bank and social capital.* London: Anthem.

Harriss, J., and de Renzio, P. 1997. Social capital: Missing link or analytically missing? *Journal of International Development* 9(7):919–937.

Hashemi, S.M., and M. Hasan. 1999. Building NGO legitimacy in Bangladesh: The contested domain. In *International perspectives on voluntary action: Reshaping the third sector,* edited by D. Lewis. London: Earthscan, pp.124–131.

Karim, L. 2001. Politics of the poor? NGOs and grassroots political mobilisation in Bangladesh. *Political and Legal Anthropology Review (PoLAR)* 24(1):92–107.

Lewis, D. 1991. *Technologies and transactions: A study of the interaction between new technology and agrarian structure in Bangladesh.* Dhaka, Bangladesh: University of Dhaka, Centre for Social Studies.

Lewis, D. 1998. Partnership as process: Building an institutional ethnography of an inter-agency aquaculture project in Bangladesh. In *Development as process: Concepts and methods for working with complexity,* edited by D. Mosse, J. Farrington, and A. Rew. London: Routledge, pp. 99–114.

Lewis, D., A. Bebbington, S. Batterbury, A. Shah, E. Olson, M.S. Siddiqi, and S. Duvall. 2003. Practice, power and meaning: Frameworks for studying organizational culture in multi-agency rural development projects. *Journal of International Development* 15:1–17.

Lewis, D., and M.S. Siddiqi. 2002. Empowerment, income generation and organizational culture: Making sense of the Silk Development project in Bangladesh. Unpublished report. Washington, DC: World Bank.

Lin, N. 2001. *Social capital: A theory of social structure and action*. Cambridge: Cambridge University Press.

Long, N. 2001. *Development sociology: Actor perspectives*. London: Routledge.

Lovell, C. 1992. *Breaking the cycle of poverty: The BRAC strategy*. Hartford, CT: Kumarian Press.

McGregor, J.A. 1989a. Towards a better understanding of credit in rural development: The case of Bangladesh, The Patron State. *Journal of International Development* 1(4):467–486.

McGregor, J.A. 1989b. Boro Gafur and Choto Gafur: Development interventions and indigenous institutions. *Journal of Social Studies* 43:39–51.

Putnam, Robert D. 1993. *Making democracy work: Civic tradition in modern Italy*. Princeton, NJ: Princeton University Press.

Sinha, S. 1990. *The development of Indian Silk: A wealth of opportunities*. London: Intermediate Technology Publications.

Van Schendel, W. 1995. *Reviving a rural industry: Silk producers and officials in India and Bangladesh 1880s to1980s*. Dhaka, Bangladesh: University Press Limited.

Wood, G.D. 1981. Rural class formation in Bangladesh 1940–80. *Bulletin of Concerned Asian Scholars* 2–15.

Wood, G.D. 1997. States without citizens: The problem of the franchise state. In *NGOs, states and donors: Too close for comfort?*, edited by D. Hulme and M. Edwards, London: Macmillan, pp. 79–93.

SECTION FOUR

INTERPRETING SOCIAL CAPITAL DEBATES AT THE WORLD BANK

CHAPTER TEN

CONCEPTS: THEIR CONTEXTS AND THEIR CONSEQUENCES

Anthony Bebbington
Scott Guggenheim
Michael Woolcock

We opened the book by asking whether the concept of social capital has enhanced the leverage of long-standing substantive concerns among World Bank social scientists for participation, empowerment, social inclusion, and the role of local associations in development. The question is not an idle one. Considerable time and financial resources have been dedicated to refining and promulgating discussions on social capital and development within the institution. Some governments—in particular, those of Norway and Denmark—have invested substantial parts of their support to social development at the Bank in this project,[1] and some individuals have pursued their larger goal of "humanizing" the World Bank through making the concept of social capital more visible in the institution.

Some external observers consider these efforts a waste of time, at least in terms of the larger goal of enhancing the Bank's contributions to more socially just forms of development (or at least reducing the extent to which its interventions foster injustice). Indeed, rather than view the interest in social capital as part of a strategy to "change" the Bank, some critics appear more inclined to understand the "rise of social capital" as having been pursued by some, and allowed by others, as a strategy of inquiry that has the effect of "depoliticizing development" (Harriss 2002). This depoliticization covers broad terrain, they suggest, involving support for both Washington (Harriss 2002) and post-Washington (Fine 2001) consensus positions. At its core, though, is the excision of class and class politics from the Bank's understanding of development and the continuing refusal to entertain any serious discussion of redistribution or of the developmental state. Furthermore, these critics argue that rather than fostering a means through which social scientists might engage with economists, the effect of social capital research has been to enable the further colonization of social development with economic principles and assumptions (Fine 2001; Harriss 2002). More fundamentally still, these critics—along with many others—seem unconvinced that anything can be done to change the Bank and believe that to seek reform from within the institution is to be on the wrong side (Harriss 2002).

These are formidable charges and merit careful assessment. The chapters in this book, collectively and individually, provide some input for this assessment. In this closing piece, we draw some conclusions from these chapters. First, we place these debates on social capital in the Bank in context, discussing how they emerged, became part of the language of different professional communities, and assumed a range of meanings in these different communities.[2] Second, we explore what the chapters reveal about the effects that debates on social capital have had—and might have—on the way the Bank operates. Third, we develop a framework for interpreting both the way in which the social capital debate emerged within the Bank and the possibility that the debate and the issues that some have intended to raise via the social capital concept will have any material effects on Bank practices. The chapter concludes with a reflection on the possible future of discussions on social capital inside the Bank.

The Uses of "Social Capital" in the World Bank

The Emergence of Social Capital Debates in the Bank

Social capital is but one concept in a longer line of concepts that have informed social development work over the last three decades at the World Bank. Its emergence, appropriations, and effects can be adequately understood only in the context of this longer history of ideas in the institution. Davis (2004) has shown how the Bank's engagement with the concept of social capital ought to be viewed in the light of earlier approaches in the social development group, approaches in which themes of social organization, social assessment, and participation were emphasized. What distinguishes the concept from these earlier themes is that it deals—however partially—with questions of social structure. This is not to say that it was only in the mid-1990s that social scientists (and others) in the institution became aware of social structure. Rather, given the political economy, leadership, and staff composition of the Bank at that time, it was less likely that people would raise issues pertaining to the effects of social and political relationships on development. It was easier to talk about the potential role of local organizations and nongovernmental organizations (Cernea 1988;, Salmen and Eaves 1989) in development, about the validity of assessing people's own views of development options and feeding this back to questions of design (through beneficiary assessments), and about the importance of facilitating people's participation in development projects as a way of improving the efficacy of those projects. These were all things that Bank project staff had the capacity to operationalize.

During the late 1980s and early 1990s, however, things changed as the Bank began to reflect more institutionally and openly on some of its disastrous experiences with dams and massive integrated rural development programs. Identifying the sources of these disasters made it palpably evident that social structures were instrumental in influencing development outcomes. The evaluations of resettlement in the Narmada Dam project (Morse and Berger 1992) and the Resettlement Review (Cernea and Guggenheim 1994) placed questions of politics, class, caste, and governance at the center of their interpretations of failure in Bank-funded interventions. Though their implications were not fully absorbed, they did help push the frontier of what was speakable within the institution in the early1990s.

Other changes in the 1990s had similar effects. As the social agenda broadened—partly in the wake of the increasing acceptance that Bank projects could have negative social impacts, and also with the arrival of James Wolfensohn as president—an increasing number of non-economists and staff with NGO backgrounds were recruited. This in itself brought in people who were more inclined to talk of structure, power, and politics and who in many cases viewed their role as one of changing the Bank from the inside. And finally, the 1990s were a post–Cold War period of Democratic administration in US government, a period in which some of the sensitivities to a sniff of anything vaguely "political" were perhaps blunted.

That said, not everything became speakable, and full-fledged notions of political economy were still not going to fly in the institution. In such a context, and for those wishing to continue broadening the social agenda so that it engaged questions of state-society relations, social capital was deemed a useful concept for a number of reasons. First, as Chapter 5, on Indonesia, shows, by drawing attention to the local-level institutions in and through which poor communities sought to manage risk and advance their interests, it was a short step to show that the efficacy of this activity was powerfully shaped by the political context in which it was occurring. Some local-level institutions (e.g., indigenous peoples' organizations) were acting in defiance of or active resistance to the state, others were forced to assume functions (e.g., security, schooling) that states were unable or unwilling to perform, and still others (e.g., credit cooperatives) were acting as complements (and potential entry points) to formal institutions. Second, as a logical corollary, the way was now clearer to argue that these organizations themselves (and civil society more generally) enjoyed a varying degree of capacity to influence public and private organizations. Supported by research from beyond and within the Bank on the role of the state in explaining the East Asia miracle and aid effectiveness, debates surrounding state-society relations more generally moved from polemical zero-sum discussions ("more"or "less" is better) to a more sophisticated inquiry into the conditions under which the complementary strengths of states, firms, and civic organizations could generate positive-sum gain. Third, social capital was a language that could be used to talk about state-society interactions (governance) in less sociological ways (as in all the work on "trust"; Knack and Keefer 1997) as well as in ways that drew attention to the social relationships underlying these interactions. Fourth, by appropriating an "assets-based" (as opposed to "deficits-based") discourse in which social capital was talked of as an asset of the poor, the discussion of social capital offered a language for talking both of governance and of poverty. The asset focus helped spark a more positive discussion of the resources and aspirations of poor communities, even as it also enabled clear contrasts to be drawn between the size and sources of "assets" possessed by the rich and poor. And finally—as all the Bank staff in this collection state clearly—dialogue on social capital helped them engage their more economistic colleagues on issues of local organization and collective action.

Appropriations of Social Capital

Although it is possible to cast a general story about the emergence of social capital debates within the Bank, accounts given here also suggest the ways in which the concept of social capital became part of the language of specific subcommunities in the institution. In the Indonesian case, the concept traveled to operations directly from a research program being conducted by the social development team located at the center of the Bank in Washington. More specifically, Guggenheim had worked in that core team and was a close colleague of Gloria Davis, who directed the team. The idea of deepening a reflection on social capital was already circulating when Guggenheim worked in the central social policy division, and a discussion was already in process over whether the concept was useful primarily for thinking about the role of local institutions in development or rather for thinking about state-society relations. In due course, Indonesia became one of the countries in which that research was undertaken because Guggenheim relocated to the newly created Environment and Social team there. In this case, then, the person was the vector through which the concept traveled to a community within the Bank. Chapter 5 discusses in more detail how the concept then informed—and was used to make the case for—a major project that gave priority to local institutions as development actors and that aimed to build mechanisms linking them and subdistrict governments.

In the cases of the professional communities working on indigenous peoples and development in Latin America and on social funds, the concept traveled in less direct ways. That is, rather than key individuals bringing the social capital concept to the discussions, the growing body of research on social capital being undertaken both by the social development team at the center and by economists in DEC made the concept visible. The written accounts do not allow us to reconstruct this process in detail, but it seems that as both social development and DEC researchers began writing more about social capital, as the discussion meetings of the social capital thematic group became more visible and frequent, and as key individuals began hawking their social capital and development seminars around the different divisions of the Bank, the idea began to be taken up by new communities. Though there were evidently social and professional relationships that linked the teams to these groups at the center, the networks were more diffuse.

For the concept to be appropriated, however, each of these professional communities had to find something useful in it, and the chapters in the book's second section suggest different (if overlapping) ways in which the various communities found the concept helpful. In her essay, Van Domelen suggests that the social funds group came a bit late to the concept of social capital and that it entered their lexicon because it resonated with their long-standing interest in local organizations. The Latin American indigenous development team—which was then trying to shift the indigenous peoples' agenda in the Bank from safeguards and policies to one of investment in and direct support to indigenous organizations—began to feel that the language offered a way of talking about indigenous peoples, their organizations, and their poverty in ways that did not seem like special pleading for a particular identity group.

The more general point here is that debates travel very unevenly within an institution as large and complex as the Bank. The chapters in the book, which demonstrate this unevenness, should not be taken as evidence that all sectors of the Bank are discussing the concept or are doing so for the same reasons and in the same ways. On the contrary, discussions vary considerably, and the transmission mechanisms for these ideas also take quite different forms and guises. Some people have actively adopted the concept to help them pursue a particular agenda; others have embraced social capital as a way of talking in new ways about what they were already doing. Very often, the concept has had different meanings among the different groups using it.

Meanings of Social Capital

As noted previously, one of the apparent virtues of the concept of social capital, at least within the Bank, is that it can be used in the context of sociopolitical interpretations of state-society relations, and it can be used to speak both of governance and of poverty. Indeed, groups in the Bank have interpreted the concept in varying ways. The schema in Chapter 2 offers a vehicle for mapping these different uses. The authors suggest that four views of social capital can be identified in the sociological and development literature, and that these views carry different implications for development interventions. They refer to these four perspectives as the communitarian, network, institution, and synergy visions of social capital. These different approaches to the concept are apparent in different bodies of analytical work at the Bank, as well as in the different projects discussed here.

The most basic and typical appropriation of the term has doubtless been the communitarian view, which

> equates social capital with local-level organizations, namely associations, clubs, and civic groups. This view, measured most simply by the number and density of these groups in a given community, implies that social capital is inherently "good," that "more is better," and that its presence always has a positive effect on a community's welfare. (Woolcock and Narayan, this volume)

This emphasis on local organizations as assets is apparent in much of the Bank's published research on local-level institutions (Narayan and Pritchett 1999, Grootaert et al. 2002) and empowerment, as Moore (2001) notes, as well as much of the work conducted within the Bank's Social Capital Initiative (Grootaert and van Bastelaer 2002). It is also visible in each of the case study chapters in this collection. In different ways, all the chapters emphasize (1) the extent to which projects can and should build on existing forms of social capital among poor people (generally but not always at the village level) and (2) that the further strengthening of such social capital is a legitimate and important goal of projects. In this respect there is much continuity between these projects and earlier work at the Bank emphasizing the importance of local organizations (Cernea 1988).

Though not all of the projects or authors referred to here would agree with the second sentence in the definition offered by Woolcock and Narayan, they all emphasize the importance of organizations and networks as assets of the poor, they all see (and give space to) community organizations as important actors in development interventions, and they all seek ways of transferring resources to these organizations. Where they vary most significantly is in the types of linkages they have aimed to promote between such local associations, various parts of the state, and other actors.

Social funds have sought to increase community participation in public investment and reduce the layers of bureaucracy between villages and public funds. They have not, however, been especially concerned with working with federations of local organizations or with fostering new forms of state-society relationships at intermediate levels of government. Their emphasis has been on making it easier for villages to access public resources rather than on fostering mechanisms through which villagers are able to plan the supra-village allocation and use of public resources and hold public institutions to account. It is thus perhaps not surprising that these funds have used the concept of social capital primarily to talk about village-level capacities, rather than about forms of state-society embeddedness. The communitarian view of social capital dominates the ways in which social funds operate (see also Moore 2001) and in which they appropriate the concept. A networks view is also present at times, but is rarer; indeed, it is notable how little attention social funds still pay to local-level social divisions, alliances, and power relationships.[3] Some would argue that because of this their resources are prone to capture and that groups excluded in the process have no vehicles through which to voice their concerns or pursue any coherent reform agenda. Van Domelen in Chapter 7 questions some of these criticisms. She argues that such capture is relatively rare and that the impacts of social funds on village poverty have been significant. She also argues that over time, one effect of the social capital discussion has been increased reflection among some within the social funds group on the ways in which local power relationships and social structures affect the workings of social funds in communities. It is not clear how this has translated into changes in design, except perhaps in some of those social fund–like operations that have morphed into community-driven development projects.

Of course, the communitarian view of social organization is evident not only in social funds. The Bangladesh Silk Project, discussed by Lewis and Siddiqi in Chapter 9, also focuses on local-level producer organizations and makes little effort to foster empowerment either through inter-village forms of association or through reworking the complex relationships between producer organizations and NGOs. Similarly, the rural development interventions discussed by Fox and Gershman in Chapter 8 limited their attention primarily to strengthening village groups. At a more general level, the rise of "community-driven development" (CDD) in the Bank has often involved predominantly communitarian and network views of social capital (Mansuri and Rao 2004).[4]

Other projects—even when they have shared communitarian optimism about local organizations—have sought to foster quite different sorts of change in state-society relationships and have worked with a "synergy" view of social capital, one arguing that inclusive development takes place when representatives of the state, the corporate sector, and civil society establish common fora through which they can identify and pursue common goals. Social capital is thus treated as a mediating variable; it is shaped by public and private institutions, and yet has important impacts on development outcomes. This makes "investing" in social capital an inherently contentious and contested—that is to say, political—process, one in which the role of the state is crucial, not marginal. (Woolcock and Narayan, this volume)

This approach is clearest in the Indonesian project (Chapter 5) but is also used in Ecuador (Chapter 6). In Indonesia the Kecamatan Development Project (KDP) requires collective actions within village-level groups as well as among these groups and among villages. This reflects a deliberate effort to work with sub–village-level social capital and, at the same time, to create inter-village linkages. The intent is for these inter-village spheres—and organizations—also to become an interface with external actors, particularly subdistrict (kecamatan) government. The notion is that in working at this interface, villages will learn how to engage, hold to account, and access resources from government. In Ecuador, while the Indigenous and Afro-Ecuadorian People's Development Project (PRODE-PINE) emphasized direct support to federations of indigenous base groups, it also built municipal and national-level fora at which indigenous organizations, government, and certain other actors elaborated development plans and negotiated control over and allocation of resources. While working less systematically than KDP on creating mechanisms for accountability, these fora constituted arenas in which relationships fostering both embeddedness and complementarity were to be built (cf. Evans 1996a, b; Woolcock and Narayan, this volume).[5]

In many cases, these initial goals of reworking state-society relationships have weakened during the course—and sometimes even during the design—of the project. This seems to have been particularly the case where the initial goals were not especially ambitious. This suggests that when there were conditions leading the Bank to make early commitments to ambitious governance programs, these conditions were more likely to sustain those commitments over the life of the project; conversely, when the Bank's early commitments were less strong, they were more easily squeezed out as the project unfolded. Several of the cases in Mexico and the Philippines discussed by Fox and Gershman (Chapter 8) showed diminution of such goals (see also Fox 1997). They also point to the significance of changes in Bank staffing. In some cases, project leaders continued to insist on passing degrees of power to communities as long as a particularly committed staff member task-managed the project. When those leaders were later replaced with staff who evidenced less commitment to such a goal—and were less inclined to stand up for it—projects became more orthodox, government-implemented programs.

Among the cases discussed in this collection where this commitment to empowerment objectives has been sustained over time (i.e., PRODE-PINE and KDP), a key factor appears to have been that the handful of Bank staff committed to this core idea refused to let go of the project. They continued to be closely involved in the monitoring of projects as well as in the design of follow-up phases. Their success in standing firm has been helped by the political conjuncture of the countries in question and by the Bank's position in the country. In Ecuador, the very strength of indigenous federations and confederations (and their evident ability to challenge government authority[6]) made it easier to sustain a commitment to support them directly and to involve them directly in project management. Similarly, in Indonesia, the crisis of government in the late 1990s and the related crisis of the World Bank's Country Office made it easier to argue that governance was a critical problem in Indonesia and that it should constitute the core of the Bank's program there. This meant that the space for KDP stayed open.

Thus, the concept of social capital had different meanings among different groups within the Bank, and certain meanings could be kept alive only under certain conditions. Among the most important factors was that key individuals and teams, committed to pursuing certain goals and sustaining certain meanings of their projects, remained stable—a point made strongly in Fox and Gershman's comparative treatment of six projects in Mexico and the Philippines (Chapter 8). The effects of the social capital discussion—and more generally of discussions of empowerment and participation—thus depend critically on how certain commitments are sustained over time.

The Effects of Social Capital

Social capital literature—as articulated by both its boosters and its critics—has tended to apportion too much causal power to social capital: social capital has been the source of all things good to some and all things anti-political to others. In wrapping up an assessment of what difference, if any, the concept has made in the internal dynamics of the Bank, we therefore err on the side of caution and avoid attributing too much (good or bad) to a single concept—not least because much that happens in and around Bank-supported activities still depends greatly on the political economy of the institution, its peculiar bureaucratic rules and incentives, and the political economies of the countries in which it works. In what follows we tease out certain areas in which the debates on social capital may have had some influence, usually as one among several influences. We trace effects on concepts and understandings of poverty, on governance and development in the Bank, and on project designs and material impacts in a country.

Social Capital, Poverty, and Governance

Much has been made of the relative frequency with which Bank publications have cited the idea that social capital is the "glue" that holds societies together. Though a simplified and easy-to-criticize claim, it has arguably left its mark by raising the visibility of the significance of social cohesion and by making clear the significance of social relationships as both input and output of development. The visibility of "empowerment" and state-society linkages in the World Development Reports of 2000–2001, 2004, and 2006 together suggest that the Bank now pays more attention to the significance of social cohesion than it once did.

The visibility of social capital within the 2000–2001 WDR was consciously sought by the social development team. However, it was also made possible by related shifts in thinking among certain influential economists in the Bank and proactive social scientists in the Poverty Reduction and Economic Management (PREM) network. Joseph Stiglitz, Chief Economist at the time, and Michael Walton, then director of the Poverty Group in PREM, both were overtly supportive of the empowerment agenda and were active supporters of the large and high-profile "Voices of the Poor" project (coordinated by Deepa Narayan; see Narayan et al. 2000), which was conducted in conjunction with the WDR. This group also immediately launched a follow-up sourcebook (World Bank 2002) on empowerment (also coordinated by Narayan), the most controversial of the WDR's three pillars, and the "empowerment" terminology then became one of the *two* key themes[7] that Stiglitz's successor, Nicholas Stern, adopted and actively promoted (see World Bank 2004).

Given the central role of Deepa Narayan in all of these events, it is not a stretch to argue that many of the ways in which Bank documents speak of empowerment are a direct extension of work done around the concept of social capital within the institution.[8] Pritchett and Hammer (Chapter 3) argue something similar when they claim that, although the language of social capital was largely absent in the 2004 WDR's emphasis on the role of voice and public pressure in service delivery, this emphasis was possible only because of the earlier discussions on social capital within the Bank. That said, the rise of an empowerment and voice agenda is also the outcome of the longer history of work done by the social development group within the Bank. It is reasonable to argue that throughout the group's existence, most members have aimed to alter the way the Bank as an institution understands development and have been searching for a way of framing these alternatives theoretically, and in ways that other professional constituencies in the Bank would understand. The earlier focus on participation and social assessment provided ways for making pre-project assessment, project design, and, in some cases, even policy formation more participatory and more attuned to social realities. It did not, however, provide another language for talking of and conceptualizing development at a macro level. The language of social capital has changed this somewhat. By discussing organizations, networks, and the capacity to act collectively in terms of "capital," the concept provided a bridge with more conventional Bank analyses of poverty and development that discuss it in terms of human, financial, and physical assets.[9] This was captured most importantly in publications suggesting that the wealth of nations, and the sustainability of development, can also be understood to be a function of social capital (Serageldin and Steer 1994).

The notion of social capital as "the glue" holding societies together is an effort to give a more general, almost lay, interpretation to this overall role of organizations, networks, and trust in development. Underlying this interpretation, however, are at least two reflections: one on the nature of poverty and well-being, the other on the nature of governance, and each informed by the social capital debate.

In past years social capital issues contributed to ongoing discussions of the multidimensionality of poverty in two important ways: social capital dialogues, overlapping with broader discussions of livelihoods (Scoones 1998; Bebbington 1999; Rakodi 1999), increased understanding of poverty in terms of people's asset bases, and understanding those assets as different forms of capital went hand in hand with including social capital as one of those assets (Moser 1998). Thus, people's degree of association, belonging, and involvement in society became part of the determination of their poverty—because such involvement and association was a means of managing risk, accessing other resources, managing resources more effectively, and so on. At the same time, such belonging also became part of the understanding of the experience of poverty—that anomie and alienation were as much a part of impoverishment as was lack of income. Belonging and involvement in associations—cohesion, glue—was thus part of a poverty agenda. Social capital was a language for addressing this more analytically.

Discussions of social capital also fed into changes in the ways in which governance was being framed in the Bank—increasingly as a problem of state-society relationships rather than of public management. Up to the mid-1990s, discussions of the state and of governance on the one hand and discussions of participation on the other were largely separate affairs within the World Bank—the former the domain of the public sector management team and the latter the domain of a broader group, but one anchored in the social development division. Furthermore, governance discussions were dominated by the language and concepts of public administration ("inefficiency," "corruption"), and participation debates remained project-focused and de-linked from analysis of everyday political practice and process. In neither of these discussions was the state or its interactions with citizens and subjects discussed as worthy of significant sociological or anthropological inquiry.[10] There was certainly very little thought given to how citizen participation in the processes of public management might be instrumental to the building of more accountable, transparent, and responsive state institutions or to how particular styles of public sector management might contribute to the production of citizens and citizenship. In this context, the 2004 World Development Report (World Bank 2003), *Making Services Work for Poor People*—with its explicit focus on building stronger "relationships of accountability" among clients, providers, and states—represents an important step forward.

Without claiming too much for a single concept, the fact that (at least the synergy view of) social capital focused attention on the ways in which state and society were embedded in each other helped bridge some of this divide between public sector management and participation and helped focus attention on questions of governance and accountability. For some involved in the early debates on social capital in the Bank, the concept was always primarily one for rethinking questions of governance so that governance would not simply mean "what happens in government" but would instead refer to the many interactions between state and citizens and to the ways in which these interactions affect resource allocation, government action, and the exercise of power. A concept alone was never going to achieve this, however. Rather, any such change—if it were to occur—would have to be endorsed by an operation demonstrating the validity of thinking of governance in this way. Of the projects discussed here, only KDP and PRODEPINE have done this in any significant and, at least for some involved, self-conscious way. KDP has shown that it is possible to experiment in a large-scale way with supporting new interfaces for citizen influence on the state, that this can translate into different ways of allocating public resources, and that these different allocations can have positive effects on the asset bases in and of villages. As Chapter 5 notes, KDP has had its share of difficulties, but it has been successful enough both at a village level and in an orthodox Bank sense (lending large amounts of money ahead of schedule) that it has become visible throughout the Bank, being discussed in handbooks, flagship publications, PowerPoint presentations, and elsewhere. In 2004 KDP was showcased in a high-profile meeting held in Shanghai and co-organized by the government of China, the Bank, and others whose purpose was to bring together donors, governments, and other parties to discuss large-scale projects that had successfully reduced poverty and whose "design principles" might be transferred to other contexts in support of the broader enterprise of meeting the Millennium Development Goals.[11]

KDP and PRODEPINE also have implications for thinking about development and governance as culturally loaded phenomena. The two projects make explicit the role of identity-based organizations in the governance of development—PRODEPINE by recognizing the intersections between ethnic and race-based federations and the structures of government, KDP by explicitly noting that village government legislation in Indonesia has been an exercise in Javanization and by struggling with the place of traditional *adat* institutions in local governance. Insofar as networks and organizations are also cultural forms, then, the existence, mobilization, or repression of certain forms of social capital project some *meanings* and not others and reflect certain identities and not others (Bebbington et al. 2004b). In this sense, any efforts to make certain types of organization more visible than they were before are also attempts to change what a country and its state *mean*—to Bank staff and country citizens. More specifically, demonstrating that such organizations (be they indigenous federations in Ecuador, traditional *adat* institutions in Indonesia, or others) can play significant roles in formal governance processes challenges taken-for-granted meanings of what the state should look like and of whose cultures of organization it ought to project and promote. Although it would be far too much to suggest that debates around social capital have led the Bank to recognize development and governance as inherently cultural phenomena, it may be that the concept and certain operations that work with it have at least opened space for such a reflection.[12]

Social Capital Operations and Their Effects

In a recent review of Bank operations, Francis (2002: 7) concluded the following:

> All Regions of the Bank are, of course, engaged in operations with a bearing on social capital (indeed the wide definition of the concept means that few interventions would not have implications for social capital at some level). More specifically, community driven development and social funds, as well as programs in rural and agricultural development, human development and poverty alleviation, almost always draw upon and affect social capital at the community and local level. Most Regions have made some use of the concept of social capital in analytic or investment work. However, no Region has made social capital an orienting or strategic concept for its work.

The implication of this observation is that while social capital debates have made some inroads into operations, they are not yet substantial. On the other hand, the new generation of Bank community-driven development projects—poverty reduction interventions of which KDP, PRODEPINE, certain social funds, and other selected "star" projects were forerunners—appear to take many of the themes in the debates around social capital and aim to operationalize them on a large scale. The roles of local associations in defining local development agendas, handling finances directly, and contracting their own service providers feature strongly in the design of these projects. Indeed, in a review of the Bank's community-driven development portfolio, Mansuri and Rao (2004) note that an explicit aim of many CDD projects is to "build the social capital" of poor people's organizations. It is not for nothing, then, that Van Domelen ends her chapter by concluding that much of the social fund and social capital agendas come together in the current move toward community-driven development.

This might be deemed an important effect of the social capital debate, but the chapters also make it quite clear that simply getting a concept into the design of a project is nowhere near enough to ensure a significant pro-poor or pro-empowerment effect (as Chapter 8 notes so clearly). The chapters demonstrate just some of the factors that can neutralize projects that on paper are innovatively pro-poor. Governments might reject the idea outright; intermediary NGOs, expected to be vehicles of empowerment, might have disempowering agendas that are primarily oriented toward institutional survival and growth (Bangladesh); Task Managers may be replaced by more conservative and risk-averse Task Managers (Mexico and Philippines); local elites may just be too clever and find a way to ensure they can still capture project benefits (Indonesia); government project staff may simply not understand or may have no interest in seeing the idea through; or Country Directors may become less supportive of a risky pro-empowerment project. The list is long. Though changing the conceptualization of a project is important, by itself it is no guarantee of any change of interest to the poor.

Several of the chapters make clear how much Task Managers who do want to do things differently endeavor to set up systems to ensure that their ideas and intentions are carried through. The Indonesia and Ecuador chapters in particular demonstrate the extent to which the devil is in the details—showing that design matters immensely in keeping open spaces for change. In particular, the insistence on certain indicators of process, transparency, and impact matters, as does establishing monitoring systems that are independent of major stakeholders. Getting audit arrangements right, without being bureaucratic or interventionist, and working out how exactly to transfer money to villages in ways that are less likely to allow theft—these are the details that, though apparently boring, keep task managers awake at night. More significantly, they are the vehicles that determine whether concepts of empowerment, good governance, and collective action will be embodied in actual practice.

Where the stars line up, some of the chapters suggest that things can be done differently and that there can be material effects on pro-poor empowerment. Even though they are all tentative in the claims they make about impacts, several of the chapters do point to cases in which projects have fostered: increased supra-village linkages and organization among villages; increased pressure on local government from village-based and federated organizations; and increasingly assertive villager relationships with the state. More modestly, but still important, some chapters suggest that at certain points the very process of doing projects differently has had an impact on the reciprocal attitudes among Bank, civil society, and certain state actors.

The question arises, Did these impacts derive from the use of a notion of social capital to help frame the project or pre-project research activities, or were these impacts an effect of the people involved? We cannot know this, though many of the chapters—perhaps most insistently, Fox and Gershman's review of Bank-funded rural development projects in Mexico and the Philippines—do imply that *who* the Task Manager is matters a great deal. However, it is interesting that the authors insist that the concept mattered, too, and did help them at certain times in specific ways: to see things they might otherwise have missed (Van Domelen); to reflect on state-society relationships (Guggenheim); to think through the nature of market and state failure (Pritchett and Hammer); to think about the relationships among social organization and the quality, significance, and productivity of other assets (Uquillas); and so on. Individuals promoting pro-poor change can, it seems, be served more by some languages than others, and—albeit at different points in the project cycle for different people—the language of social capital became useful for many of the authors writing here.

Another question is whether the concept had materially significant, political effects. At one level, it is clearly the case that politics are not central to the concept of social capital; social capital sidesteps discussions of class and political economy and does not per se raise themes of redistribution or the links between asset bases and social power—hence the criticism that this is ultimately a depoliticizing concept. That said, a number of the projects discussed here, which have drawn on the concept, have politicized discussions of development—whether by throwing open the whole issue of corruption, by fostering more participatory and deliberative forms of democracy both within the state and around resource allocation, or by broaching questions of transparency head-on. But it is just as clear that other projects—including some social fund operations—have used the concept and completely sidestepped questions of power and politics. The lesson, perhaps, is that the concept per se is not inherently strong enough to force either politicization or depoliticization; the final political effects that might accompany the deployment of the concept in Bank projects depend entirely on who is deploying it and why. Clearly, some deploy it with a genuine concern to politicize debate, but others invoke it just to add jargon and frills to a project-as-usual. So if many of those who have adopted the social capital terminology have not (for whatever reason) also explored more detailed questions of politics and power, it is one thing to note this point, but quite another to claim that the terminology itself is responsible for (or at least wholly encourages) the omission.

Given that many of the power differentials in the world are created and sustained through exclusive networks that manage to wrest control over the state and large private sector firms—as Bourdieu's (and others') conception of social capital makes explicit—it is entirely plausible to regard social capital theory and issues of political economy as complements, not substitutes (as the harshest critics argue).[13] But the concept of social capital does not on its own do the job of political economy. It does not make visible all the factors that drive difference and inequality, even if it is more effective than other languages circulating within the Bank for illuminating some of the relationships and forms of organization through which inequality is maintained. Indeed, in their own ways, most of the chapters in the book argue and demonstrate that concepts of social capital are best deployed within a broader (perhaps more generic) political economy analysis of the problem at hand.

Interpreting Social Capital Debates: A Framework

Beyond any inherent interest of their own, social capital debates at the World Bank provide a case of a broader phenomenon—namely the struggles over ideas and meanings that occur within development agencies and that serve as venues for broader struggles over the directions to be taken by those organizations. Such struggles are always taking place within development organizations, yet they are poorly understood in the literature. This is the case both because it is so difficult to get inside these organizations and because so much of the struggle happens "off-camera"—that is to say, in corridors, over coffee, and (as Guggenheim in Chapter 5 notes) behind closed doors.

This collection—and certainly our interpretation of the chapters— offers inputs for developing simple frameworks to help understand these struggles over ideas and institutional trajectories. At the core of this framework are actors more than ideas. In focusing on "enthusiasts, tacticians, and skeptics," Michael Edwards's chapter gives prominence to the actors behind the social capital debates, rather than to the idea itself. This is important, for much of the critique of the way in which the Bank has discussed social capital has focused on ideas—and appears at times to give those ideas causal power. In texts such as Fine's (2001), social capital appears as an actor with causal powers of its own—powers enhanced by similarly imputed structural logics and political interests underlying the way the institution works. That "external" interpretations should take this tack is completely understandable—again, because from the outside it is so difficult to identify and follow such actors. Our position, as insiders and outsider-insiders, helps in this regard, for it allows some insight into the dynamics of human agency within the Bank. Of course, this advantage has a corollary risk. This position as insiders, where we are also actors in the phenomenon we are aiming to understand, can just as easily lead to an overestimation of the potentials of human agency and can also lead to misinterpretations of certain manifestations of agency because of concerns to defend and appreciate people who are colleagues and at times friends.

That said, in our interpretation of the social capital debate at the Bank, agency is central. People within the institution have motivations, assets, and commitments. They mobilize ideas in pursuit of those commitments, and the success of their efforts depends a great deal on the assets that they have at their disposal. The essays here suggest that the most important assets in these struggles are financial and social. Money is essential in any effort to foster change in the institution. Activities (research, pilot projects, etc.) must be mounted around the idea being promoted if the idea is to become at all visible and persuasive in the institution. Contacts, networks, and coalitions are as important as money; as Fox and Gershman note in Chapter 8, the "social capitalists" had to have a social capital of their own if they were to progress in their efforts to foster new ways of working and understanding development. Individuals cannot possibly foster change in an institution like the Bank; they need to find kindred spirits and then find ways of enrolling others in the same project. Much of this enrolling occurs through broadening and blurring the core ideas associated with the project, in order to make it intelligible, interesting, and motivating to others who may not be quite kindred, but who are at least pulling in a similar direction. In the cases pursued in this book, the meaning of social capital was quite clearly broadened and blurred at an early stage in order to enlist different people in the broader program. At the same time, the concept itself broadened the purchase of earlier concerns for participation and social assessment, and in so doing helped enroll others who would have felt less inclined (for professional and normative reasons) to tie their flag to the mast.

This process of coalition building and of making alternatives visible within an institution is inevitably affected by the broader rules and practices of the institution. Indeed, to a considerable extent the process has to work through those rules and practices. In the case of social capital debates at the Bank, this has been reflected, above all, in the need to link the concept with operations—ideally, large operations. "Operationalizability" counts a great deal within the Bank, where the professional incentives are still to get projects approved, and the bigger the project, the better. Social development professionals are under pressure to respond to such demands (Mosse 2004). This is the significance above all of KDP, but also of PRODEPINE; these projects have succeeded in this regard and have become highly visible as a result. However, as the chapters by Fox and Gersham and by Lewis and Siddiqi—and even the one by Van Domelen—remind us, incentive structures within the Bank also pull in other directions and can easily dilute any efforts to do things differently.

The rules and structures that affect agency are not only internal to the Bank as a development bureaucracy. They also depend greatly on the political economy of the Bank and of the countries in which it works. At the Bank level we have suggested that some of the space that opened and made the social capital debate possible—both in general and in particular country offices—reflected shifts in the political economy of the institution. Institutional (e.g., post–Resettlement Review) and country-specific (e.g., post–Indonesia financial crisis) moments of deep uncertainty and crisis for the Bank helped create space for different ways of working. That a president sympathetic to social development was in charge also helped create a propitious climate for this (and was itself no political accident). The ability of certain member countries (wittingly or not) to introduce financial resources in ways that allowed people within the Bank to take advantage of those spaces was also critical: It provided the essential financial resources at the right time. But such spaces are not stable, and as politics shifts within the United States, it is just as likely that in years to come, the space for Bank staff to, for instance, frame and address governance as a sociopolitical problem and to fund projects in ways that directly challenge economic elites in particular countries (as PRODEPINE and KDP have done) will be reined in.

Country-level political economy is an equally critical determinant in the extent to which the social capital debates fostered significant change in particular places. The Ecuador and Indonesia chapters are explicit in stating that projects such as KDP and PRODEPINE were possible only because of conjunctures in national politics. They were not just a consequence of Bank staff being *in the right place*; they were consequences of Bank staff being in the right place *at the right time*. These national political economic spaces are also unstable, and spaces that opened at certain times for (Bank and other) reformists can also close (cf. Fox 1996, 2004), reducing the extent to which either governments or Bank management will be inclined to be significantly pro-poor or to build on, for example, governance experiments such as those of KDP.

What comes through in all this is the notion of unevenness over space and across time. The Bank is uneven internally. Staff members have different (if overlapping) motivations and normative commitments, and different country programs and teams have differing predispositions. The quality and quantity of social development staff and ideas also vary across the institution. The political economic contexts—at country and regional levels—in which teams and staff work and pursue their normative as well as professional goals also differ greatly. Some are far more propitious than others with regard to promoting particular ideas about social development, and how propitious they are changes with time. Finally, the extent to which the overall environment of the Bank fosters any such orientation is not constant over time (just as it is not constant across units of the Bank). Struggles over ideas, debates, and processes of institutional change, in the face of such unevenness, will inevitably take different forms and guises and have different effects. Clearly, the odyssey of social capital shows how and why the debates took hold in some parts of the Bank while remaining invisible in others, and it also throws some light on the processes through which these debates did not travel uniformly within the institution. Methodologically, this makes ethnography, or at least participant observation, critical to any inquiry into the politics of ideas within the Bank; politically, it makes disaggregated knowledge of the Bank's internal dynamics and of the location of pro- and anti-reform actors and coalitions within the institution critical for any external actor pushing for change from outside the institution (see also Fox and Brown 1998).

The Bank remains a large and powerful organization driven by the twin imperatives of rendering complexity legible (through technocratic and bureaucratic means; Scott 1998) and lending large volumes of money. Structure and institutional rules therefore matter. But it is also the case that many members of its staff take seriously the organization's avowed mission of helping bring about "a world free of poverty" and that the more pragmatic among them are relatively open to adopting demonstrably superior ways to realize that objective; different types of agency therefore also matter (as Edwards in Chapter 4 also insists). All of this is to say that while fully acknowledging the real institutional and political constraints, we are somewhat more hopeful than Ferguson (1990), Fine (2001), and Harriss (2002) about the possibilities and potential for change within the World Bank, about the operational leverage that discursive shifts can open and nurture, and about the capacity of strategic (and disciplinarily hybrid) terms such as "social capital" to facilitate and legitimize that leverage.[14]

Beyond Social Capital Debates

If the discussion to this point has been dominated by considerations of how the idea of social capital gained intellectual purchase and policy traction within the World Bank, it is worthwhile to conclude by applying the logic of that analysis to a brief consideration of social capital's future. Has the idea run its course, or does it still have a useful role to play? Should it be abandoned in favor of more precise language, or can it continue to help introduce "social" themes into those realms of the Bank (and elsewhere) in need of a starting point?

Our answer, perhaps not surprisingly, is yes to both of these seemingly opposing perspectives. That is, there is a real sense, we argue, in which the idea of social capital has helped to introduce and legitimize serious discussions around a host of important social issues that were previously ignored (by design or default) within the World Bank; it is a separate matter, however, as to whether social capital has the capacity to sustain and expand those discussions. If the issue is *sustaining* a discussion around a specific policy issue, we suspect that social capital lacks the depth and rigor to inform a long-term agenda and needs to be successively replaced (as Hammer and Pritchett document in Chapter 3 with respect to service delivery); in these cases, social capital has largely done the work it was intended to do and is capable of doing. If, however, the issue is *to expand* a discussion of social themes into arenas that otherwise lack such a discourse—and that terrain remains very large—the concept of social capital may well continue to play an important role in ushering in such themes. Our own experiences talking to practitioners, policymakers, and academics working on issues ranging from health care to homelessness confirm this point. In order to move any political agenda—but especially one whose inherent subject matter is hard to define—it is crucial that the agenda be informed by a broadly accessible and intuitively appealing language that both galvanizes internal support and "speaks to power"; social capital, at its best, has provided that language for "tacticians" (in Michael Edwards's words) inside the World Bank, but it should always be seen as an interim language, deployed as part of a broader reformist strategy.

There is a third communicative task in which social capital's role is more ambivalent, and this concerns those domains where the constituency itself has a long-standing and internally coherent language for articulating its social concerns and aspirations, but finds that language being ignored, misunderstood, or distorted by those they are trying to influence. Here, in-group members seeking greater external influence may find themselves confronting something of a Faustian bargain, namely an imperative to change their language in order to "speak to power," but at the risk of undermining the galvanizing coherence of their own internal discourse. Indeed, it has been our experience that the introduction of a social capital discourse can just as easily meet with resistance because it is deemed to water down (politically) an existing way of framing social relations. We clearly cannot and do not recommend a uniform response to these situations, since the efficacy and salience of a given discourse is, in these instances even more than usual, so powerfully shaped by its political context. Even (or especially) if difficult discursive trade-offs such as these have to be made, the point remains that different discourses are required for different political purposes, and that effective change agents are often judiciously, and tactically, "multilingual" in this sense.

If we are partially calling for the abandonment of social capital, then, it has little to do with the scathing critiques to which the concept of social capital has been subjected, even if some of the weaknesses identified in those critiques are related to the principle that other languages are needed for social development. Instead, we suspect that, social capital has achieved its goal, at least in certain key areas and respects, and that, indeed, its explosive growth has potentially undermined its capacity to continue doing the work for which Edwards's tacticians initially sought to use it. It has helped bring local organizations and state-society relationships more forcefully onto Bank agendas; it has helped broaden conceptions of poverty in the institution; and it has helped link concerns for participatory processes with themes of governance and state transformation. These effects are most clearly articulated in the World Development Report of 2000–2001, *Attacking Poverty,* which explicitly made the case for conceiving of social relationships both as assets *and* as something whose efficacy is inherently a product of the state-society relations in which it is embedded. This work, in turn, helped to make possible a number of subsequent programmatic and analytical shifts, from projects on empowerment and community-driven development to new approaches to conceiving poverty analysis and service delivery (World Bank 2003).

The rationale for seeking to influence the WDR on poverty (initially, and on other matters subsequently) was that such documents help crystallize particular currents of thought in the institution in ways that become critical points of reference for what the Bank does subsequently. This appears to be occurring, as the Bank shifts to large-scale community-driven development programs that, in many regards, aim to operationalize the empowerment agenda. More direct forms of support to local organizations, coupled with a reworking of local state-society relationships to make them more accountable, are now a far more prominent part of Bank practice.[15] The great risk, of course, is that in the rush to achieve the Millennium Development Goals (MDGs), the community-driven development agenda will be distorted and operations will be made too massive too quickly. In this regard, there is perhaps some historical analogy with the way the Bank promoted integrated rural development projects far too quickly in its aggressive pursuit of a poverty agenda under the presidency of Robert McNamara. And more generally, others have already worried that the MDGs will distort the poverty agenda in undesirable ways (Hulme and Shepherd 2003). It will therefore be important that these new initiatives aiming to work more explicitly with ideas of empowerment be watched closely, from within and without the Bank, in order to assess the extent to which they deliver on what they promise.

Community-driven development, however, only touches certain types of power relationships and certain forms of exclusion. And at the same time as the Bank expands this area of activity, identity-based forms of exclusion, mobilization, and violence continue, and levels of overall inequality seem to change little, and in many countries are getting worse (CPRC 2004). As critics have emphasized, the concept of social capital has little to say about such issues. Different languages, concepts, and theories are also needed, and at the core of these ought to be notions of citizenship, rights, identity, and social structure.

Yet it is still the case that organizations "learn" unevenly across time and space and that there will inevitably be "leaders" and "late adopters" regarding the extent to which social development ideas are taken up. Just as new operational frontiers have been opened that undeniably require a more precise and powerful language to justify, explain, improve, and promote their pro-poor activities, much of the organization has yet to have any significant engagement with social development themes. For these latter constituencies—as with the "frontier" ones before they became frontier—it will remain the case that a place is needed for a social science term that can provide an intuitively appealing and strategic language for beginning conversations about the social dimensions of development.

The Ideas-Practice Nexus Beyond the World Bank

Although a focus on the World Bank is not, as we said at the outset, "any old case study," we suggest that the chapters in this collection do have a broader relevance for thinking about processes of change and the production of discourses in other large development institutions. In the simplest sense, the cases have shown the utility of heeding Campbell's call for research that focuses on "identifying the actors who seek to influence policy making with their ideas, ascertaining the institutional conditions under which these actors have more or less influence, and understanding how political discourse affects the degree to which policy ideas are communicated and translated into practice" (2002: 21). These processes are not only of interest in and of themselves; they also illuminate our understanding of the causal processes involved in institutional change. Even in an entity as large as the World Bank, this focus suggests that there is significant contingency in the determination of specific forms of institutional action and that, furthermore, the scope for such contingency is at times struggled over by particular actors both inside and outside the institution whose policies and actions they are seeking change. Human agency—and its role in both reproducing and changing "normal" practice—needs, therefore, to be at the heart of our understanding of institutions.

That said, the cases here—all of them—emphasize that actors *must* be viewed in the context of the networks of which they are a part and in whose production they sometimes play a role. In these chapters the networks have been viewed primarily as social networks, though there is clearly much overlap here with actor-network theory and its emphasis on the constitutive role of networks that embrace people, ideas, things, technologies, and so on. Human agents reproduce and change institutions—and the discourses associated with those institutions—not simply through human action, but more importantly through *networked* forms of action. The chapters here have repeatedly suggested the importance of networks, of varying sizes, in fashioning actions executed through the World Bank. These networks have been ones in which members are joined primarily on the basis of sociopolitical affinity. They have been effective because the shared sociopolitical motivations have been grounded in a general form of humanism and a generally shared sense of the real limits of any particular academic discipline in offering an adequate framing of development.

Various authors have emphasized the importance of networks in fashioning organizations' discourses and the practices of development organizations (Riles 2000), social movements (Escobar 2001), and NGOs (Bebbington 2004); others have emphasized the importance of networks (or epistemic communities) of professionals and technocrats in fashioning policy change (Haas 1992). This collection falls very much within the same tradition, suggesting the significance of such networks and epistemic communities in the workings of institutions. The focus here has been on those networks fostering pro-poor change and social development. These are, of course, not the only networks that exist; others mobilize for quite distinct sources of change, or at least against the activities of the networks documented here. In this sense, Long and Long's (1992) notion of a "battlefield of knowledge" is not just helpful, but quite apposite in addressing struggles over discourses and other sources of power within institutions. What the chapters here also suggest is that in these encounters, the *type* of concept mobilized by networks can have great influence on the extent to which they are effective: In the battlefield of knowledge, some weapons are more effective than others.

Notes

1. Just some of the publications deriving from this support include the essays collected together in Grootaert and van Bastelaer (2002), Grootaert and Narayan (2004), and Grootaert et al. (2002).
2. We develop this theme much more fully in Bebbington et al. (2004a).
3. This is a criticism also made by Tendler (2000), Moore (2001), and others.
4. Mansuri and Rao (2004) also stress that there is actually little "rigorous" (defined by them as data derived from formal, independent, peer-reviewed project evaluations) evidence to support the "social capital building" (or many other) claims espoused by CDD adherents.
5. More generally, the rise within the Bank of "community-driven development" approaches that combine elements of the community, network, and synergy views has also been helped by the rise of a broader interest in decentralized forms of rural and area-based development promoted early on by Hans Binswanger.
6. This was made most palpably evident when they led a successful attempt to overthrow the government in 2000, although their strength (and thus the viability of PRODEPINE) has declined in recent years.
7. The other pillar was building a favorable "investment climate" (World Bank 2004).

8. Importantly, the 2005 WDR, on equity, gave even more space to thinking about questions of inequality, fairness, power, and history (World Bank 2005). Notably, some of the same actors were involved in this report—which were led by Michael Walton.

9. Furthermore, the interpretations that emphasized how such organizations and networks helped people manage risks and gain access to information resonated with ongoing concerns among Bank economists.

10. By the same token, they never became objects of any significant reflection in Bank-funded operations. The social capital debate—especially the turn toward understanding state-society synergies that authors such as Peter Evans (1996a, b) and Jonathan Fox (1996) gave it—offered a different way to talk about state-society interactions and to consider the effects of inequality and political economy on the quality of these interactions (Evans 1996b).

11. The meeting was titled "Scaling Up Poverty Reduction," May 25–27, 2004.

12. See Rao and Walton (2004) for one such reflection.

13. That the field has largely chosen, wittingly or unwittingly, to embrace Coleman's more individualist conceptualization of social capital perhaps says more about the political climate of our time and the vacuum of usable social theoretical ideas connecting micro and macro levels of analysis than it does about inherent flaws in the terminology itself.

14. It should be said that the authors of this chapter differ in *how* hopeful they are in this regard—but are able to agree on this text.

15. They are not necessarily always done well, and the problems of corruption, poorly accountable governments, and elite capture of institutions all continue. However, the case for addressing such questions has been more clearly made in the institution.

References

Bebbington, Anthony. 1999. Capitals and capabilities: A framework for analyzing peasant viability, rural livelihoods and poverty. *World Development* 27(12):2021–2044.

Bebbington, Anthony. 2004. NGOs and uneven development: Geographies of intentional development. *Progress in Human Geography* 28(6):725–745.

Bebbington, Anthony, Scott Guggenheim, Elizabeth Olson, and Michael Woolcock. 2004a. Exploring social capital debates at the World Bank. *Journal of Development Studies* 40(5):33–64.

Bebbington, Anthony, Leni Dharmawan, E. Farmi, and Scott Guggenheim. 2004b. Village politics, culture and community driven development: Insights from Indonesia. *Progress in Development Studies* 4(3):187–205.

Cernea, Michael. 1988. *Non-governmental organizations and local development.* World Bank Discussion Paper No. 40. Washington, DC: World Bank.

Cernea, Michael, and Scott Guggenheim. 1994. *Anthropological approaches to resettlement.* Boulder, CO: Westview Press.

CPRC. 2004. *Chronic poverty report.* Manchester and London: Chronic Poverty Research Centre.

Davis, Gloria. 2004. *A history of the Social Development network in the World Bank, 1973–2002.* Social Development Working Paper No. 56. Washington, DC: World Bank.

Escobar, Arturo. 2001. Culture sits in places: Reflections on globalization and subaltern strategies of localization. *Political Geography* 20:139–174.

Evans, Peter, ed. 1996a. *State-society synergy: Government and social capital in development.* Berkeley, CA: Institute for International Studies.

Evans, Peter. 1996b. Government action, social capital and development: Reviewing the evidence on synergy. *World Development* 24(6):1119—1132.

Farr, James. 2004. Social capital: A conceptual history. *Political Theory* 32(1):6–33.

Ferguson, James. 1990. *The anti-politics machine: Development, depoliticization and bureaucratic power in Lesotho.* Cambridge: Cambridge University Press.

Fine, Ben. 2001. *Social capital versus social theory.* London: Routledge.

Fox, Jonathan. 1996. How does civil society thicken? The political construction of social capital in rural Mexico. *World Development* 24(6):1089–1103.

Fox, Jonathan. 1997. The World Bank and social capital: Contesting the concept in practice. *Journal of International Development* 9(7): 963–971.

Fox, Jonathan. 2004. Empowerment and institutional change: Mapping "virtuous circles" of state-society interaction. In *Power, rights, and poverty: Concepts and connections,* edited by Ruth Alsop. Washington, DC: World Bank; London: UK Department for International Development.

Fox, Jonathan, and L. David Brown. 1998. *The struggle for accountability: The World Bank.* Cambridge, MA: MIT Press.

Francis, Paul. 2002. *Social capital at the World Bank: Strategic and operational implications of the concept.* Report to the Social Development Department, World Bank, March 31, 2002.

Grootaert, Christiaan, and Thierry van Bastelaer, eds. 2002. *Social capital and poverty: An empirical assessment.* Cambridge: Cambridge University Press.

Grootaert, Christiaan, and Deepa Narayan. 2004. Local institutions, poverty and household welfare in Bolivia. *World Development* 32(7):1179–1198.

Grootaert, Christiaan, Gi-Taik Oh, and Anand Swamy. 2002. Social capital, household welfare and poverty in Burkina Faso. *Journal of African Economies* 11:4–38.

Haas, P. 1992. Introduction: Epistemic communities and international policy coordination. *International Organization* 46(1):1–36.

Harriss, John. 2002. *Depoliticizing development: Social capital and the World Bank.* Wimbledon: Anthem Press.

Hulme, David, and Andrew Shepherd. 2003. Conceptualizing chronic poverty. *World Development* 31:403–424.

Knack, Stephen, and Philip Keefer. 1997. *Does social capital have an economic payoff? A country investigation.* IRIS Working Paper 197. College Park: University of Maryland.

Long, Norman, and Ann Long, eds. 1992. *Battlefields of knowledge: The interlocking of theory and practice in social research and development.* London: Routledge.

Mansuri, Ghazala, and Vijayendra Rao. 2004. A critical review of the community driven development literature. *World Bank Research Observer* 19(1):1–39.

Moore, Mick. 2001. Empowerment at last? *Journal of International Development* 13:321–329.

Morse, Bradford, and T. Berger. 1992. *Sardar Sarovar: The report of the independent review.* Vancouver, BC: Resources for the Future.

Moser, Caroline. 1998. The asset vulnerability framework: Reassessing urban poverty reduction strategies. *World Development* 26(1):1–19.

Mosse, David. 2004. Social analysis as product development: Anthropologists at work in the World Bank. In *The development of religion/the religion of development,* edited by A. Kumar Giri, O. Salemink, and A. van Harskamp. Delft: Eburon Academic Publishers.

Narayan, Deepa, et al. 2000. *Voices of the poor: Can anyone hear us?* New York: Oxford University Press.

Narayan, Deepa, and Lant Pritchett. 1999. Cents and sociability: Household income and social capital in rural Tanzania. *Economic Development and Cultural Change* 47(4):871–897.

Pritchett, Lant, and Michael Woolcock. 2004. Solutions when the solution is the problem: Arraying the disarray in development. *World Development* 32(2):191–212.

Rakodi, Carole. 1999. A capital assets framework for analysing household livelihood strategies: Implications for policy. *Development Policy Review* 17(3):315–342.

Rao, Vijayendra, and Michael Walton, eds. 2004. *Culture and public action: A cross-disciplinary perspective on development policy.* Stanford, CA: Stanford University Press.

Riles, Annelise. 2000. *The network inside out.* Ann Arbor: University of Michigan Press.

Rose, Richard. 1998. *Getting things done in an anti-modern society: Social capital networks in Russia.* Social Capital Initiative Working Paper No. 6. Washington, DC: World Bank.

Salmen, Lawrence, and A.P. Eaves. 1989. *Between public and private: A review of non-governmental organization involvement in World Bank projects.* Policy, Planning and Research Working Paper WPS 305. Washington, DC: World Bank.

Scoones, Ian. 1998. *Sustainable rural livelihoods: A framework for analysis.* Working Paper 72. Brighton: Institute for Development Studies.

Scott, James. 1998. *Seeing like a state: How well-intentioned efforts to improve the human condition have failed.* New Haven, CT: Yale University Press.

Serageldin, Ismail, and Andrew Steer. 1994. Epilogue: Expanding the capital stock. In *Making development sustainable: From concepts to action,* edited by I. Serageldin and A. Steer. Environmentally Sustainable Development Occasional Paper No. 2. Washington, DC: World Bank.

Tendler, Judith. 2000. Why are social funds so popular? In *Local dynamics in an era of globalization: 21st century catalysts for development,* edited by S.J. Evenett, W. Wu , and S. Yusuf. New York: Oxford University Press.

World Bank. 2002. *Empowerment sourcebook.* Washington, DC: World Bank.

World Bank. 2003. *World development report 2004: Making services work for poor people.* New York: Oxford University Press.

World Bank. 2004. *World development report 2005: Building a favorable investment climate*. New York: Oxford University Press.

World Bank. 2005. *World development report 2006: Equity and development*. New York: Oxford University Press.

INDEX

Also from Kumarian Press...

Governance, Civil Society and NGOs

Development and Management: Experiences
in Value-Based Conflict
Edited by Deborah Eade, Tom Hewitt, and Hazel Johnson

Development and Social Action
Edited by Deborah Eade

Going Global: Transforming Relief and Development NGOs
Marc Lindenberg and Coralie Bryant

Managing Policy Reform: Concepts and Tools for
Decision-Makers in Developing and Transitioning Countries
Derick W. Brinkerhoff and Benjamin L. Crosby

Nongovernments: NGOS and the Political Development
of the Third World
Julie Fisher

New Kumarian Press Titles

Coming of Age in a Globalized World: The Next Generation
J. Michael Adams and Angelo Carfagna

Transnational Civil Society: An Introduction
Edited by Srilatha Batliwala and L. David Brown

Non-State Actors in the Human Rights Universe
Edited by George Andreopoulos, Zehra Arat, and Peter Juviler

Visit Kumarian Press at **www.kpbooks.com** or
call **toll-free (800) 289-2664** for a complete catalog.

Kumarian Press, located in Bloomfield, Connecticut, is a forward-looking, scholarly press that promotes active international engagement and an awareness of global connectedness.